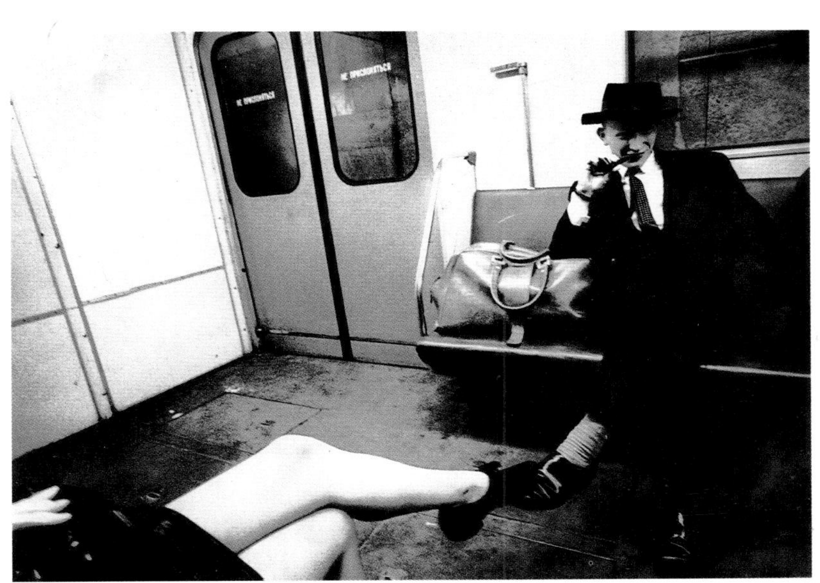

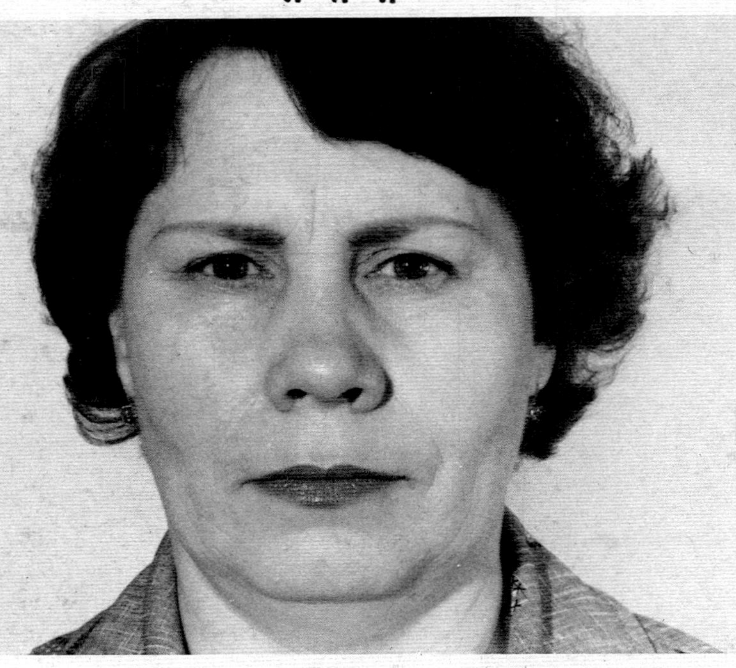

Погасло дневное светило;

* * *

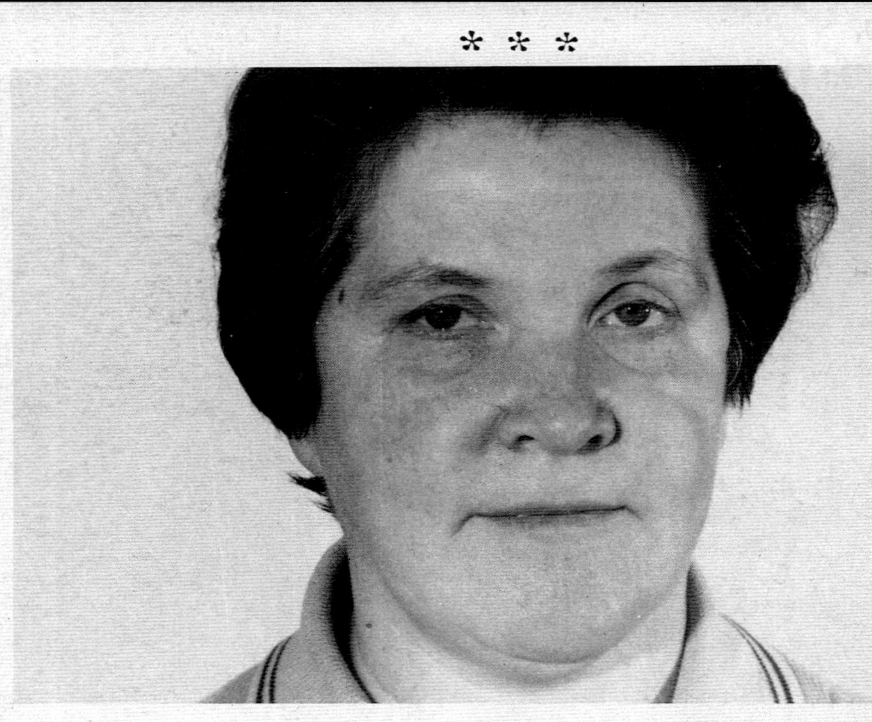

На море синее вечерний пал туман.

* * *

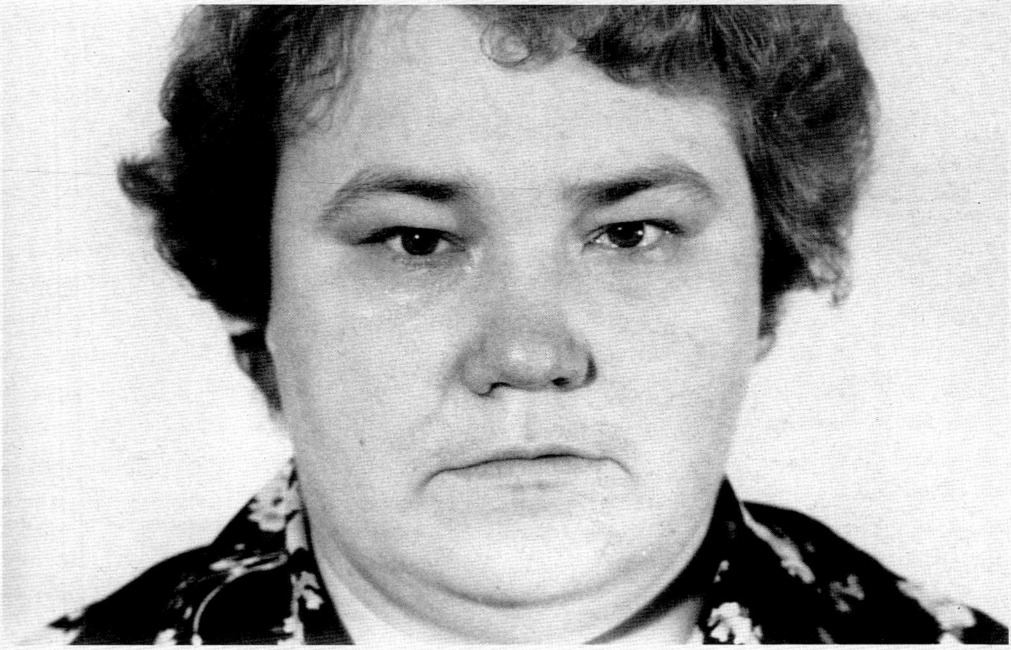

Шуми, шуми, послушное ветрило,

* * *

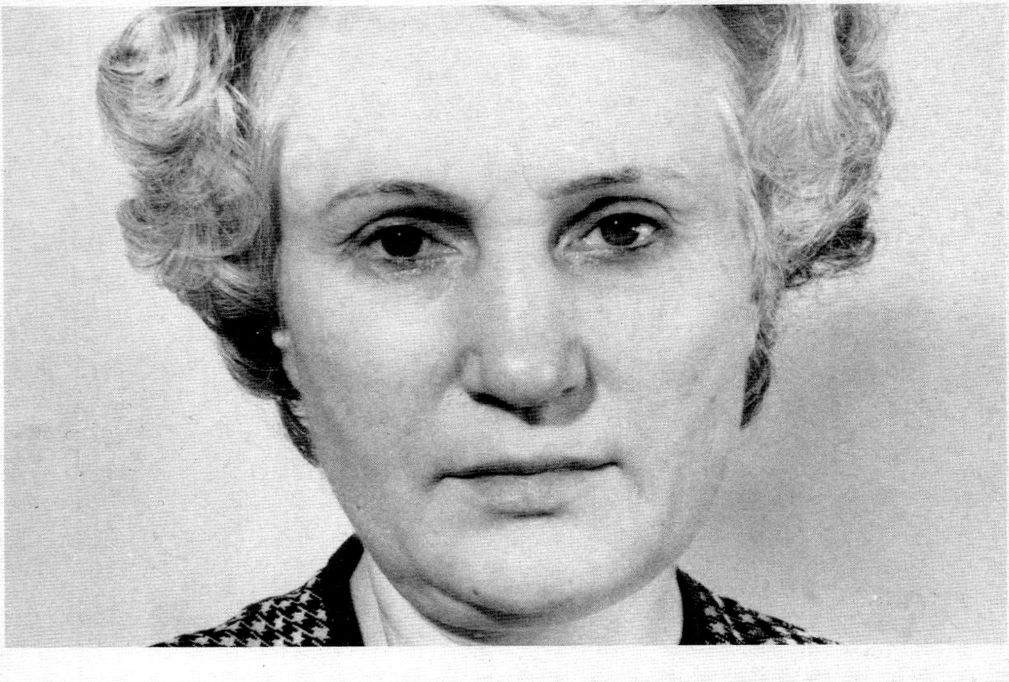

Волнуйся подо мной, угрюмый океан.

* * *

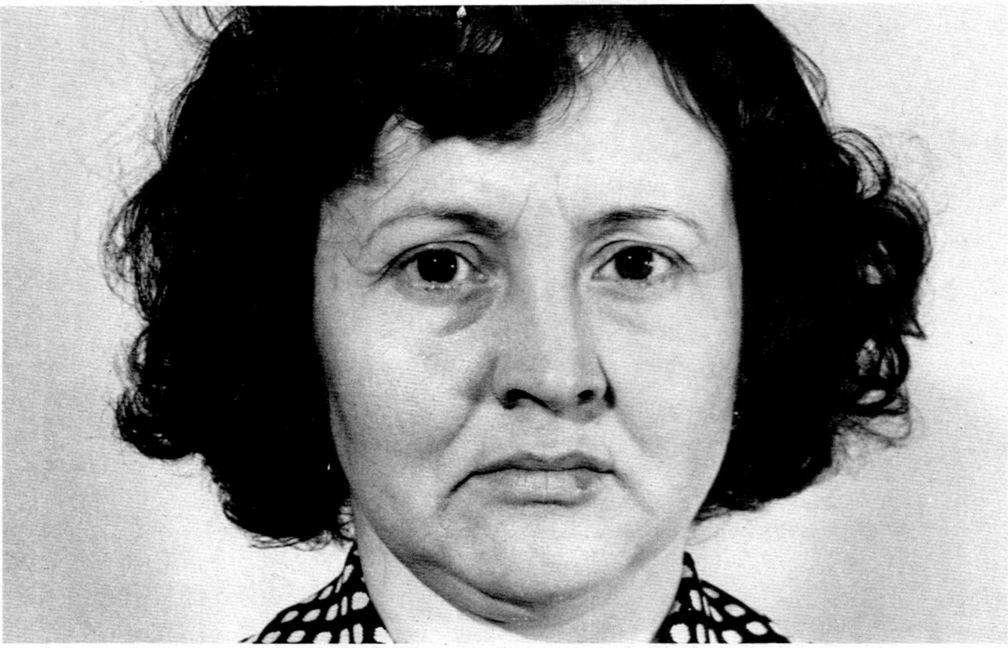

Я вижу берег отдаленный,

* * *

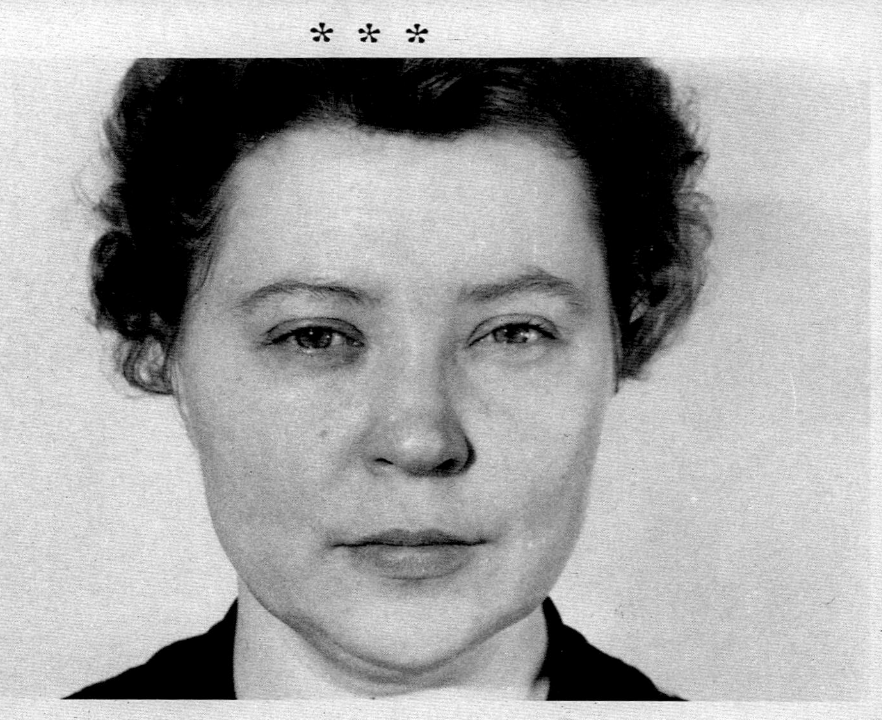

Земли полуденной волшебные края;

* * *

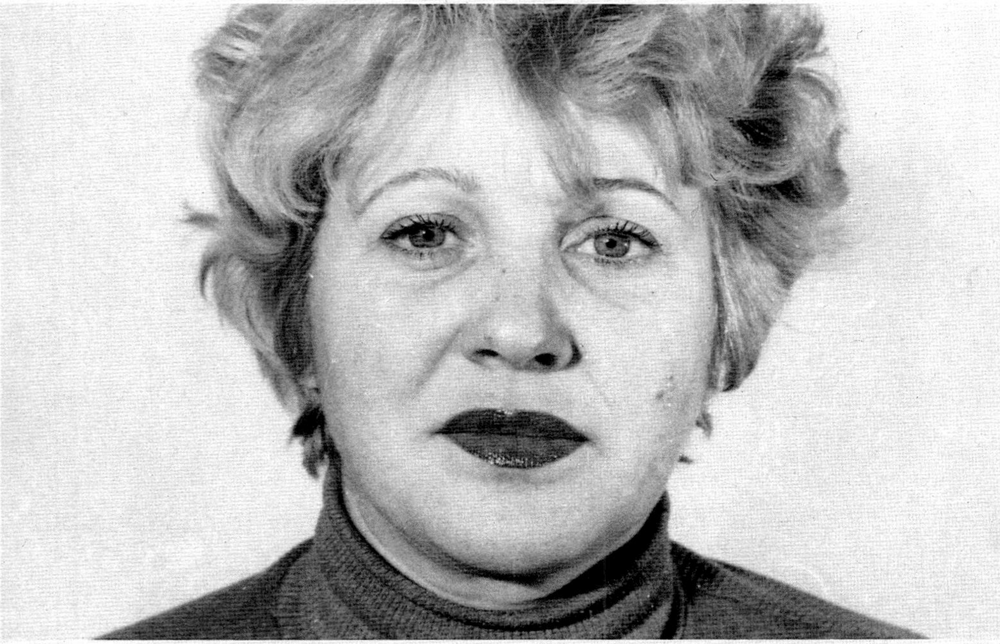

С волненьем и тоской туда стремлюся я,

* * *

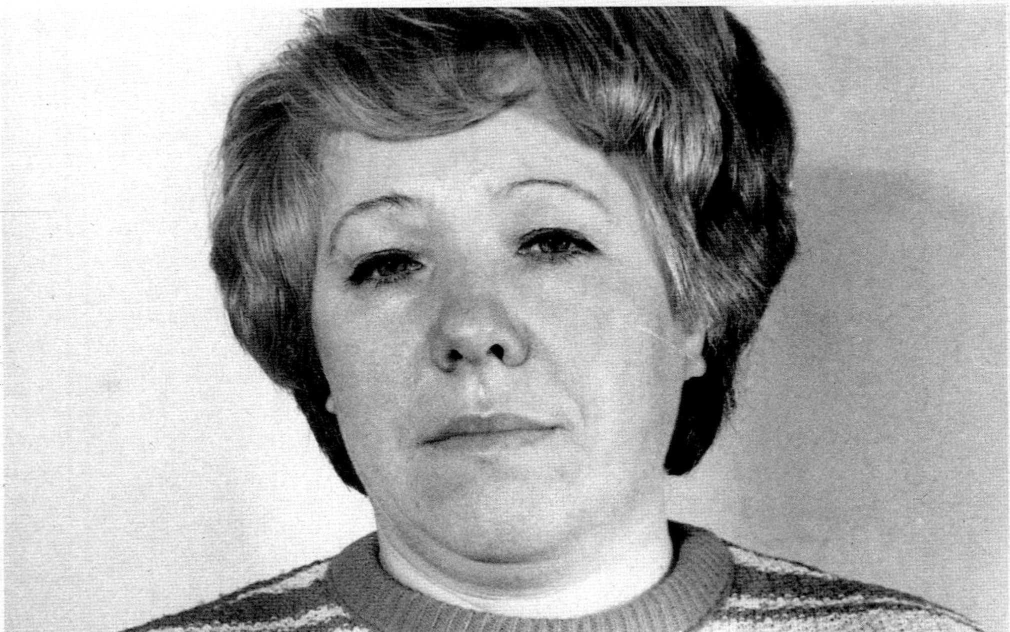

Воспоминаньем упоенный...

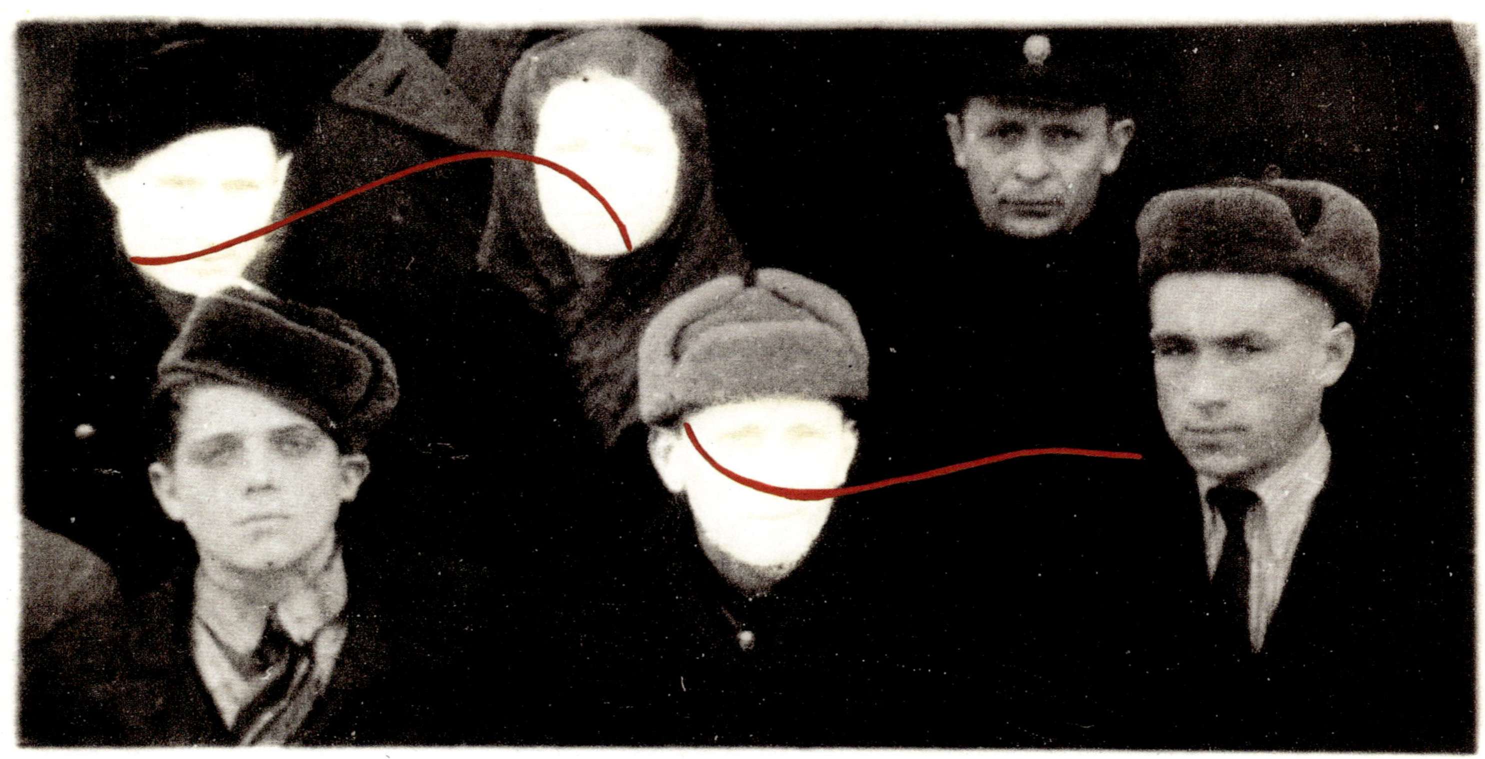

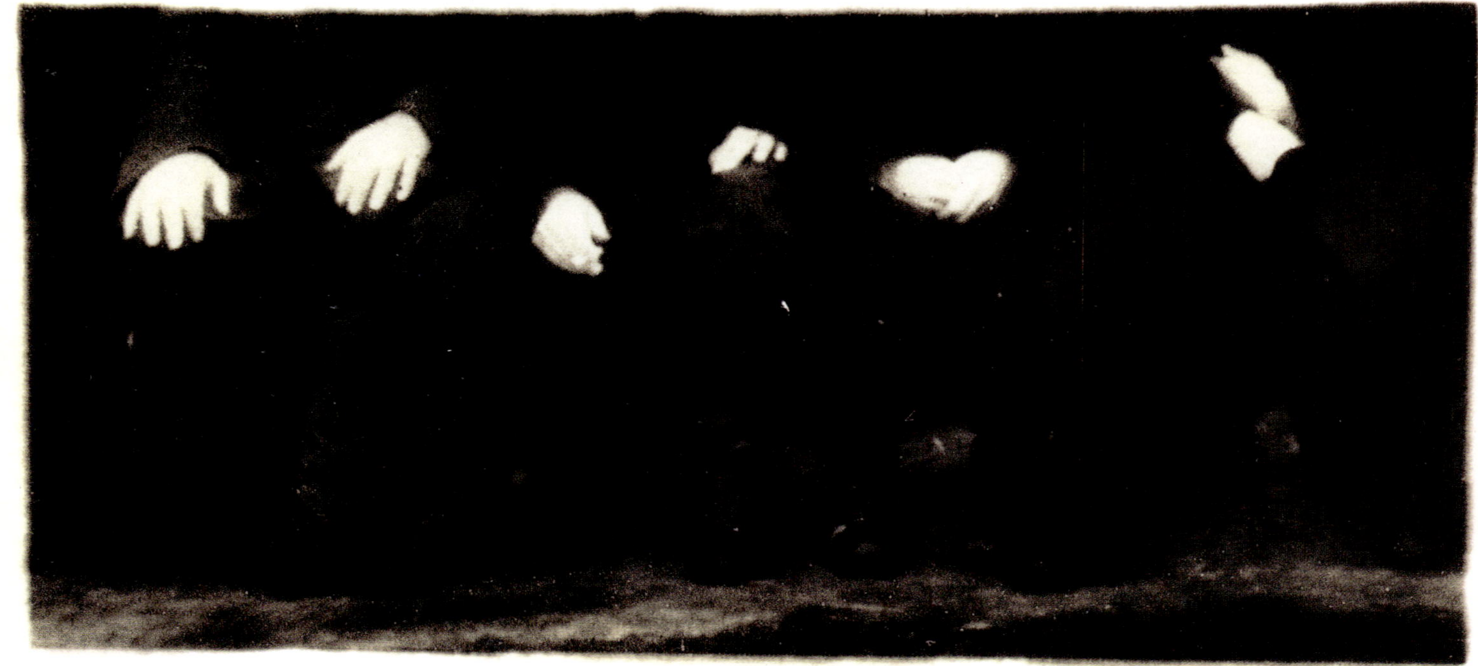

PHOTO MANIFESTO

CONTEMPORARY PHOTOGRAPHY IN THE USSR

WALKER, URSITTI & McGINNISS

WITH ESSAYS BY ALEXANDER LAVRENTIEV,
VALERY STIGNEEV, GRANT KESTER,
AND IRINA RACHEYEVA

FOREWORD BY MICHAEL BOTWINICK

STEWART, TABORI & CHANG
NEW YORK

"Photography Since the Revolution: An Historian and Participant's View" translated from Russian by Elena Kulagina

Published in 1991 by Stewart, Tabori & Chang, Inc.
575 Broadway, New York, New York 10012

Library of Congress Cataloging-in-Publication Data

Photo manifesto : contemporary photography in the USSR / Walker, Ursitti & McGinniss ; with essays by Alexander Lavrent'ev . . . [et al.] ; foreword by Michael Botwinick.
p. cm.
Includes index.
ISBN 1-55670-199-3 (cloth)
1. Photography, Artistic. 2. Photography—Soviet Union. I. Lavrent'ev, Aleksandr Nikolaevich. II. Walker, Ursitti & McGinniss.
TR654.P4678 1991
779'.0947'09048—dc20 90-28912
CIP

Distributed in the U.S. by Workman Publishing,
708 Broadway, New York, New York 10003
Distributed in Canada by Canadian Manda Group,
P.O. Box 920 Station U, Toronto, Ontario M8Z 5P9
Distributed in all other territories by
Little, Brown and Company, International Division,
34 Beacon Street, Boston, Massachusetts 02108

Printed in Italy

10 9 8 7 6 5 4 3 2 1

PAGE 1:
VICTORIA STRANADKO
THE LENINGRAD METRO, 1990
6½×9″

PAGES 2–5:
VLADIMIR KUPREJANOV
from the series: IN MEMORY OF PUSHKIN, 1985
(left to right, top to bottom): "The lights of the day extinguished," "The evening mist fell over the blue sea," "Let's hear you, let's hear you, obedient wind," "Storm on under me, somber ocean," "I see a distant shore," Magical parts of the afternoon earth," "Excitedly and yearning I hurry there," "Stunned by the memory . . ."
9½ × 12″ (each)

PAGE 6:
IGOR V. SAVCHENKO
Top: 9.89-16.2, bottom: 9.89-15.1, 1989
Top: 4½×8″, bottom: 3½×8″

PAGE 9:
VICTOR SHUROV
BOYS, 1990
7½×5″

PAGE 10:
ANONYMOUS
ALEXANDER RODCHENKO

PAGE 11:
© 1961 ELWOOD BAKER
PETER C. COSTAS

PAGE 12:
ANDREY CHEGIN
MAY 9, VICTORY DAY, 1990
6×15½″ (each)

PAGE 34:
LEWIS HINE
POWERHOUSE MECHANIC, 1925,
Courtesy of PACE/MACGILL GALLERY, New York
13½″×9¾″

PAGE 38:
BARBARA KRUGER
"UNTITLED" (I SHOP THEREFORE I AM)
111″×113″
Photographic silkscreen/vinyl, 1987
Collection: Private Collection.
Courtesy: MARY BOONE GALLERY, New York.

PAGE 41:
SHERRIE LEVINE
"UNTITLED" (AFTER ALEXANDER RODCHENKO: 9)
20″×16″
Photograph, 1987
Collection: DON/MERA RUBELL, New York.
Courtesy: MARY BOONE GALLERY, New York.

Photographs by Vladimir Filonov (pages 35, 36, 196–99), Vassily Kravchuk (pages 166–71), Sergey Leontiev (pages 143–47), Boris Mikhailov (pages 163–65), Vladislav Mikhailov (pages 190–91), Igor Moukhin (pages 154–57), and Boris Smelov (pages 194–95) with courtesy of COMPTOIR DE LA PHOTOGRAPHIE / Paris

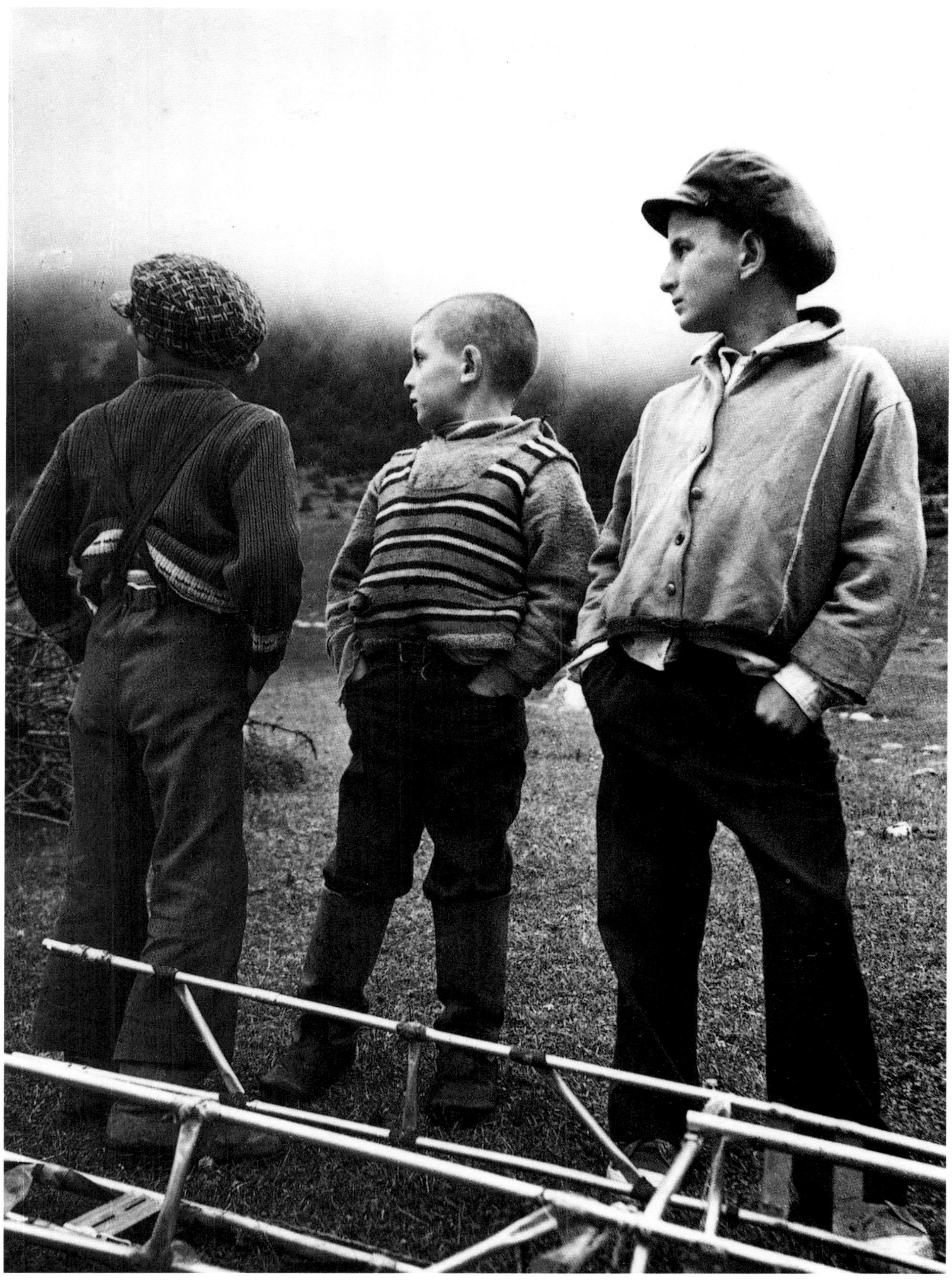

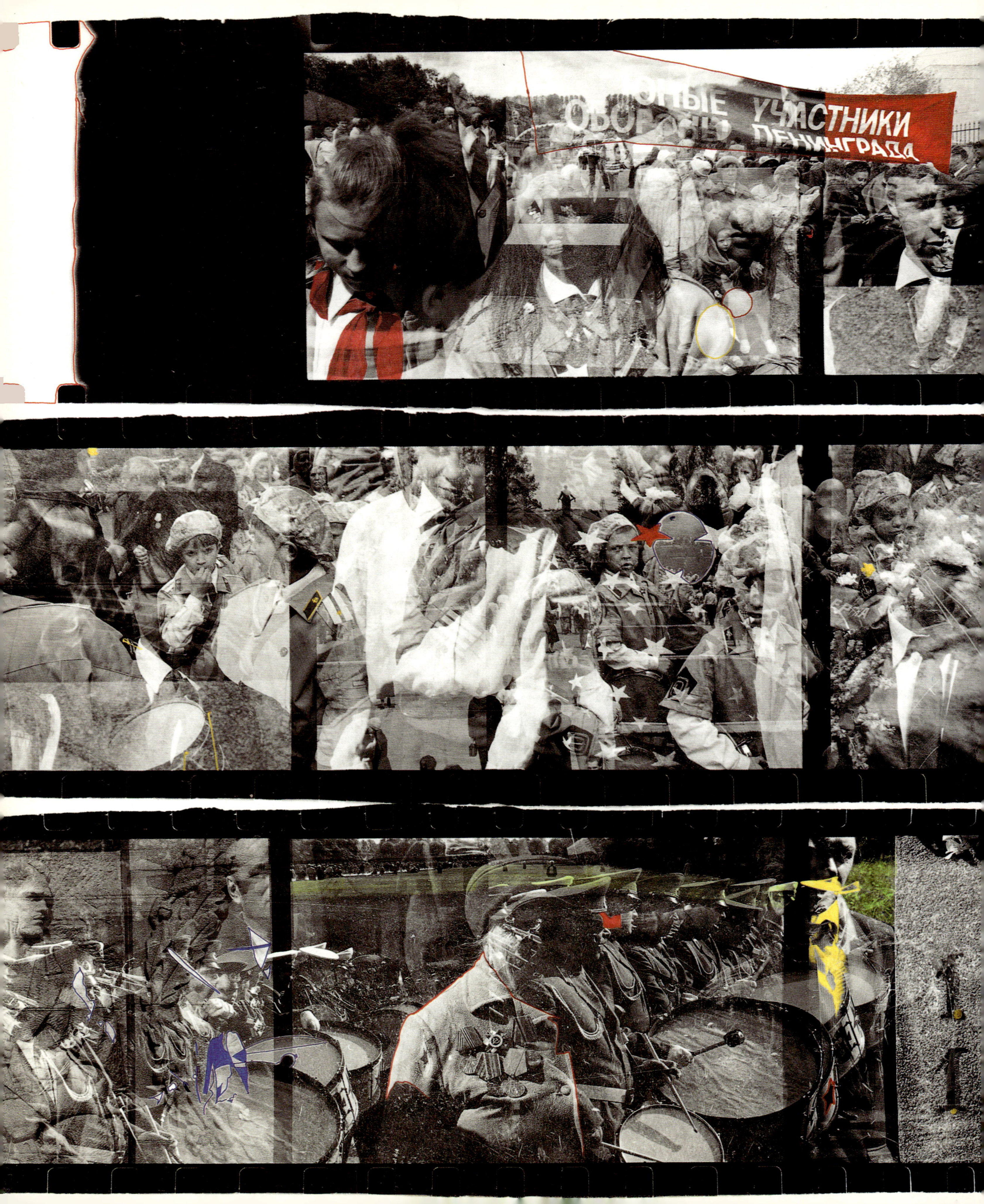
УЧАСТНИКИ
ЛЕНИНГРАДА

CONTENTS

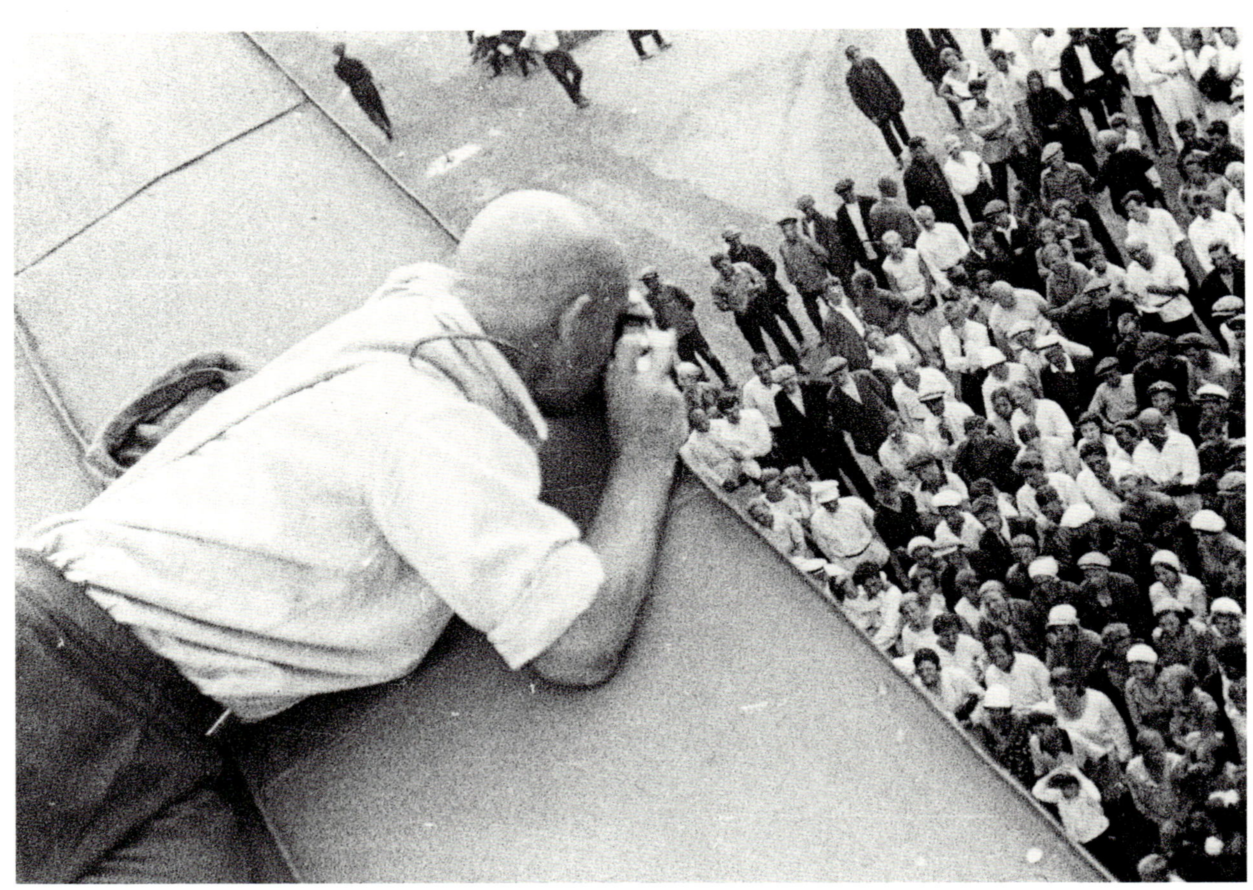

DEDICATED TO

ALEXANDER RODCHENKO

AND PETER C. COSTAS

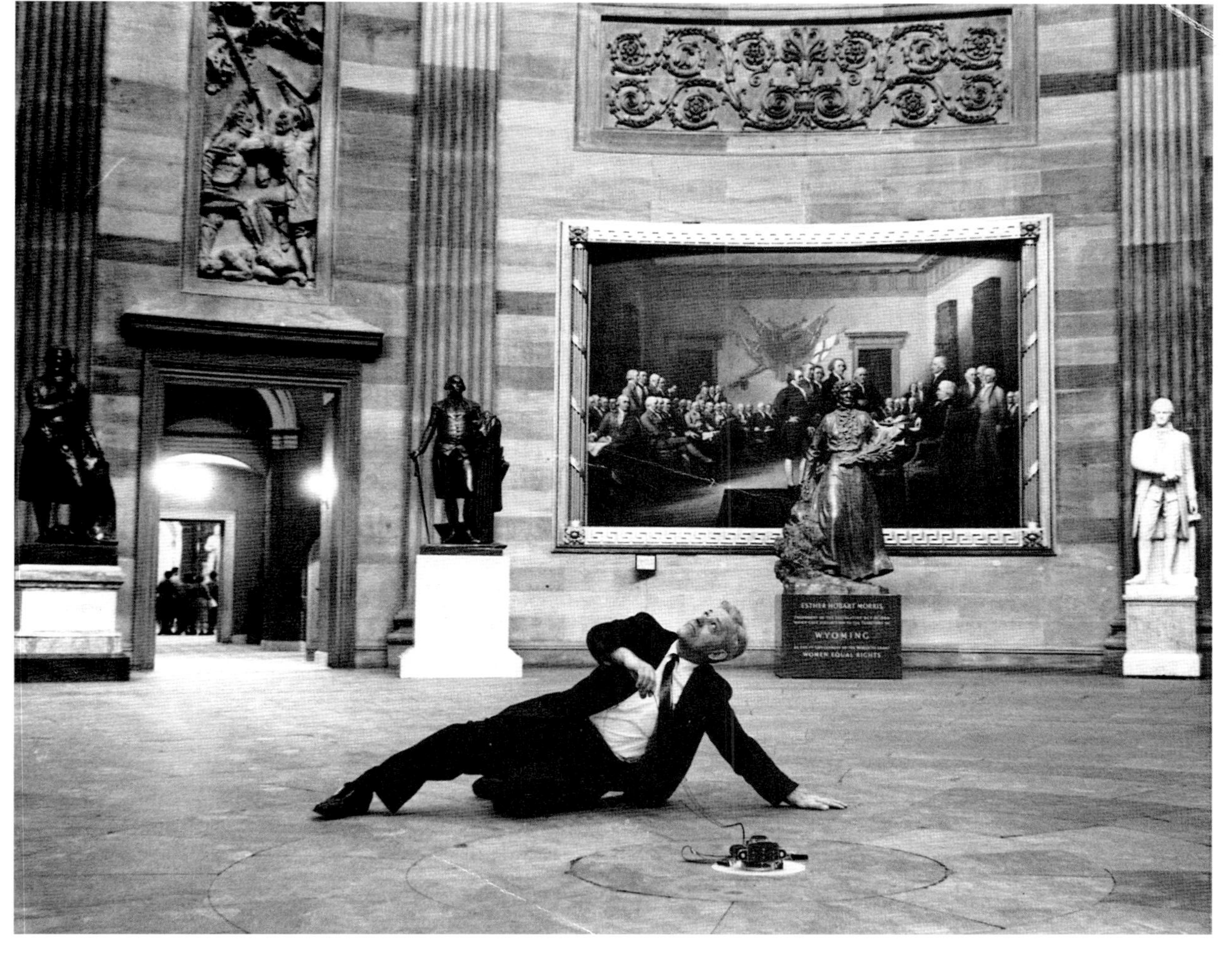

LIST OF PHOTOGRAPHERS

GALINA MOSKALEVA
IVAN PETROVICH
VADIM KACHAN
GENNADY SLABODSKY
VLADIMIR SHAKHLEVICH
IGOR V. SAVCHENKO
HELEN MULYUKINA
ALEXANDER SINYAK
SERGEY KOZHEMYAKIN
SERGEY KOVALYOV
VLADZIMIR P. PARFIANOK
GENNADY RODIKOV
VALERY D. LOBKO
SERGEI SUKOVITZIN
ALEXEY PAVLUTS
ALEKSEY ILYIN
YURY MATVEEV
ANDREY CHEGIN
DMITRY SHNEYERSON
TAK
LUDMILA FEDORENKO
VALENTIN SIMANKOV
VALERY POTAPOV
ALEXANDER IGNATJEV
SERGEY LEONTIEV
VLADIMIR KUPREJANOV

ALEXANDER SLIUSSAREV
TANIA LIEBERMAN
IGOR MOUKHIN
VLADISLAV EFIMOV
ALEXEY SHULGIN
BORIS MIKHAILOV
VASSILY KRAVCHUK
TATIANA DANILOVA
VALERY STIGNEEV
VICTOR SHUROV
LUDMILA IVANOVA
EDWARD STRANADKO
VICTORIA STRANADKO
LEV MELIHOV
IGOR STOMACHIN
MARIA SNIGIREVSKAYA
VLADISLAV MIKHAILOV
NICHOLAI BACHAREV
BORIS SMELOV
VLADIMIR FILONOV
SERGEY OSMACHKIN
PAVEL KISELEV
MIKHAIL LADEISHIKOV
ALEXANDER LAVRENTIEV
NIKOLAI LAVRENTIEV
IRINA PRESNETSOVA
VARVARA RODCHENKO
KATYA LAVRENTIEVA

FOREWORD

MICHAEL BOTWINICK

The progress of change in the world increases with each generation. But in the last decade the process has achieved a kind of critical mass. The speed with which cultural or historical realities are turned on their head is nothing short of breathtaking. Nowhere is this more evident than in the overturning of the comfortable notions of our relationship to developments in the Soviet Union. What could have been more solid for this generation than the idea of the balance of the Soviet Union and the United States as two opposing value systems? It was a clear picture in black and white. The heady days (at least in the West) of glasnost and perestroika have created a veritable circus of new images, sound bites from the six o'clock news that give us glimpses of reality behind the political façade. It is not always comforting.

One of the pernicious tools of the Soviet state in its evolution from Revolution to cold war was the subversion and then the suppression of the creative act. Creativity, in all its forms—drama, poetry, painting, photography—first had to be harnessed to the hard goals of the Revolution, and even then, when it had been co-opted and suborned to the needs of the state, it could not be trusted. The effect on us in the West has been to put some considerable distance between us and a movement that at one time had the promise of being a great intellectual force: the Russian avant-garde movement of the generation that came out of the Revolution. It is instructive to rediscover now the zeal of the photographs of Alexander Rodchenko and then follow the way in which his work was drawn into the propaganda needs of the regime. He survived, but we lose the sharpest part of his radical thought. After a long hiatus, his other work is just now re-emerging.

The lessons of the subversion of this earlier generation of artists seem not to have been lost on the current generation of photographers to whom we are about to be introduced. It is an encouraging surprise to discover behind the political realities that for so long separated East and West a ferment, a diverse pool of talent resistant to categorization, doggedly individualistic, and toughened by a climate of repression we can only vaguely guess at. If there is a quality that draws this diverse generation together it is the pursuit of a more intensely personal vision than that of their revolutionary forebears. There is no chance that the state, or any successor state, will rise up and appropriate the visual iconography of these photographers for its own purposes. They have created a private language, an internal contemplation that is rich in surrealism, allegory, manipulation of the image, and interior dialogue. It is deliberately poor in images of achievement, moments of heroism, triumphs of the collective.

That this should be the chosen path is not surprising. What is surprising is the extent to which the suffering, inequity, and capriciousness of life in the Soviet Union has become banal so that it is not the focus of these photographers. They have liberated themselves by turning inward. We cannot tell by the progress of their works when, or indeed whether, they will turn their lens outward. They keep us removed from their work by a variety of means. The "aesthetic of defect" is widely practiced. Negatives are often defaced and scratched, anything to deprive the photograph of its almost magical ability to capture a moment of reality in airless, timeless, high-contrast relief. Instead of those totemic images of reality, we see texture, double imaging, and panoramic sequences in motion. It is the desire of this generation to force the viewer to deal with the texture of the medium. Rarely do they allow the purity of the classical photographic surface to assert itself. The works we are introduced to in this volume are like the first glimpses of hidden manuscripts, the murmurings of the clandestine conversations that have been held in secret in the last forty years. They are not the direct descendants of constructivist works, but rather an indirect view of the process by which creativity has been kept alive in the Soviet Union, not unlike that of the medieval monasteries which kept much of the creative tradition alive by turning inward rather than looking outward.

These photographers and their works have been coaxed forth by an unusual group of men. Joe Walker, Chris Ursitti, and Paul McGinniss joined forces in Washington, D.C. some years ago because they believed that artists needed to be nurtured on some direct level in order for galleries to really connect with young and undiscovered talent. Because of their openness to new ideas they were involved in some early exchange programs with the Soviet Union. From the first their style, their directness, and the freshness of their vision won them access to Soviet artists. First in Moscow and then in an increasingly wide geographical circle they were introduced and passed from one artist to the next. At a time when entrepreneurs and hustlers of every artistic persuasion were trying to catch the next Russian fashion, they created relationships based on respect for their response to what they were seeing. They have brought us a picture of a generation of emerging photographers. It is not romanticized. This body of work blinks awkwardly in the unaccustomed light. It shows us the musings at the end of a long night.

PREFACE

"To find yourself, think for yourself."
SOCRATES

Photo Manifesto exists without the burden of preconceived expectations. The book is the culmination of a series of seemingly unconnected events that began in Washington, D.C., in the winter of 1986. On the eve of Soviet-American reconciliation our gallery, once located in our nation's capital, presented a lifetime of photographic works created by Mr. Ursitti's grandfather Peter Costas. A review of the exhibition attracted the attention of Charolette Goodwin, director of a USA-USSR cultural exchange program.

Inspired by Mr. Costas's visual interpretation of our capital's monuments, Ms. Goodwin suggested we pursue a photographic exchange with Moscow. Preliminary negotiations with Soviet exchange officials resulted in the suggestion that Alexander Rodchenko's architectural studies of Moscow would counterpoint the Costas perspective exemplified in his studies of Washington, D.C. As President Reagan and Mr. Gorbachev pursued their summit dialogues, we attempted to work within the complicated official exchange bureaucracy—to no avail.

Determined to succeed, however, Mr. McGinniss independently pursued an understanding of the Soviet system that would prepare us to conduct our proposed exchange in an appropriately diplomatic manner. In the course of his research and study, he discovered a review of a small exhibit of Rodchenko's works curated by Ms. Alessandra Latour for the American Institute of Architects in New York City. Our angel had been found.

Ms. Latour generously gave her time and effort to guide us. Instinctively she trusted our intentions and introduced us to the family of Alexander Rodchenko. Alexander Lavrentiev, Rodchenko's grandson, enthusiastically supported our initiative. Arrangements were swiftly concluded and in the spring of 1989 a small Rodchenko exhibit served as the concluding presentation at our four-year-old Washington, D.C., gallery. In September, 1989 the largest exhibition of Rodchenko photographs in America inaugurated our new gallery in New York City.

On Ms. Latour's recommendation, the director of the Shchusev Architectural Museum in Moscow agreed to host the first retrospective exhibit of Peter Costas's work. Thus our objective to initiate a photographic exchange was realized.

The fateful pairing of Costas and Rodchenko was, in hindsight, fortuitous. Motives aside, each man pioneered new ways to view the familiar. They pursued their deep patriotic convictions, seeking to capture the idealism of their disparate times and milieus. Each survived, driven by a singular need to elucidate his compelling vision, despite the hardships this compulsion engendered. While each represented the artistic virtues of his time, each also stood apart from accepted practice, fired by a desire to expand on possibility. In dedicating this book to these two grandfathers we acknowledge those who have inspired us to search, to advance our thinking and our understanding of the times and places in which we live.

What began as an exchange between two families anxious to share the fruits of their grandfathers' labor has evolved into more than we could have anticipated. The Soviet Union has become a vital part of our lives and the small role we play in cultural relations between our two countries is a responsibility we take very seriously and with great pride. That *Photo Manifesto* was completed in less than one year's time is a result of hours of listening, learning, and responding to our Soviet counterparts. Garnering such a high level of cooperation from so many in a society where trust is hard earned is not, however, a testament to us, but rather is indicative of the respect our Soviet colleagues have for Alexander Rodchenko and the Rodchenko family, and those, like us, fortunate enough to be associated with them.

Our work has taken us to the Soviet Union at a time when innovation is once again aggressively sought and fiercely debated. During the past two years of our visits to the Soviet Union we have witnessed the results of censorship and artistic repression and the artists' struggle to understand, forgive, and move forward.

The past subjugation of the artistic process to the manipulative aims of the state was a notorious effort to reinterpret the cultural heritage. In order to direct the growth of cultural heritage, the artist as a vehicle for such growth was targeted for state control. Thus the act of thinking for oneself—artistically and otherwise—was discouraged by violence, exile, and isolation.

The current deconstruction of the state ideology that restricted the artist was an unexpected occurence but, in retrospect, inevitable as a building block for renewed growth. Traditionally, the Soviet artist is accorded deep respect for the ability to inspire and reflect the people's sentiment. Now, as the Soviet Union emerges from the shadows of its past, it is once again "liberating" its artists, and follows their lead in search of an expanded cultural consciousness that presumes individual thought and responsibility. Artists are being given a pivotal role in helping to heal the damaged national psyche and to rouse independent thought; the potential for significant change driven by their creative minds is explosive.

Photo Manifesto reports the first photographic results of this search, this Soviet effort to push individuals to think for themselves, and also explores the painful introspection—bordering on narcissisism—currently gripping the Soviet national consciousness. This introspection has a quality of the self-reckoning of warriors who center their minds and spirits so that their choice of action will result in victory that advances their society. It is raw and without pretense, but carries as well a striking uncertainty. In contrast to the definitiveness of the warriors' self-reckoning, a quality of almost passive surveillance in the artistic introspection reveals a restive, tentative spirit. What is certain is that the society is on the path to some denouement. Whether it is reached in anger or in peaceful resolve is not yet determined.

The impact of this deep soul-searching, the discovery in real terms of the potential and power of individual choice, will reverberate far beyond the borders of the Soviet Union. It presages a redefinition of both national and individual roles in the new social evolution wherein our fate is intertwined with all who inhabit this planet.

Photo Manifesto is our contribution to the cause of artistic freedom, not only in the Soviet Union but throughout the world. Now is a time to take risks and to be open to criticism, for fearlessness and freedom are the strengths of the individual who strives for truth. It is not as important that an individual idea reign supreme as that the artistic dialogue promote the growth of ideas. With an expanded base of fearless and unrestricted individual expression, the prospects for this constructive dialogue increase.

ACKNOWLEDGMENTS

Andrew Stewart and Stewart, Tabori & Chang, Inc. deserve our deepest thanks for allowing us to create *Photo Manifesto*. Special thanks is given to Sarah Longacre and Jose Pouso for facilitating the authorship of this book. Ann Campbell, our editor, Sarah, and Jose have given us a valuable education in publishing with patience, wisdom, and enthusiasm for which we are very grateful. We commend designer Diana Jones for her sensitive, creative treatment of the material and production director Kathy Rosenbloom for her skillful and demanding eye. We salute all members of the Stewart, Tabori & Chang team for their professionalism, commitment to excellence, and superb creative instincts.

The authors of the photographs and essays in *Photo Manifesto* are due special thanks for their generous contributions. The extraordinary efforts of Alexander Lavrentiev, Valery Stigneev, and Irina Racheyeva were instrumental to the timely completion of this project. The enthusiastic assistance given to our cultural exchange program by Edward Gurkov manifests a sincere love for Soviet culture we find truly inspirational. Additionally, we would like to give special mention to the following individuals who provided support, friendship, or inspiration to this project: Ambassador and Mrs. Jack Matlock, First Secretary and Mrs. Lev Orekhov, Valery Lobko and the Union of Art Photographers of Byelorussia, Dmitry Shneyerson and The Photo Gallery, Leningrad, Lev Liubimov, Antonina Manina, Tatiana Bozhutina, Alexei Shchusev and the Shchusev Museum of Architecture, Valery Sazonov and the Penza Art Gallery, N.F. Markov and the Leningrad Mukhina College of Art and Design, Z. Scopiutzova, Marina Kuzina and the Tula Arts Museum, Victor Penzin and the Museum of Peoples Graphics, Michael Sidur and the Sidur Museum, and Svetlana Strijniova and the Mayakovsky Museum.

Also: the family of Alexander Rodchenko and Varvara Stepanova, Claudia Ignatovich, Anatoli Chajhet, Ely Bielutin, Lev Melihov, Alexei Rossal, Vacheslav Koleichuk, Alexander Kozhanov, Michael Saksin, Vladimir Fleurov, Jack Fleurov, Tanya Timanovskaya, Veronica Rossal, Tatiana Salzirn, Egle Jasmkuniene, Vitaly V. Gan, and Servolot Salzonov.

We thank the board of directors of the Museum for Contemporary Arts in Baltimore, Maryland and the director, George Ciscle, for agreeing to host the first *Photo Manifesto* exhibit.

We express continuing gratitude to our business associates the Fine Arts Group, Daniel Pritzker, Angeline Ursitti, Gerald and Anita Ursitti, Judith Sipes, and Joyce Poindexter.

Our colleague Michael Botwinick has lent a gentle hand of guidance to us over many years. His confident belief in our abilities has been demonstrated in many ways. We thank him for his friendship, his unwavering support, and his significant contribution to our success. We are forever indebted.

Support is given in many ways and for their special contribution to our efforts we would like to acknowledge and thank the following: the Walker family, the Ursitti family, the McGinniss-Moylett family, Angela Adams, Teresa and Bruce Anderson, Sherrie Arnaiz, David Autry, Tatiana Bachuretz, Marilyn and John Barrett, Rae Bayer, Amy Berkeley, Leon Berkowitz, Maureen Berkowitz, Harriet Botwinick, Linda Cady, Denise Carroll, Mark Dayvault, Cohn Drennan, Marge and Anthony Fernandes, Patrick Finnegan, Joy Freathy, Judi Giannini, Roger Gilroy, Charolette Goodwin, Cynthia Grenier, Anthony Harvey, Alan D. Hirsch, Essie Ilkhan, Deborah Ismond, Lisa and Joseph Kirk, Carl Kramer, Courtney and Karen Lord, Lee Kimche McGrath, Patrice and Herbert Miller, Mary Ortner, Madeleine Reberkenny, Lou Rojas, Jaimie Sanford, Josef Schutzenhofer, Sylvia Snowden, Bene Svitavsky, Alice Thorson, Kim Walker, Washington House Photography, and Carrie Zenzefillis.

Also: Pierre Apraxine, Martin Bondell, Bobbie Duke, Terence Eagleton, Scott Ellard, Aaron Etra, Deidre Belle Finley, Juliette Galant, Gilman Paper Company, Hal Goldstein, Patricia Harnedy, Simon Hiscock, Brian Hotchkiss, Janna W. Josephson, Igor Jozsa, Leon Klayman, Alessandra Latour, Angela Lucas, Queva Lutz, Peter MacGill, Debbie Marino, Maxine Marshall, Earl Morgan, Tina Muller, Dr. Patricia Thompson, Roger Thompson, Margarita and Victor Tupitsyn, and Thomas Walther.

Our final thanks we reserve for our special friends who have shared so much of our rich experience with the Soviet Union and to whom we express our deepest gratitude: Marte and Ken Newcombe.

PHOTO MANIFESTO

JOSEPH WALKER, CHRISTOPHER URSITTI,
AND PAUL McGINNISS

To look at any art out of its social context is to deny the fullness of its appreciation. While in the long run perhaps only aesthetic criteria will define what remains as great art, it is essential now to analyze art not in a vacuum but within the overall framework of history. John Bowlt stated in the book *New Art from the Soviet Union,* "For the Western historian to attempt to evaluate modern Soviet art . . . is a hazardous venture especially if he lacks an adequate knowledge of the political structure of the Soviet Union." This is especially so for photography from the USSR. It is important to analyze the photographs in this book not just within the context of an individual photographer's work, or within a formalistic artistic-technical context of creation, but in comparison with their historical antecedents.

While we will not attempt to present a complete overview of the political structure or history of the USSR in this essay, we will highlight the way in which photography and politics have interacted in the USSR since the Bolshevik Revolution of 1917. For within the history of the Soviet state lies the history of Soviet photography, and in many ways photography helped shape the course of the Revolution and the Revolution helped shape the course of photography.

The 1917 Bolshevik Revolution and the political events which resulted from it brought photography and film to the forefront of the arts. The Bolshevik Revolution was captured on film, perhaps better than any pre-

BORIS IGNATOVICH
YOUTH, c.1937
9 × 12″

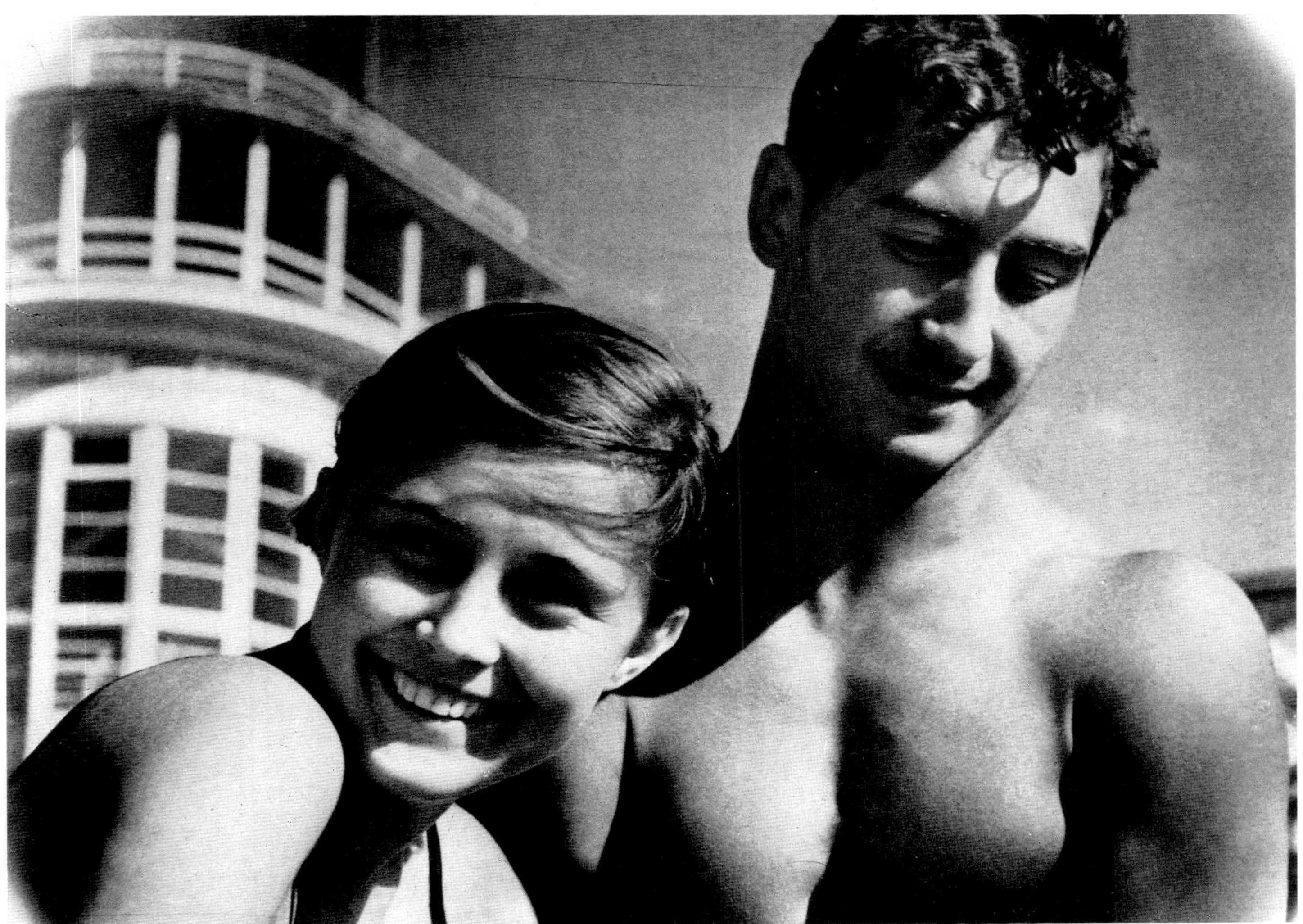

vious event in history, by a dedicated group of politically conscious artist-photographers who documented its progress and communicated its ideals to the masses. One of them was Alexander Rodchenko.

> "Art has no place in modern life. It will continue to exist as long as there is a mania for the romantic and as long as there are people who love beautiful lies and deception.
>
> "Every modern cultured man must wage war against art, as against opium.
>
> "Photograph and be photographed!"

In 1928 the great Russian avant-garde artist Alexander Rodchenko wrote the above lines in the Moscow publication *Novy LEF: New Left Front of the Arts.* In his essay entitled "Against the Synthetic Portrait, For the Snapshot," Rodchenko argued that photography was the true art of modern times. He believed that art forms such as painting and sculpture were outdated and could not as truthfully express the reality of the revolution of society in the USSR. Although now acclaimed for his formalist talent as a photographer, Rodchenko always expressed the social benefits of photography as its pri-

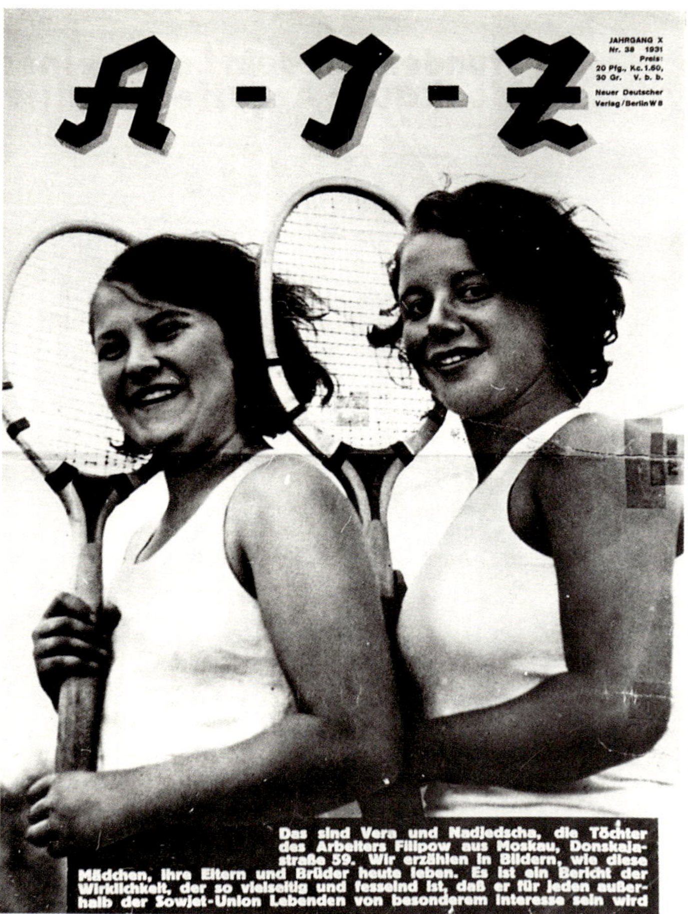

MAX ALPERT and ARKADY CHAJHET
from the series: TWENTY-FOUR HOURS IN THE LIFE OF THE FILIPPOV FAMILY, 1931
7 ¾ × 5 ¾″

mary goal, believing that photography was a utilitarian medium whose purpose was to educate and inform the public.

"Against the Synthetic Portrait, For the Snapshot" can be interpreted as a statement against the censorship of information conveyed through the arts. Rodchenko stated, "By means of a photograph and other documents, we can debunk any artistic synthesis produced by one man of another. So we refuse to let Lenin be falsified by art. Art has failed miserably in its struggle against photography for Lenin." Ironically, as Rodchenko was pioneering an artistic photo documentation of the new utopian regime, the regime was beginning its own censorship of artists, dictating to them the policies of bureaucracy. Indeed, the new censorship had been introduced a decade before Rodchenko's essay, immediately after the Revolution, and solidified in 1922 with the formation of a committee to oversee the unification of all censorship efforts.

The photo essay *Twenty-four Hours in the Life of the Filippov Family* (page 24), created in 1931 by Max Alpert and Arkady Chajhet, is a good example of how the state influenced what the public saw of the USSR. In the essay the Filippovs were photographed as a model family living well in Moscow. The photographic sequence, approximately eighty photographs in all, captured the family in a supposedly documentary truth. The Filippovs were photographed in idyllic poses while shopping, at leisure, and at the infirmary.

At the same time, the state was in the midst of Stalin's brutal attempt at the forced collectivization of the country's farms: by 1931 hundreds of thousands of people had been sent into forced labor, starved, and killed. Meanwhile, the Filippovs were exhibited abroad as if they were a truly typical family. The deception was so effective that the family received greetings from hundreds of impressed well-wishers abroad.

The Filippov family series shows how officials manipulated the sincerity of artists to create propaganda. Although such well-being as the Filippovs displayed was not widespread, the family truly existed; the photographs have a theatrical, staged quality but the subjects were not actors. In the early

1930s the general public was unaware of the nature of the political situation. It still believed that the Revolution's political and social transformation would have all families resemble the Filippovs. What made the Filippov family such a powerful tool of propaganda was that they were real and that the photographers believed wholeheartedly in the image they were projecting. The propaganda bureaucracy merely capitalized on the photographer's vision, co-opting it for their own purposes.

The Filippov family series also highlights the difficulty in appraising a particular artwork or artist without knowledge of the artist's intent and the context of the work's creation. The state decided the political correctness of an artist's work, perhaps arbitrarily. The photograph *Youth* (page 23) taken by Boris Ignatovich around 1937 shows that without insight into the interaction between Soviet cultural officials and the artists, the intent and content of a piece of art can be easily misinterpreted. Ignatovich's *Youth* has been seen as a romantic glorification of Stalin's Russia. Yet the picture is in fact an innocent portrayal of two youths that the photographer met by chance on the beach near the Sea of Azov. The youths did not even know each other, and Ignatovich asked them to stand together for the picture. Ironically, *Youth*, a photograph that depicts a beautiful, healthy innocence at a time of terror and corruption in Soviet history, was not used for propaganda purposes by the state and was even criticized and condemned by Soviet officials as an example of corrupt formalism.

Thus, through the arts, the USSR exercised its dehumanization of the public in its attempt to create the perfect *Homo sovieticus*. The collectivization of intellectual thought, like agricultural collectivization, helped to destroy the place of the individual in society. Writer Evgeny Zamyatin had predicted this in 1920 when he said, "We have lived through the epoch of suppression of the masses. We are living in an epoch of

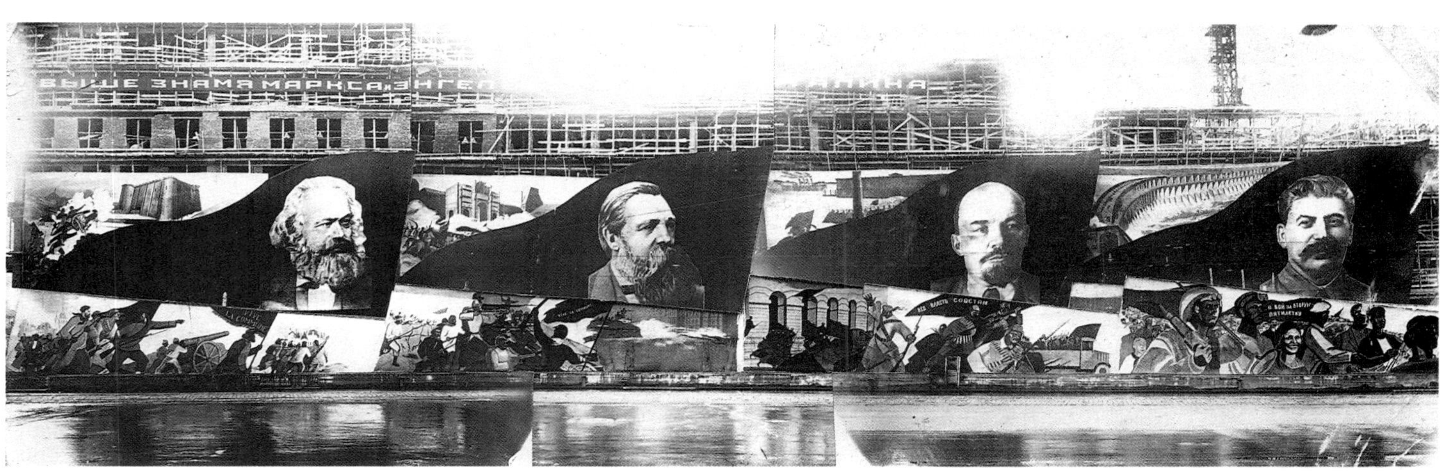

GUSTAV KLUTSIS
HOTEL MOSCOW COLLAGE, 1933
4 ½ × 14 ½"

suppression of the individual in the name of the masses." Soviet political theorist Nikolay Bukharin went so far as to state in 1925, "Yes, we will produce standardized intellectuals, produce them as though in a factory." Bukharin was successful in his fight to eliminate the value of the individual: not surprisingly, later in his political career he was ordered executed by Stalin. With the illegalization of all independent intellectual and artistic organizations in 1932, the Soviet government completed its campaign to take control of the arts for the benefit of the Revolution.

With the Stalinization of the society, photography became a powerful tool of the state—a means of propaganda—and its resemblance to the truth grew distant. It was in the 1930s, when Stalin finalized his consolidation of power, that the techniques of photomontage and collage were fully developed for the benefit of the propaganda machine. During this time, photographic artists such as Gustav Klutsis used these techniques to create an advertising platform for the government: large-scale political decorations designed for display in public areas, such as the huge photographic sign—based on a small photo collage developed by Klutsis specifically for the purpose—displayed on the side of the Hotel Moscow under construction in 1933 (page 25).

Further, it was not unusual for the photographs of this period to have faces blacked out or inserted depending on who was in favor at any point in the progressive reigns of terror. Images presented to the public as real were in fact designed, hand-sketched by artists who then took staged photographs and montaged them to look like the "real" drawing first created. In the decades after the Bolshevik Revolution, an unparalleled expertise was developed in manipulating photography to control history.

While early explorations of the photographic medium and its manipulation were for creative purposes, such experimentation in the 1930s was not primarily aesthetic or formalistic. The manipulation of photography was a means to an end, not an end in itself, and the end was complete political and artistic control. Rodchenko's fear of false representation in the arts was realized, and ironically most effectively, through the use of photography.

Photographs taken by Soviet World War II correspondents, however, are an exception to the massive stifling of photography. Arkady Chajhet, who was imprisoned from 1935 to 1936 because he photographed Kirov before he was assassinated, truthfully captured the war on film. His photographs, such as *The Carpathian Mountains in West Ukraine* (page 27), *The Forging of the River Oder* (page 28), and *Unexpected Meeting* (page 29), which captures an unexpected reunion of a soldier, his wife, and sister in war-torn Byelorussia, are effective documents of the war, honest and moving.

In the decades after the Revolution, the pioneering experiments of earlier photographers were harnessed for the benefit of the Soviet government. Klutsis's art had broken creative barriers and under the jurisdiction of the political machine had helped to create the image of the Revolution for the masses.

ARKADY CHAJHET
THE CARPATHIAN MOUNTAINS IN WEST UKRAINE, 1945
15¼ × 11½"

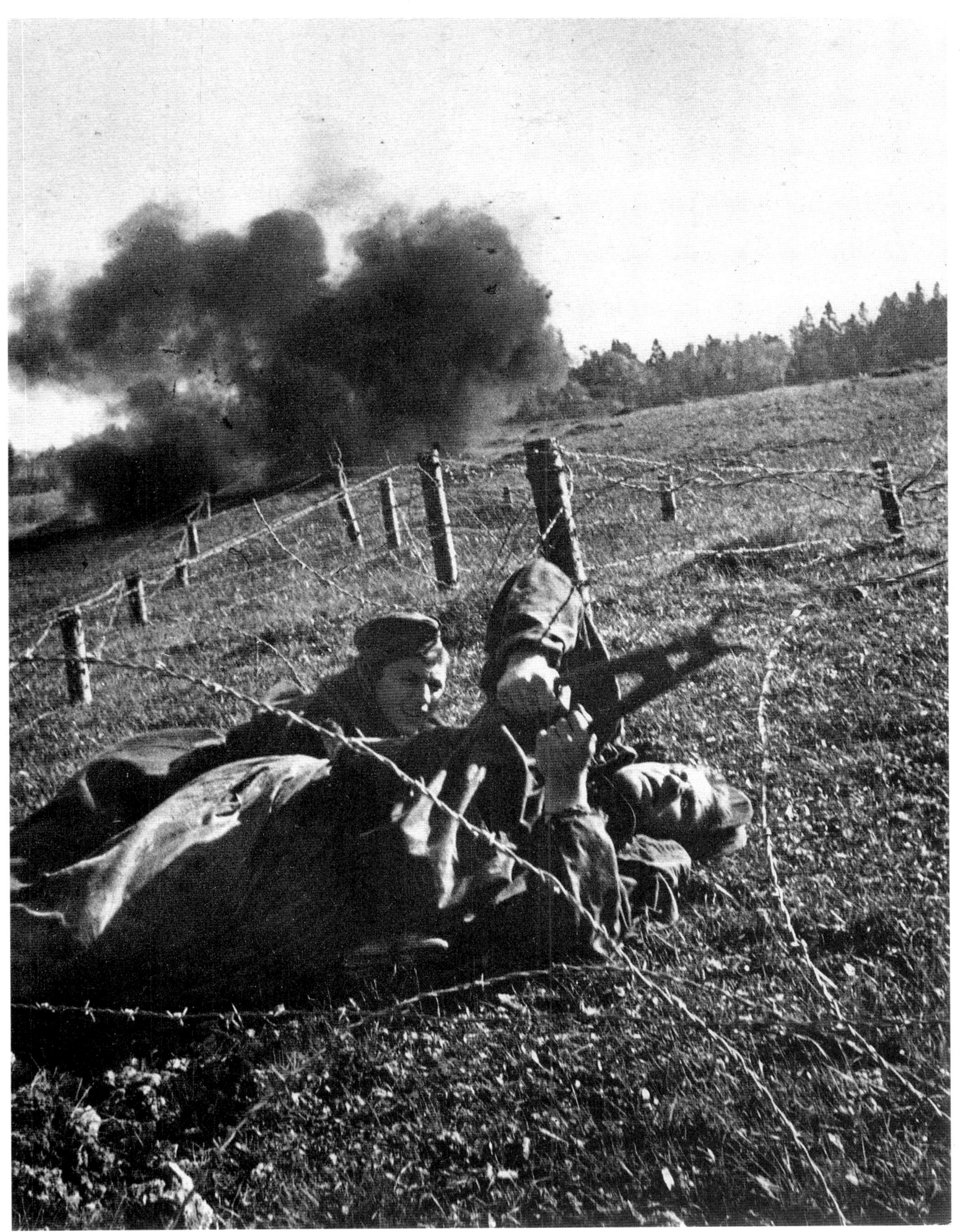

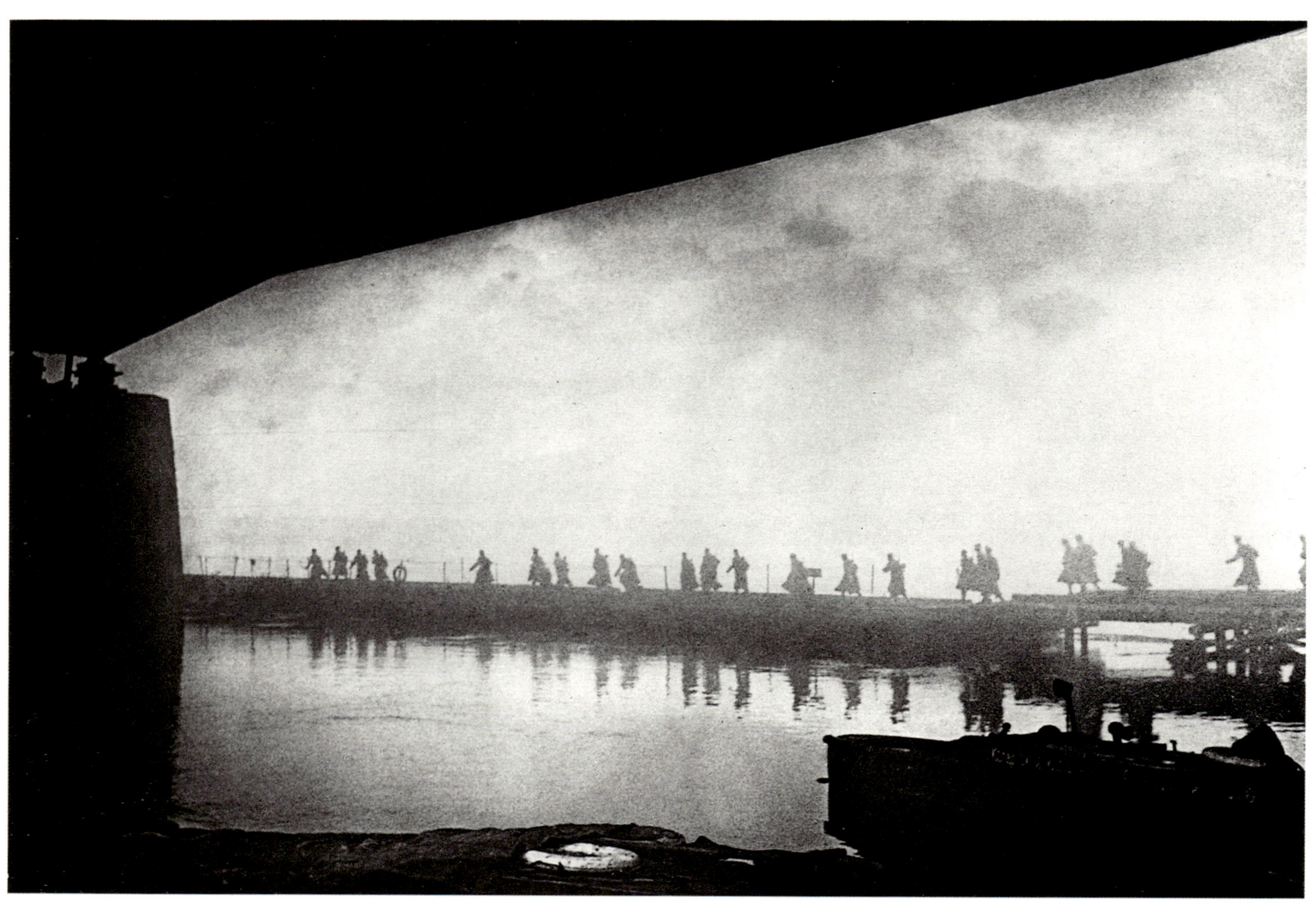

ARKADY CHAJHET
THE FORGING OF THE RIVER ODER, 1945
11 × 15½″

He was arrested in 1938 and died while in confinement; it is unclear precisely when or how he died. Culminating in 1932, Rodchenko was harshly criticized for the formalist quality of his work, and although he continued to photograph throughout the 1930s, eventually he greatly reduced his photographic output and returned to painting. The connection between his new vision in art and the new vision of society had been severed. Art had become official and the true artist unofficial. The synthetic portrait became the standard image for the Soviet masses.

The USSR is currently experiencing a time in many ways similar to the post-revolutionary avant-garde period. There has been an outburst of creative activity, and artistic and political opinions, platforms, and manifestos have proliferated. Photography is once again playing a major role. However, instead of the Soviet state becoming more centralized, as it became in the 1920s, the new society is decentralizing and loosening control. Censorship of the arts is taking a backseat to the explorations of the new avant-garde thinkers who are attempting to lead the country into the future.

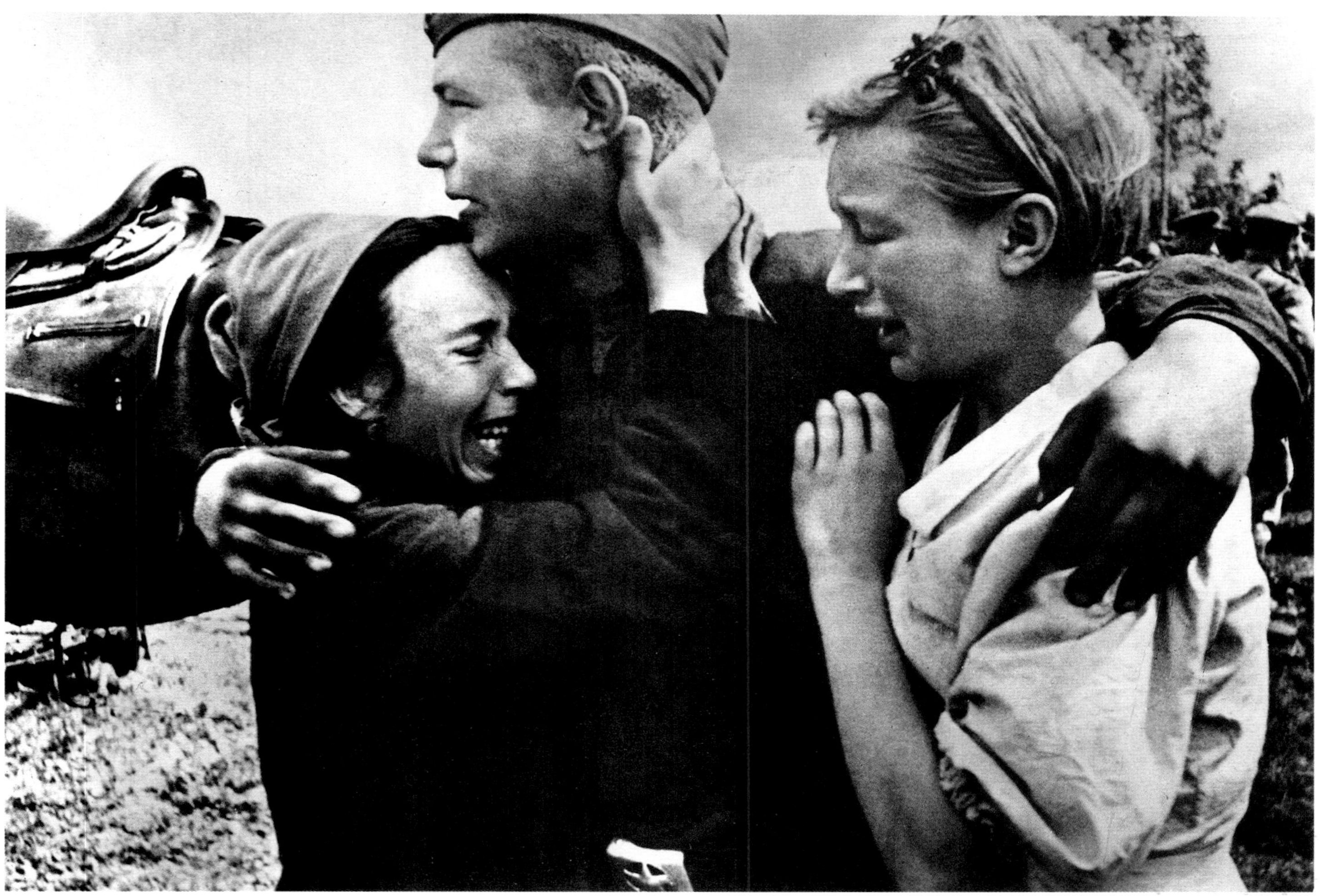

ARKADY CHAJHET
UNEXPECTED MEETING, c.1943
10¾ × 15½"

Art critic Margarita Tupitsyn states in *Margins of Soviet Art,* "This agitation creates an atmosphere rather similar to the post-revolutionary period, the difference being that then the Soviet Cultural apparatus had not been built and now it has not been dismantled." Contemporary photography in the USSR displays the dismantling of the Soviet apparatus and reflects the new freedom, the return to individual expression from the state as author. It rejects the co-option of art and the synthetic portrait manufactured by the state.

Since 1985, Soviet society has been permitted an ongoing openness that reveals the brutality and falsehoods of the past. With the dismantling of the strictures placed on society, the distinction between official and unofficial culture has become blurred, but in the pre-glasnost era creative experiments in art were banned as un-official, dangerous experiments. Contemporary photographers can well remember—even in the very recent past—art taken off the walls of exhibits and whole exhibits being closed on orders from the authorities. While a fertile and exciting underground culture did develop, photography as an artistic, truthful, and

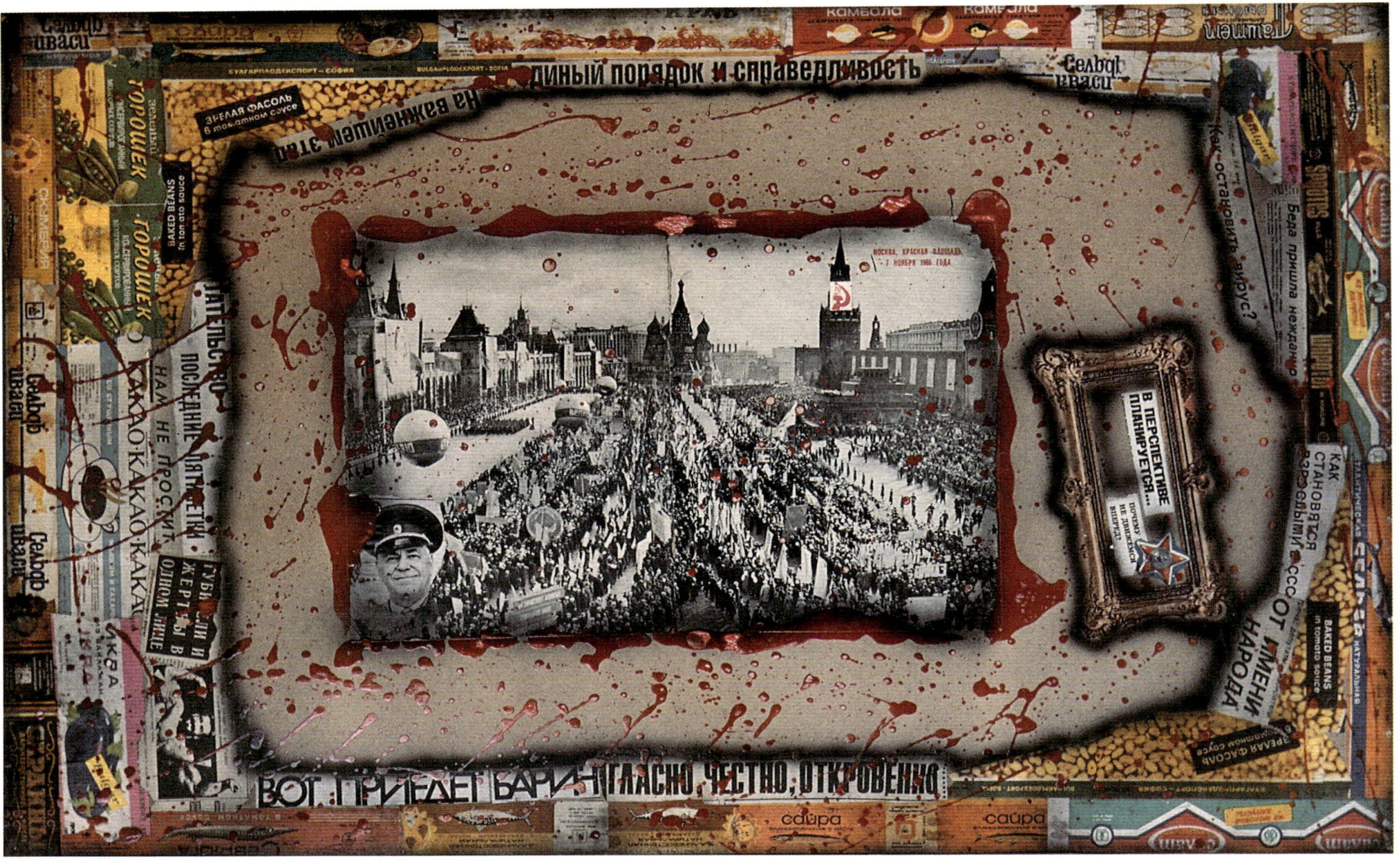

ALEXEI ROSSAL
from the series: REPENTANCE, 1990
30 × 20″

creative medium did not openly exist for the almost sixty years between Stalin and Gorbachev. The idea that photography was anything but a nonartistic entity in the service of the current bureaucracy was forgotten. Healthy workers were presented as model citizens flourishing in the new state as people throughout the country had to struggle for each meal; Kremlin leaders were arranged and rearranged in a Byzantine fashion understood by only the highest members of the Politburo: appearances were everything as reality was simulated for public consumption.

Moscow art critic Victor Misiano stated in 1989, "There is no photography in the Soviet Union. In a country where the idea of glasnost represents a political innovation, the notion that photography is not merely a simple analogue of reality but an analysis of it has not had much chance to be realized." But with the advent of the recent political changes in the USSR, the use of photography for true analysis and artistic expression has begun. Photographs can once again explore various perceptions of the truth and be a part of real social change.

Like their pioneering forebears, contemporary Soviet photographers have begun to work in creative series, using multiples of photographs to express their feelings and opinions. Combining avant-garde artistic

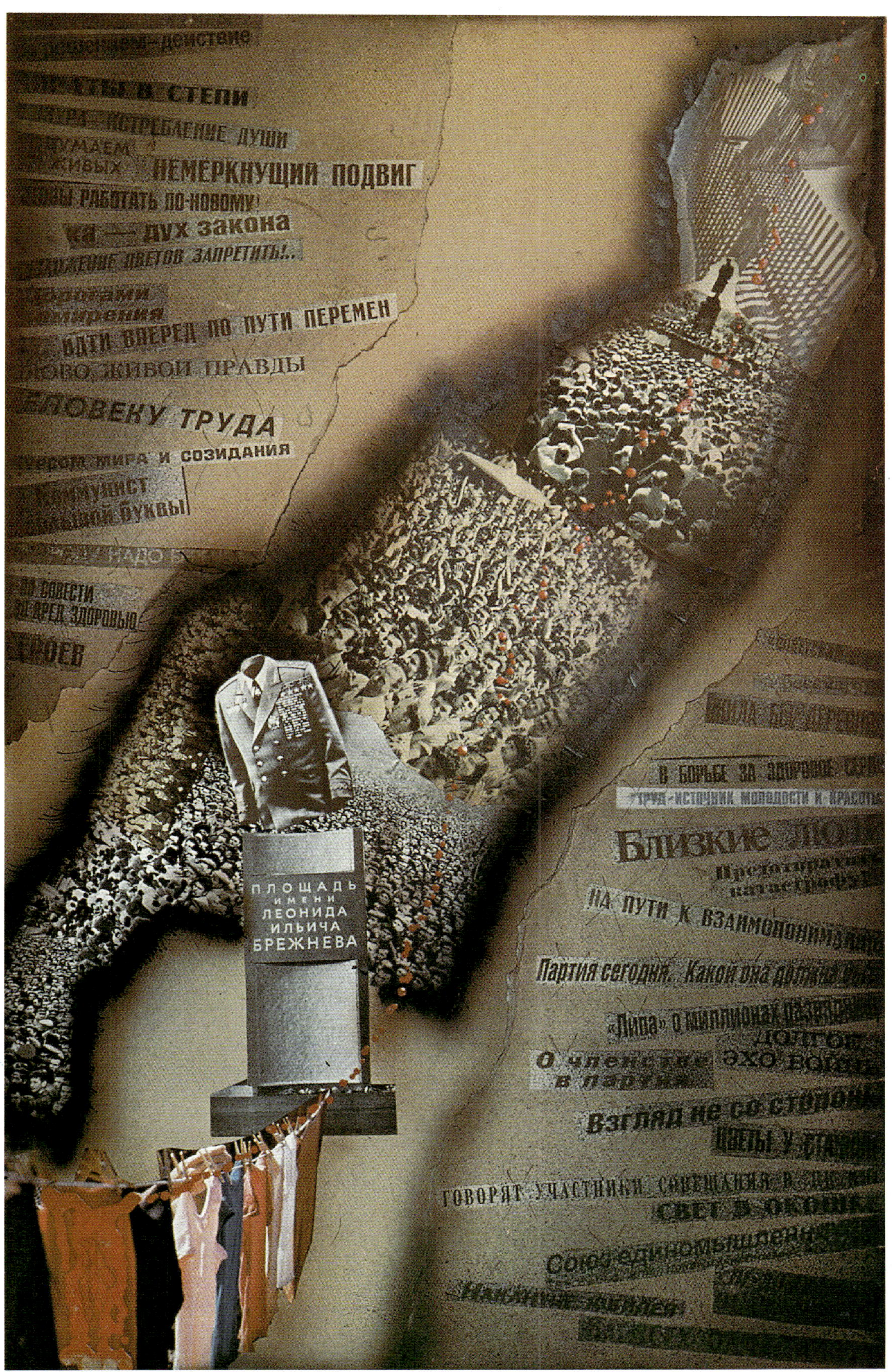
В СТЕПИ
ИСТРЕБЛЕНИЕ ДУШИ
НЕМЕРКНУЩИЙ ПОДВИГ
РАБОТАТЬ ПО-НОВОМУ!
ДУХ ЗАКОНА
ЦВЕТОВ ЗАПРЕТИТЬ!..
ИДТИ ВПЕРЕД ПО ПУТИ ПЕРЕМЕН
ЖИВОЙ ПРАВДЫ
ТРУДА
МИРА И СОЗИДАНИЯ
ПЛОЩАДЬ
ИМЕНИ
ЛЕОНИДА
ИЛЬИЧА
БРЕЖНЕВА
В БОРЬБЕ ЗА ЗДОРОВОЕ
ТРУД – ИСТОЧНИК МОЛОДОСТИ И КРАСОТЫ
Близкие
НА ПУТИ К
Партия сегодня. Какой она должна
«Липа» о миллионах
О членстве в партии
ЭХО
Взгляд не со
ЦВЕТЫ У
ГОВОРЯТ УЧАСТНИКИ СОВЕЩАНИЯ
СВЕТ В
Союз

developments in photography with the pre-revolutionary styles of Russian photo-reporters such as Maxim Dmitriev, Pyotr Otsup, and Karl Bulla, the new photographers present to the viewer artistic photo documentation of contemporary life.

For example, like Mikhail Napplebaum in the 1920s, Lev Melihov has recorded the portraits of the entire artistic intelligentsia of his era: the 1980s (pages 184–85). Napplebaum photographed artistic figures such as Vladimir Tatlin, Boris Pasternak, and Vsevolod Meyerhold. Melihov has photographed such eminent figures as painters Ilya Kabakov, Eric Bulatov, and Grisha Bruskin. In a parallel vein of portrait photography, Sergey Leontiev's oversized photos of strangers on the Arabat capture the faces of everyday citizens on Moscow's public gathering place for street artists and performers (pages 143–47).

Artist Vladzimir P. Parfianok created the continuing series of works called *Persona Non Grata* (pages 112–13), a series about youth in the Soviet Union who are in limbo between the student's life and the worker's life, between being an adult and growing up.

Moscow artist Vladimir Kuprejanov has created a series called *Middle Russian Landscape* (pages 148–49, 225), which captures vividly the oblique pain and suffering of contemporary Soviet life. Like Klutsis, Kuprejanov first makes small photo collages as studies for larger pieces. Then he develops his images on oversized material and enlarges them to the size of small billboards. In contrast to the propaganda of the past, Kuprejanov's photo installations portray everyday people and emotions, not the staid, emotionless public images of leaders such as Marx, Engels, Lenin, and Stalin.

As in the past, the manipulation of photographs is widespread in contemporary photography in the USSR. Many photographers hand-color, collage, superimpose, and otherwise manipulate photographic images in many different ways. But their reasons for manipulating photographs are different from those used by the Soviet government in the past. Contemporary photographers' manipulation has more to do with freedom of expression and the re-exploration of old techniques than with the idealization of reality in a state-approved form.

The new photographers manipulate photography not to censor but to explore the truth. Instead of creating a make-believe reality for the news, they explore their own inner reality and reaffirm their significance as individuals within the state. Their photographic series often capture the alienation within the present society and are a vivid reminder of the independence of spirit that has remained despite the efforts to extinguish it: for example, Igor Moukhin's *Fragments* (pages 156–57) and Alexey Shulgin's *TV Set* (pages 160–61).

Andrey Chegin's *Black Square* series (pages 130–31) shows the unique mix of the avant-garde and photo documentation while it captures the alienation inherent in the modern Soviet situation. The artist pictures the subject as a fragment of art history, portrayed as a disintegrating figure tattooed with a black square. In an homage to Kazimir Malevich, the artist in this series is lost within a hybrid of past visual influences.

Contemporary art in general in the USSR exemplifies an often anguished return to personal meditation and the reinterpretation of history. In a *New York Times* review of the 1990 exhibit Between Spring and Summer: Soviet Conceptual Art in the Era of Late Communism, Michael Kimmelman points out that "while the constructivists advocated art in the service of the masses, the conceptualists in Between Spring and Summer seem to return often to the notion of art as a private occupation." Even when addressing political issues, Soviet photographers, as well as painters, poets, and sculptors, today do so from a perspective that is intimate, emotional, subjective, and personal.

The Moscow artist Alexei Rossal, who uses photographic images he finds in mass publications to paint on and collage, combines private and public issues through his art. His recent *Repentance* series (pages 30–31), consisting of forty poster-sized pieces, juxtaposes manufactured photographic images from papers such as *Pravda* with newsprint and paint to shock the viewer into reading between the lines of history. His *Repentance* series asks for forgiveness, and, like Kuprejanov's series, begs God, "Please don't abandon us."

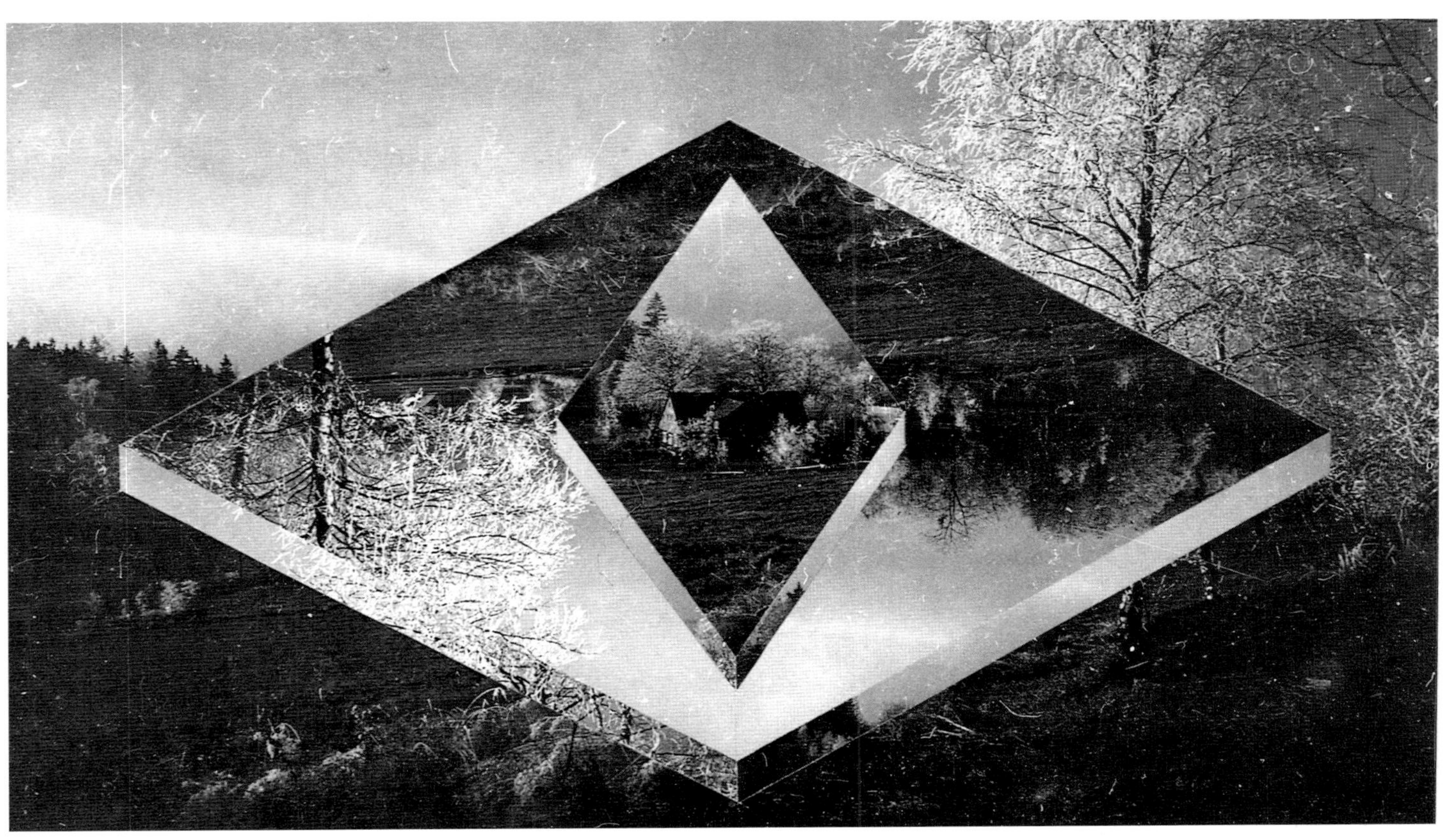

VACHESLAV KOLEICHUK
COLLAGE, 1982
5 × 8¾″

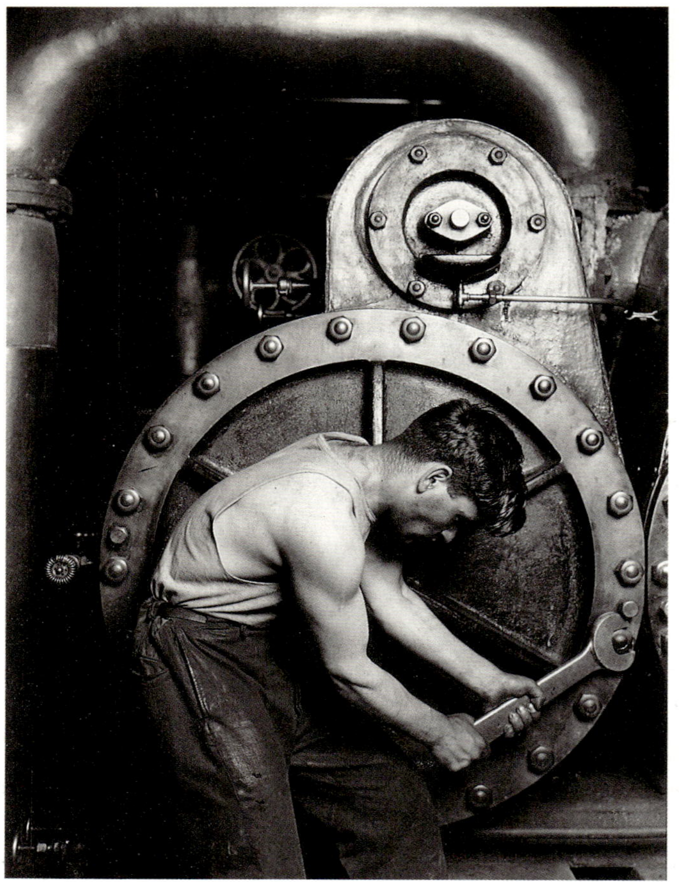

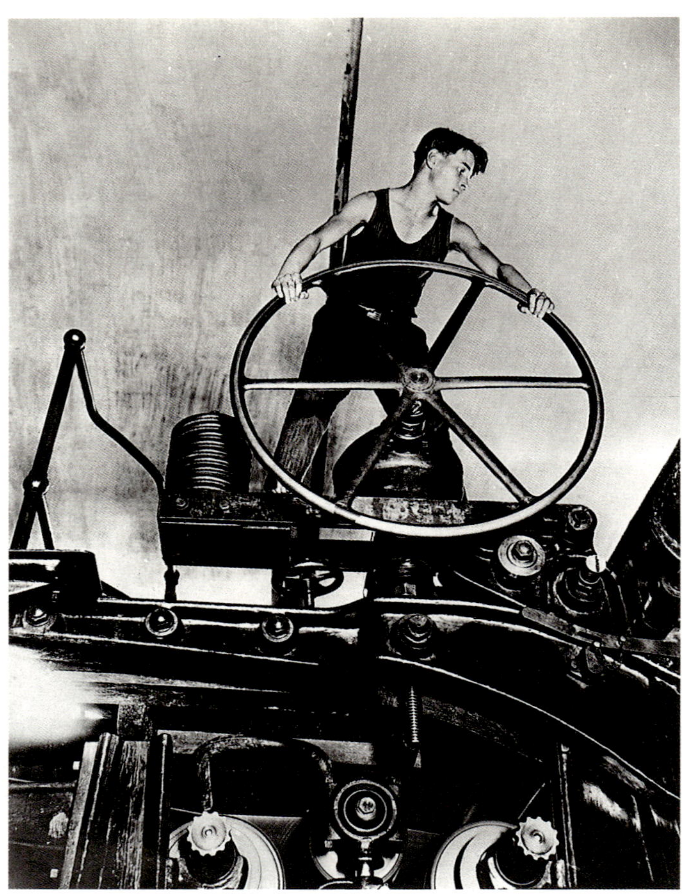

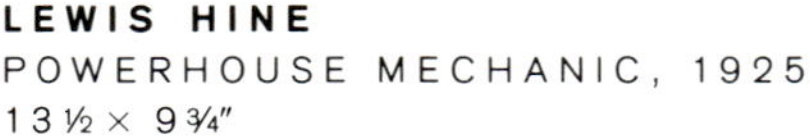

LEWIS HINE
POWERHOUSE MECHANIC, 1925
13½ × 9¾″

ARKADY CHAJHET
A KOMSOMOL AT THE WHEEL, c.1931
15½ × 11½″

Yet within the wide range of contemporary photo-art styles optimism is also expressed. Kinetic artist-photographer Vacheslav Koleichuk perhaps best captures this optimism in his fascination with form and space (page 33). By exploring the nature of visual reality in such a beautiful and simple way, Koleichuk reminds us that not only lies and deception but also an intricate and wonderful order wait to be discovered beneath the surface. Koleichuk looks at photography and life with awe, as if he were an astronaut on a distant planet seeing the earth for the first time.

The recent photograms of Varvara Rodchenko, the daughter of Alexander Rodchenko, also offer an uplifting glimpse through personal experimentation (pages 220–22). Composing her photograms with flowers and leaves, she echoes photo experiments of the past while creating a world of her own. Her work, neither dramatic nor political, reflects quietly on nature and lets the viewer rest from the bombardment of contemporary images.

VLADIMIR FILONOV
from the series: LONG, LONG DAY, 1987
8½ × 6″

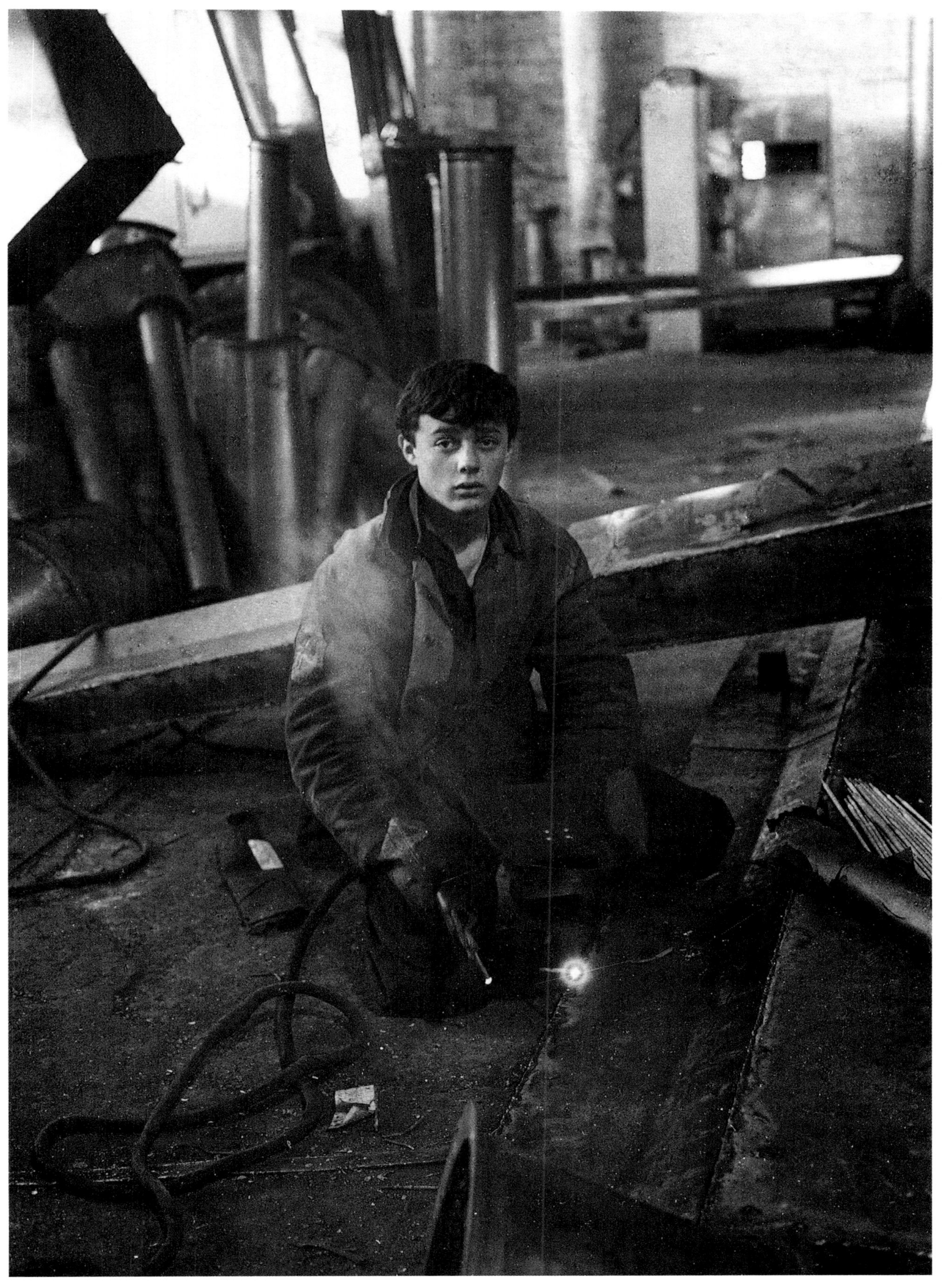

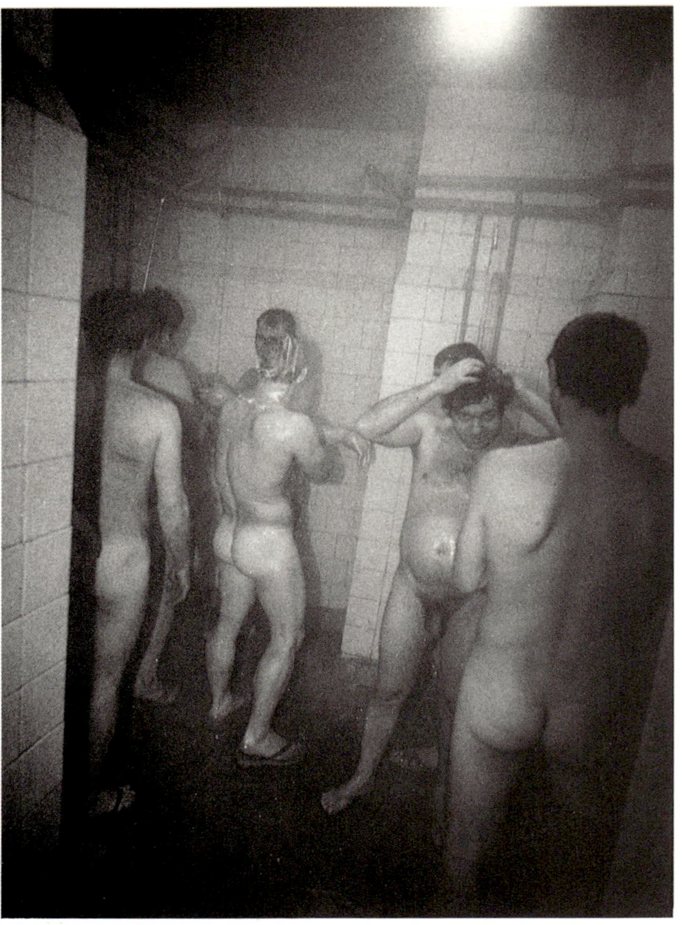

VLADIMIR FILONOV
from the series: LONG, LONG DAY, 1987
8½ × 6″

The comparison of photography done in the USSR with photography done in the West over the past century yields interesting similarities. In the March 1990 *Harvard Law Review,* Judge Pierre N. Leval wrote, "All intellectual activity is in part derivative. There is no such thing as a wholly original thought or invention. Each advance stands on building blocks fashioned by prior thinkers." While myriad influences have been traded back and forth between generations of photographers, the important issues to remember when making cross-cultural comparisons in art are not only who did what first and where, but the specific personal and political context of creation.

The interchangeability of Lewis Hine's *Powerhouse Mechanic* (page 34) and Chajhet's *A Komsomol at the Wheel* (page 34) demonstrates how unique photos can appear to be derivative of each other. The young Komsomol who turns the wheel of Soviet industry looks like a cousin or brother of the handsome American worker. The fact that Hine's image predates Chajhet's does not imply that Soviet photographers were mimicking their Western associates: both photographs originally capture the germination of the machine age. As both the United States and the USSR underwent industrialization, the photographers captured the epic event in different versions of alternative utopias.

The photographs of contemporary photographer Vladimir Filonov can be compared to the work of both Hine and Chajhet. A photograph from his series depicting a steel factory in Zaporozhye, Brezhnev's birthplace, shows the present state of industrialization in the USSR. In contrast to the two photographs by Hine and Chajhet, Filonov's photograph of a young worker reveals despair (page 35). The older photographs project a positivity toward the future, while the Filonov image captures a present with no future.

As well, Filonov's photograph of men showering at the steel plant (page 36) contrasts with Boris Ignatovich's *The Shower* (page 37), taken in 1948. The Ignatovich work almost has no characters: from a distance it emphasizes the atmosphere surrounding the men rather than the men themselves. The image is misty, soft, and romantic. In the Filonov photograph, the reality of nakedness and separateness is revealed.

Visual and philosophical comparisons of work done by American advertising photographers and Soviet propagandists have also been made. In the West the development of a stylized, manipulated, commercial hyperreality paralleled the movement of Soviet photography, reaching the height of style in the 1950s, not surprisingly at the height also of the cold war. After World War II, when the sanitized picture of the USSR was held up against the style of American photography that we call the Clean Kitchen Cabinet genre, happy suburban housewives in the United States were presented as both the antithesis and mirror image of the enemy Soviet housewife.

In a more contemporary context, the art of Barbara Kruger has obvious, if not deliberate, similarities to Soviet photography, specifically to the avant-garde. In Kruger's work one sees parallels with the innovative photo-graphic design developed by artists such as Klutsis. Kruger's 1987 montage of a hand with the words "I shop therefore I am" (page 38) is reminiscent of Klutsis's 1930 design for a political poster that proclaims "We will realize the plan of the great project" (page 39).

Both Klutsis and Kruger utilize bold red backgrounds, the human hand, and words to proclaim ideologically incompatible concepts that somehow look similar today: Klutsis's promotion of communism as Stalin gained control and Kruger's embodiment of capitalism out of control. Here both Kruger and Klutsis make advertising an art and art advertising. Each artist captivates the viewer through a collective-unconscious col-

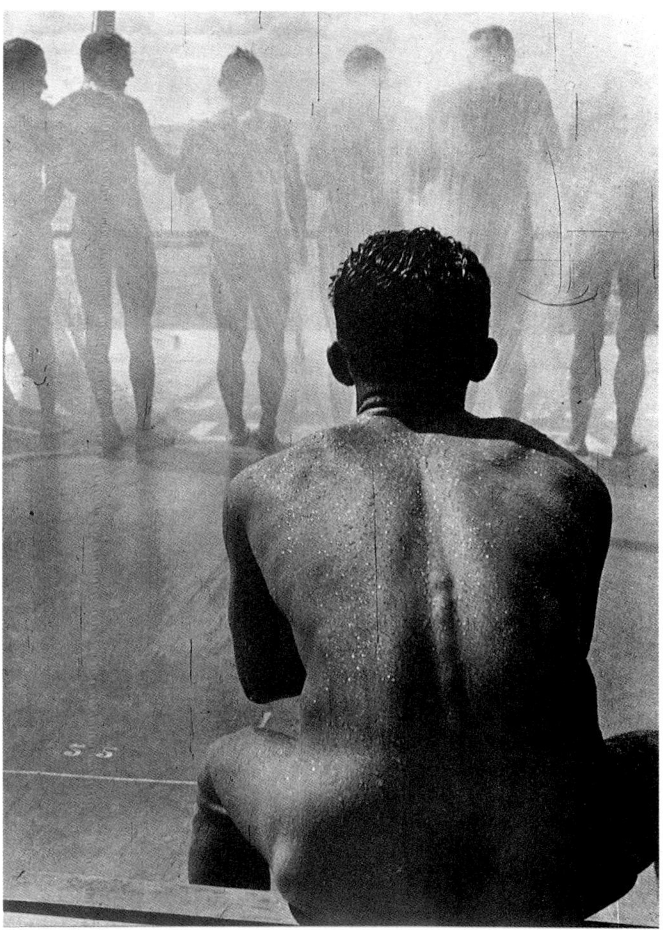

BORIS IGNATOVICH
THE SHOWER, 1948
15¾ × 10¼"

lage of words and images that becomes pictorial propaganda.

Comparing the portrait of Alexander Rodchenko's mother done by Sherrie Levine (page 40) with the portrait of Rodchenko's mother done by Rodchenko (page 41) demonstrates that in the postmodern context the debate over whose work is derivative of whose is moot. Levine argues that the Rodchenko image is her original, adopting a postmodern stance, creating ambiguity over authorship.

Levine's art stresses the importance of the act of creation in its context: the reason for creating and the method of creating art is as

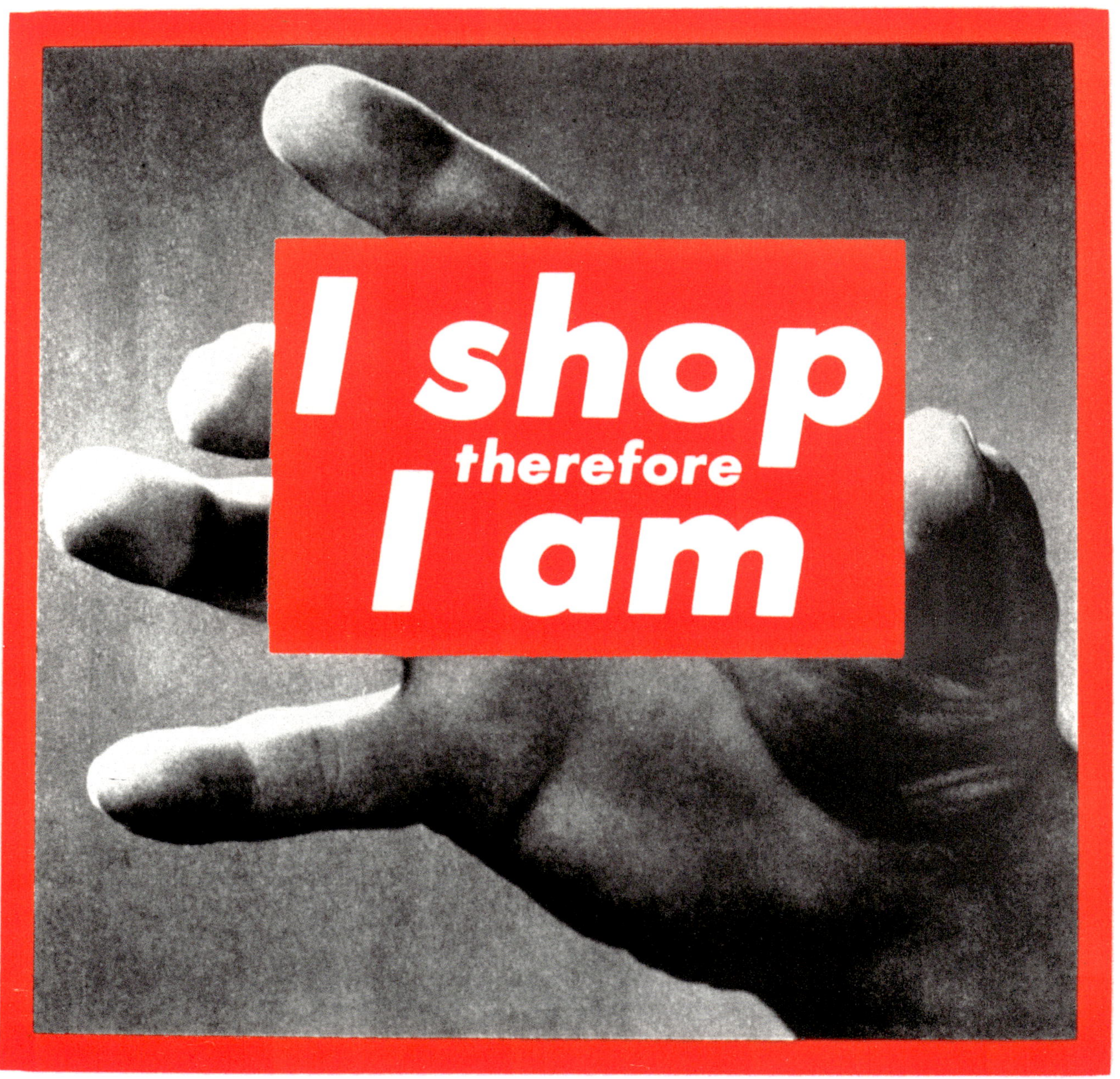

BARBARA KRUGER
UNTITLED (I SHOP THEREFORE I AM), 1987
111 × 113″

important as what is created. In fact, the art objects Levine creates are less important than the ideas that generated them. Levine's success supports the idea that art must be looked at within a framework that goes beyond pure formal criteria. It's the same image. Or is it?

The use and manipulation of found negatives by contemporary Soviet photographers accents as well the postmodern questioning of authorship and originality. Photographers all over the USSR are developing negatives created by anonymous photographers and claiming the results as their own. Sometimes the photographs are printed directly from the negatives without any changes, but usually the photographer scratches, hand-paints, or collages the negatives or prints to create new images from the old. To the photographers, this approach to photography is as important as the object created.

As well as anonymous negatives, many photographers, such as Sergey Kozhemyakin and Galina Moskaleva, use negatives from family archives as the source material for new works. In this way, they re-create their own history. Their photographic artwork, derived from the statements made by another's photographs, is as original as the photographs from which it is created.

Undoubtedly, one of the major recent trends in the USSR has been the formation of groups of individual photographers and artists who support one another's creative activity. Although these groups are often loosely defined and not specifically founded on a dominant ideology, they still serve as a major influence on contemporary Soviet photography. The photographers collaborate both creatively and technically, sharing ideas and working together on series as well as sharing cameras, film, and darkroom equipment. There is, however, no possible generalization of the nature of photographic groups in the Soviet Union. Each works differently, with diverse goals and methods, from providing a loose network of information to more extensive artistic collaboration. The lack of rigidity in these groups promotes interaction between them, between their individual members, and also with the many independent photographers. For example, the Photo Gallery in Leningrad featured the works of Igor Moukhin of Moscow's Immediate Photography group in one of its first exhibits. Valery Stigneev, an independent photographer, art critic, and historian in Moscow,

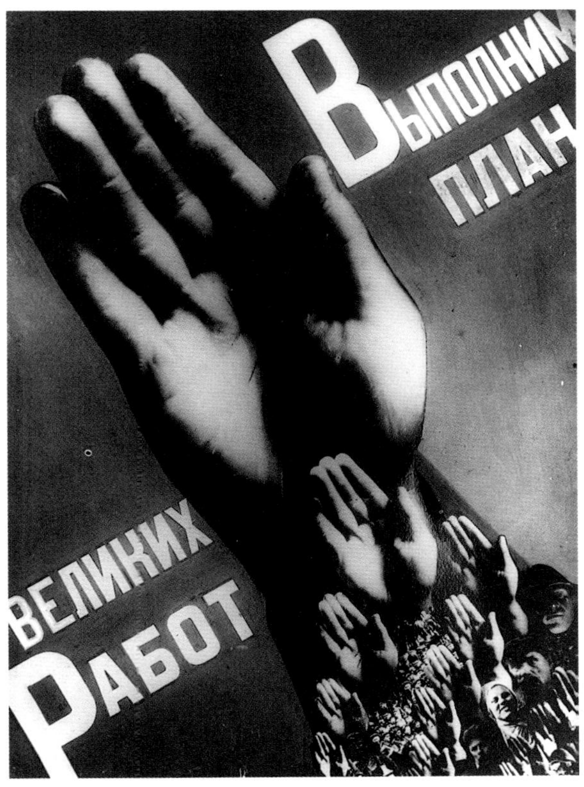

GUSTAV KLUTSIS
WE WILL REALIZE THE PLAN OF THE GREAT PROJECT, 1930
8 ¾ × 6 ¼"

helps to connect the various pockets and outposts of photographic activity in the USSR. Boris Mikhailov, an independent photographer from the Ukraine is also considered a member of the Moscow group.

While most of the photographers included here live and work in major cities within the republic of Russia, many were born or are part of families from other Soviet Republics. Together their photographs in some way capture the entire country once confidently called the Union of Soviet Socialist Republics.

Most of these artists groups exist in the USSR as an extension of the pre-glasnost underground art era when nonunion, or unofficial, artists secretively gathered in one another's apartments and studios where their intellectual experimentation could be hidden

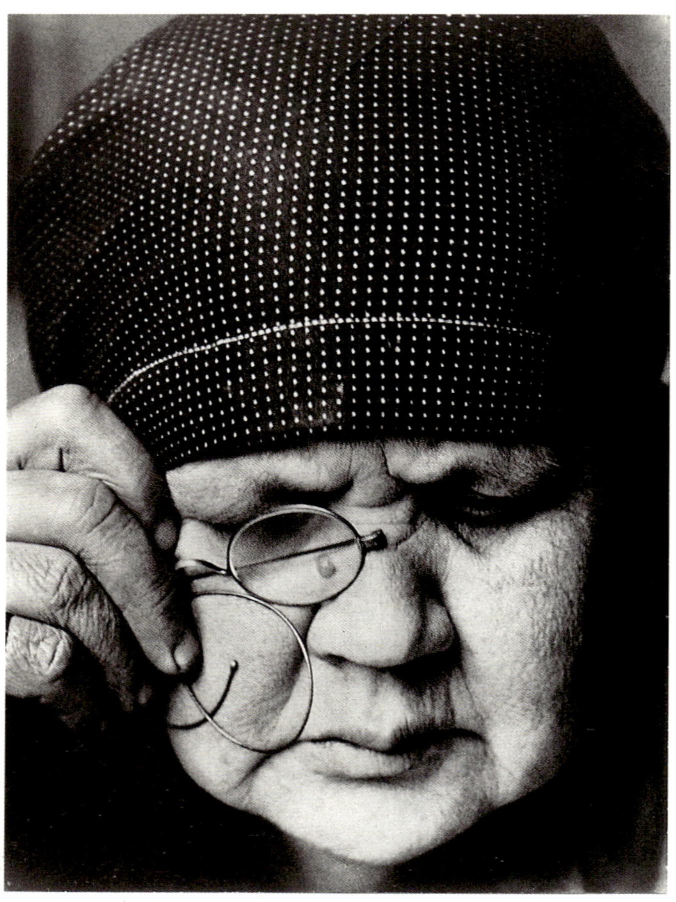

ALEXANDER RODCHENKO
PORTRAIT OF MOTHER, 1924
15½ × 11¼″

from the authorities. Now these groups come together to share insights, create contacts, and explore exhibition opportunities in the USSR and abroad. The difficulty in finding supplies is also still a major obstacle to overcome and artists groups continue to support each other to this end.

In his 1928 essay "Against the Synthetic Portrait, For the Snapshot," Alexander Rodchenko asked, "What ought to remain of Lenin?"—a question appropriate for today. His answer: "A file of photographs. . . . I don't think there is any choice." What remains of Lenin must be a composite whole. The variousness of his reality, as of Stalin's, must not be denied. There lies a parallel in the current removal of Lenin from the popular culture to the decimation of Stalin's presence in public spaces. But with the dismantling and deconstruction of Soviet society, it is imperative that the monuments of the past not disappear out of anger. If all the monuments to Lenin and Stalin are removed and their influence denied, those eradicating their presence are acting as did the totalitarian leaders of the past. The history of the Revolution should no more disappear than the history of prerevolutionary Russia. Idealistic Soviet artists once attempted to creatively build a new utopia proclaiming to abandon the past, but this utopia was not realized. Even if distasteful, the images of history and of reality need to remain, if only to remind us of how we came to be. So the collection of photographs gathered in this book as a photo manifesto, showing a reality documented by the variety of images, should remain a part of the ever-expanding file of photographs from the Soviet Union.

The nature of reality is infinitesimally debated, defined, redefined, and questioned. Photography as a sequence of images questions life's sequence of events. In its myriad expressions, whether color, black-and-white, hand-colored, staged, hand-altered, electronically manipulated, journalistic, or artistic, photography as a whole can capture the essence of everyday life and transform our view of the world.

Mikhail Heller and Alexander Nekrich state in their book *Utopia in Power*, "Memory makes us human. Without it people are turned into a formless mass that can be shaped into anything the controllers of the past desire." *Photo Manifesto* is also a manifesto of memories, a manifesto affirming the strength of the individual over the masses.

Not all of the photographs in this book are light, pretty pictures. Many reveal serious and dramatic moments, and some may even be considered onesided, perhaps ugly and overly focused on the harshness of life. But they are real and touch a raw nerve that cannot be denied.

After the Revolution the creative optimism, techniques, and sincerity of artists were used as a propaganda tool by the government. Today one could ask if the creative dissent of contemporary Soviet art is being used as a propaganda tool by the new state. Contemporary Soviet art has become a major export—a powerful public relations tool to show the changes occurring in the Soviet Union. How real are these recent changes and what is their future?

In many ways the changes in the era of glasnost are much more real to the West than to those still living in the USSR. Now there is greater freedom of expression, but the restructuring, perestroika, has not been fully realized. In fact, it can be argued that the average Soviet citizen was more comfortable during the years of stagnation than today. It is important that the Western audience not perceive the changes in Soviet society through the new trends in Soviet art as in the 1930s the general public mistook art as a reflection of a society that had truly reversed itself. The USSR has not transformed—it is transforming, day by day, snapshot by snapshot.

While we have tried to make sense of

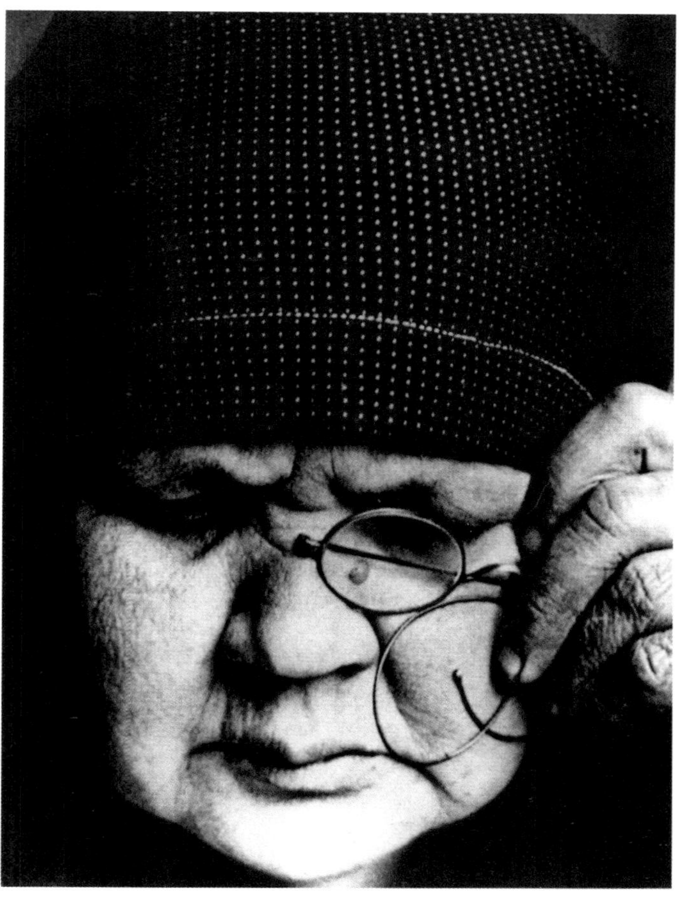

SHERRIE LEVINE
UNTITLED
(AFTER ALEXANDER RODCHENKO : 9), 1987
20 × 16″

contemporary Soviet photography within the framework of overall sociopolitical developments, in the end this book is not about perestroika. It is about how each photographer has tried to capture his own rhythm in his own time. It is true that art and society are inextricably bound and that the history of photography in the USSR is interwoven with the history of the Soviet government. But in the end only personal feeling, artistry, and intellect within this intermingling create a style, an art form that is enduring and beyond the temporal concerns of everyday life.

PHOTOGRAPHY SINCE THE REVOLUTION:

An Historian and Participant's View

ALEXANDER LAVRENTIEV

". . . photography sets imagination free . . ."
SALVADOR DALI

The quotation from Salvador Dali seems an important statement which reflects in a very condensed form the artistic independence of photographic visual language. Photography's competitiveness with the older visual arts such as painting, graphics, and sculpture is the result of its development from these older visual arts, a development in which Russian and Soviet photography played an important role.

Such development, however, looks different when observed from historical distance than when viewed directly from the position of an eyewitness. Thus, the art scene of the 1920s and 1930s looks more definite and purposeful than the contemporary situation, which seems uncertain and full of casualties. With this awareness, we can evaluate in a different way not only the historical precedents but also the recent events, trends, exhibitions, and newly recognized artists.

While in the past there were strong leaders who stimulated the activity of others, current Soviet avant-garde photography seems less dependent on leaders than on events and opportunities: the art and photographic exhibitions, thematic publications, and competitions of the 1970s and 1980s. These events were organized mostly by artists and art critics, for just as the ideas of conceptual value and artistic intention in photography were developed under the influence of other art forms, photographic events were organized by people whose

MAXIM DMITRIEV
SPOON-MAKERS, c.1890–1900
8 1/4 × 5 1/2"

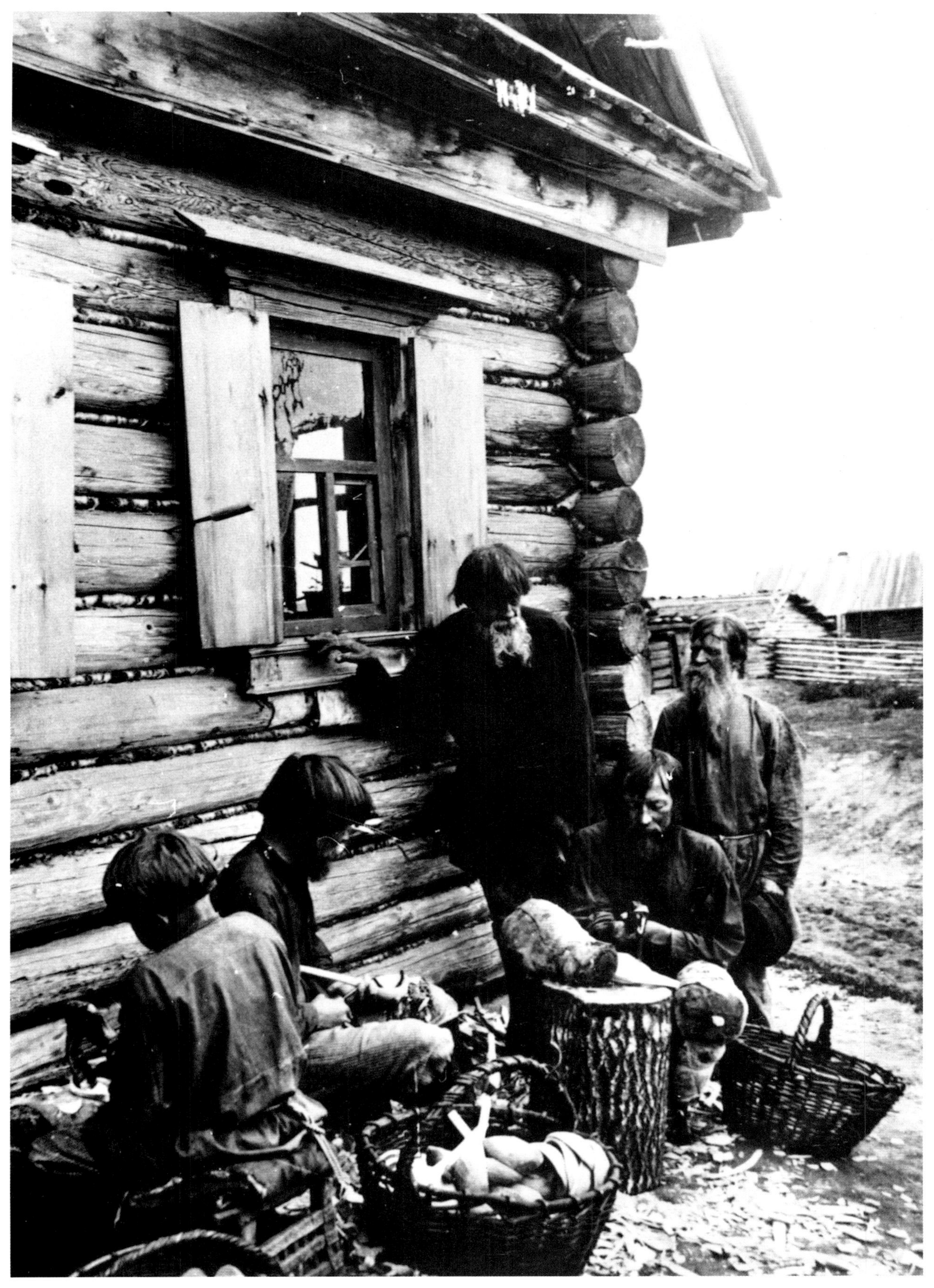

main profession was not necessarily photography.

The major events mentioned here were themselves like manifestos—conceptually independent and new. In 1977 and 1978 two exhibitions of young designers were organized by Alexander Jermolaev, an architect and photographer, and included photography. In 1978 and 1979 there were two exhibitions of the avant-garde artists of the 1960s, one in the House of Scientists and one, called Form and Space, at the trade union organization of graphic artists. At these exhibits Francisco Infante showed photographs of his mirrored installations which he called *Artifacts*. Since 1980 many of the graphic designers' exhibitions have included photography, mostly conceptual photography, as used in book illustration. In 1981, in cooperation with the editorial board of the magazine *Teknicheskaya estetika*, art critic Elena Chernevitch organized a three-day roundtable discussion on "Possibilities of Photography." It was tied to the ninetieth anniversary of Alexander Rodchenko's birth and for the first time introduced to a wider public such photographers as Boris Mikhailov and Georgy Pinkhasov. The following year's major event was the competition Photography and the World of Objects, announced by *Teknicheskaya estetika* and, in 1983, publicly displayed in an exhibition designed by Jermolaev.

Among the prizewinners of Photography and the World of Objects were Igor Berezovsky, for a series of powerful images of details of bookbinding using rolls of rope and iron cord, and Jermolaev, for a series that included shop windows, dilapidated buildings, and amateurishly painted signs on walls, fences, etc. With these images Jermolaev focused attention on the artistic features of the common visual reality that surrounds everyone but remains unnoticed because it is considered ugly and not worth seeing. For Jermolaev, however, it was full of attraction because of its rich visual qualities and truthful presentation.

In 1986, the competition Graphics in the City was announced by the same organizers. The exhibition showed both the state of graphic art in the USSR and the inventiveness of the participating photographers. In 1988 there were numerous exhibitions in which photography played an important role: Designer as Artist, Art and Geometry, The Second Exhibition of Contemporary Artistic Consciousness, and Photography in a Book. All these events helped to create an unusual artistic atmosphere around photography and to formulate new concepts which by the end of the 1980s had crystallized as purely photographic systems distinct from other forms of art.

Strong, original, and personal declarations are something new in contemporary Soviet experimental photography, but they have a long and rich history in Soviet culture. Kazimir Malevich, for instance, declared his Suprematist concept at the 1915 exhibition 0.10 through a performance. He drew the figures 0.10 on his forehead and pasted the declaration "I am an apostle" (a priest of new belief) on his back. Early practicing photographers, however, generally did not need to announce their work—they simply created it. They took the pictures that they saw. The innovative photographers in nineteenth-century Russia, for instance, used existing channels to introduce their work, i.e., photo salons, friends, etc., although they did not always receive acknowledgment for their progressiveness. During this period Andrei Karelin was the first to create staged photography, which he sent to international photo salons and for which he received gold medals. Through the Russian Photographic Society and various publications Maxim Dmitriev became well known for his photo landscapes and journalistic photography. Independent of the fine-art society, photography had quickly developed a professional circle that included magazines, societies, shops, and ateliers.

With the beginning of the twentieth century and the development of avant-garde photography in France, Germany, and Soviet Russia, many things changed. Artistic manifestos, declarations of purposes and themes, became an essential part of photography because rather than reproduce reality, photographers were creating their own worlds. Photography was becoming independent from its material—reality—and a new reality was being built (as in other avant-garde arts as well) by means of installations, photomontage, or purposeful framing of selective objects and events.

Before Alexander Rodchenko, the Soviet Union's well-known photographer and art theorist, took up photography he had great experience in producing artistic declarations. In 1918 he announced his series of paintings with planes—compositions called *Concentration of Color, The Line, Black on Black, Three Basic Colors,* and others—and proclaimed his manifesto by presenting the new painterly series at the opening of an exhibition, supplying each picture with a text (often written directly on the wall), and publishing a brief declaration. Many of Rodchenko's first visual experiments in photography had to be announced and explained, and he had a distinctive talent for explaining and convincing. His statements were brief and clear, like slogans, which later facilitated the task of criticism.

Rodchenko had to thus proclaim himself because there were no skilled photo critics who could explain his work and, in general, there were no developed criteria by which to evaluate his experimental work. In fact, such criteria are always created by the artist's work and its concomitant artistic statements. These criteria include the artistic possibilities opened by the artist's originality.

Photomontage, shots taken at an abrupt angle, mobility of the camera, photo illustration, and snapshot photography were among Rodchenko's inventions which he had to announce. Additionally, he made statements defending his right to independent artistic work and justifying his own creative experience.

The idea of photo experiments came to Rodchenko from early family games with a camera. Together with his wife, Varvara Stepanova, and other relatives, he created humorous situations that were full of meaning, but only for the participants. In such group portraits one can always find exaggeration of the principles of photography—as when somebody is posing or looking into the camera.

Rodchenko's more serious attempts at exploring photographic principles, in 1925 and 1926, were stimulated by these early probes and very soon were aimed at achieving certain compositional results in photo-

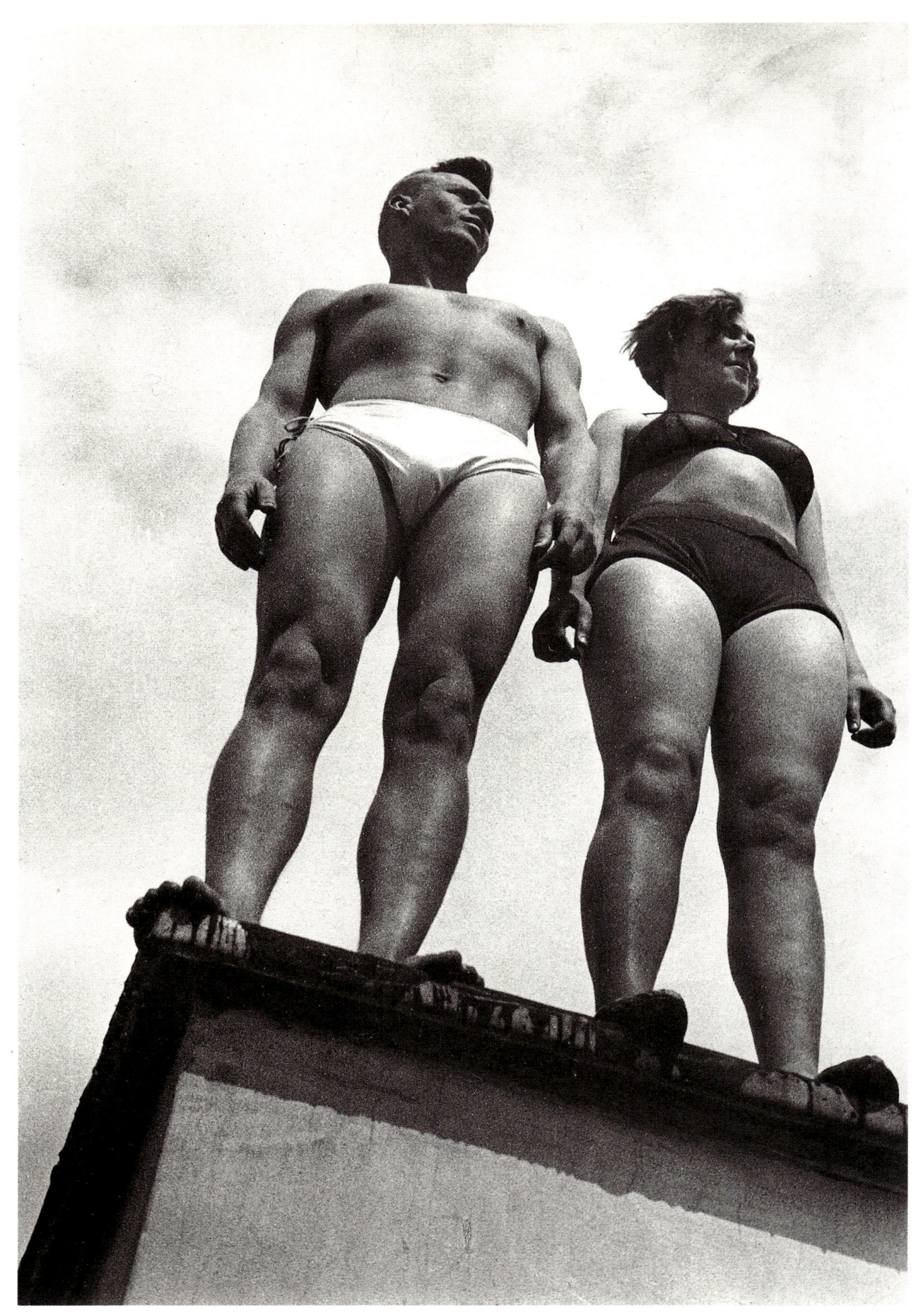

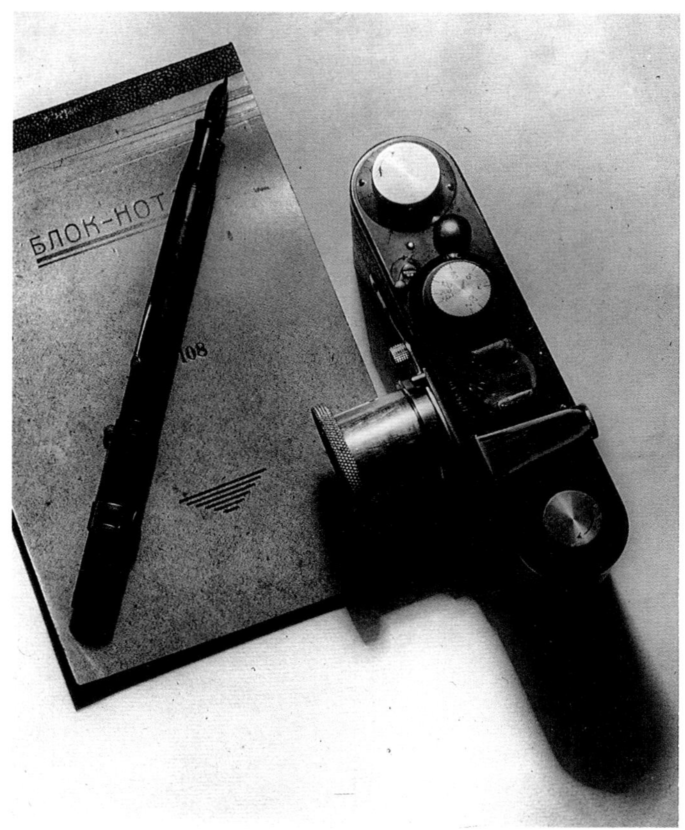

ALEXANDER RODCHENKO
STILL LIFE, PORTRAIT, 1928
12 × 9½″

Opposite:
ALEXANDER RODCHENKO
THE STUDENTS' TOWN OF LEFORTOVO—TOGETHER, 1932
15¾ × 10½″

graphs of houses, still lifes, and technical objects. Rodchenko later explained that these experimental photographs were half-nonobjective, leading from the world of forms to clear geometric schemes. In the face of severe criticism of his shots of houses in exaggerated perspective, Rodchenko published five articles in the magazine *Novy LEF* to explain and defend his work. Had there not been such negative reaction to these shots, he would probably not have answered his opponents in such a detailed way that his response later formed a distinguished photographic system.

Rodchenko was the first among Soviet photographers to use so much of his literary talent to describe his intentions as an artist and photographer. He understood that the situation in art, as in science and technology, was moving toward a valuation of very quick change and momentary perception, and that it was photography that could help to establish this new, active way of seeing the world.

In 1929, a new organization called October emerged, an association of workers

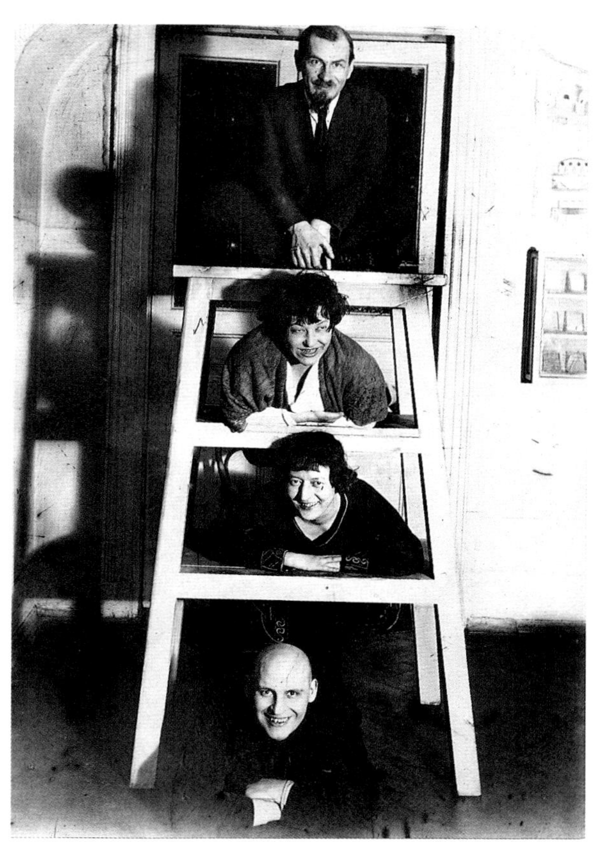

ALEXANDER RODCHENKO
FAMILY GAMES, 1924
11½ × 8″

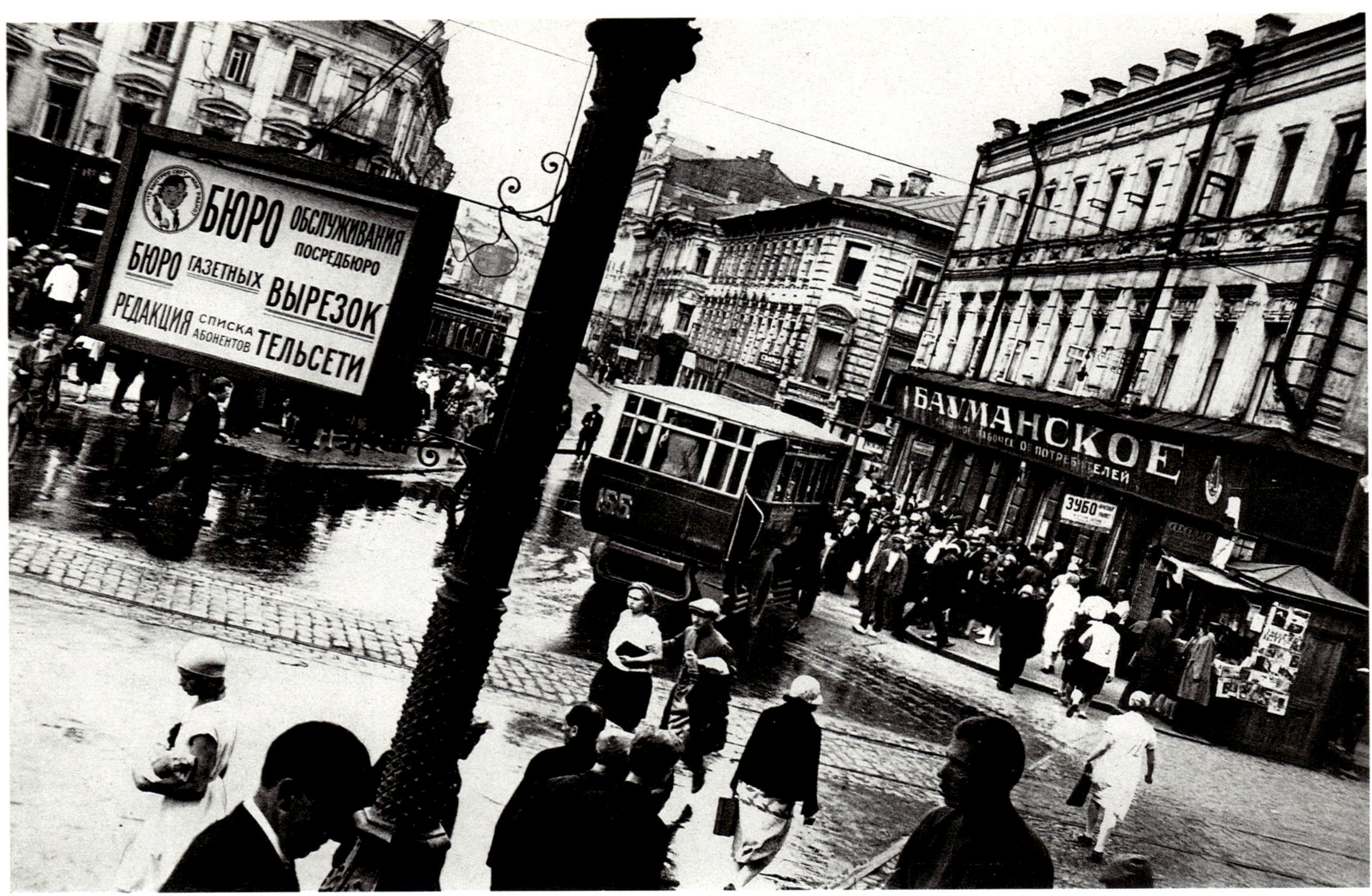

ALEXANDER RODCHENKO
MOSCOW STREET SCENE, c.1928
10¼ × 15¾″

from all the branches of art: architecture, theater, film, typography, etc. Art critics and sociologists declared that the idea was to unite all art professionals in building the new environment for the Socialist society. Rodchenko first joined October as a member of the section of interior design, but in 1930 he formed a photo section.

The members of the group intended to sponsor photo exhibitions and, in general, to develop new artistic possibilities in photography. They were against pure documentary imitation of events and objects in photography. Instead, unusual angles and diagonal composition were used to stress visually the new facts of life that the photographers were selecting in the outside world.

After a group exhibition in 1931, members of the photo section formed a separate group, independent of October. This splinter group, which called itself the October Group, was led by Rodchenko, Boris Ignatovich, and to some extent Eleasar Landman and Vladimir Gruntal. They published their manifesto in the magazine *Soviet Photo* together with a number of photographs. The result was heavy criticism: all the members of the group were accused of formalism and uncritical uses of bourgeois Western photography.

Opponents of the October Group from the Russian Society of Proletarian Photographers also published their photographs and their manifesto, in which they declared mostly political purposes for their work. *Soviet Photo*'s photo critics sided with the opponents. The October Group's work was rejected by the critics as simply the wrong approach to reality. And letters from workers and angry pioneers confirmed that the masses of people did not understand such photography.

Viewing the situation from an historical distance, we cannot find much justification for all the evils of which Rodchenko and the October Group were accused. The themes of their photographs were the same as their opponents': construction, new buildings, workers, sportsmen. The differences were in a very slight degree of "bending" the camera, in some feeling of the composition, and in the presence of acute perspective, all

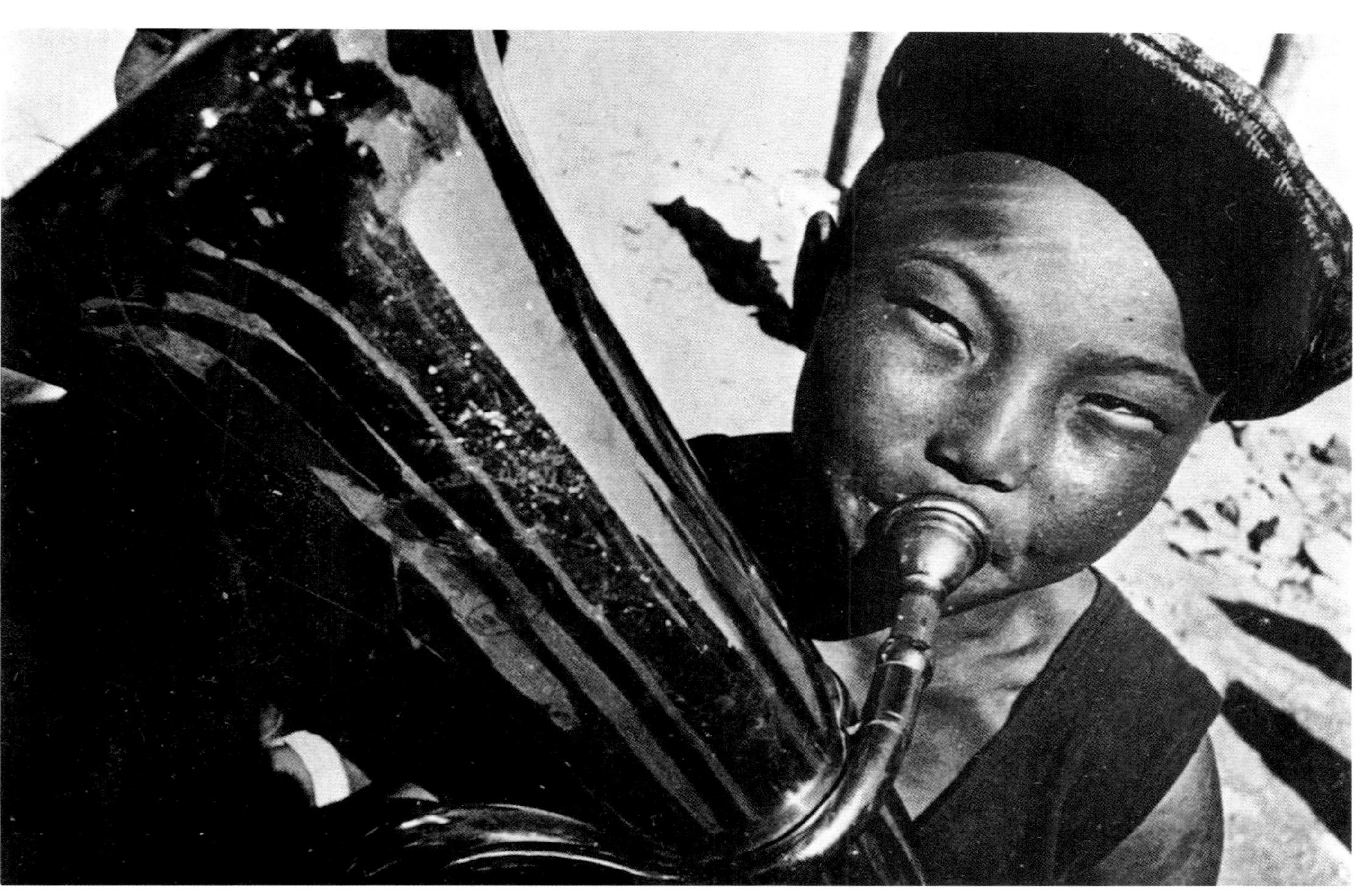

ELEASAR LANDMAN
KAZAKHSTAN, 1934
5 3/4 × 8 1/4″

of which made the October Group's photographs not only examples of photo reportage but also visual statements establishing a new culture of seeing.

In the 1920s and 1930s photographers and artists intensively produced strong visual and verbal statements to announce their works. Later, when this sort of creative declaration was replaced by political texts and editorials, nobody dared to announce his or her personal credo aimed at solving artistic and visual problems if it stood in opposition to the dominating principles of art. In the late 1930s and 1940s photographic credos were not so popular. The photo manifesto was a forgotten genre until as recently as the 1960s and 1970s.

It is the contemporary art situation that has made photographers aware of the necessity for detailed statements that reflect the changes in artistic style and work, and show the relationship of newly proclaimed artistic systems to their predecessors. Interestingly, in the 1980s each new system is presented as distinct from all the others. The individual photographers go in all different directions, each one trying to create his or her own photographic world.

The boundaries of art are always in motion, pushed by artists who thus increase the territory of what is aesthetically familiar. Within wider artistic concepts there always exist very narrow branches of creative experimentation.

Boris Pasternak, in his 1925 introduction to futurist poet Alexei Kruchonikh's book *Kuranti* (*The Clock*), described the process of artistic development as a nonstop movement from the unknown to the habitual, from the mad to the banal. He wrote that at one end of the spectrum is the groundbreaking work of the contemporary artist and at the other, art that with the passage of time has become a common statement, well known and understood by the masses. Pasternak appraised Kruchonikh's experimental sound poetry as in no danger of becoming a banal artistic statement.

Kruchonikh exemplified a specific point on this spectrum of artistic development from madness to banality. While the works of certain writers and artists might very quickly become assimilated into mainstream aesthetic culture, this might never occur with the works of others, such as Kruchonikh. Or, such artists' madness would be validated in the aesthetic culture only after followers had entered the same territory and used the same material for expression.

With its momentary flashes of metaphors that suddenly give light to common scenes and subjects, Pasternak's poetry is akin to photography. And his theory of artistic development holds true for photography as well as for poetry. The 1990 Moscow exhibition devoted to the 150th anniversary of photography contrasted the work of two distinct eras: photographs taken in Russia some hundred years ago and contemporary avant-garde pictures, many of which were only recently taken and on view for the first time. The exhibition showed that this boundary establishing what is artistically valued expands not only in consideration of works created by contemporaries but also in evaluation of works created in the past.

Photographs which previously were con-

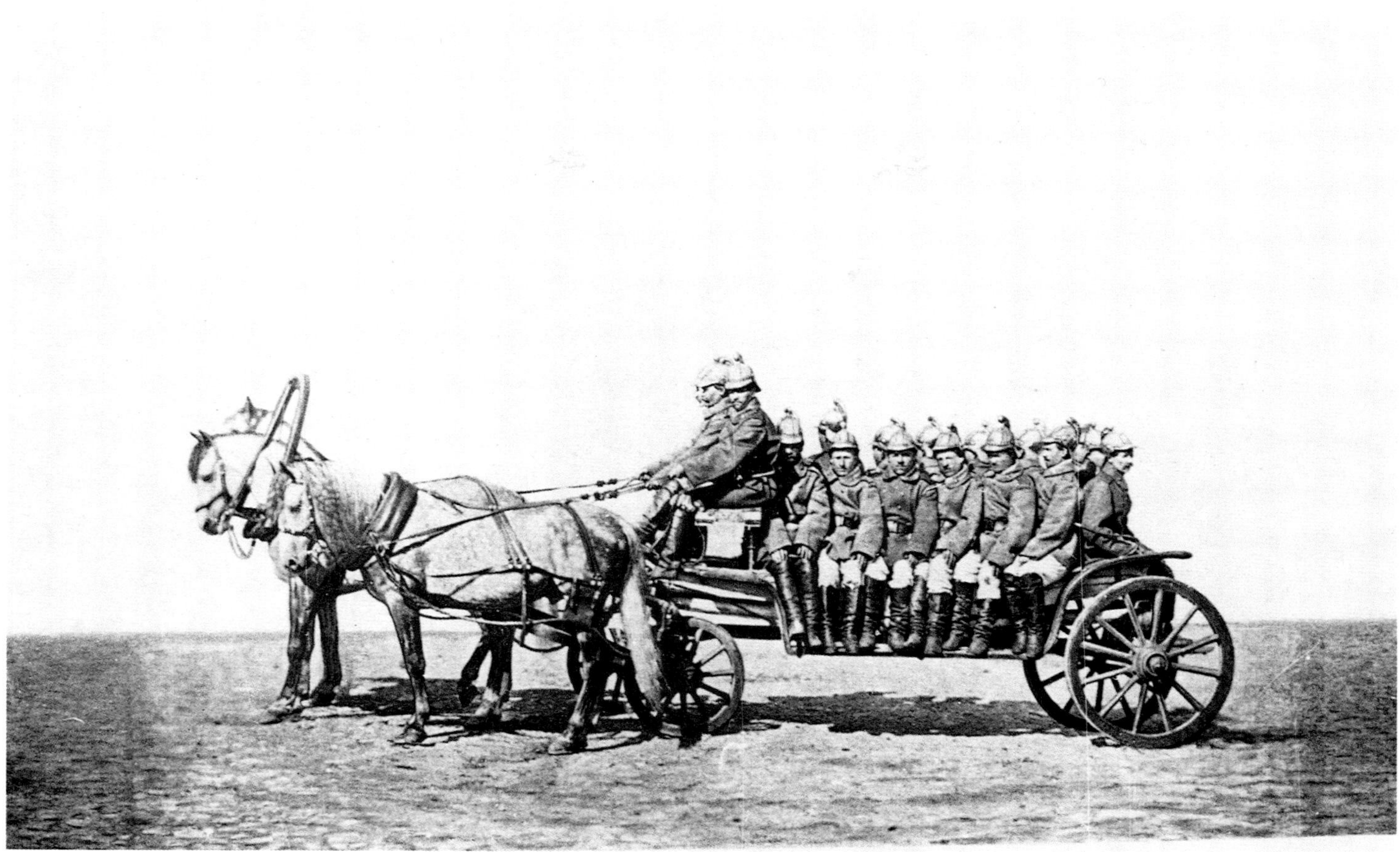

ANONYMOUS
from the series: MOSCOW FIREMEN SERVICE,
1871
7 × 9¼″

sidered mere curiosities could, in fact, be acknowledged as art, in part because of contemporary concepts and works of art which draw on the past. For me personally, one such result of the expanding boundary of art was a new appreciation of the anonymous photography of the 1880s and even earlier: sailors sitting with a picture of a ship; stablemen; and finally a fire brigade (page 51). In these shots, despite their naive character, there is something solid and convincing.

In turn, these old examples of "direct" photography correspond to some of the experiments done in the late 1980s in the USSR. In the direct photography done by a group of young Moscow artists, there is some element of staging and design, but this is always aimed at stressing the real, routine character of the situation. One can even note an element of imitation of folk, nonprofessional photography intended to renovate the professional photographic canons, to encourage the viewing of life as if through the eyes of a newly born baby. But what the contemporary artists are doing is only now becoming art, building on the graduation of nineteenth-century anonymous photography from curiosity to art. And the appreciation of this nineteenth-century artistry lies not only in the technical

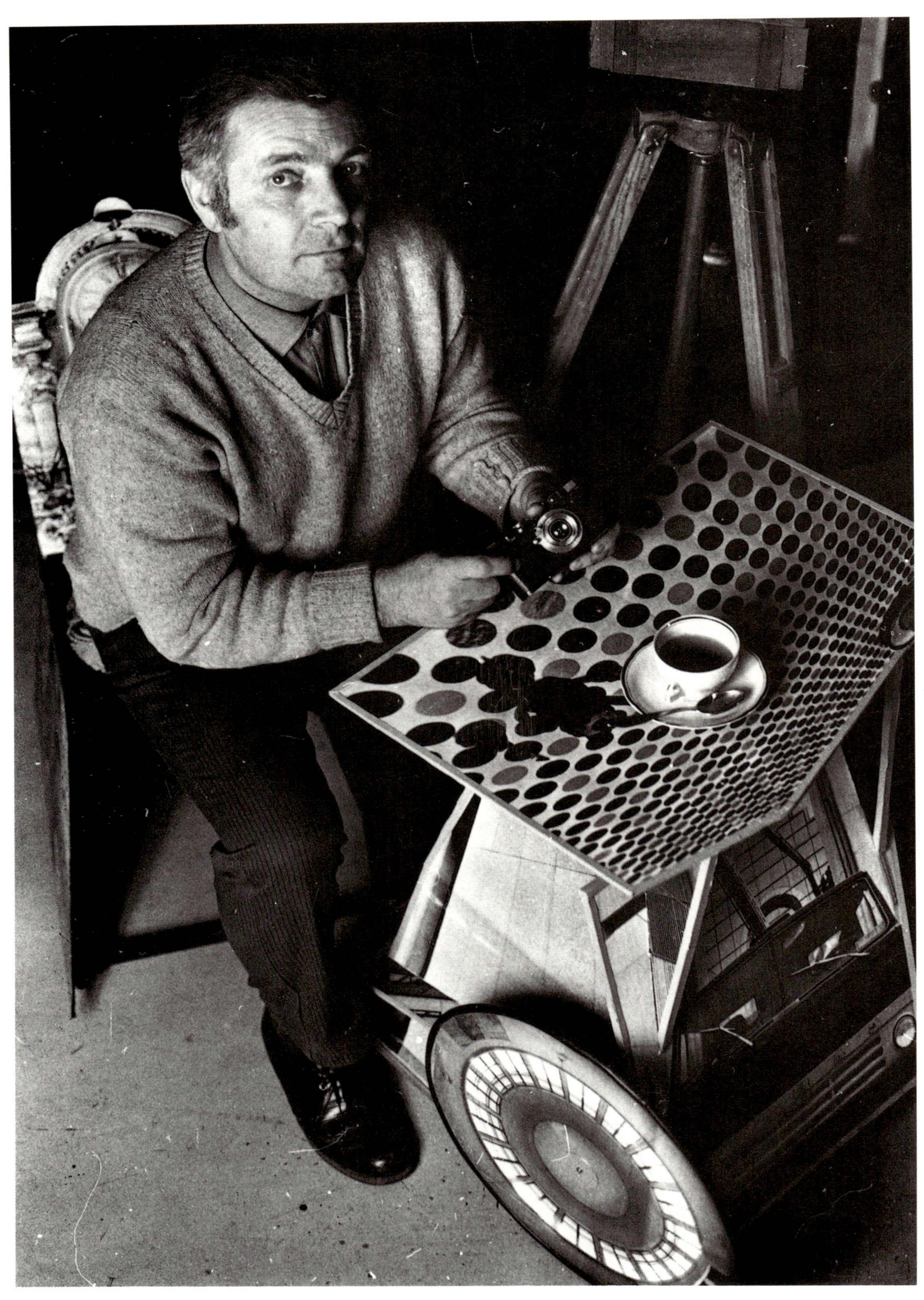

quality of old, large-format cameras but in the truthfulness of the situations being photographed: everyone before the camera believes in this prearranged situation, and the photographer seems to be just one of the folk.

In contemporary Soviet performance photography we seldom find direct links with the photo atelier of the nineteenth century. That photo atelier was an artificial theater of high culture and nobility, with strict rules of posing. While our contemporaries sometimes imitate such style in their works, they use the laws of this theater to express themselves more than to express their model's status, as happened in the classic photo atelier. They construct another world, one with its own logic and scenery. The aim may be to create a visual paradox, a geometric installation, or a surrealistic game with happy or sad characters. Sometimes it is even hard to say who plays the main role in achieving the result: the man with the camera or his friend-models who are living within this constructed situation, trying to persuade us that it is real and quite routine.

I like these games. This attachment came as a result of mastering the situation before the camera during numerous installations of my own design objects. Quite often I placed photographs into these small installations and thus my photographic puppet theater was born. Heroes of this theater were photographs of people, houses, cars, plants—everything. They were put together almost as a photomontage, the only difference being an added dimension: pictures were placed in various planes, facing the central object, one behind the other.

There is always magic when a photograph is photographed. The photograph of the photograph keeps all the tonal, textural, and optical features of the original print, and in the new situation it seems no less real than the people or other objects which surround it. From my point of view, Sherrie Levine has stressed this strange magic of a photograph of a photograph by reproducing works of famous photographers. Of course, this sort of art is connected with postmodernist interest in the context of this or that artistic situation. But the fact that somebody conducts such experiments with the physical, optical, and contextual qualities of photography seems quite important.

Such experiments exploring the objective essence of photography were on view at the Moscow Jubilee Exhibition in 1990. There, Ilya Piganov created a piece on the theme of the photo message, with photographs printed on intriguingly closed mail envelopes; and, by printing photographs on crumpled photographic paper, Vladimir Kuprejanov created works reminiscent of photo sculptures, or photo objects.

By photo sculpture or photo object, I mean a new environment or object created not by the usual methods and materials of painting or collage but primarily by means of photography: for instance, three-dimensional geometric figures that have photographs at their sides; photo enlargements that cover walls, ceiling, and floors, thus changing the character of the space. Sometimes the artist provokes visual con-

ALEXANDER LAVRENTIEV
PHOTOGRAPHER VICTOR ACHLOMOV SITTING AT MY PHOTO FURNITURE, 1988
7 ½ × 5 ¼″

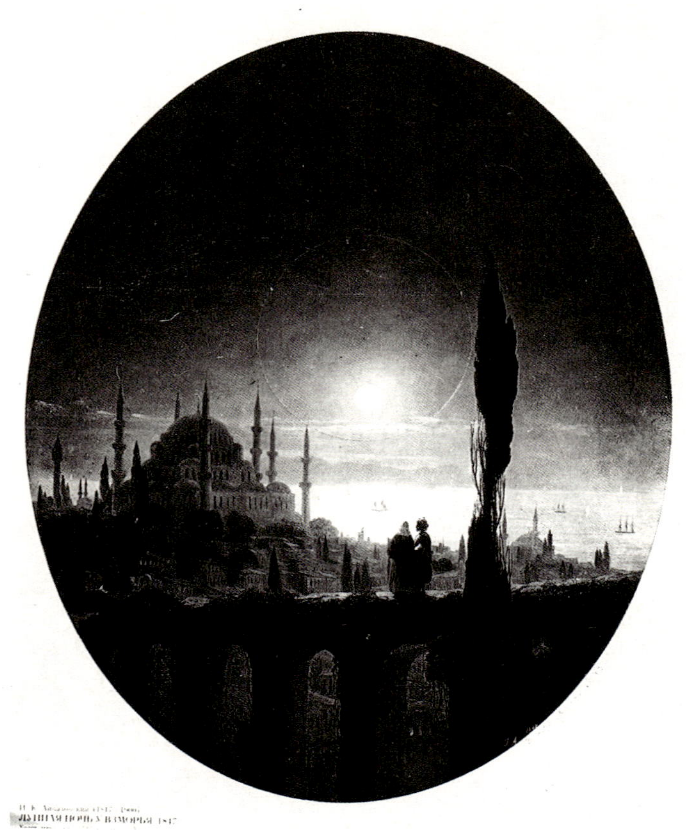

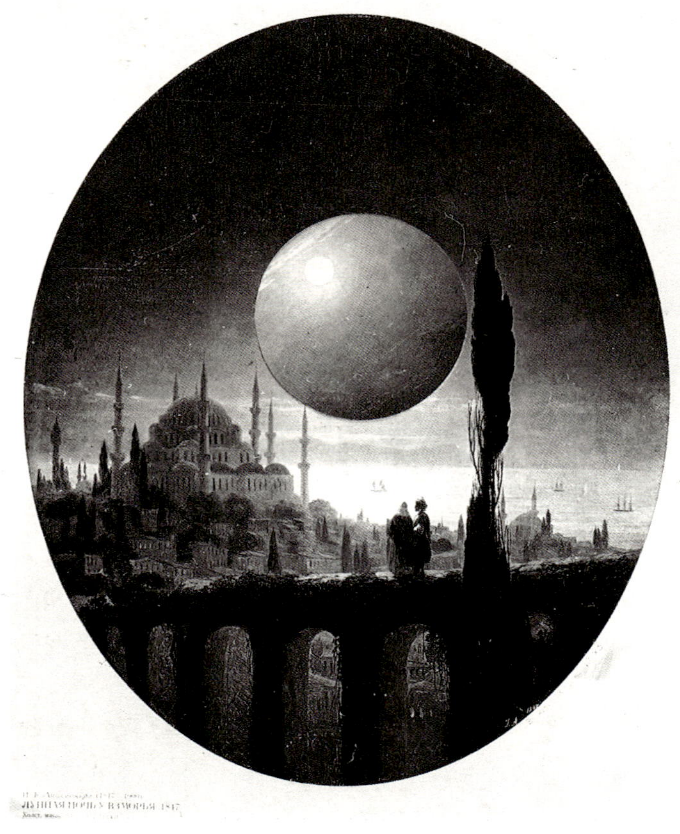

flict between the three-dimensional base and the subject of the flat photographic image. Not only exhibition installations but even functional furniture can be constructed on this principle, realizing a strange synthesis of design and photography in which both sides act as equal partners. We can imagine photo chair and photo table, photo lamp and photo clothes, photo book and photo dinners . . . It is a matter of artistic choice which subjects should be used for the panels of the object: a still life, a landscape, a house, a window, a picture of grass and soil, a wall, etc. We can bring into people's everyday environments historical styles, nature, architecture—anything—and create a photo life.

Sometimes this new visual effect and context can be achieved with a minimum of effort, as in the series of collages by Vacheslav Koleichuk. Koleichuk uses colored photographs from oversized calendars, and by cutting out certain geometric shapes in these images and changing their positions, he creates a kaleidoscopic image within the photograph. In the simplest variant of his constructions, *Sphere* (page 54) Koleichuk cut a circle in the middle of a photograph of a landscape picture and rotated the circle slowly within the picture by means of a motor. This photograph was thus very simply transformed by Koleichuk into a kinetic object. At only one point does the image look untouched. But as the circle moves, its configuration slowly changes into a strange, spherical object on an idyllic sky. By means of this art technology, which the artist calls self-collage, one can find many miracle objects inside a quiet and banal image.

VACHESLAV KOLEICHUK
SPHERE, 1984
7½ × 5¾" (each)

I have conducted another sort of experiment in interfering with the photo subject. My series, in which the photographer also acts as performer, started in 1987 with an exploration of the possibility of "touching" objects at a distance. Using a wide-angle lens with a deep area of sharpness and controlling the position of one's hand through the viewfinder, one can create strange effects when something huge is touched or picked up as a relatively small thing. At first this was no more than an intriguing visual trick, but through further exploration of the relationship between photographer and nature, the essence of this game slowly emerged. It became evident that each situation and each landscape had its own potential for interference such that the whole picture formed a unity, a combination of the stable situation and the fragile gesture of a man performing visual wizardry viewed through the lens. With this gesture the photographer discovers himself as an object within the photograph. He stresses the fact of his efforts in taking this or that image. As he tries to grasp faraway objects, to control his gesture through the lens, he imitates the way reality is being variously grasped by the lenses of millions and millions of photographers.

In all these cases, photography breaks its boundaries, constructing a heretofore nonexistent reality, a new object for perception, a revolutionary context. It belongs to the orbit of contemporary art.

SOVIET ARTISTIC PHOTOGRAPHY

VALERY STIGNEEV

The foundations of modern Soviet photography reflect changes arising from the renewal of Soviet society. This renewal began several decades ago on the eve of the 1960s, during the time of Khrushchev's thaw. After the Twentieth Congress of the Communist Party of the Soviet Union, in 1956, art began to open up and to reflect a reality that was much more diverse and complex than the reality that heretofore had been presented as clear and simple.

The aspiration to know and explore the truth which came as a result of the thaw gave birth to a general taste for the documentation of reality, greatly influencing all kinds of art. Photography was no exception, but this renewal of society, as reflected in the new taste for photo documentation, was not as straightforward as it appeared.

In articles and discussions on photography in the late 1950s and early 1960s, photo reporting was considered the most vivid method of capturing reality, and staged or manipulated photography was reprimanded. This was not the first time photo reporting had gained precedence as the sanctioned development of Soviet photography; its first endorsement had occurred during the photographic reforms of the late 1920s and early 1930s.

During the eras both of the thaw and of the earlier reforms, photography was seen as an essential means of mirroring reality. In the 1920s journalistic photography had been considered superior to the artifices of

LEV SHERSTENNIKOV
LISTENING TO MOZART, c.1965
9½ × 10″

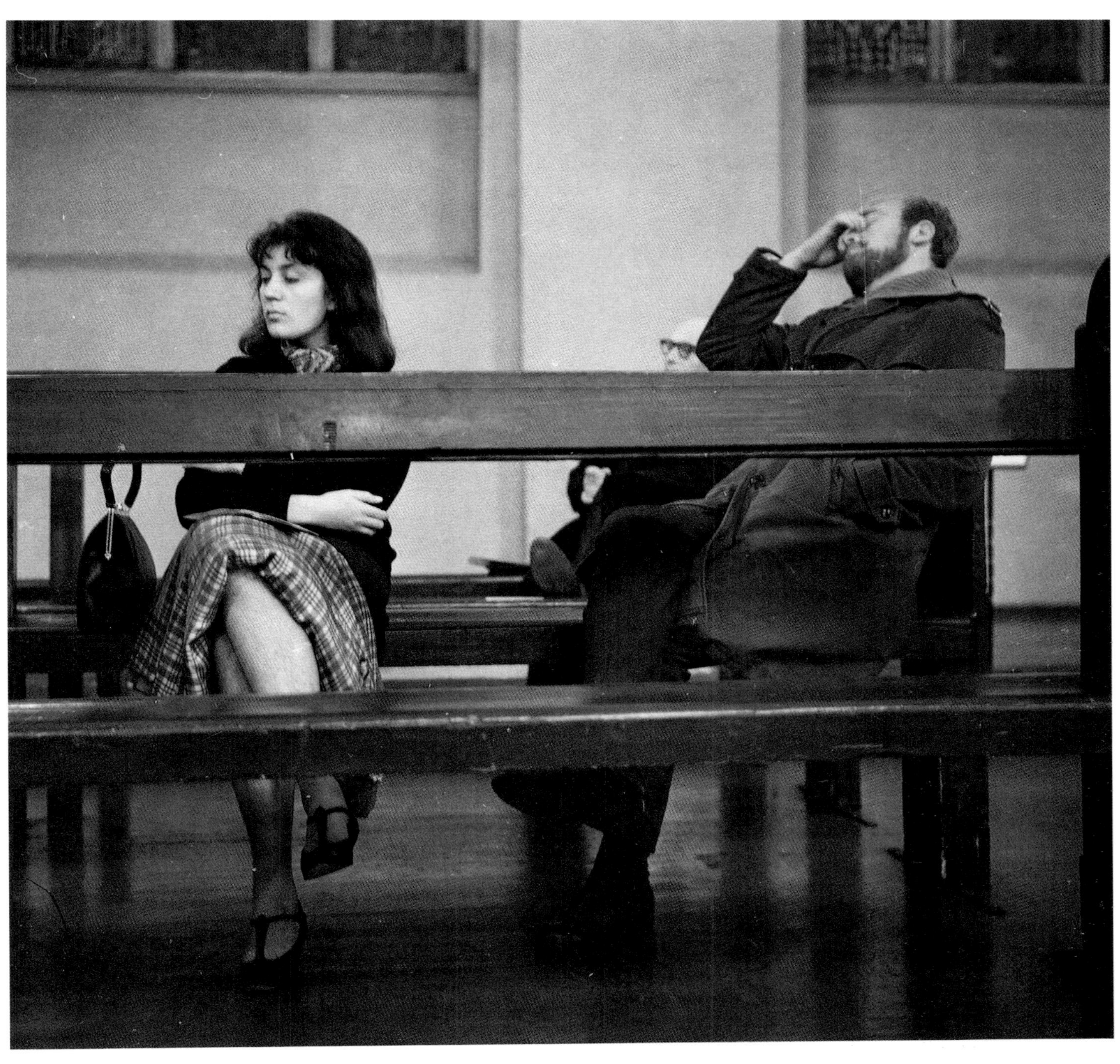

early experimentation in photographic art. During the thaw, however, the new journalistic photography was considered superior to the social and political artifices that had been presented as photographic reality.

Soviet photography in the 1960s was marked by the aesthetics of the "decisive moment," under the influence of Henri Cartier-Bresson's pictures and opinions on photo reporting, which were published in the magazine *Soviet Photo*. For many people Cartier-Bresson's photographs became the standard for the photo documentation that was at that time almost the sole expression of the art of photography.

But there was also a rapid growth of photography clubs such as Novator in Moscow, sometimes under the influence of older photographers who had survived the reforms of the 1920s, the repression of the 1930s, World War II, and the postwar climate. These older artists, such as Boris Ignatovich, Sergei Ivanov Allillyev, and Alexander Khlebnikov—who often had practically stopped working before this period—began to share their knowledge and experience with the young photographers, prompting a genesis of new photographic artists amidst the amateurs and proponents of the decisive moment.

The majority of these young photographers had other professions. They had no formal education in photography and most did not attend art school. But to a great extent, modern Soviet artistic photography was created through the efforts of these young artists and their mentors. The new young artists developed their own creative styles. For instance, in Moscow and Leningrad genre photography developed out of the desire to depict everyday life. In Latvia photographers emphasized the use of symbolic images. In Lithuania "direct photography" was explored, but with an increasingly expressive visual style. And by the end of the 1960s, first in the Baltics and then elsewhere, photographic schools had been founded as an outgrowth of the more informal photographic clubs.

Despite their increasing stylistic differences, photographers in the 1960s shared a common principle: to portray reality humanely. They believed that their photographs gave an objective picture of the world and that their moral core as artists was essential to expressing a positive example of reality in its humanity, with all of its demands and problems. After the long reign of smiling heroes, the presentation of life through rose-colored glasses had ended. The new photography was a revelation.

The 1970s brought a change in the understanding of the nature of photography. While in the 1960s photographers discovered the complexities of reality through photography, in the 1970s they began to see the complexities within the photographic medium itself. Their new perceptions of life combined with their new understanding of photography through experimentation to create the individuality of each artist's vision.

The passion for photo reporting, for the fixation of life, flourished, but the concept of capturing the moment became more complicated. It became evident that while the decisive moment and the subject of the photograph were certainly important, the individual photographer's approach to that moment and that subject was crucial.

Photographers set about trying to capture the subtle nuances of life's daily situations and the inner nature of their subjects.

The photo series *Surgeon Nikolai Amissov* by Max Alpert, a photographer who began his career in the 1930s, exemplifies this new approach in its attempt to depict the incompleteness of a man, not revealing all, but only portraying the unexplainable, essential part of a man's character. Photographers Gennady Kolossov and Lev Sherstennikov also explored this style, concentrating on fragments rather than the whole.

Photographic experimentation led many people to doubt the simplistic integrity of direct photography: the capacity to distill an instant of life from the movable context of reality began to seem vulnerable. The principle of fixation of a moment became superficial and the content of a photograph was no longer accepted as fact. Photographic images previously had told simple stories; now they were built on associative and imaginative thinking, depicting metaphors of reality. Photographers used their own subjective visions to create compositional schemes that delved beneath what was superficially apparent.

The works of Western photographers such as Robert Frank, William Klein, Lee Friedlander, and Garry Winogrand influenced Soviet photographers of this era and were a strong impulse in developing a new photographic language. New photo compositions appeared that contained unusual arrangements of figures and objects, which were sometimes photographed off center of the film still, and photographs were taken to be seen as a small imprint of the immense area behind them. These compositions stressed the fragmentation of reality and the "undecisive moment."

By treating the picture area this way, photographers were echoing photographic styles developed before the photographic reforms of the 1920s, when Alexander Rodchenko and other photographers had treated film stills creatively by foreshortening and by using strange angles and diagonal compositions. Rodchenko had viewed subjects through his lens from every imaginable point of view and both visually and verbally had proclaimed a revolution in photography. Ignatovich had expounded, "A fixed fragment of reality is cut out. This uneven process creates the impression that the fragment is more dense than the whole. Reality seems more dynamic." Victor Shlovsky, Rodchenko's companion at the avant-garde magazine *LEF: Left Front of the Arts*, had devised a theory of photography called "moving away," which he described as "a device or sum of devices making the information about a subject unusual, strange, which in its turn breaks the automatism of perception and helps one to perceive the subject itself better."

The 1970s works of photographers such as Alexander Matsiauskas from Lithuania, Vladimir Filonov from the Ukraine, Peter Tooming from Estonia, and Leonid Tugalev from Latvia created shock waves as each photographer individually reinterpreted Shlovsky's device of moving away. But moving away does not necessarily imply a sharp break with reality. In Lithuanian photographer Algemantes Kunchus's series *Sunday* (page 62), for example, there is only a slight movement of the object within the film still. This subtlety helps to explain why Kunchus's works were initially considered straight ethnographic photography.

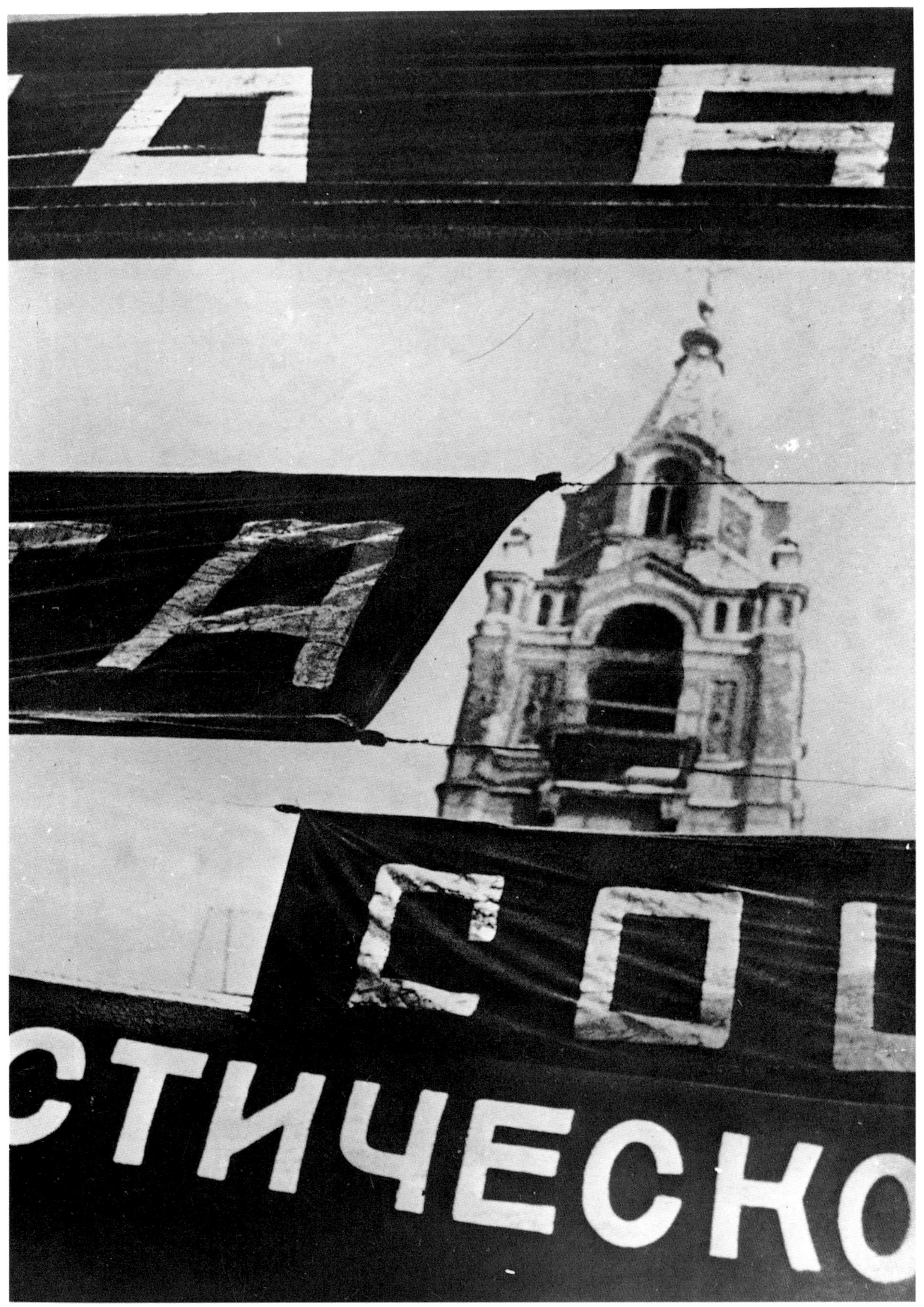
СТИЧЕСКО

The development of a new photographic language during the 1970s led as well to the rehabilitation of experiments and conventions older than those of the avant-garde era. Staged photography returned, but with a more meaningful aim, and costumes and theatrical posing resumed a role.

This renaissance of avant-garde and older techniques resulted from the artists' desire to explore reality to its fullest extent. Their work revealed that which was hidden behind the ordinary mist of daily life. Through the subjective visual vocabularies of the artists, the fixed image became a symbol for hidden meanings; and the moment, a transformation of the dynamics of reality into the rhythm of inner life.

The openness of the 1960s led to the experiments of the 1970s which reintroduced the artistic potential of photography. But photographic art remained relatively underground until the beginning of the 1980s.

The photographic underground criticized not only the canons of pure photography but also the photographic norms and standards established by the cultural and ideological bureaucracies of the Soviet government. No one style of photography, however, typifies current underground photographic art. The various photographers are joined not so much by shared aesthetic principles as by ethical ones: independent authorship and the right to self-expression. Recent exhibitions of their works, both in the USSR and abroad, contain a vast spectrum of styles of work, from social documentary to extreme experiments in photographic visualization.

In the early 1980s, however, innovative works were denied, or were not submitted for, exhibition or publication. For instance, works produced by the members of the Kazan photo club Tasma, the Cheboksary club Fact, and the Novokuznetsk group TRIVA were labeled "negative photography." These photographs, similar in style to the Depression-era works of some of the Works Progress Authority (WPA) photographers in the United States, attempted to portray an unidealized view of life, capturing what were considered unphotogenic and forbidden subjects. Under perestroika and glasnost the situation has changed, and so-called underground photography is now widely published and exhibited. It could be said that the two branches of Soviet photography—that of the official culture and that of the unofficial subculture—are in the process of uniting.

With the blending of the official and unofficial, photographic artists are discovering complexities beyond those realized in previous decades. Belief in the decisive moment seems ever more remote and naive, and while photographers continue to abandon the constraints of direct photography to concentrate on the act of creation, the reinterpreted innovative techniques of the avant-garde have become transparent to the viewer, losing their effectiveness.

Through intentional use, the clichés and stereotypes of the photographic language—

BORIS IGNATOVICH
STRASTNAYA SQUARE, 1930
9¾ × 6¾"

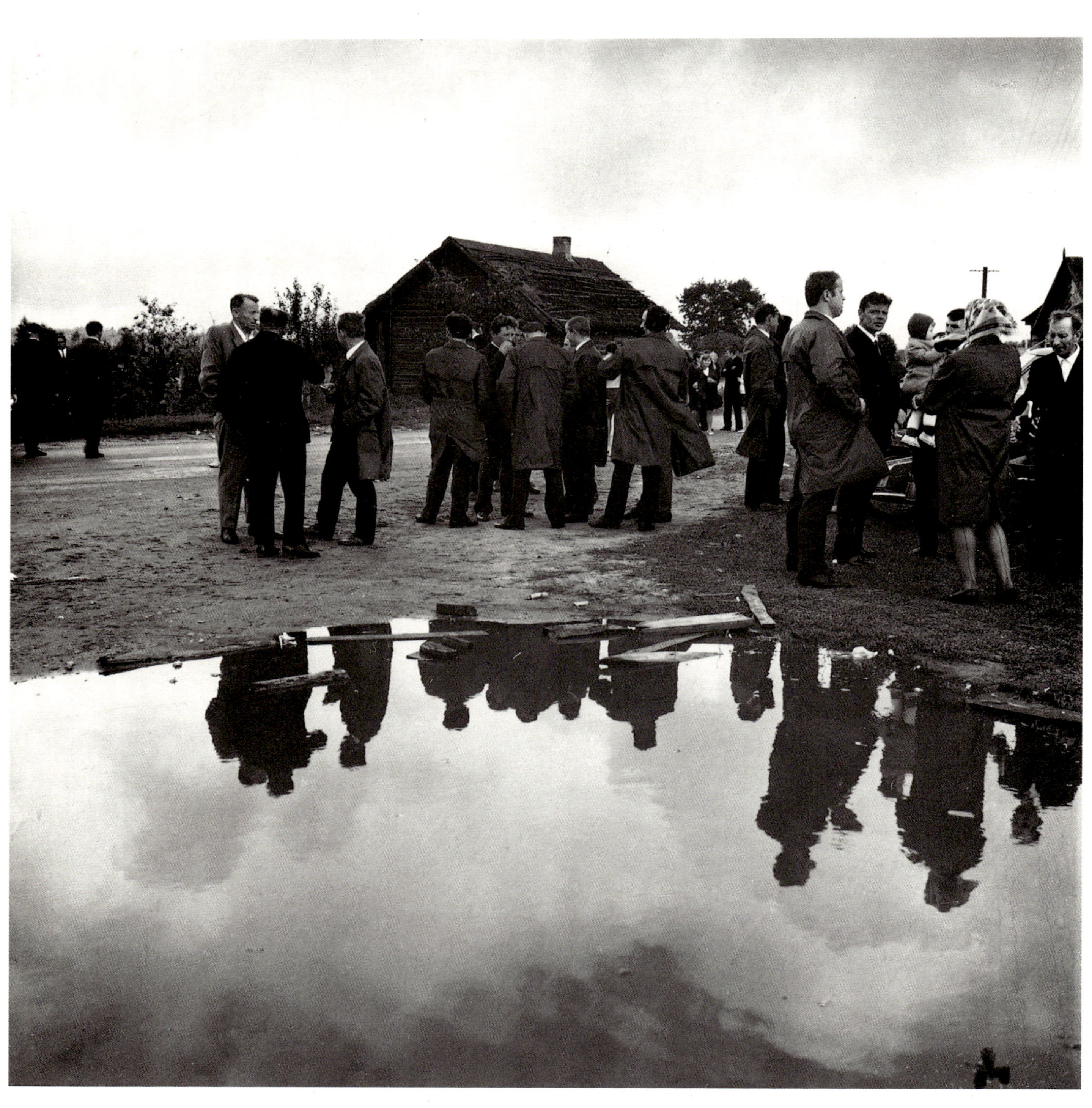

compositional scheme, manner of posing and staging—can still provide material for artistic investigation. For instance, artists working in a photojournalistic or technical style will frankly and deliberately exploit a clichéd artistic device, juxtaposing a pretense of artistic value and the quality of pure documentary in order to reinterpret and move away from visual stereotypes. This helps to revise the boundaries between photographic art and official photography and begins to obliterate the differences between high and low languages, but begs the issue of a new photographic language.

To meet the need for a new photographic language that intertwines the present and the past but is also distinct, some photographers have developed the "aesthetic of defect." In its many variations, it has become one of the canons of contemporary avant-garde artistic photography and is predominantly a reflection of the artist on the technical nature of photography. In this aesthetic, imperfections on the negative are intentionally left on the print—sometimes the imperfections are deliberately created—rather than the photographer retouching the negative to produce a picture-perfect image. In the aesthetic of defect, the scratches, spots, and glare are all signs of the truth of the picture as a document: it was just so, or, I scratched it so it became so. This photography requires double vision of the viewer. The object of the photograph itself is viewed, but also the mixture of lines and spots on the surface. The picture declares itself at once documentary and artistic.

A variation on the aesthetic of defect is to print an image with the entire negative, including the frame number and film perforation, which also carries a double meaning. One sees the picture taken by the camera and also the image of the film, a representation of the artist's involvement. The photograph becomes a new object, as in Sergey Leontiev's portrayals of strangers on the Arabat (pages 143–47).

Another trend in contemporary Soviet photography is the attempt to imitate the naive style of amateur photographers, as in the photography of Algirdas Seskus. The photographers deliberately try to show a technical unprofessionalism in their prints, sometimes signing the work in an awkward or cute manner, the idea being that the amateur snapshot is more accessible than professional photography because of its frankness and vivacity. While it is not difficult to imitate unprofessionalism, it is very difficult for a professional photographer to capture the essence of naive creativity. In order to succeed, the artist must discover how to use another's metaphorical language.

The use of anonymous photography—pictures by unknown amateurs, or archival or official stills—takes the adoption of another's style further. A new integrity is composed from the old, framed by the artist's conception and the artist's contemporary approach to Shlovsky's principle of moving away. It is the conception that attracts attention as the artist extracts the old plot hidden in the image and intertwines it with the new. This technique brings to life photo-

ALGEMANTES KUNCHUS
from the series: SUNDAY, c.1968
7 × 6¾″

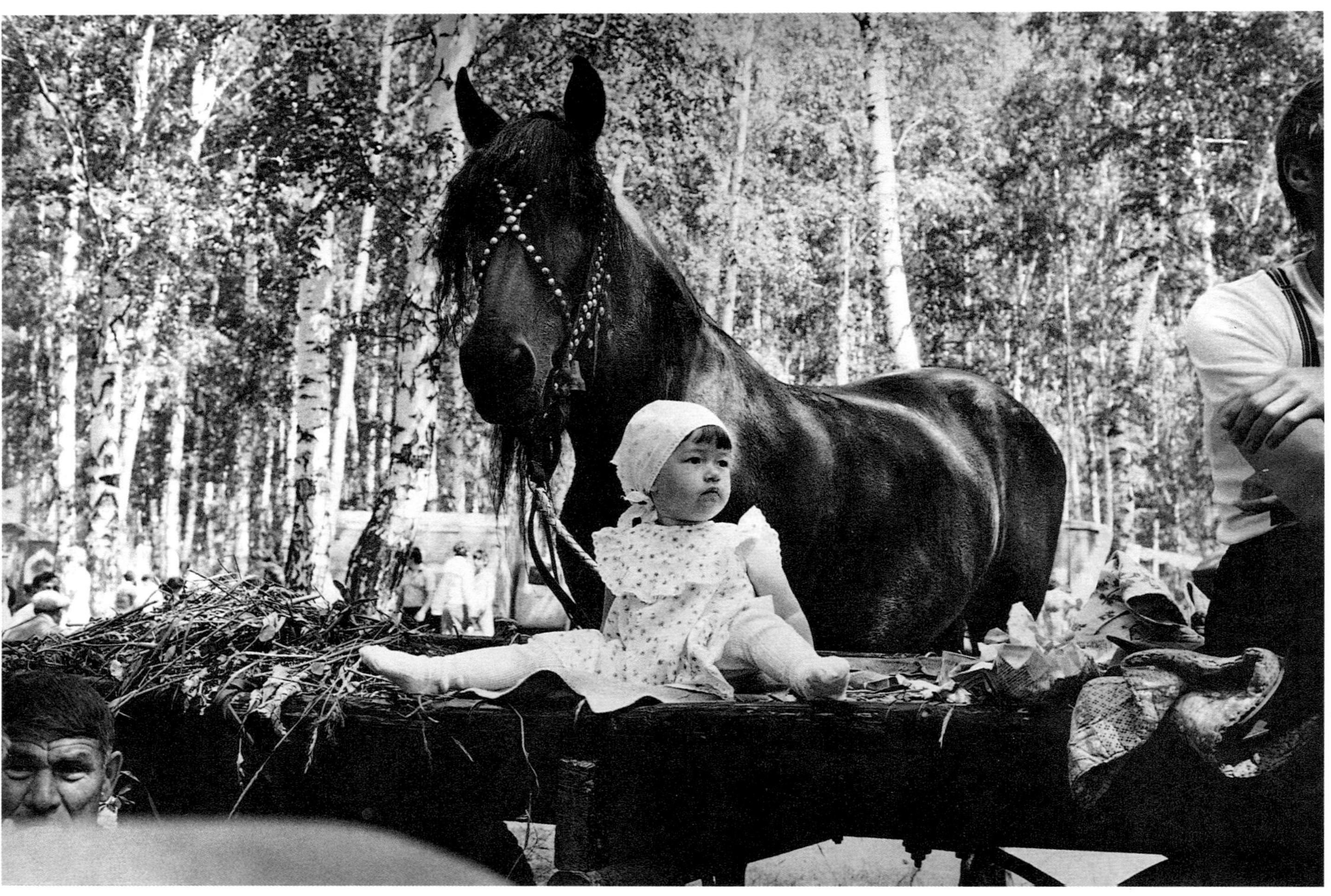

VALERY SHCHEKOLDIN
TATAR NATIONAL HOLIDAY, c.1988
10¾ × 15¼"

graphic folklore and finds nonstandard values in its layers.

Conceptual photography, like anonymous photography, stems from the exploration of the technical and physical characteristics of the photographic medium and of the psychological games within the photograph. In conceptual photography, the medium itself frequently becomes the primary subject of the photograph. While the idea of conceptual photography has myriad creative manifestations, most of these realize the author's conception with the help of text.

Such text goes beyond mere titling of the piece to actively participate in the construction of the image, to comment on the idea of the work, to establish the context within which the photographs exist. Thus the text becomes an integral part of the whole, creating an image of densely layered meanings that shows subtle connotational shades in the photograph as well as in the world. It is in this context that visual images start to live apart from the space of the photographs. Every detail of the composition is important: the location of the text, its dimensions, the technical characteristics of the still, the spatial relationship of text to image, and even the drawing of the letters.

Vladimir Kuprejanov's photo series *In Memory of Pushkin* (pages 2–5) is an excellent and widely cited example of conceptual photography. The work contains sixteen head shots of female Moscow telephone operators taken in the faceless style of a passport photograph. Under each photograph Kuprejanov set a line from Alexander Pushkin's poem "Farewell to the Sea." The lyrical content of each line of Pushkin's poetry enters into a rather complicated relationship with the human face above it, these relationships becoming more vivid in the context of the whole. The captions, the faces, the repetition of both in the plastic confines of portraiture unite to speculate on human life and our common predicament.

Boris Mikhailov can no doubt be considered one of the pioneers of conceptual photography. He made a number of innovative works in which repetition of a portrait in varying scale created a peculiar visual series. Like Kuprejanov, Mikhailov plays with images of a person to perceive that person's inner life anew. Mikhailov also pioneered the use of hand-coloring in conceptual photography. He hand-colors black-and-white prints, some given to him explicitly for this purpose, others found or taken by himself. This process of introducing color where there was none is widespread in the Soviet Union and supplies rich connotational layers by means of seemingly arbitrary and fragile color flourishes, highlights of different forms, and expressive dabs on the photographs. Hand-coloring has become extremely popular and experiments have been fruitful, resulting in a number of artistically valuable works.

The foundations of contemporary photo art were laid in the 1980s. Earlier photography, even if staged, attempted to record a fact. Now the photographic print itself becomes the subject, to be played with and analyzed visually. The physical matter of the photographic still has become the source and material of art.

The straight social photography which exposes the pain of our society has disappeared during the last two or three years. Visual narratives about the USSR's conflicts, queues, alcoholism, prisons, prostitution, etc., have disappeared. The depictions of the immorality of life, of life where double standards thrive, where there is no mercy and no tolerance have disappeared. The more artistic and adept attempts at this form came from photographers such as Pavel Krivtzov, Yuri Rybchinsky, Igor Gavrilov, and Valery Shchekoldin, but the more they impressed, the stronger the bitterness at the impossibility of correcting the error, punishing the evil, and restoring justice.

As the role of aesthetic origin grows and that of social origin is slurred, as the photographer's gesture expands, beautiful in its artistic impression and subtle psychology, photographic works turn into the pure art of photography. The desire to metaphorically interpret visual reality has drawn photographers to a photographic theater where human figures and objects perform. This

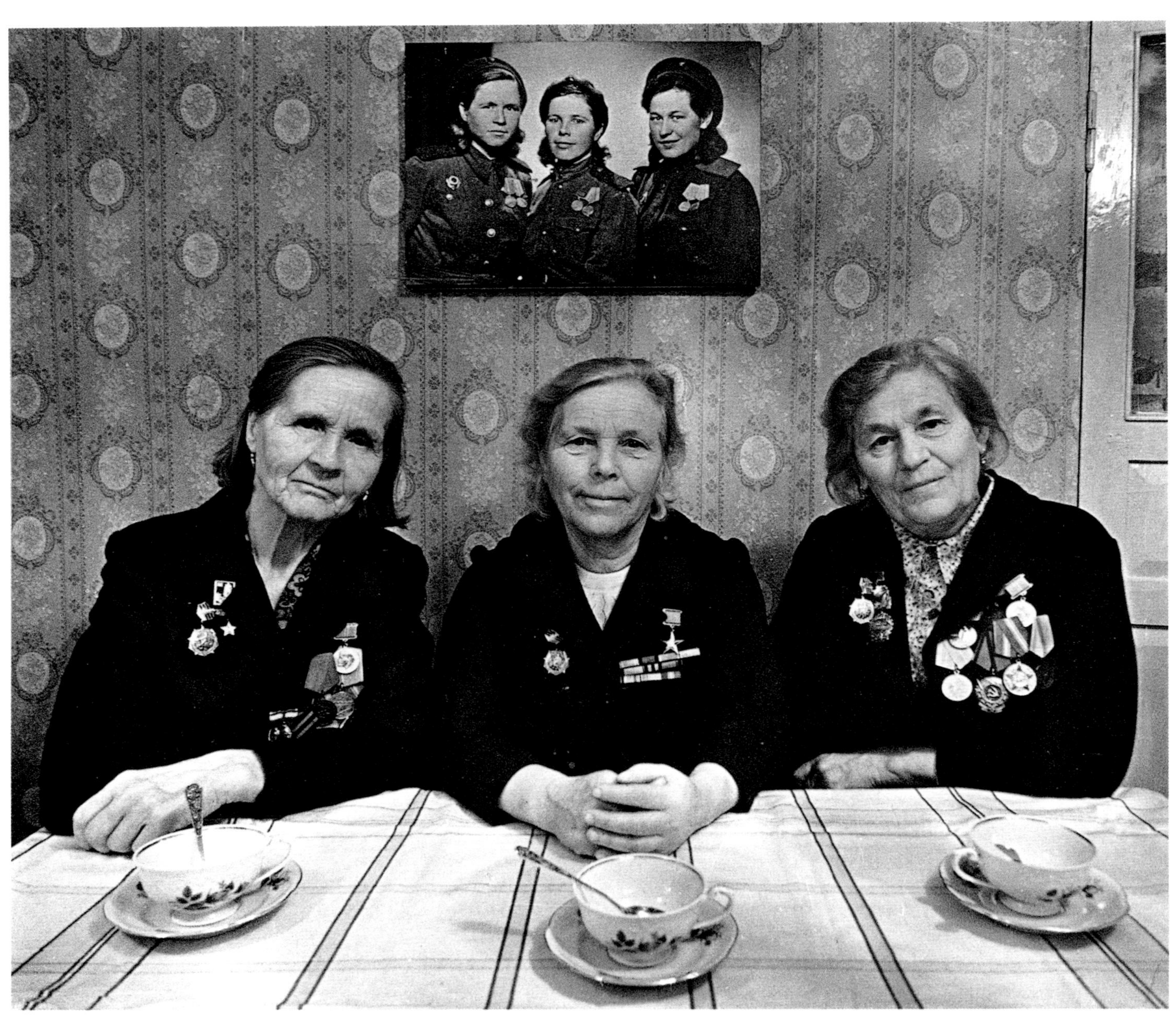

PAVEL KRIVTZOV
THE WAR FRIENDS, c.1985
7 ½ × 8 ½″

photographic performance takes place as if onstage; the frame of the still designates the stage, the performance takes place inside the camera.

The development of Soviet artistic photography has not been painless. Today most people accept photography as an art. Though this does not mean rejection of its utilitarian function, this shift in perception has met with opposition from conservative photographers. Conservatives have criticized modern photography for focusing on subjects unworthy of attention and for seeking new expressions of the photographic language. Critics still form opinions based on cultural and ideological stereotypes that retain the border between official and unofficial photography.

In *Soviet Photo* an older photographer issued a call to his colleagues:

> Wash the dirt away from your negatives. Close your umbrellas, for it is foolish to sit under an umbrella inside. Throw your television set frames into the garbage, for if you frame nothing, nothing is what you will get. Don't torment the spectator with garrulous inscriptions. Don't cut a bad photograph into the shape of a fan, for it won't become better. Don't shoot backsides and other parts of the human body—it isn't interesting for healthy people.

This comment on the works of avant-garde photographers shown at the All-Union Exhibition at the Manezh exhibition hall in 1989 demonstrates quite vividly the polarization of aesthetic purposes and tastes and the complete unacceptance of another type of art in spite of announced pluralism.

The art of photography is to balance its technical nature with the reproduction of life in a creative process. Art photography simultaneously manifests reality and the photographer's vision, and opens up new opportunities to be an artist.

A WESTERN VIEW

GRANT KESTER

"Spurred by the boredom of one-dimensional lives, thousands if not millions of people found the means of individual expression in the camera."

VICTOR MISIANO

One of the many cultural by-products of the glasnost era, along with Russian army watches and "Gorby" t-shirts, has been the widespread importation of "unofficial" Soviet art to the United States. Artists who clustered in isolated groups in Moscow, Leningrad, and Minsk anxiously awaiting smuggled copies of *Artforum* now find themselves courted by stylish New York galleries. Their work, initially created for a small circle of fellow artists bonded together by the shared experience of material privation and state harassment, is now reproduced in lavish ads for Absolut vodka. The artists themselves often feel adrift, their sense of solidarity replaced by confusion and anxiety. They begin to experience unfamiliar sensations of jealousy and competition: Who stays behind and who gets to go to New York? Who gets an exhibition and who will be this year's Komar and Melamid, or this year's Grisha Bruskin?

The work itself, detached and abstracted from its original context and audience, is transformed. Its meaning shifts to meet the ideological needs of the curator or critic of the moment. For some Western commentators Soviet art represents the triumph of the creative individual over the bureaucratic regularization of the Communist state, for others it provides an ironic foil for the growing state control of art in the United States. For some its deconstruction of political myths marks it as a variant of postmodern conceptual art, while others

VLADZIMIR P. PARFIANOK
UNTITLED, 1988
4 3/4 × 7 1/4"

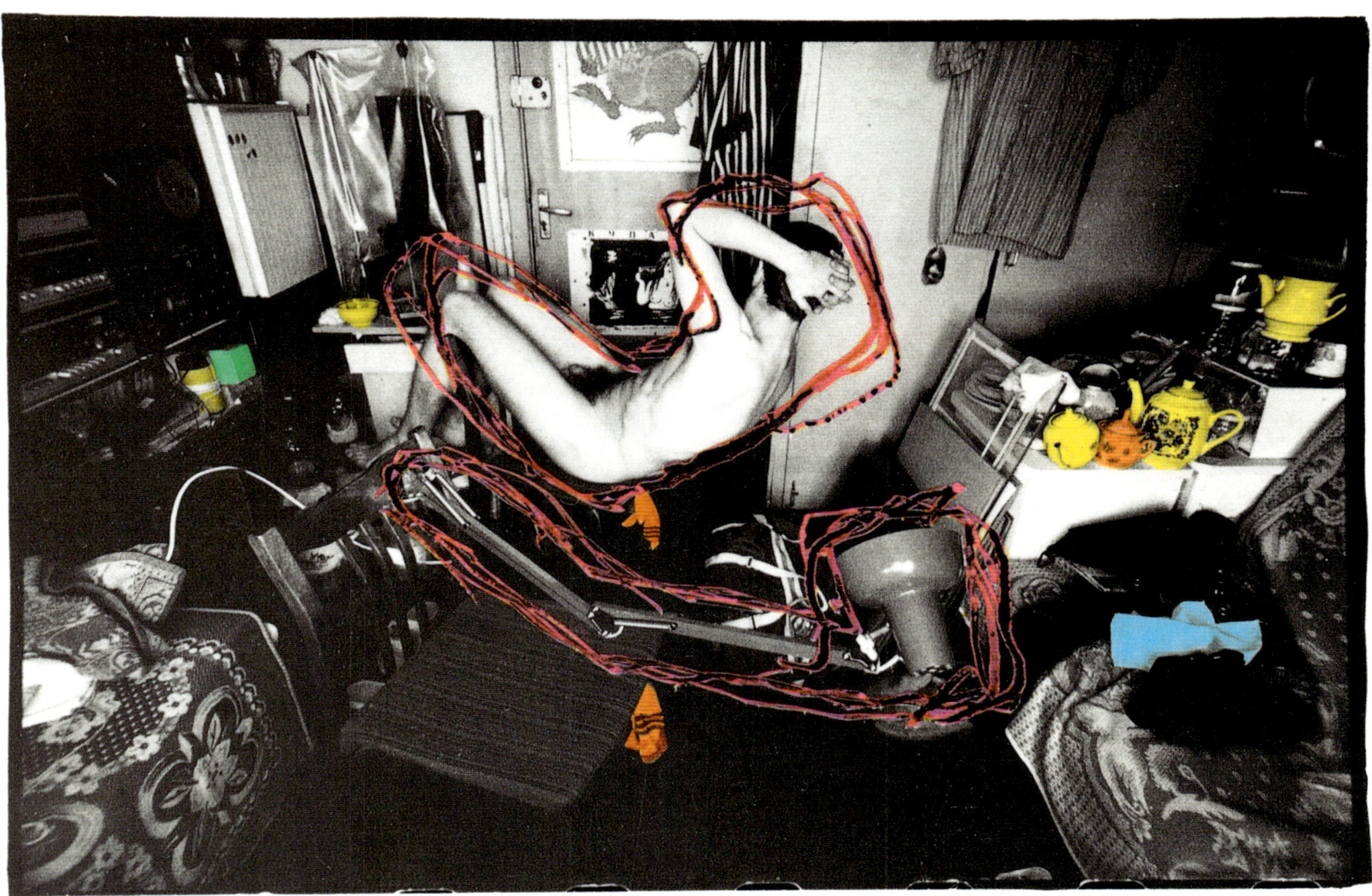

view it as a reaffirmation of modernist notions of authorship, expression, and authenticity.

The very proliferation and range of these interpretations suggest the extent to which this work eludes our understanding, and to which the actual conditions of its creation and original meaning are often secondary or irrelevant to its role in the art market. The influx of Soviet art promises a veritable gold mine of new and interesting material to be arranged, cataloged, framed, collected, authenticated, advertised, criticized, curated, archived, bought, sold, auctioned, and reproduced by the international fine art apparatus. Moscow curator Victor Misiano evokes this fantasy with his allusion to the thousands of repressed Russian photographic auteurs laboring in obscurity to effect the alchemical transmutation of ennui into creative self-expression. But how many of these potential Atgets make interesting art? And how do we judge what makes it interesting in the first place? By the evaluation standards of market-driven Western criticism?

How can we hope to reproduce the communal significance of that committed audience of friends and fellow artists for whom much of this work was originally made? The very act of bringing this material "to light" destroys something of its essence. The situation has something in common with the apocryphal story about the opening of an Egyptian tomb sealed for thousands of years: with the breaking of the tomb's seal and the inrush of fresh air, the mummified contents crumble into dust. Even as the critical, curatorial, and financial mechanisms of Western culture attempt to grasp unofficial Soviet art, it ceases to exist. At the same time, the very conditions of official proscription and cultural neglect that led to the formation of the close-knit communities of unofficial artists are being replaced by open support and encouragement. What kind of art do they make now? Will recognition from the West cease without the frisson of official disapproval?

The current explosion of interest in Soviet art caps an expansion that began with Komar and Melamid's 1976 exhibition at the Ronald Feldman Gallery in New York. Along the way, the strongest impressions have often been made not by the art

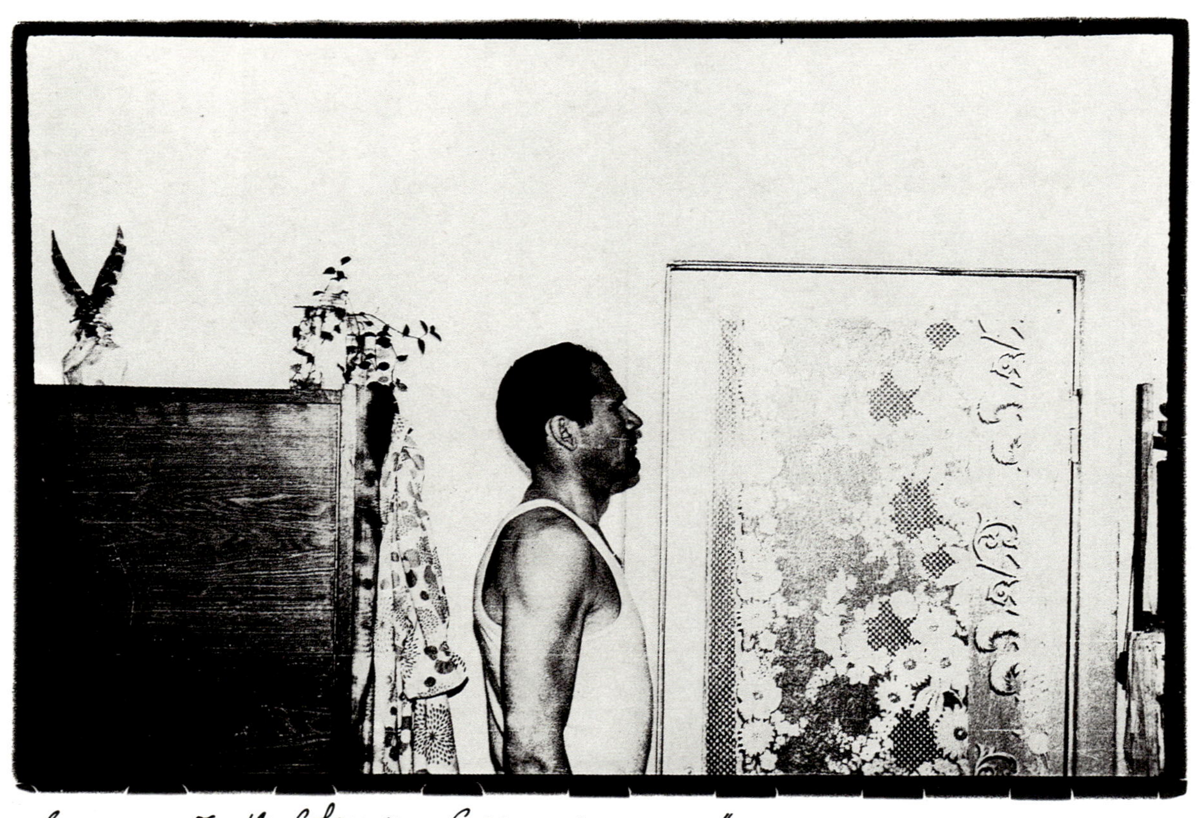

IGOR V. SAVCHENKO
THOSE WHO ARE NOT IDENTIFIED or
TERRIBLE TRIAL, 1990
6½ × 8½" (each)

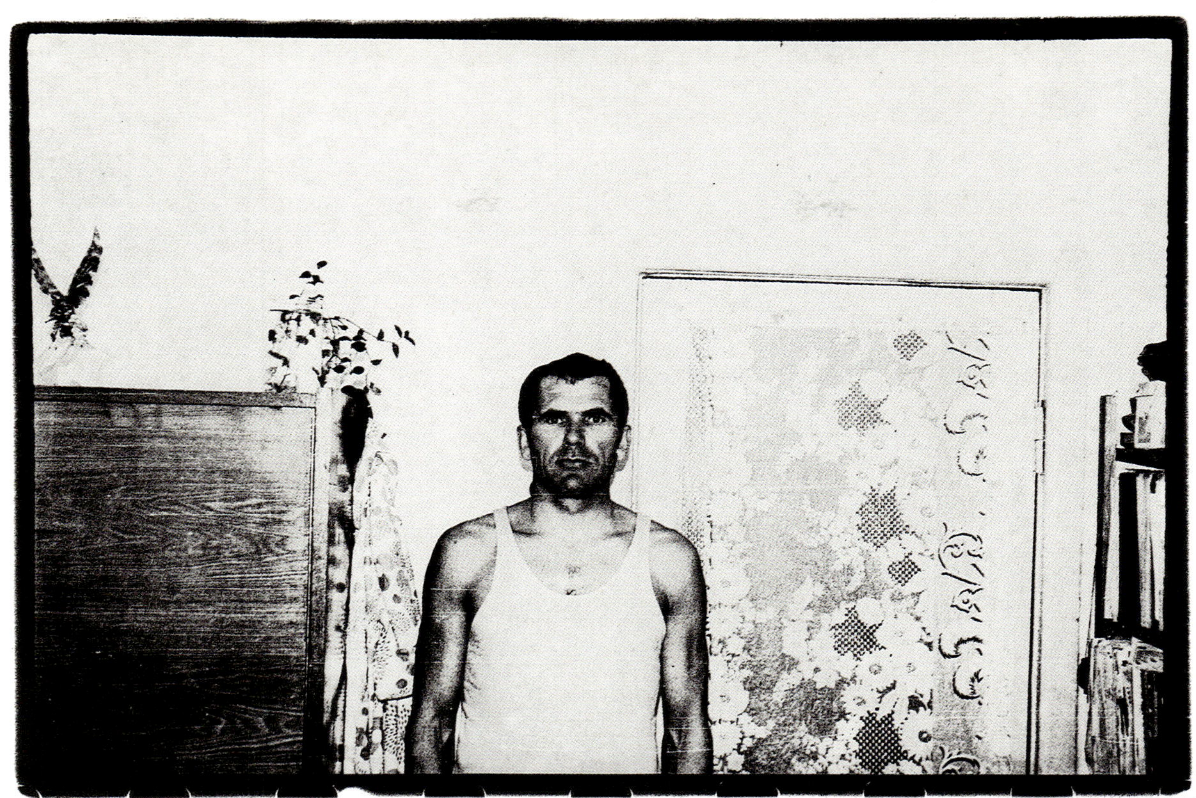

в папку N 7 „На Страшном Суде не опознано"
РЕЗОЛЮЦИЯ
No 2107/5

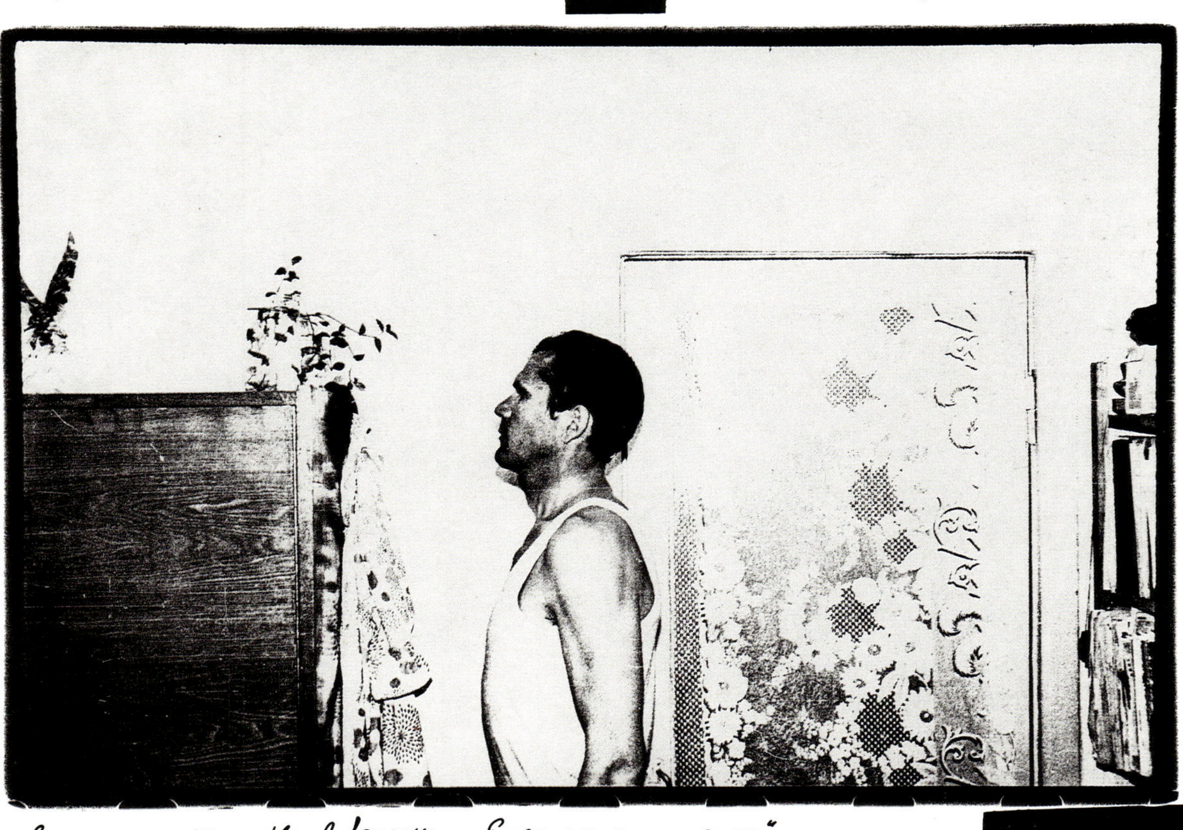

в папку N 7 „На Страшном Суде не опознано"
РЕЗОЛЮЦИЯ
No 2107/7

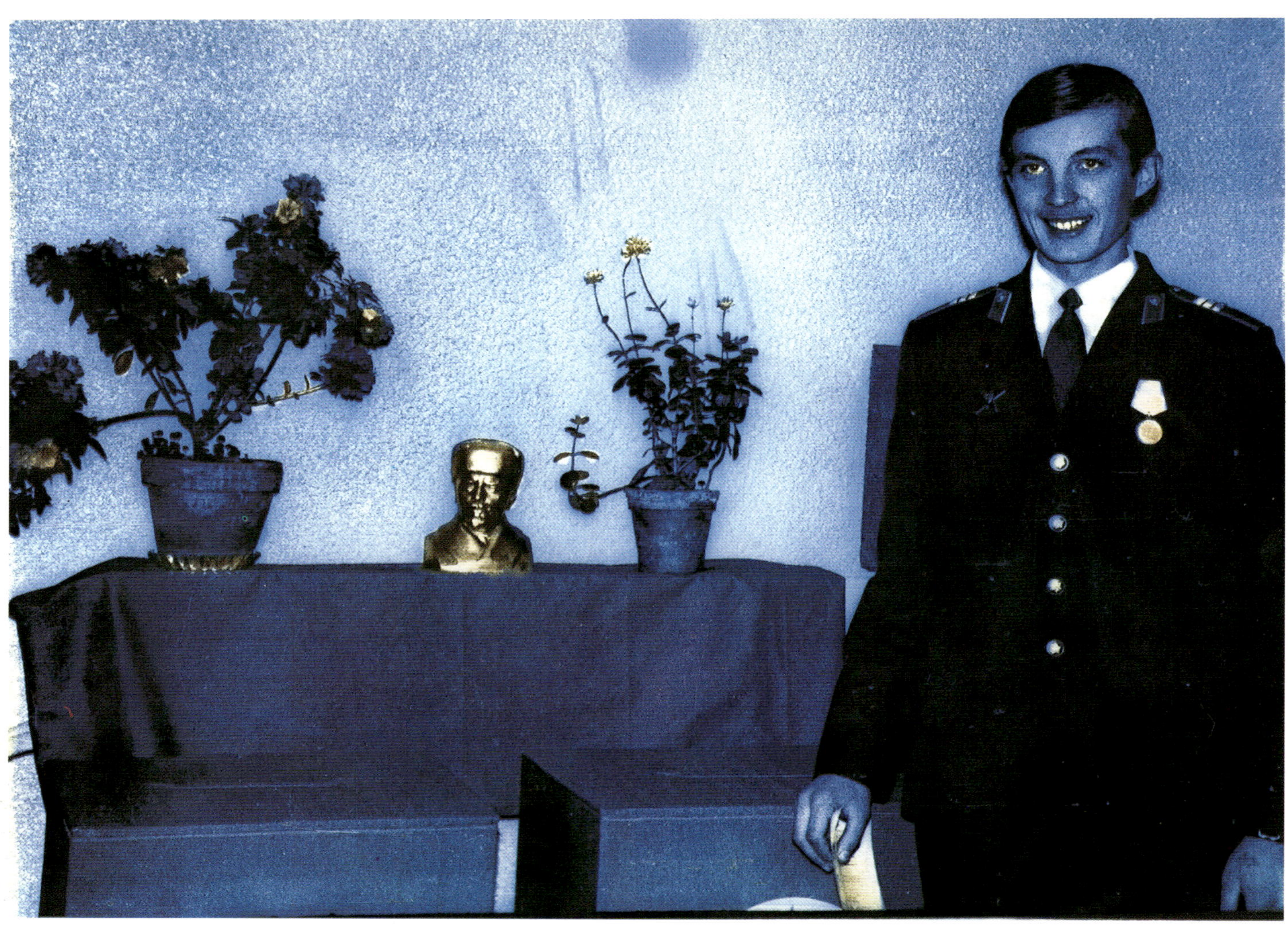

but by the artists themselves. We consume the body and lifestyle of the artist-as-outlaw in the form of photographic images in books and exhibition catalogs: grainy, black-and-white snapshots of bearded, brooding conceptualists meeting over vodka and tea beneath a bare light bulb, or performing some esoteric art project in the suburbs of Leningrad. These images satisfy our vampiric lust for aesthetic purity in an art world that seems dominated by cynical opportunists. They indulge our nostalgia for a time when artists struggled and suffered not for financial reward but for spiritual survival.

The photographs in this book share some of this fascination. In a number of these works, the human figure acts out a symbolic defiance against the personal and social prohibitions of the state. The top half of Vladimir Shakhlevich's grid *Act with a Portrait* (pages 90–91) includes four head-and-shoulder images of a man performing the parable of the Chinese monkeys who could hear no evil, see no evil, and speak no evil. The speak no evil segment, in which he holds a Communist party insignia in his

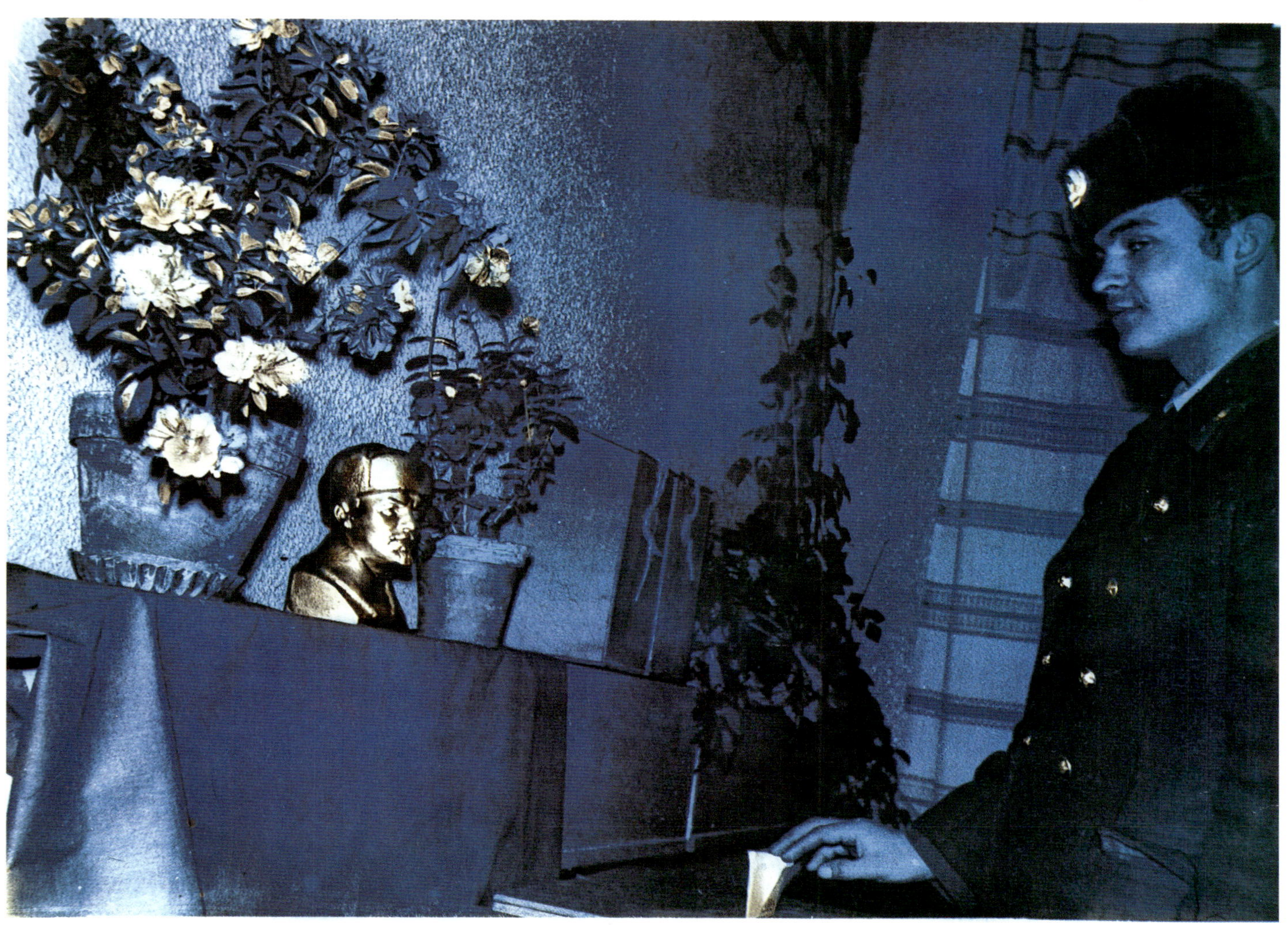

GALINA MOSKALEVA
from the series: ELECTIONS, 1989
7 × 9½″ (each)

mouth, suggests the scene in Günter Grass's novel *The Tin Drum* when Oskar's father chokes on a Nazi party pin he is attempting to conceal from Russian soldiers. In the bottom row—extreme close-ups of various folds, creases, and labia—the body stands as a fleshy landscape, immune to the authoritarian regime of the state.

Shakhlevich's *Act I–IV* (pages 92–93) includes photographs of a dramatically posed nude figure in the middle of a desert. The prints have been worked over with toner so that the figure appears to be engulfed in flames or radiating some kind of aura. Here we see parallels with other Eastern and Central European artists, particularly Austrians Arnulf Rainer, Otto Mühl, and Herman Nitsch, who use their own bodies in performances designed in part to come to terms with Austria's fascist past. The rhetoric of the sacrificial ritual, the dramatization of personal and interior experience, the exploration of physical and social boundaries and themes are all ways for Soviet artists to reaffirm individual consciousness and to acknowledge the body as a site of resistance to an invasive bureaucratic apparatus that seeks to control every aspect of daily existence.

The dramatic rituals and symbolic acts which regularly appear in the work of unofficial photographers are often staged in natural or domestic settings—deserts, forest glades, apartments—that provide an ideologically neutral ground. In a series of untitled photographs by Vladzimir P. Parfianok, the human body contorts itself to conform with the surrounding physical environment (page 69). In each image the pose of the partially clothed figure mimics the form of a nearby object in his apartment. In one image he executes an inclined sit-up, flexing his body to match the shape of a swing-arm lamp in the foreground; in another he lies on the floor with his jacket unzipped, next to an open gym bag. The photographs have been hand-colored, with erratic markered outlines of the man and selective coloring of other objects in the room.

The apartment is also the backdrop for Parfianok's *Persona Non Grata* series (pages 112–13), which grew out of his encounters with young Soviets living in state-sponsored dormitories. Too old to live at home with their parents, yet unable to find regular work and afford their own apartments, they exist on the margins of Soviet society. Parfianok has produced semidocumentary images of these untouchables, as well as staging them in such satirical tableaux as a nude figure wearing a gas mask while reading a newspaper headlined "Soviet Culture." Shakhlevich also stages photographic events in apartments. His *Happy Sunday (Ironically)* (pages 94–95) plays out a domestic scene in which an older man welcomes a visitor to his apartment only to have the visitor pull out a gun. This enigmatic sequence of photographs evokes the nightmarish climate of mutual distrust and suspicion in a heavily policed society. The pervasiveness of state surveillance is also suggested in Igor V. Savchenko's three-part image showing a dour man in an undershirt in left and right profile and frontal poses in his apartment (pages 70–71). A handwritten caption at the bottom of the image reads "At the last judgement not identified," followed by an official stamp and number.

The reliance on various forms of narrative in unofficial Soviet photography suggests a dissatisfaction with the relatively indiscriminate nature of straight photography and a suspicion of its apparent self-evidence. This skepticism toward photographic veracity has been fueled by the fact that a denuded socialist documentary was virtually the only form of photography that received any official sanction prior to glasnost. Photographers such as Shakhlevich, Parfianok, and others want now to speak through photographs, not with them. Dramatized performances, writing on the print, and images in grids or sequences allow them to thicken the level of social reference around the photograph in order to produce meanings that are at once more articulate and infinitely more subtle than those available in the single "straight" image.

Additional narrative possibilities opened up by work in grids and sequences are evident in an untitled piece by Parfianok that

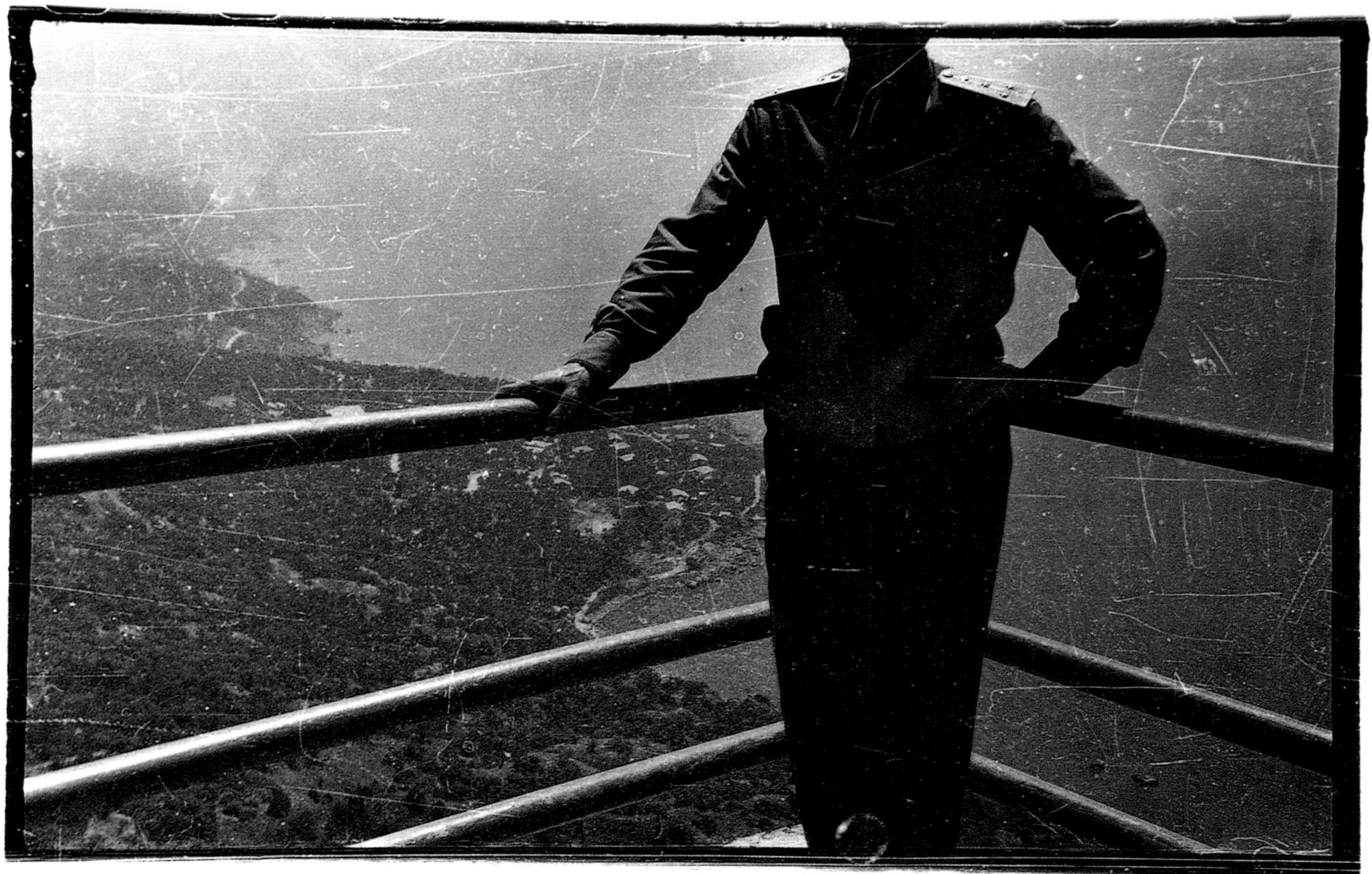

SERGEY KOZHEMYAKIN
from the series: PRESENCE, 1990
6 × 9″

explores the repercussions on Soviet society of the disaster at Chernobyl (pages 116–17). This complex work combines nine separate images in three rows. The top row features two blurred, slightly out-of-focus images, a flower and a plant on the left and right, with an image of a sectioned fish on a plate in the center—possibly a reference to the irradiation of plant and animal life and damage to the food chain. The blur and lack of focus produce a kind of blasted look in the prints, not unlike some of Ralph Eugene Meatyard's later works. The body figures again in the images in the middle and lower rows, which include close-ups of a man's eye, throat, and face, and toes, wrist, and feet respectively.

Sergey Kozhemyakin also employs sequencing quite effectively in his work, particularly in *Presence* (page 75) and **** (pages 102–03). In ****, four consecutive images of a heroic statue of Lenin grow progressively darker and more troubled. Here the ideological and monumental body of Lenin is frozen under gathering storm clouds, like Rodin's Balzac in Steichen's photograph. Curiously, in the darker prints the image of Lenin with his arm gesturing rhetorically toward the sky resembles the Statue of Liberty. *Presence* is a set of four almost identical snapshot images of a uniformed man, possibly on holiday, posing on a balcony. The man's head has been cropped out in each of the images. This compositional violence contrasts with the almost ethereal appearance of the backlit figure standing in a hazy fog with its back to a distant coastline.

Unofficial photographers' obvious disregard for the documentary function of photography is evident in their tendency to obsessively work the print surface in various ways. Almost every image in this book has been toned, bleached, drawn on, written on, scratched, or colored. Galina Moskaleva's use of garish toning is particularly effective in *Elections* (pages 72–73), a series of four photographs taken at what appears to be an official Soviet election, the ceremonial site of one-party democracy. The elaborate, almost funereal arrangement of flowerpots and imagery around the voting box is heightened by Moskaleva's use of lurid dark blue toner on the print. The attending election official appears appropriately cadaverous next to a meticulously gold-toned bust of Lenin. The scene becomes a literal shrine to (the death of) democracy.

The frequency with which Soviet photographers mark and work the surfaces of their prints may have something to do with their extremely limited access to photographic materials. With paper and chemicals scarce commodities, the idea of turning out an extended edition of a single image is impractical, so each print becomes an artifact. At the same time, the laboriously worked surfaces, the gestural, handwritten titles and stories, and the careful selective toning are all procedures that reflect a cathartic investment of self and subjectivity in the artwork.

Soviet photographers are particularly conscious of the roles photography has played in both preserving and distorting their own history. Only now are they beginning to fully recover the long-suppressed heritage of Soviet avant-garde photography from the 1920s. They are familiar with the malleability of historical truth in the hands of the state, particularly during the Stalin era, when purged political figures were literally painted out of official photographs. Nevertheless, they are also aware of the role photography has played in preserving the personal histories of Soviet citizens.

Several works in this book suggest the ambivalent, and often ironic, relationship unofficial photographers have with historical imagery. The photographers frequently use toning and scratching (of either the negative or the print) to evoke age or history. They are fascinated with images taken from family albums that seem to verify the past in some direct and indexical fashion. A number of them also use historical photographs in collages of various kinds. Savchenko alludes to the systematic distortion of history in an untitled work assembled from segments of an old group portrait (page 6). The image on the top shows the faces of the group, several of which have been bleached out. A thin red line snakes through the image, connecting only the bleached-out faces.

Both Moskaleva and Kozhemyakin have produced series of works utilizing images from family albums. Moskaleva photographed pages from an old family album showing pictures of soldiers and various family members (page 84). The images have been selectively toned and overprinted with a rough cutout of a human figure and a red star. Kozhemyakin's *The Museum of Military Fame* (pages 77–78) uses old family album pictures of a group of soldiers gathered around a cannon in what appears to be a town square. In the first images the soldiers assume various formal poses around the gun, in the final image collapsing over and around it in a scene of mock carnage.

Photography, more than any other medium, reiterates the prototypical conditions of the Soviet unofficial artist. The isolation, the enforced self-sufficiency, the privation, and the lack of any kind of institutional support network—until very recently—are almost inconceivable to those of us accustomed to the relative plethora of photographic books, magazines, galleries, schools, funding agencies, and collectors in the West. While photography was often used by Soviet artists to document performances and installations that, by necessity,

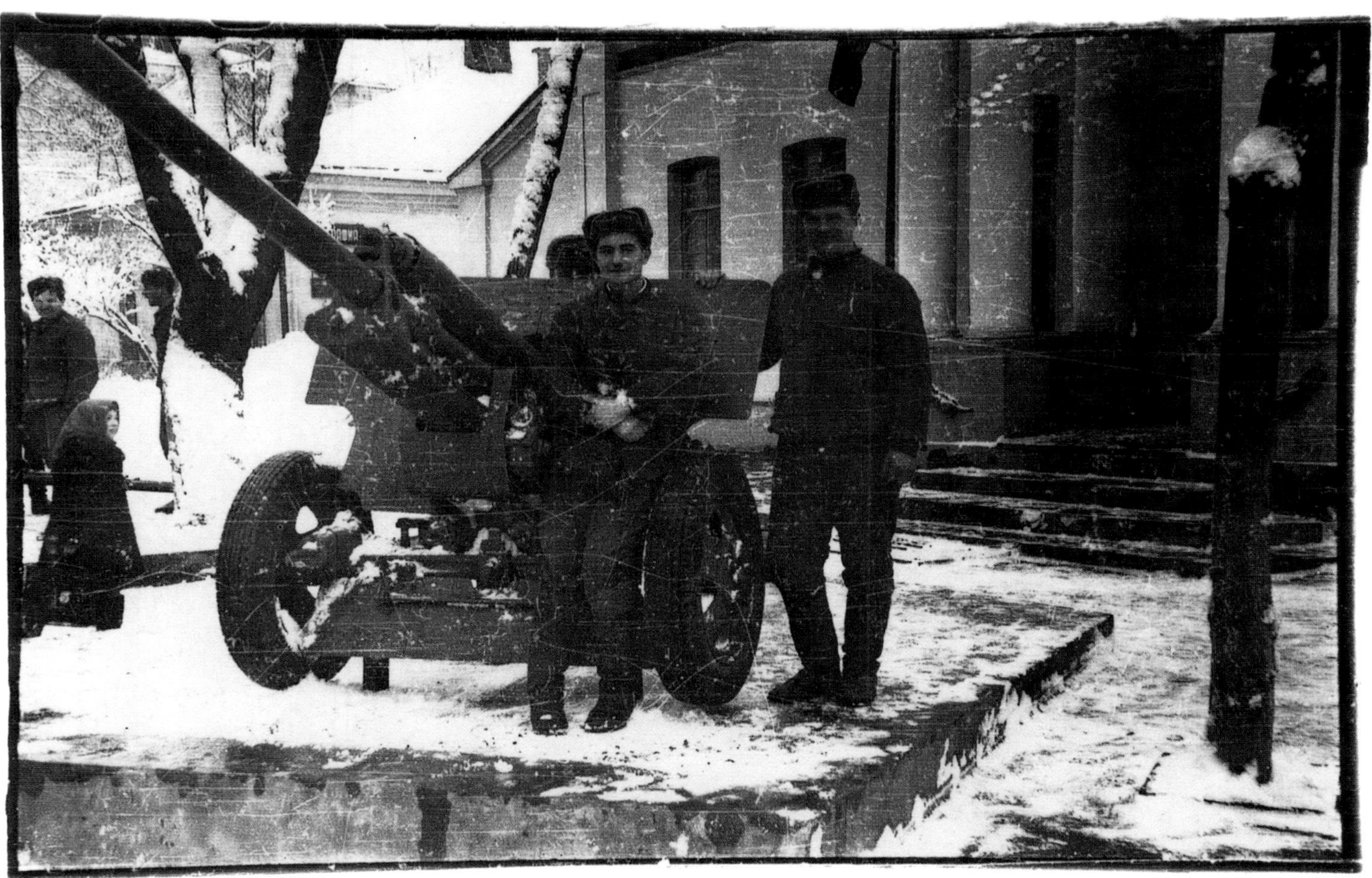

SERGEY KOZHEMYAKIN
from the series: MUSEUM OF MILITARY FAME, 1990
8¼ × 11" (each)

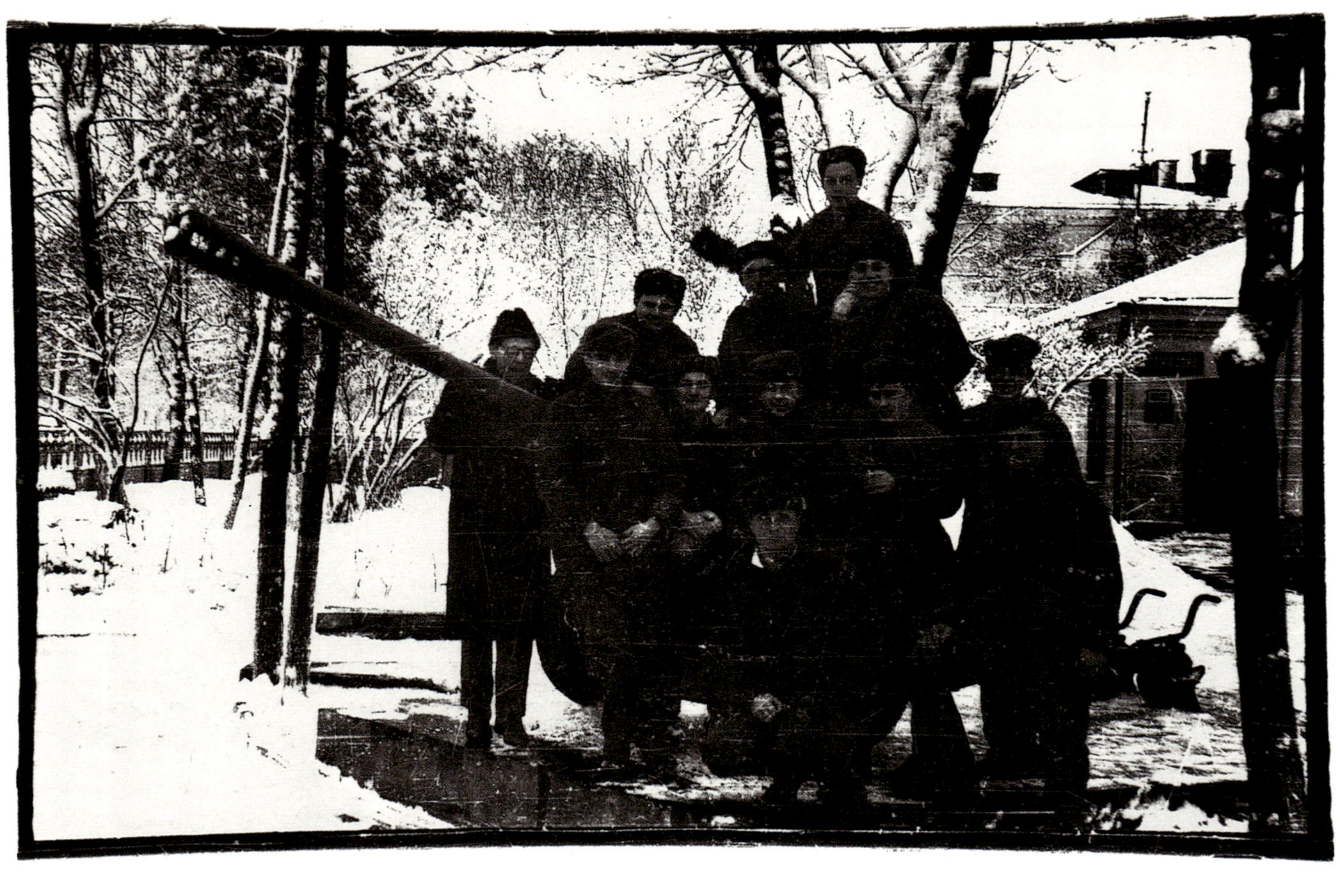

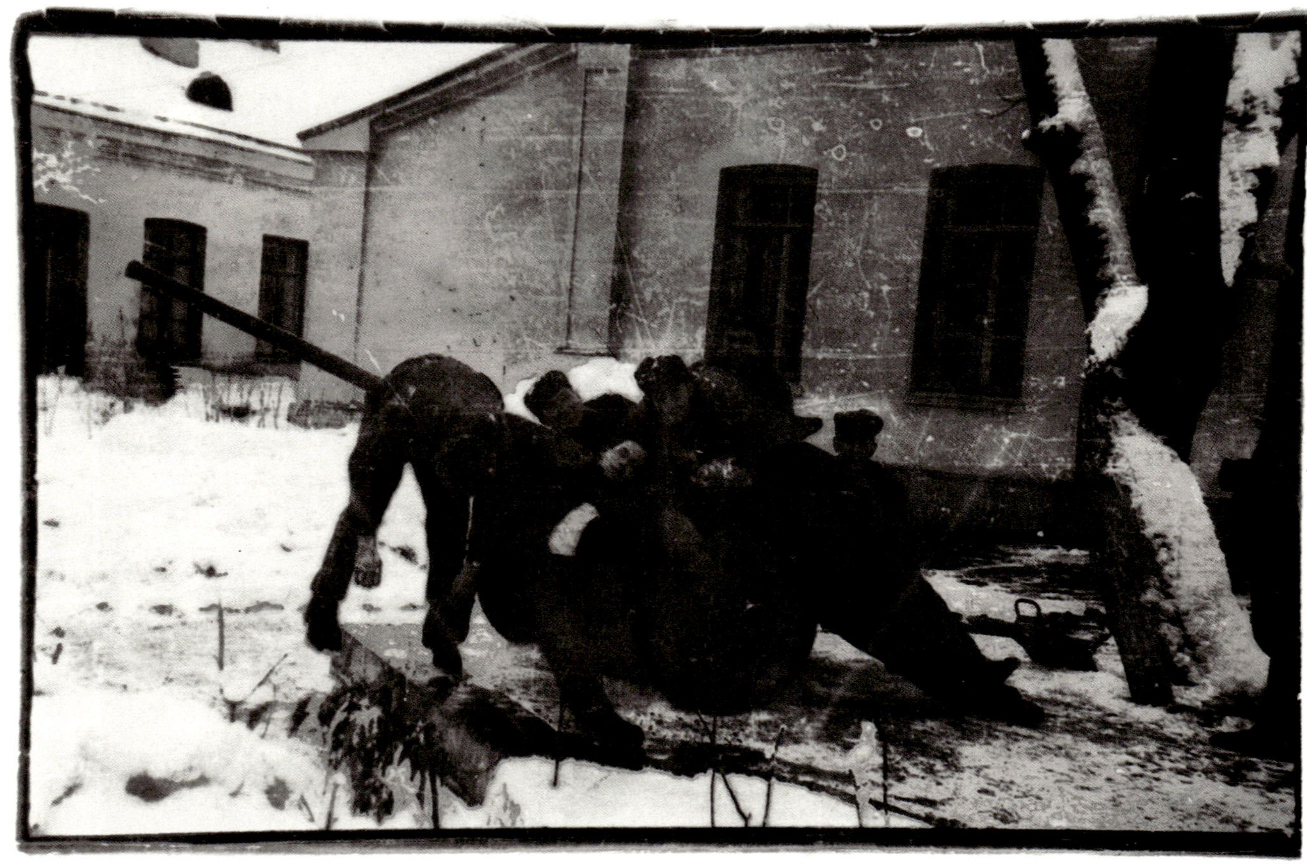

had to remain ephemeral and impermanent, it has gone virtually unrecognized as an art form in its own right. Thus, while painters and sculptors have begun to emerge into the Western limelight, much of the work in this book is being seen for the first time outside of the Soviet Union.

Surprisingly, for all its isolation, the work in this book shares many characteristics with current photographic practice in the West. The images in sequences and grids, the use of the artist's body in various dramatic tableaux, the incorporation of autobiographical materials and handwriting on the print itself: all these strategies appear in the work of contemporary artists in the United States such as Cindy Sherman, John Baldesarri, and Jim Goldberg, among many others. It is unlikely that these formal correspondences stem from a widespread familiarity among Soviet photographers with contemporary Western art. Rather, Soviet artists seem almost preternaturally drawn to explore the very issues of subjectivity and ideology that have come to dominate current Western art under the rubric of postmodernism. These artists are united by a set of shared conceptual concerns: the problematic status of photographic truth, the relationship between the personal and the political or the individual and the state, and the cultural construction of identity.

The interest of artists such as Cindy Sherman and Barbara Kruger in issues of subjectivity and representation is rooted in a critique of the culture of the marketplace—advertising, movies, fashion, etc. It is a culture in which the individual merges into an anonymous stream of shoppers whose unconscious dreams and desires have been harnessed to the consumption of deodorants, shoes, and microwave ovens. In a similar way Soviet artists respond to the culture of politics. In the Soviet Union all possible utopias are fulfilled in the posters and billboards of the Communist party, eternally progressive, dynamic, and forward-looking. The ideological operations that take place within both systems depend on the effacement of individuality, the redirection of desire and subjectivity, and the effortless manipulation of truth and representation. What has become increasingly clear in the post–cold war era is the extent to which both Western and Eastern political systems exert power over the individual on the quotidian level of daily existence and personal identity.

As this work continues to move outside the Soviet Union, and away from its original audience, it will undoubtedly begin to reveal new meanings for Western viewers. Shakhlevich's fascination with the body and state control suggests connections to Foucault's study of the carceral realm in *Discipline and Punish*. More generally, much of the work in this book could be productively analyzed within the framework of a poststructuralist critique of the polarities that characterize Western thought. From this perspective Soviet unofficial photography can be seen as effecting a series of strategic disruptions or inversions of the boundaries and oppositions that structure and define contemporary life in the East as well as the West: between public and private life, the body and the spirit, the individual and the state, and between the artist's own imagination and the banal cultures of consumerism and politics.

GALINA MOSKALEVA • IVAN PETROVICH • VADIM KACHAN • GENNADY SLABODSKY • VLADIMIR SHAKHLEVICH • IGOR V. SAVCHENKO • HELEN MULYUKINA • ALEXANDER SINYAK • SERGEY KOZHEMYAKIN • SERGEY KOVALYOV • VLADZIMIR P. PARFIANOK • GENNADY RODIKOV • VALERY D. LOBKO • SERGEI SUKOVITZIN • ALEXEY PAVLUTS • ALEKSEY ILYIN

MINSK

The artists in the Minsk section work closely with the Union of Art Photographers of Byelorussia, headed by Valery D. Lobko and headquartered in Minsk. All are graduates of photography schools directed by Lobko or his former students, schools which provide both a technical and aesthetic education in the photographic arts unavailable elsewhere in the USSR.

These young artists share technical knowledge and resources extensively; experimentation is encouraged, resulting in a provocative body of work whose themes are mainly personal and evolve around the human condition. The Minsk artists foster a creative, diverse photographic dialogue that counters conformity. While operating outside of the mainstream of Soviet art and removed from its center in Moscow, they have created a flourishing cultural enclave.

GALINA MOSKALEVA
from the series: NONCONFORMISTS, 1989
9 × 12″ (both)

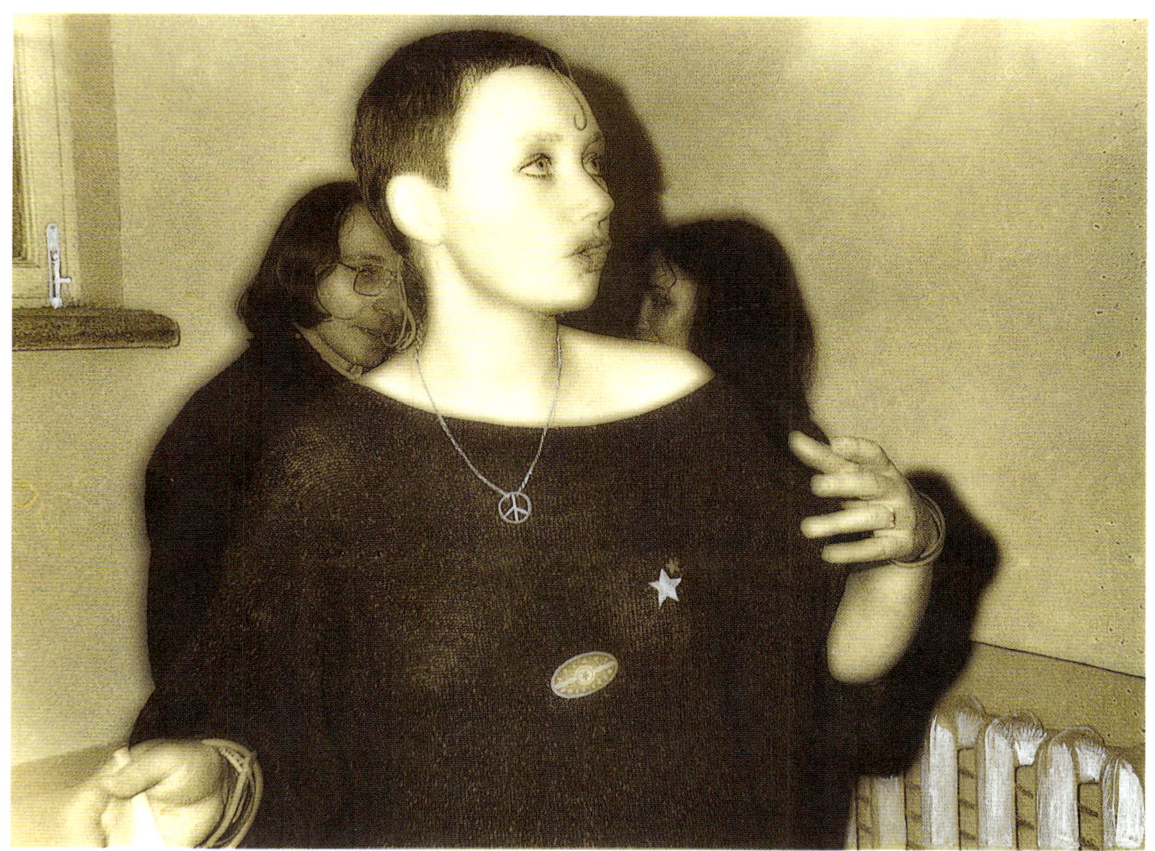

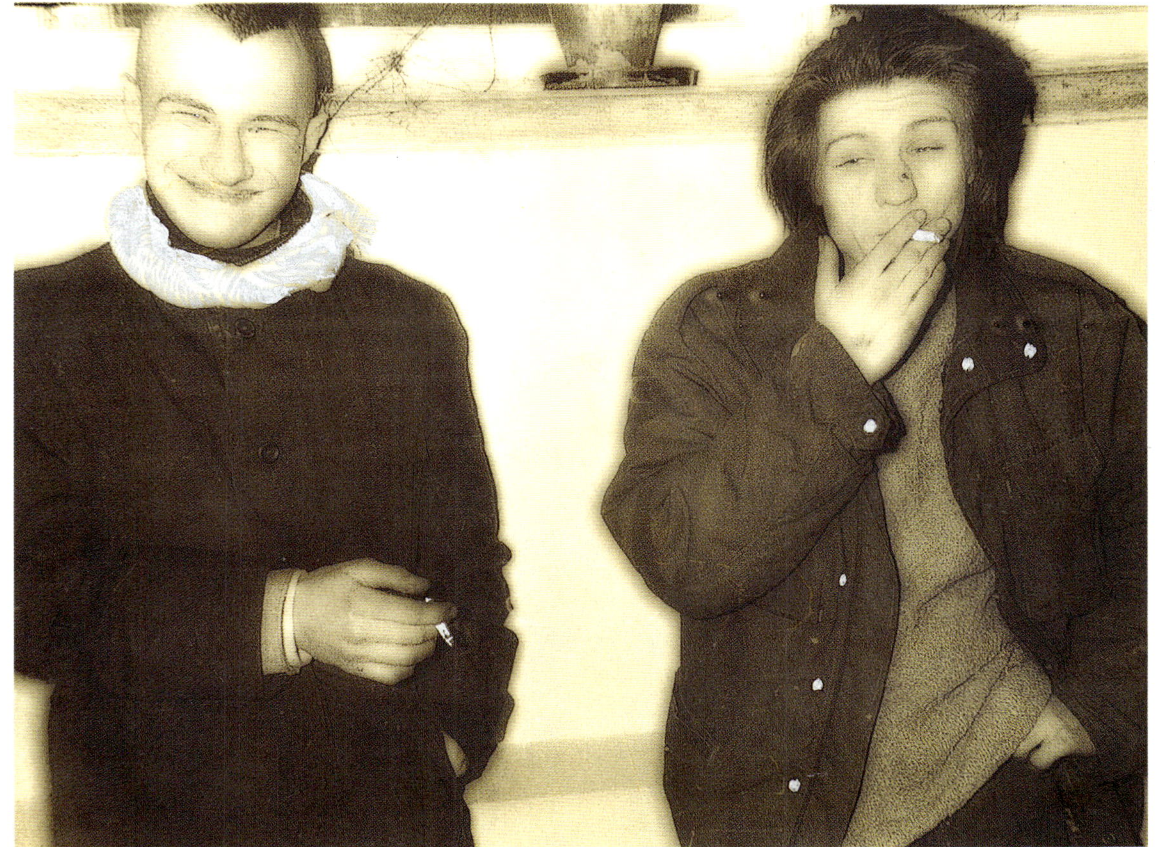

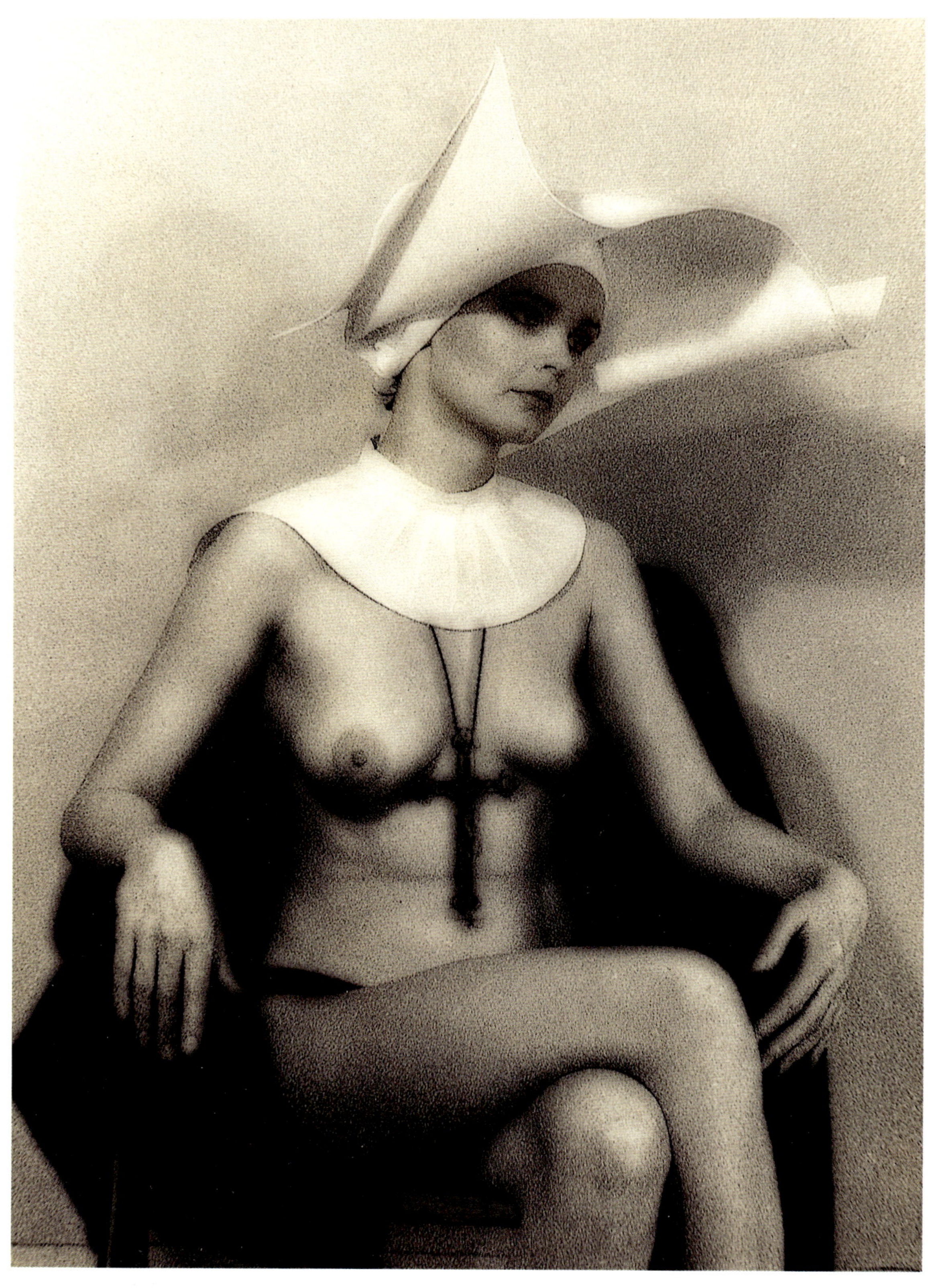

GALINA MOSKALEVA
PORTRAIT II, 1990
10 × 7″

Opposite:
GALINA MOSKALEVA
ACT I, 1990
9½ × 7″

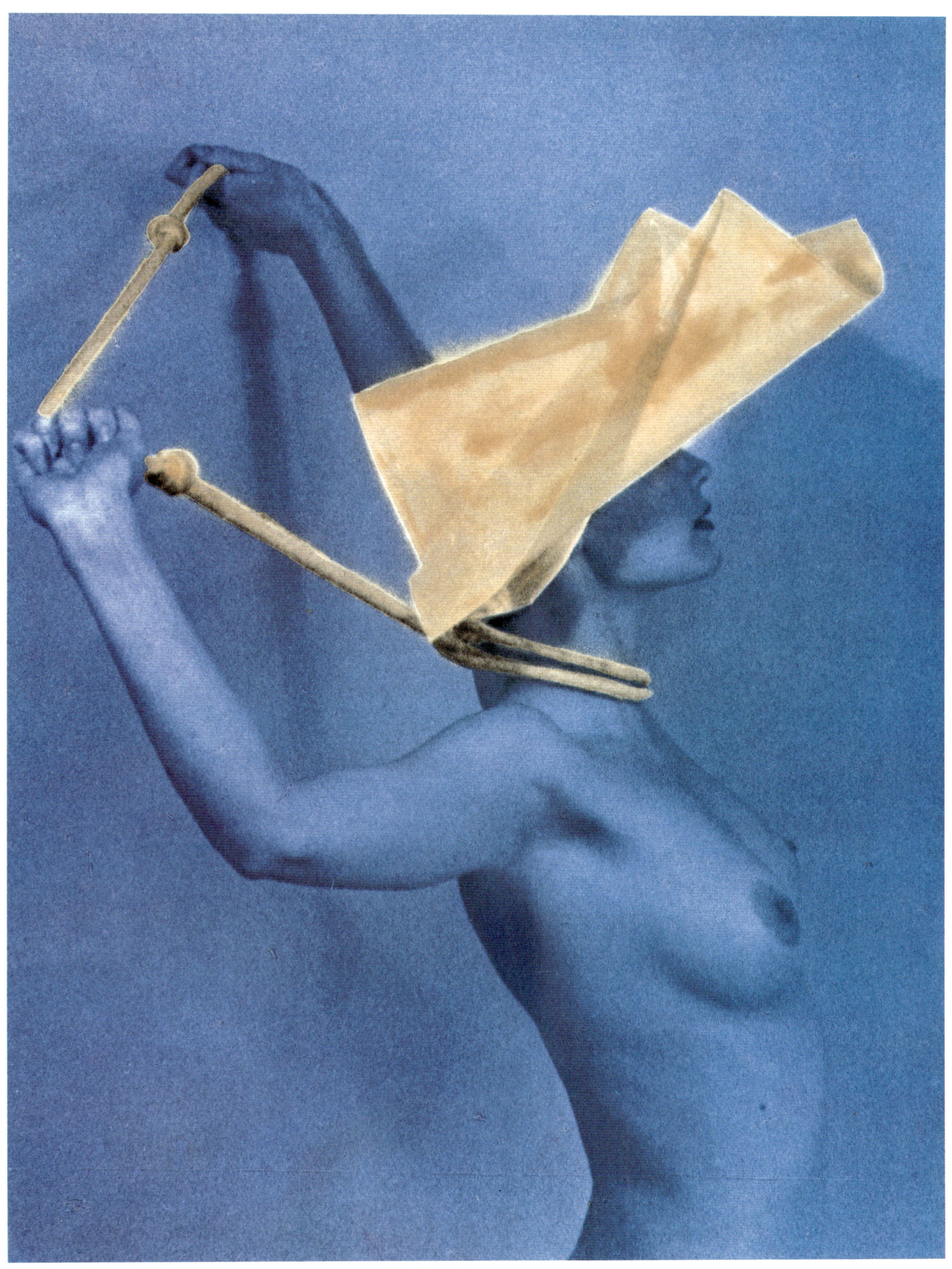

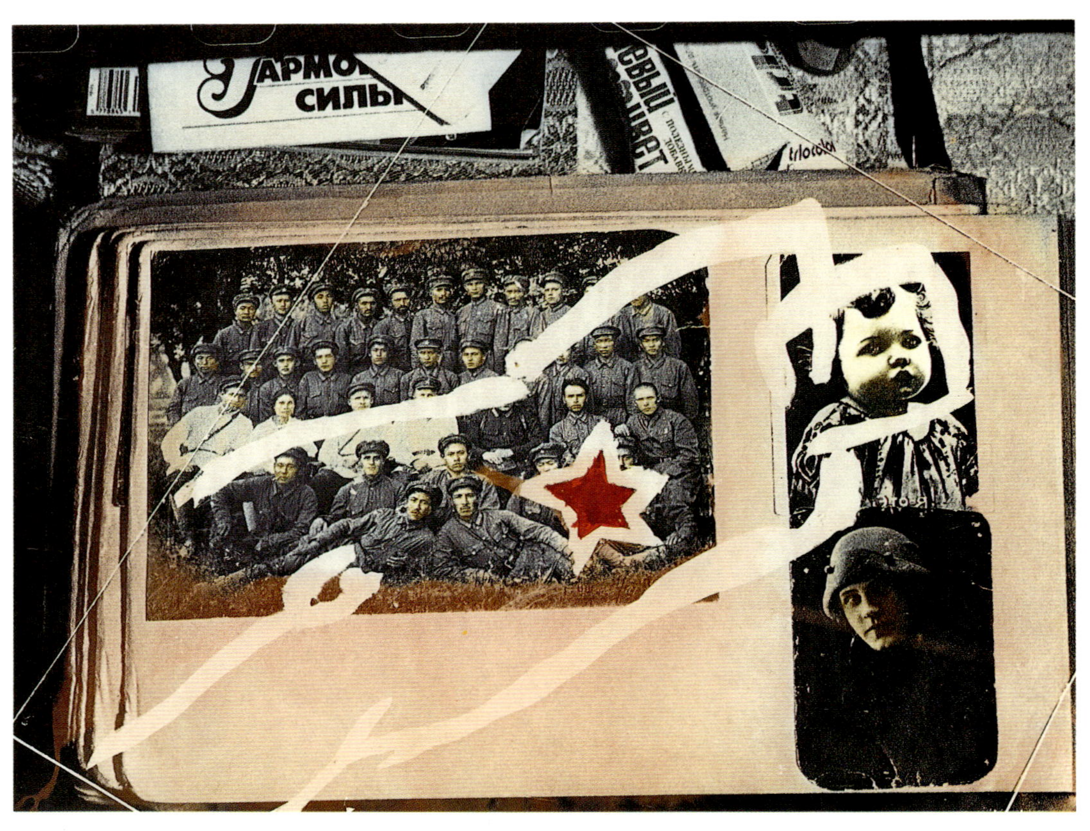

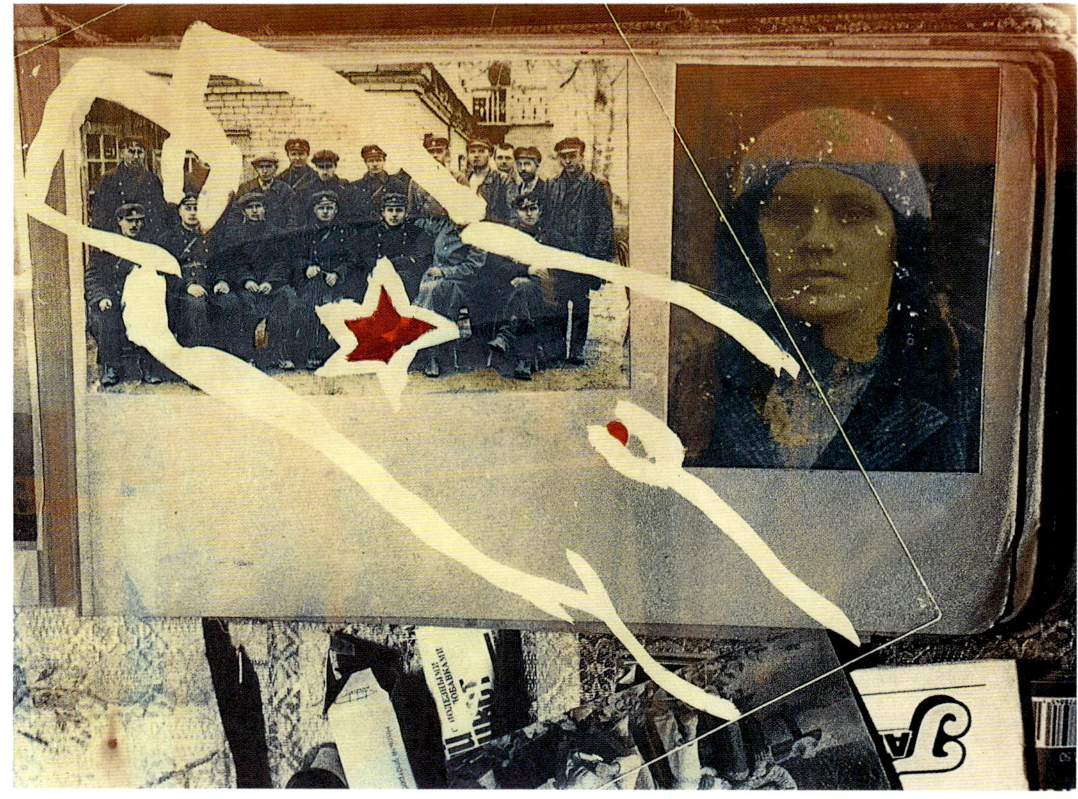

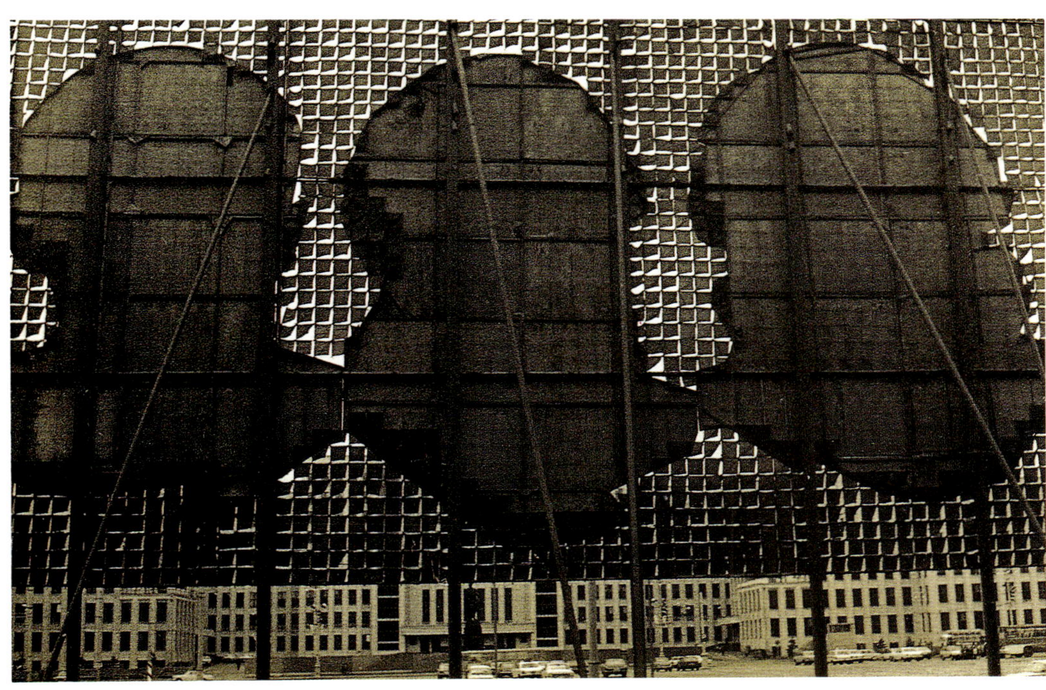

IVAN PETROVICH
SPIRITUAL CRISIS, 1990
6½ × 10″ (each)

Opposite:
GALINA MOSKALEVA
THE FAMILY ALBUM, from the series:
HARMONY OF FORCE, 1989
9 × 11½″ (each)

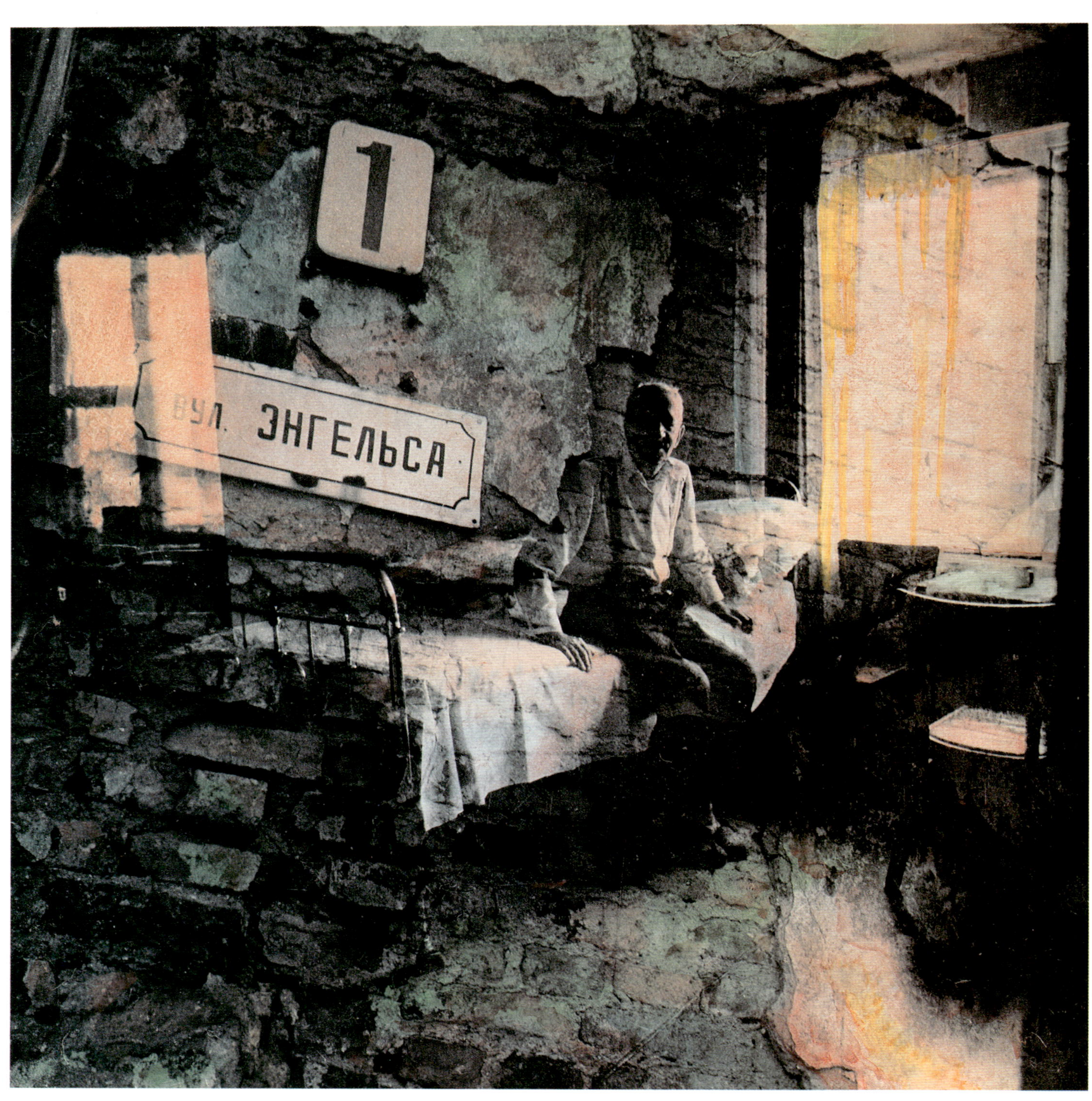

VADIM KACHAN
RED SUNSET, 1990
6½ × 6½″

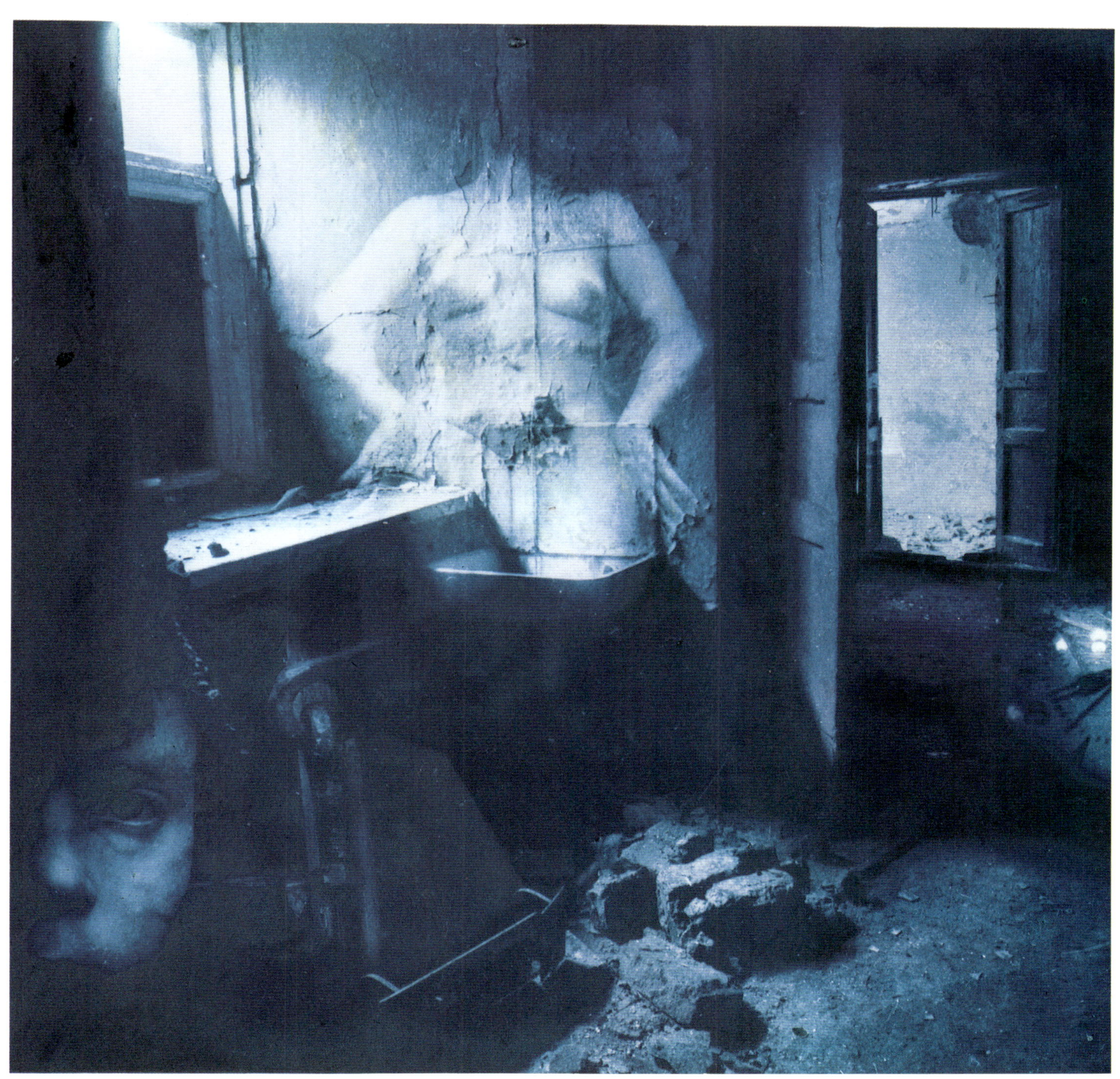

VADIM KACHAN
REMEMBRANCE ABOUT THE FUTURE, 1990
6½ × 7″

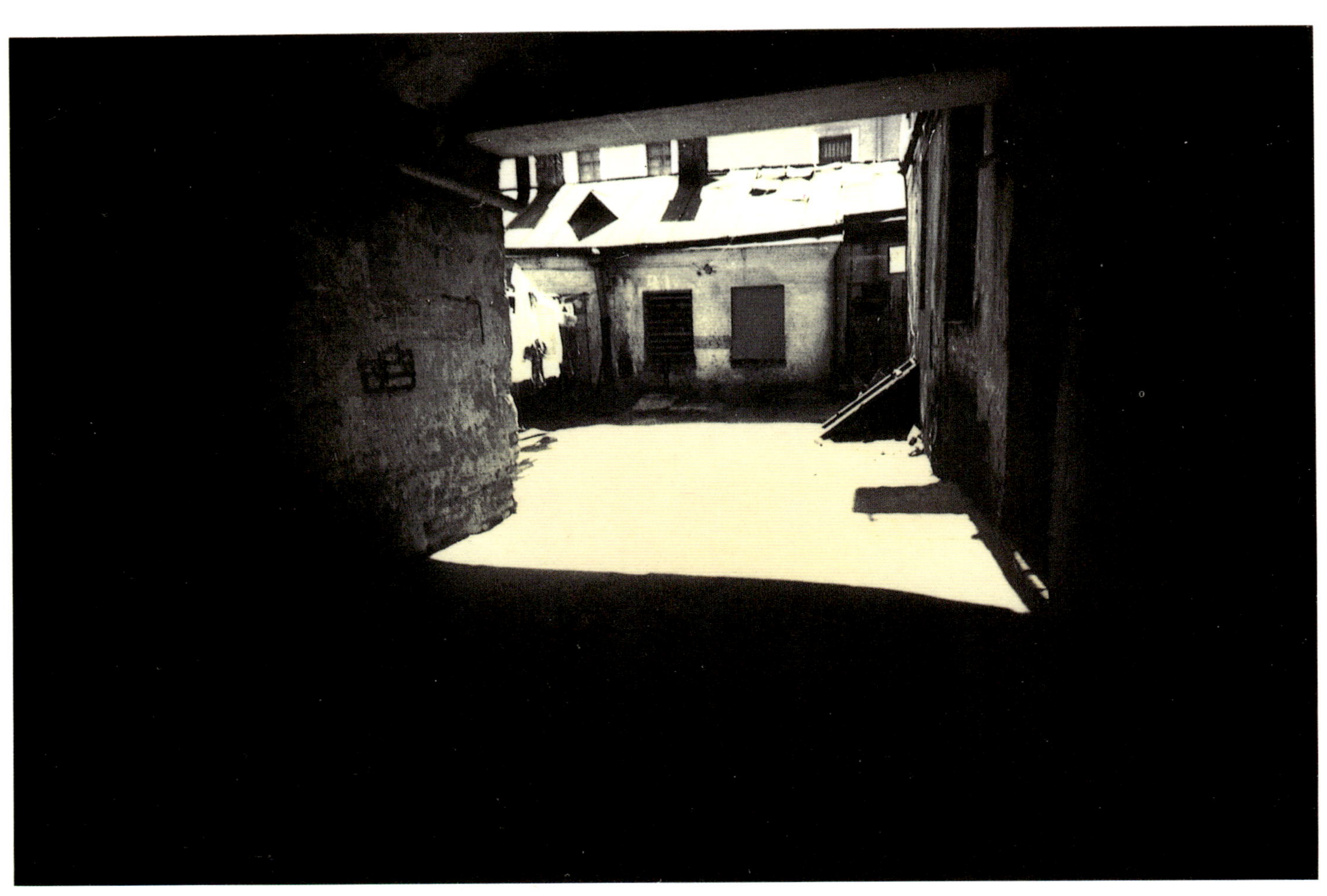

GENNADY SLABODSKY
LVOV-21, UKRAINE, 1990
3 × 4″

GENNADY SLABODSKY
LVOV-16, UKRAINE, 1990
4½ × 3″

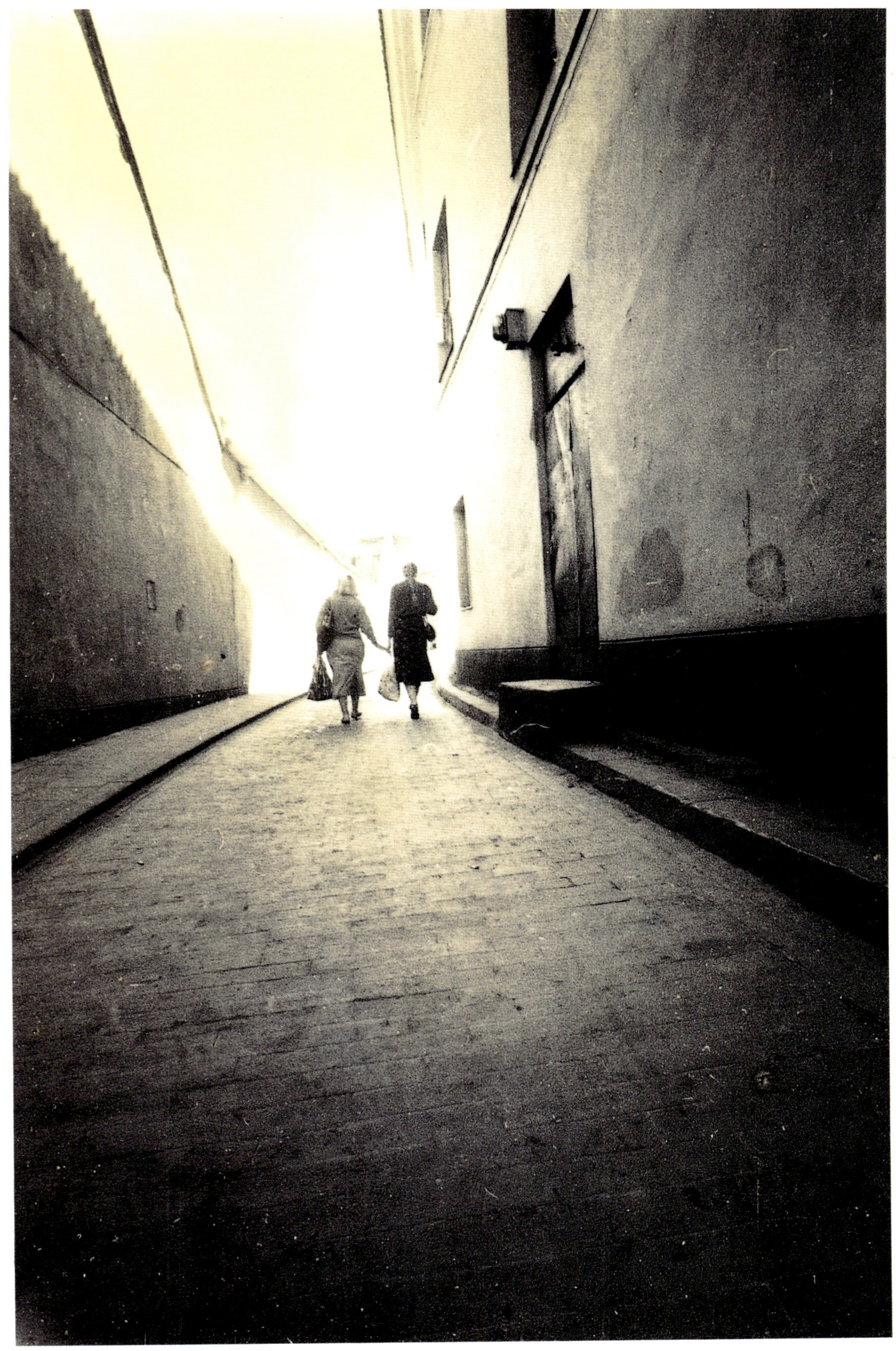

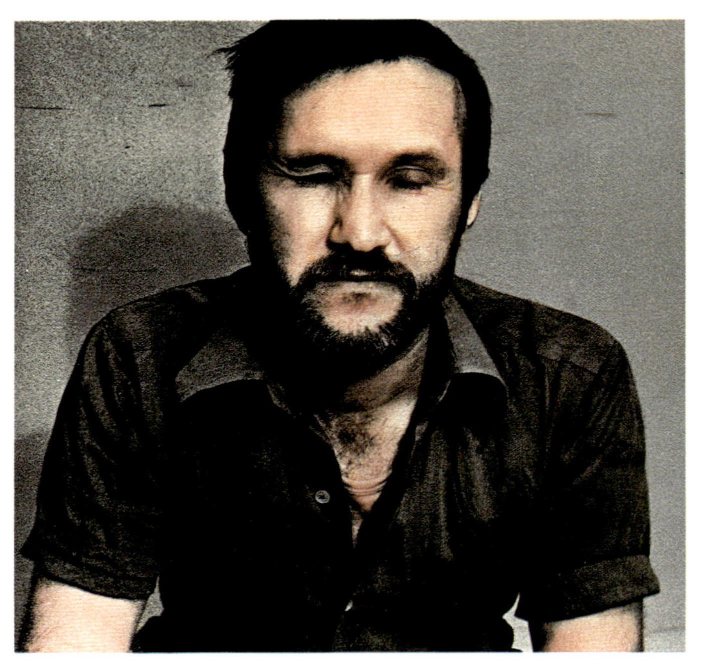
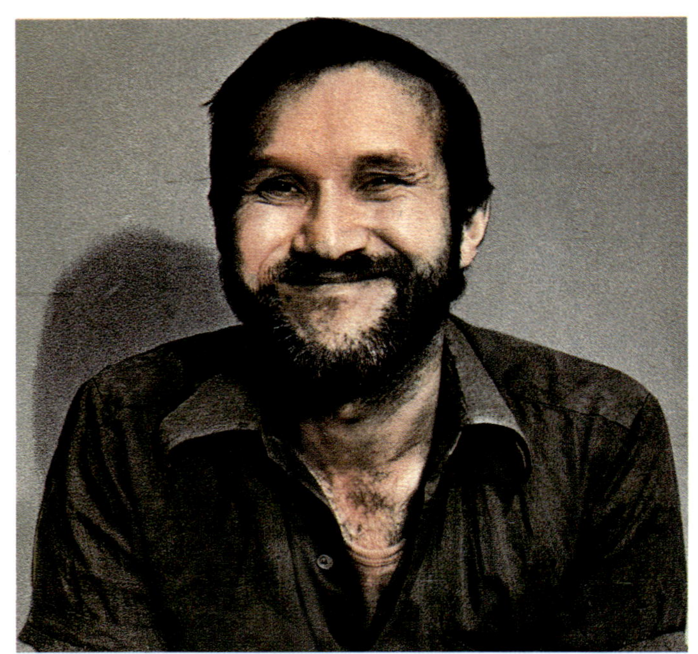
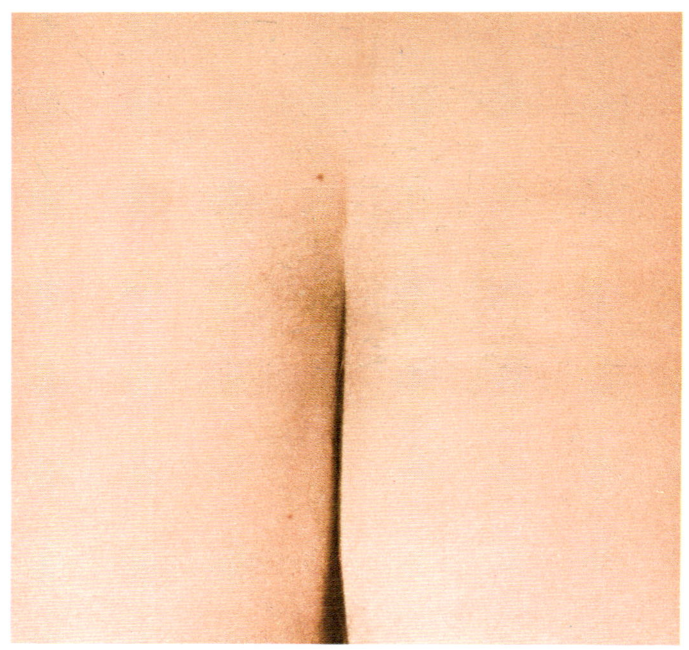
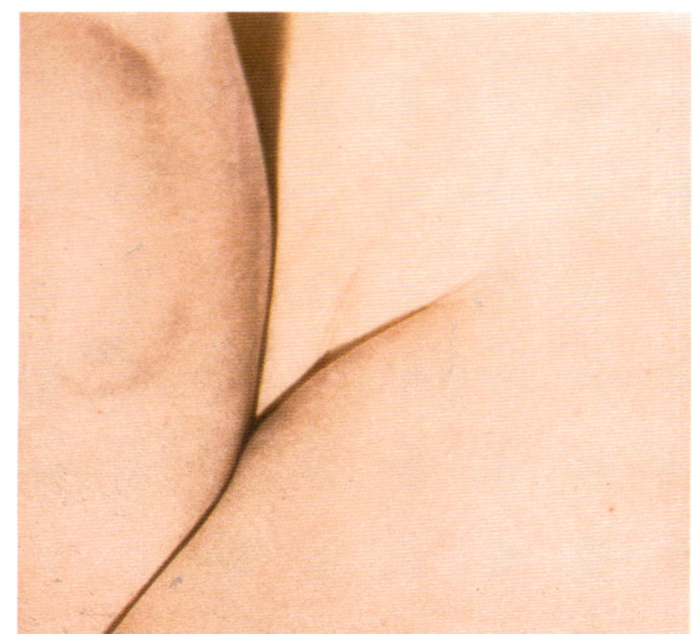

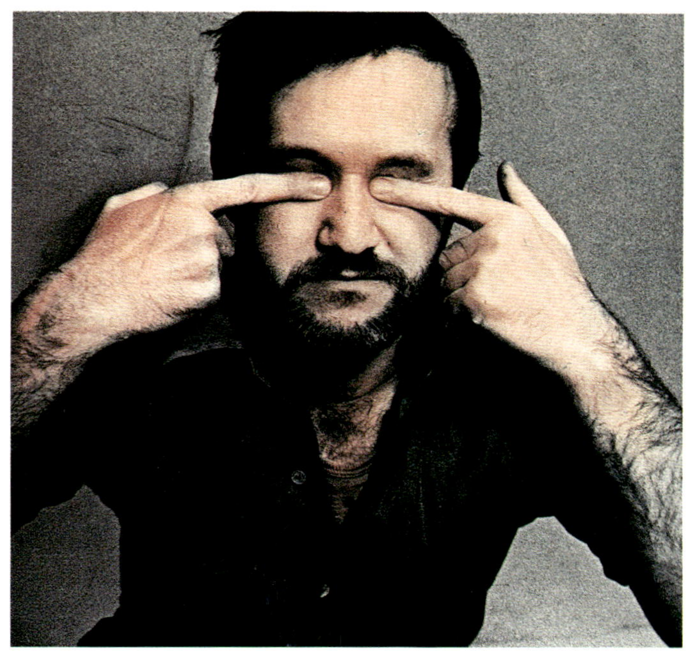

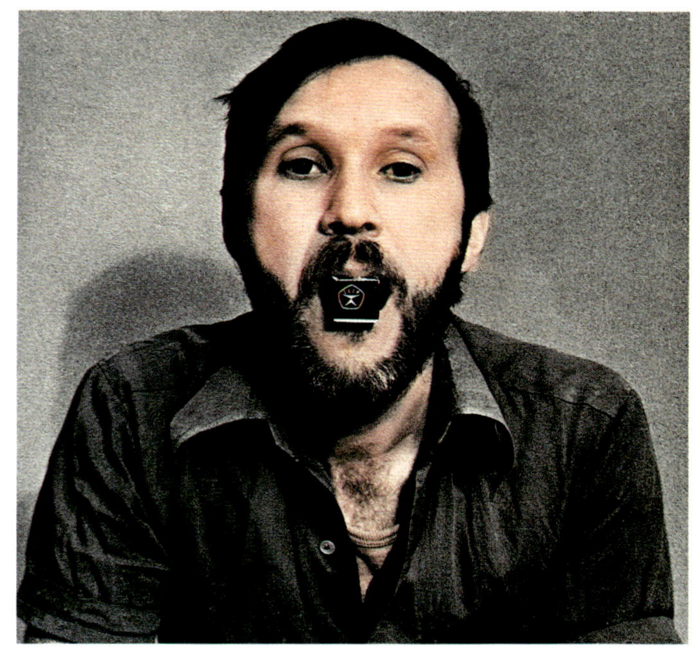

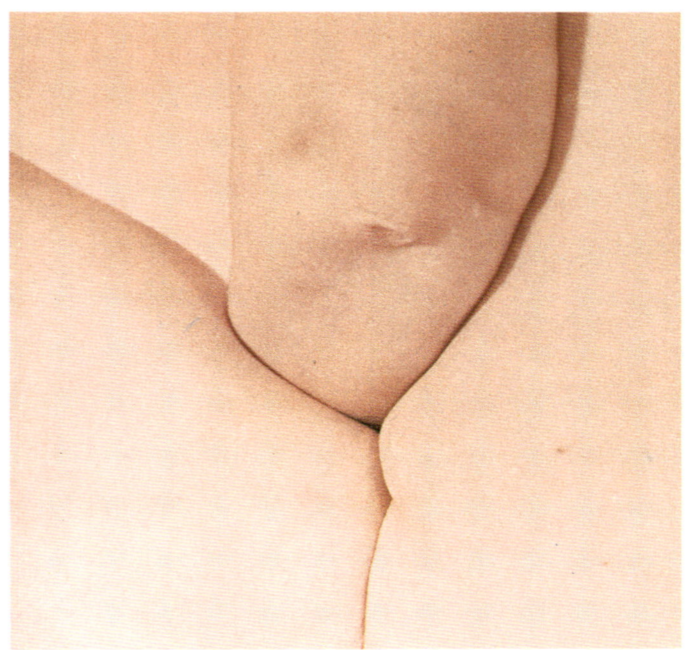

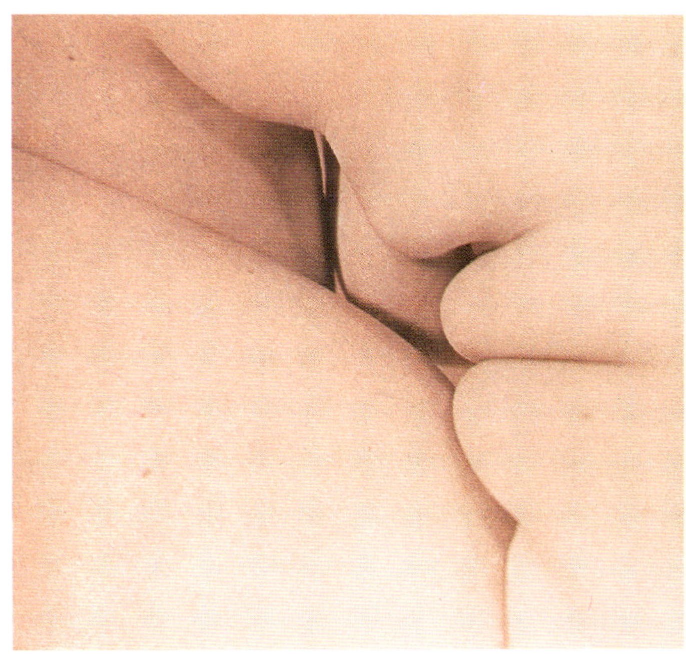

VLADIMIR SHAKHLEVICH
ACT WITH A PORTRAIT, 1990
9 × 9″ (each)

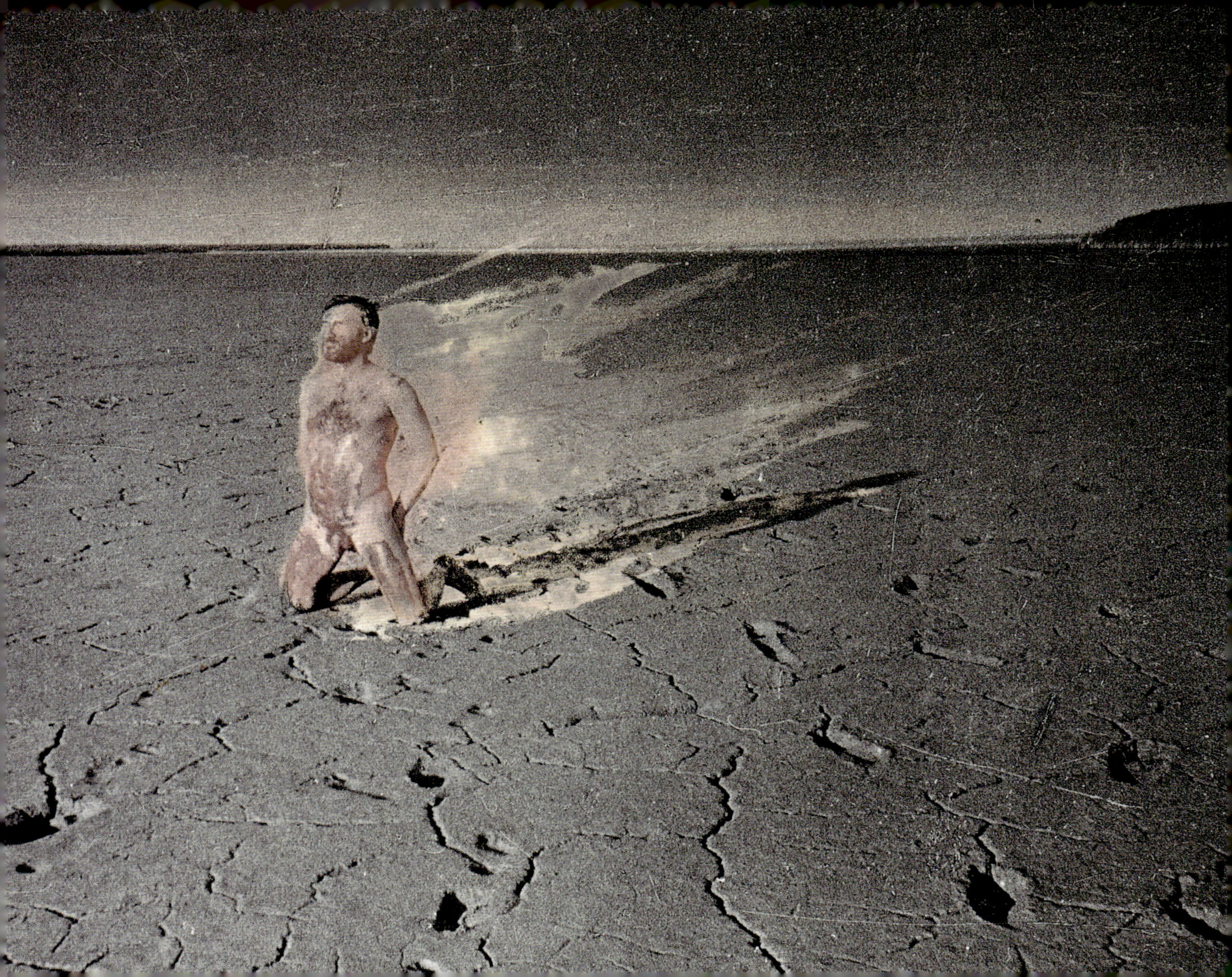

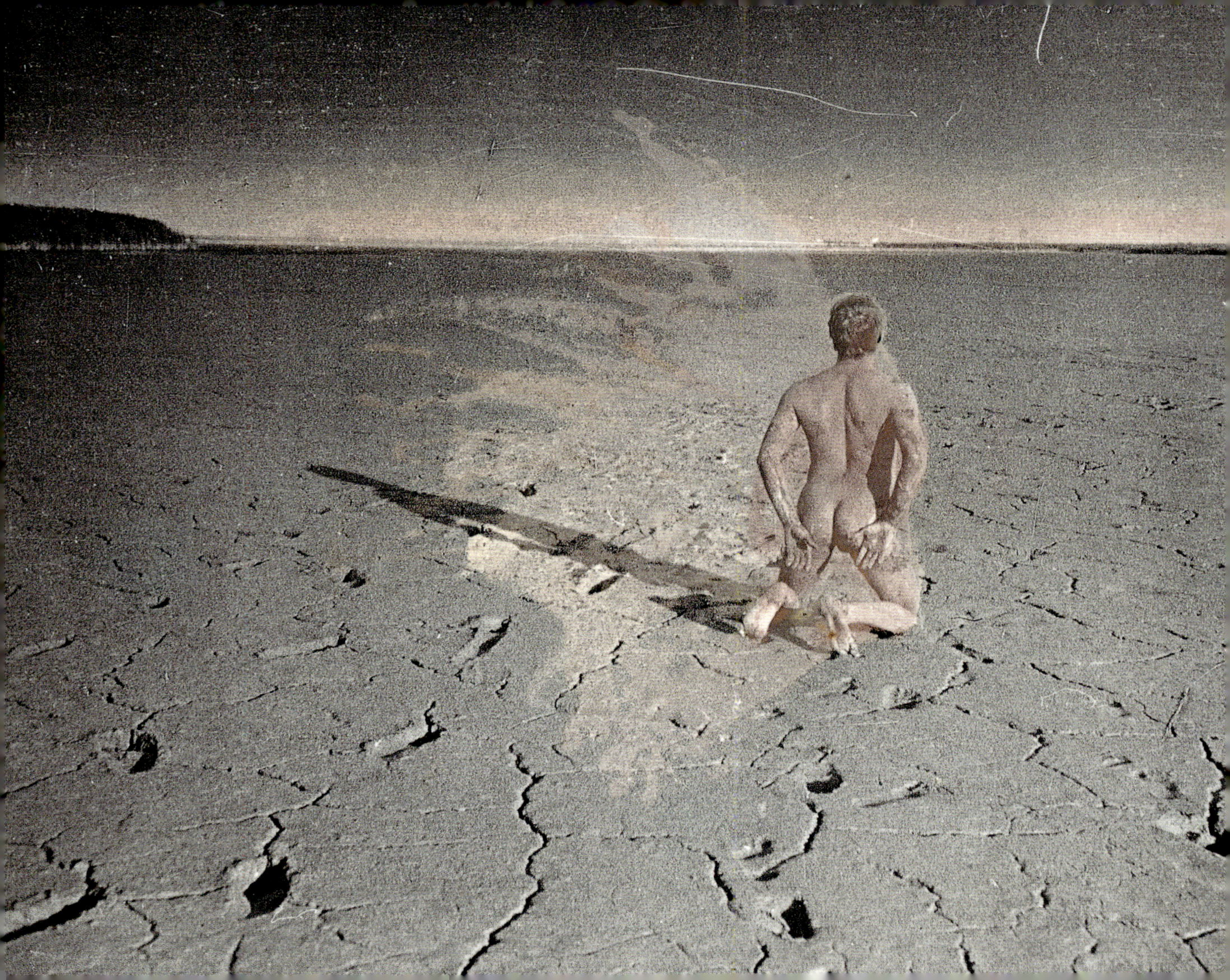

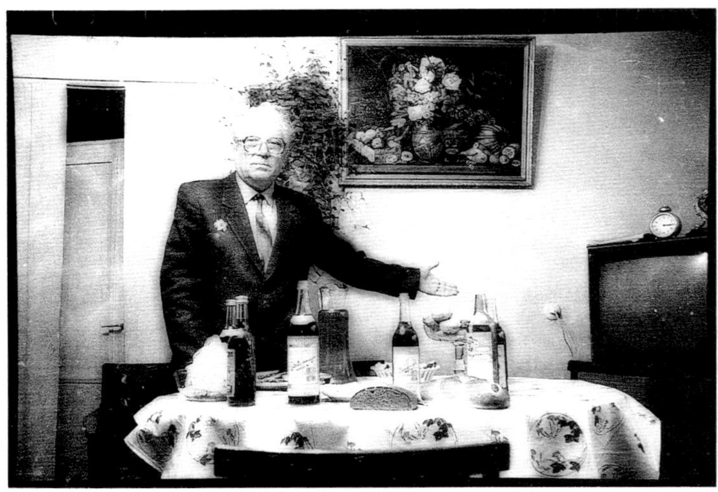

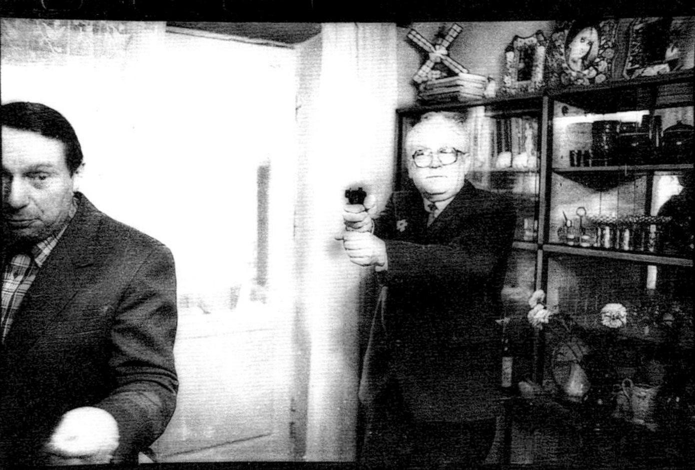

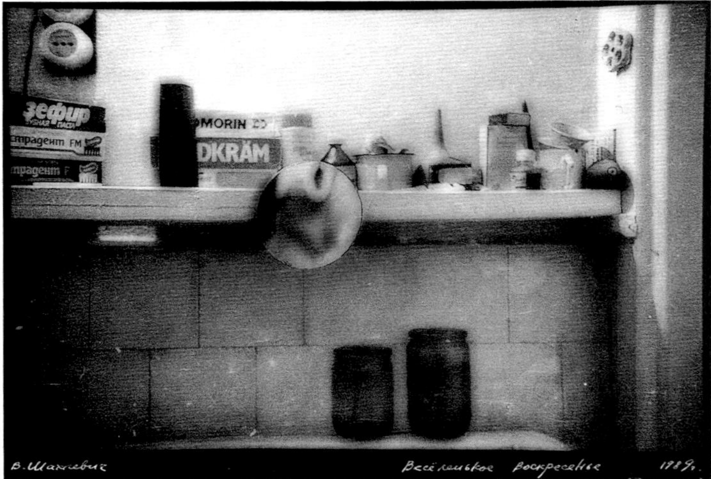

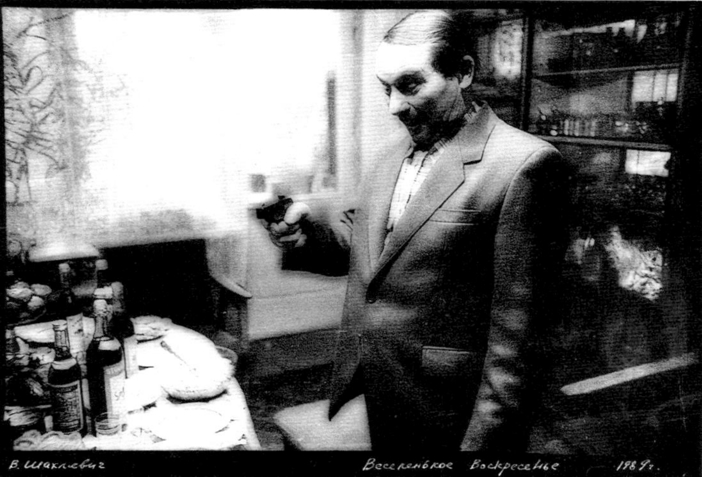

Preceding pages:
VLADIMIR SHAKHLEVICH
ACT IV, 1989
6 × 7″ (each)

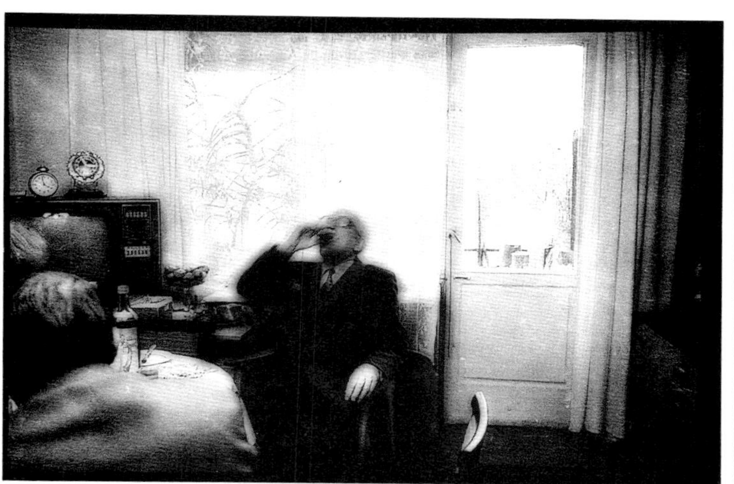

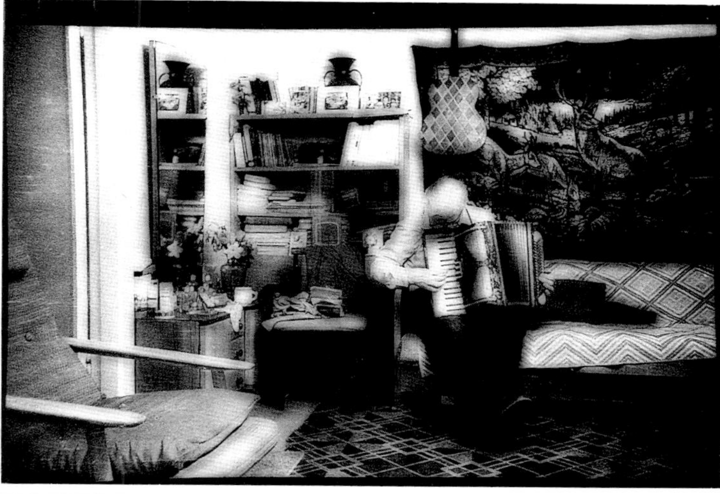

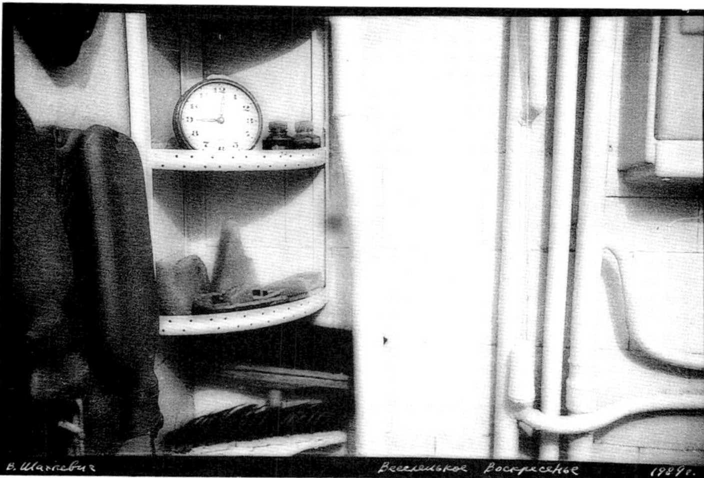

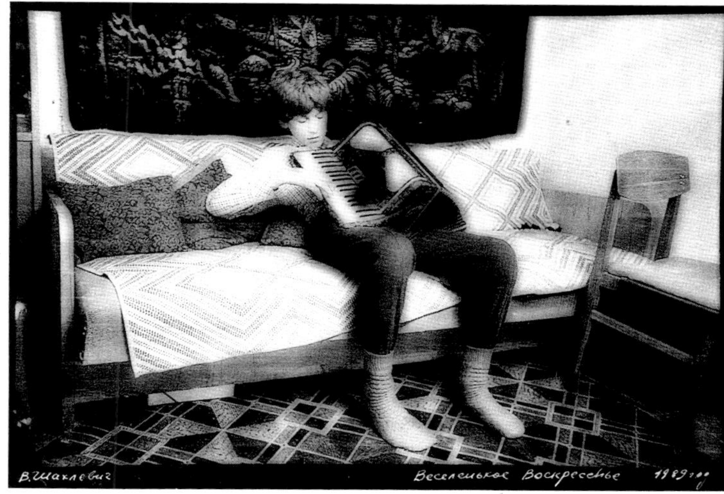

VLADIMIR SHAKHLEVICH
HAPPY SUNDAY (IRONICALLY), 1989
6 × 8½″ (each)

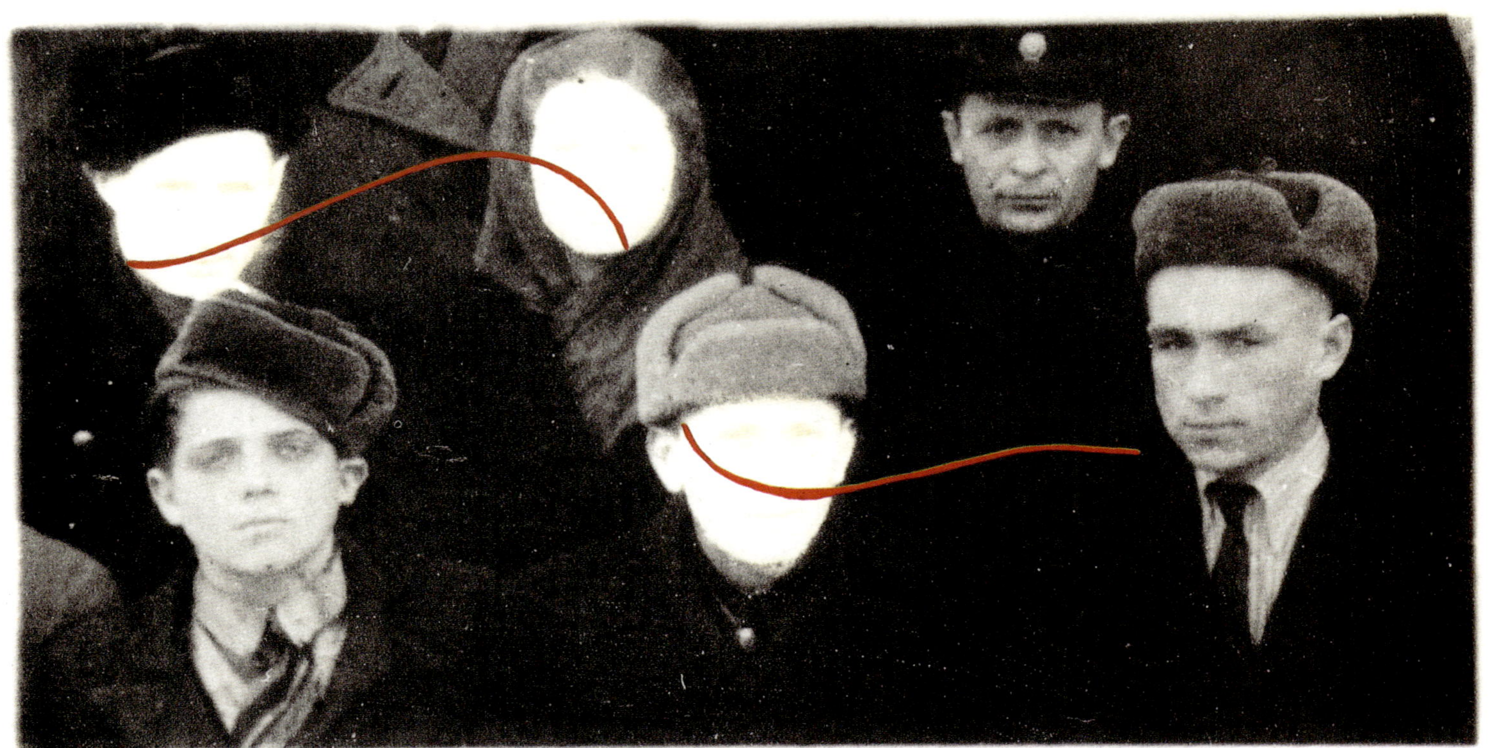

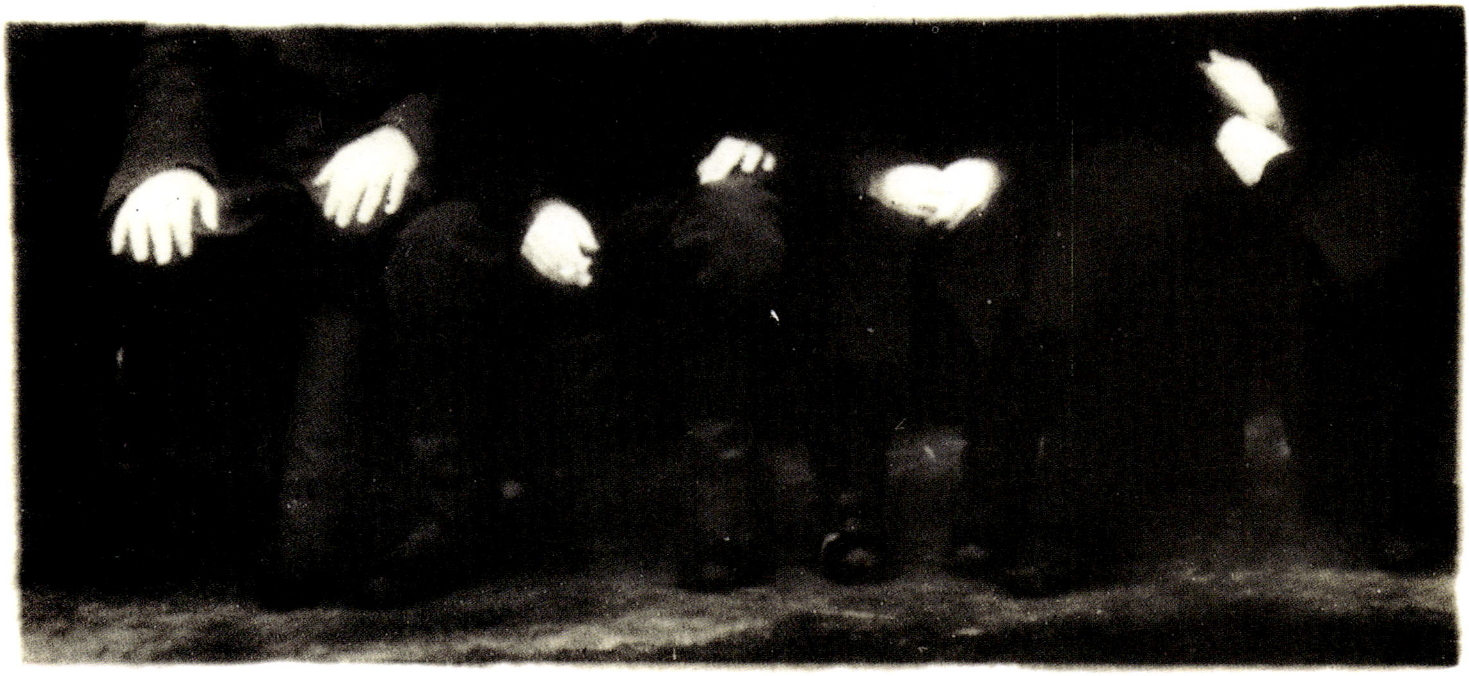

IGOR V. SAVCHENKO
Top: 9.89–16.2, bottom: 9.89–15.1, 1989
Top: 4½ × 8″, bottom: 3½ × 8″

IGOR V. SAVCHENKO
Top: 7.90–8, bottom: 7.90–9, 1990
Top: 5 × 5″, bottom: 5 × 6½

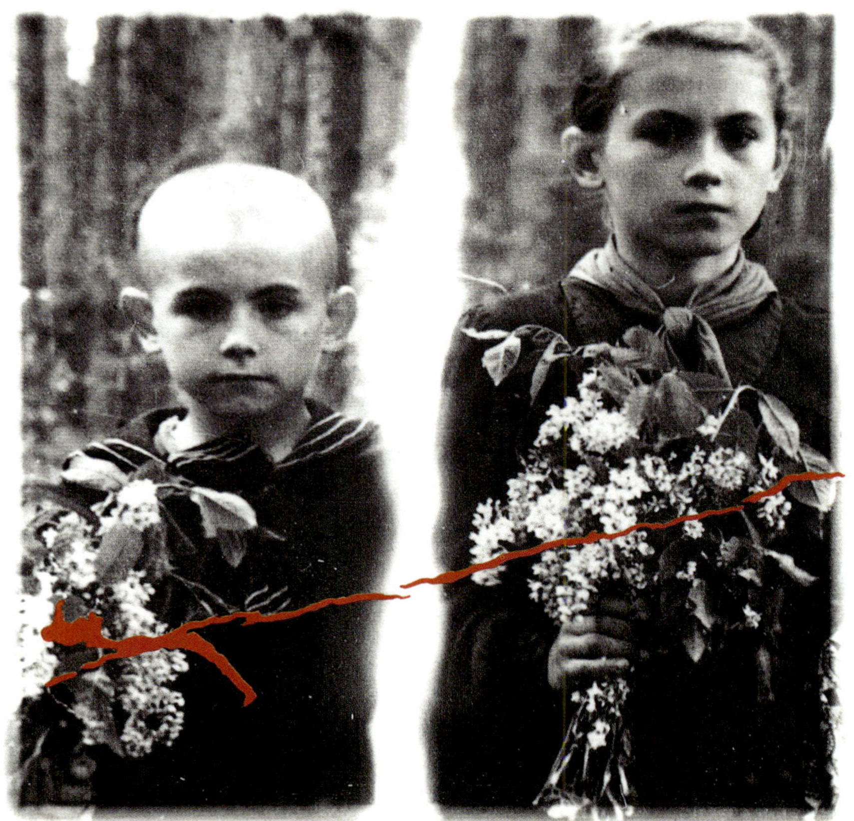

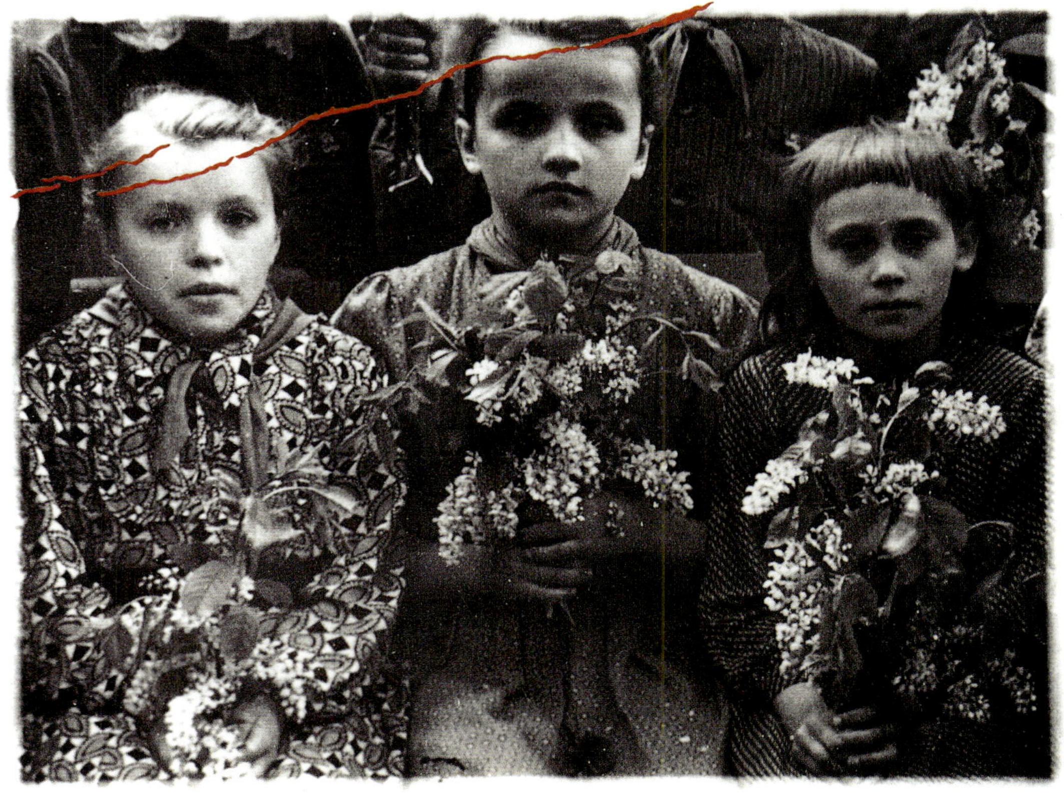

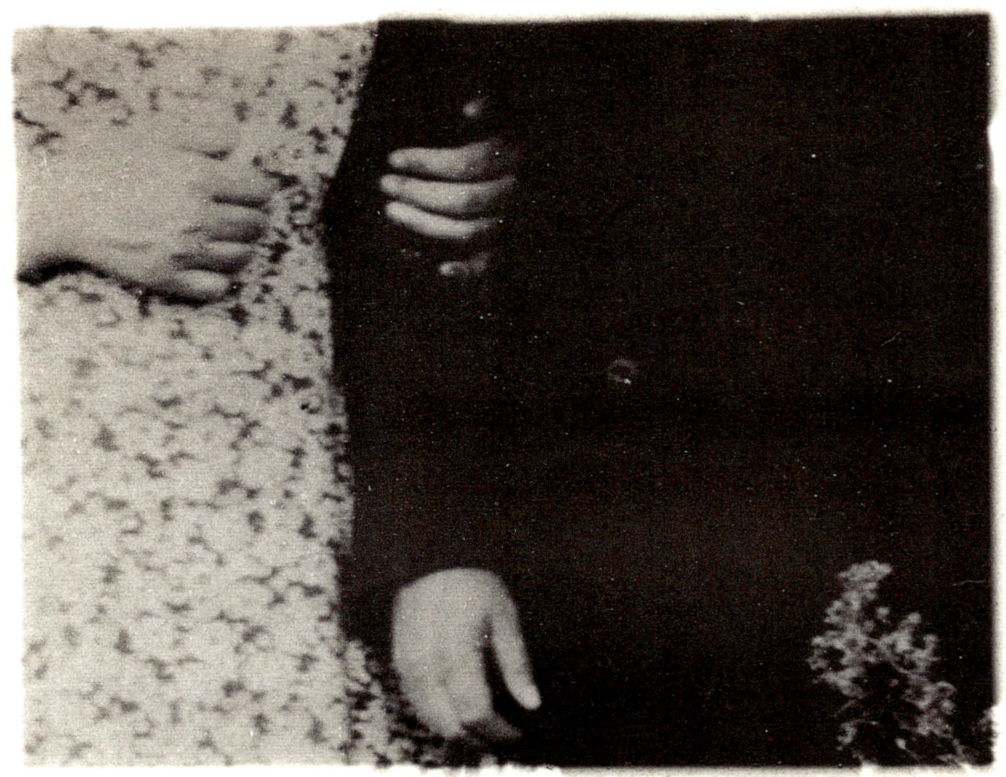

IGOR V. SAVCHENKO
11.89–9, 1989
4½ × 6″

IGOR V. SAVCHENKO
11.89–6, 1989
5 × 7″

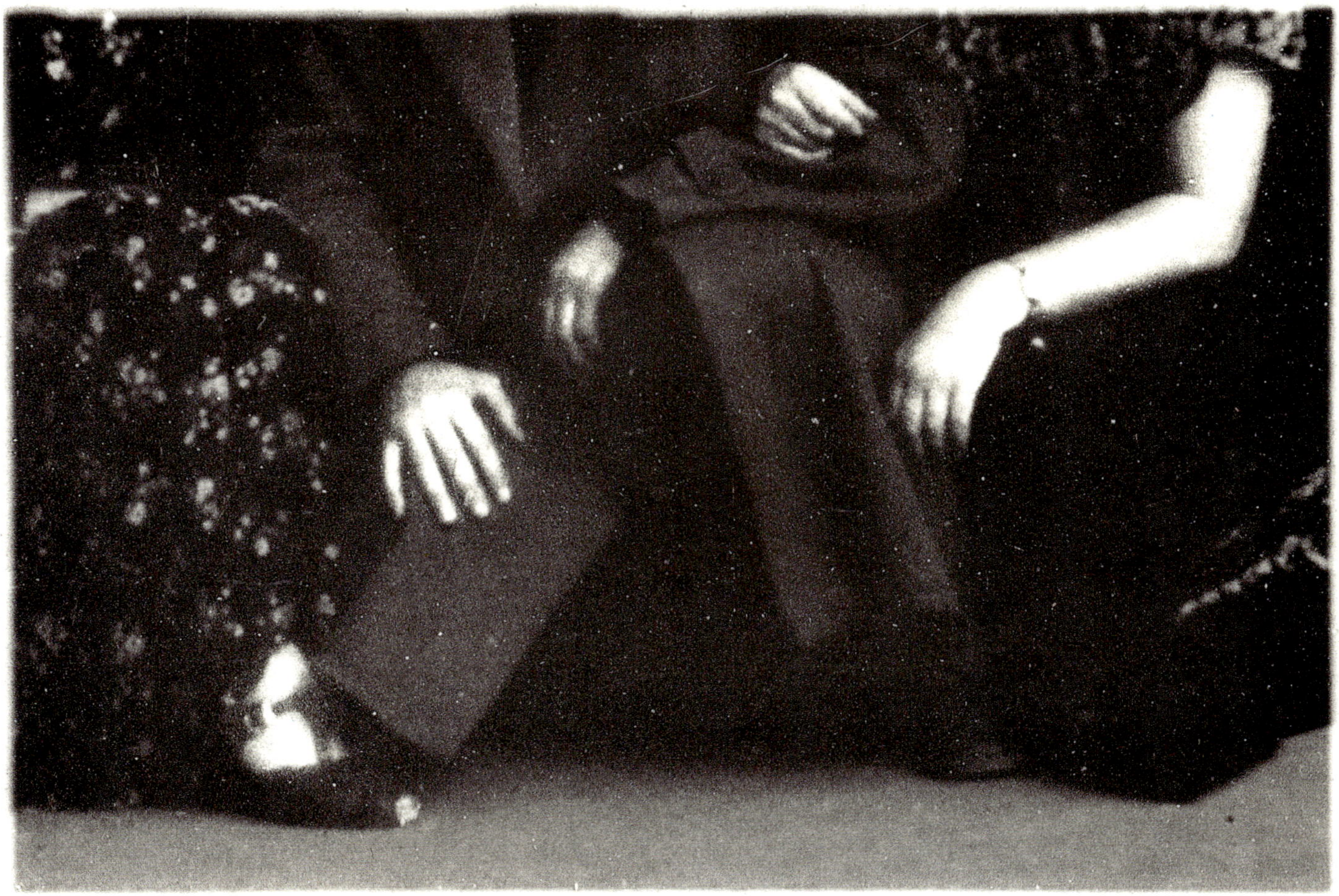

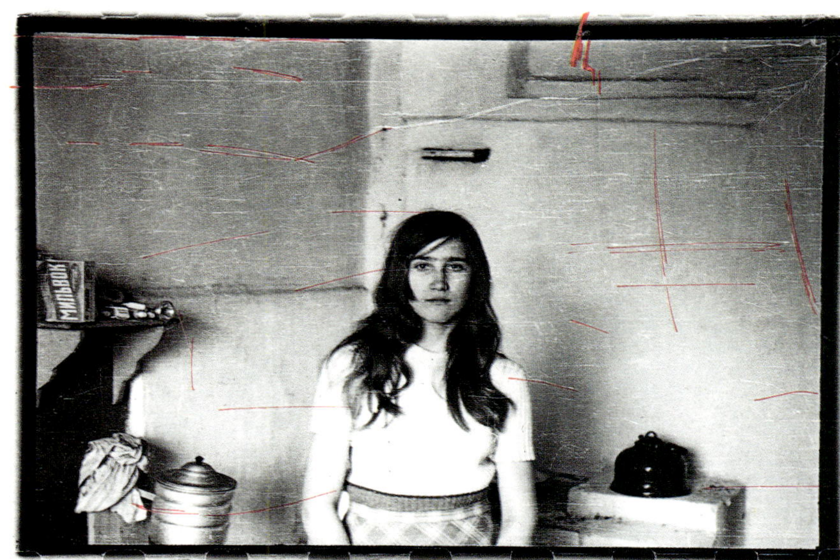

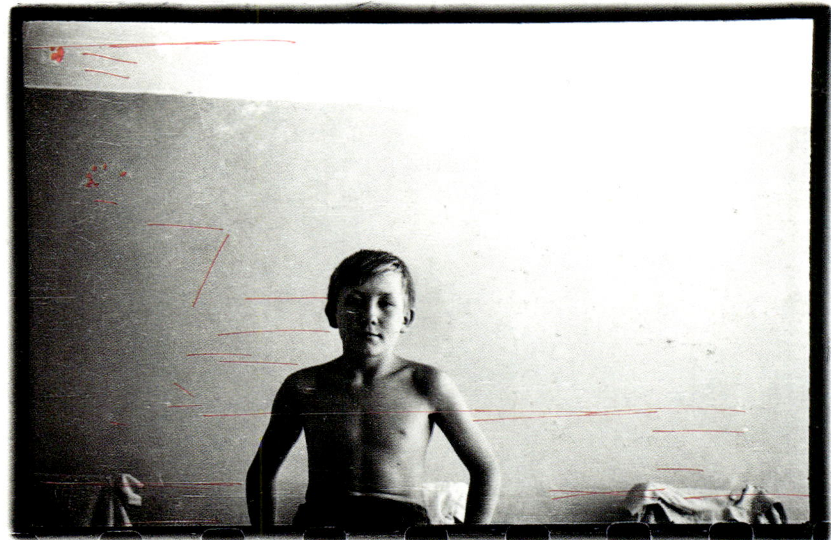

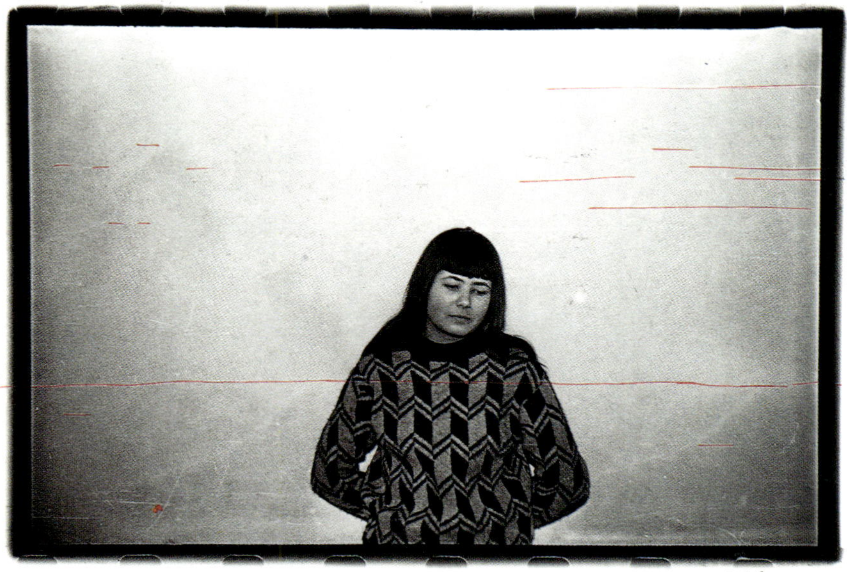

IGOR V. SAVCHENKO
1.90–4.1, 1990
"You say in many, many years life on earth will be wonderful, but if it is . . ."
9 × 11½"

IGOR V. SAVCHENKO
1.90–4.2, 1990
"You say in many, many years life on earth will be wonderful, but why . . ."
9 × 11½"

IGOR V. SAVCHENKO
1.90–4.3, 1990
"You say in many, many years life on earth will be wonderful, but how . . ."
9 × 11½"

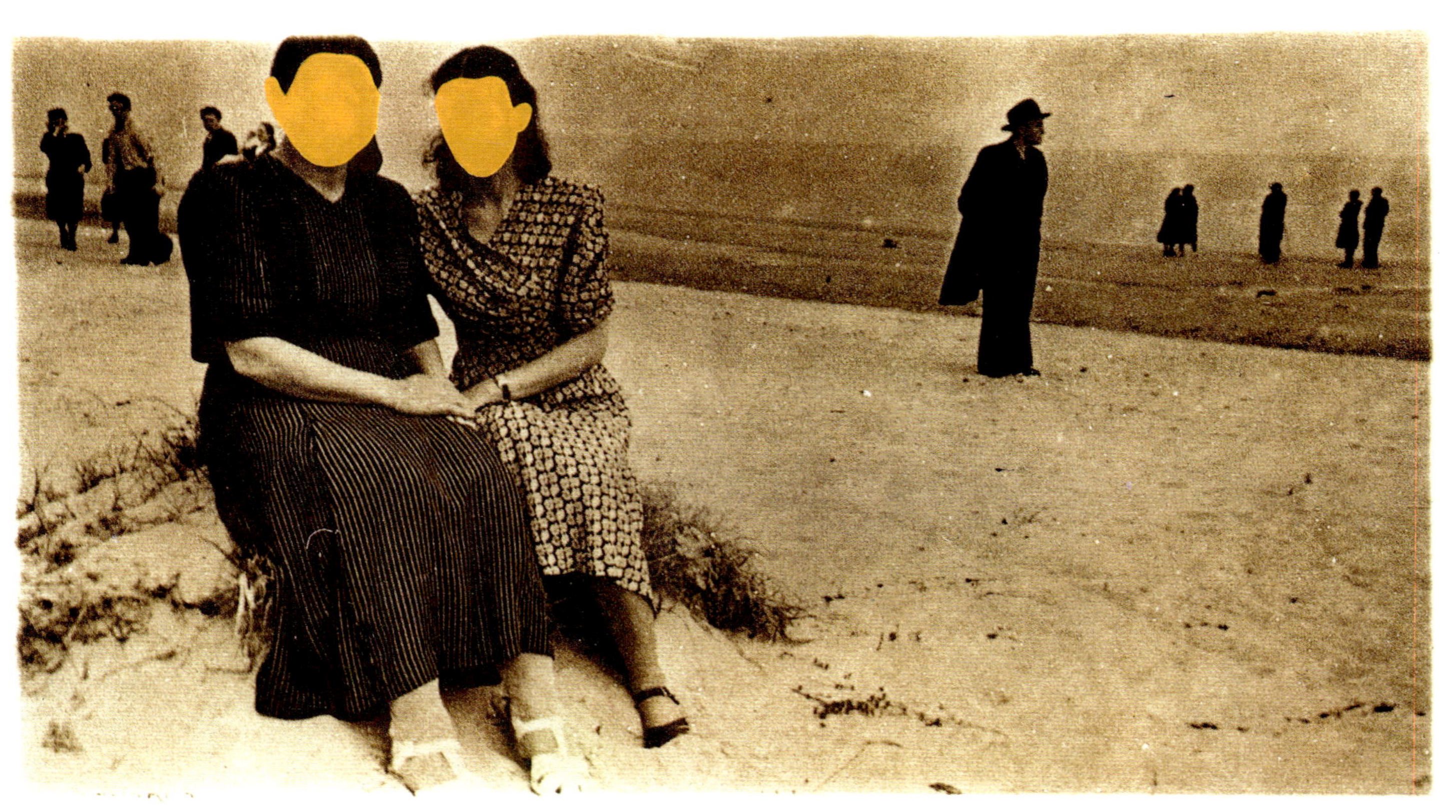

IGOR V. SAVCHENKO
4.90–22, 1990
4 × 7½″

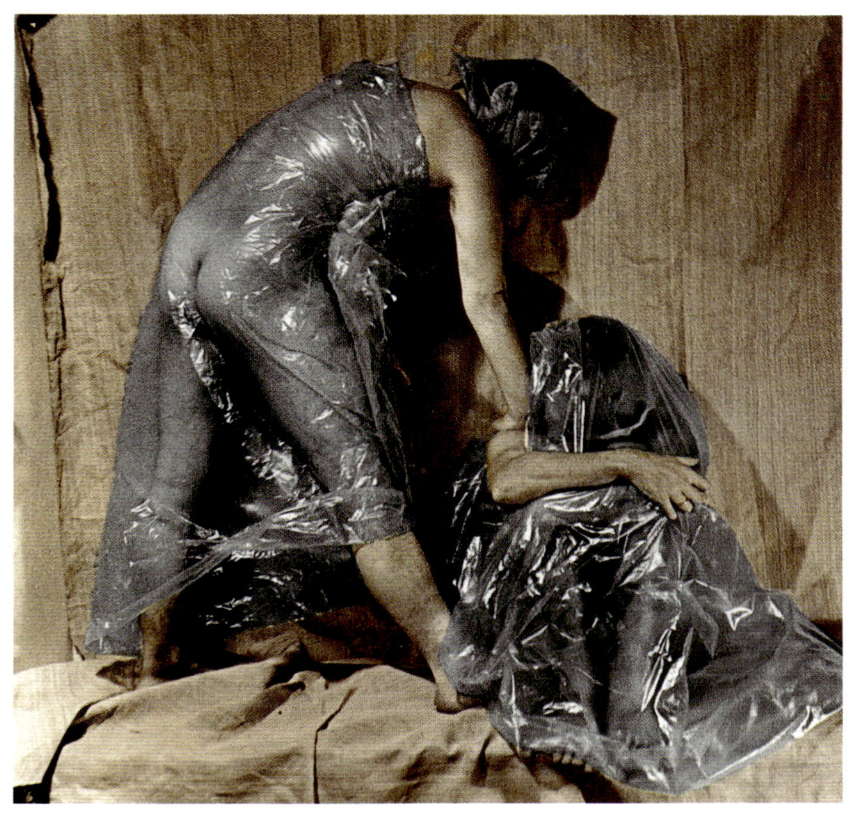

HELEN MULYUKINA
UNTITLED, 1989
6 × 6″

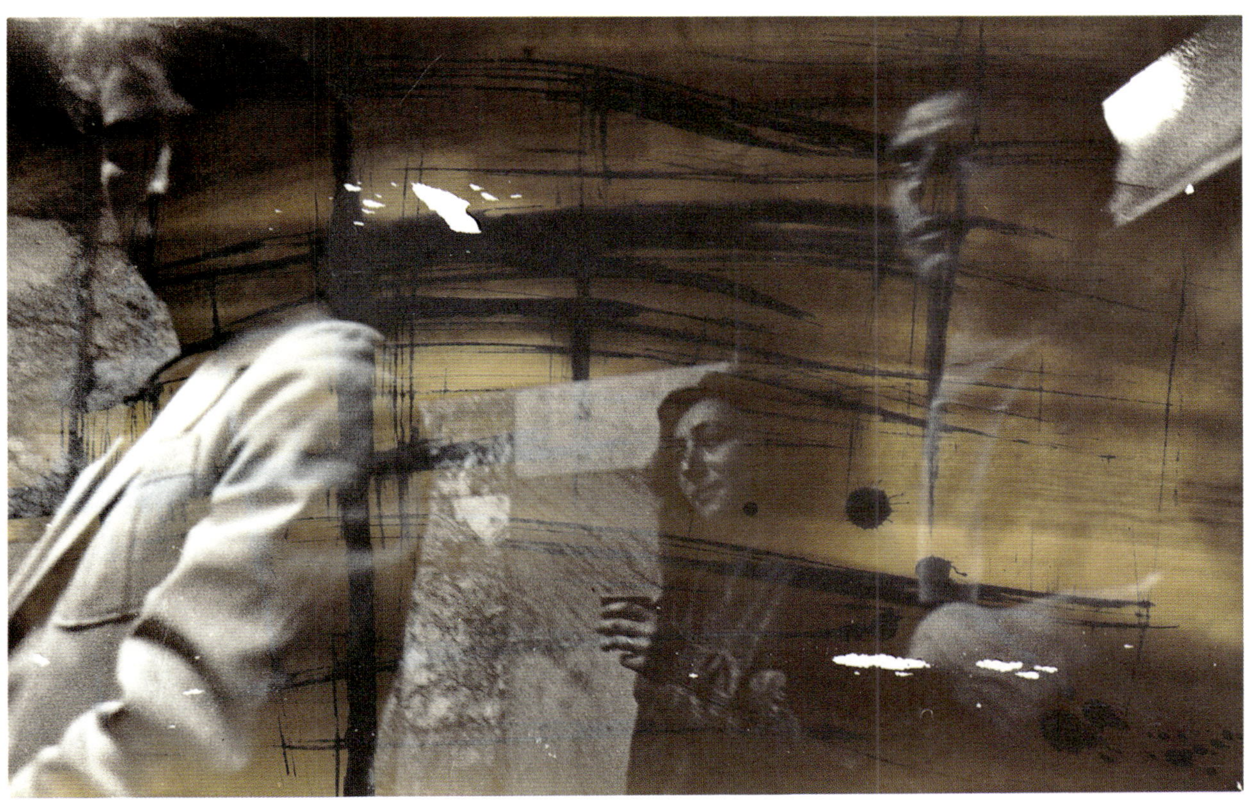

ALEXANDER SINYAK
from the series: A CUP OF COFFEE, 1990
5½ × 8½″

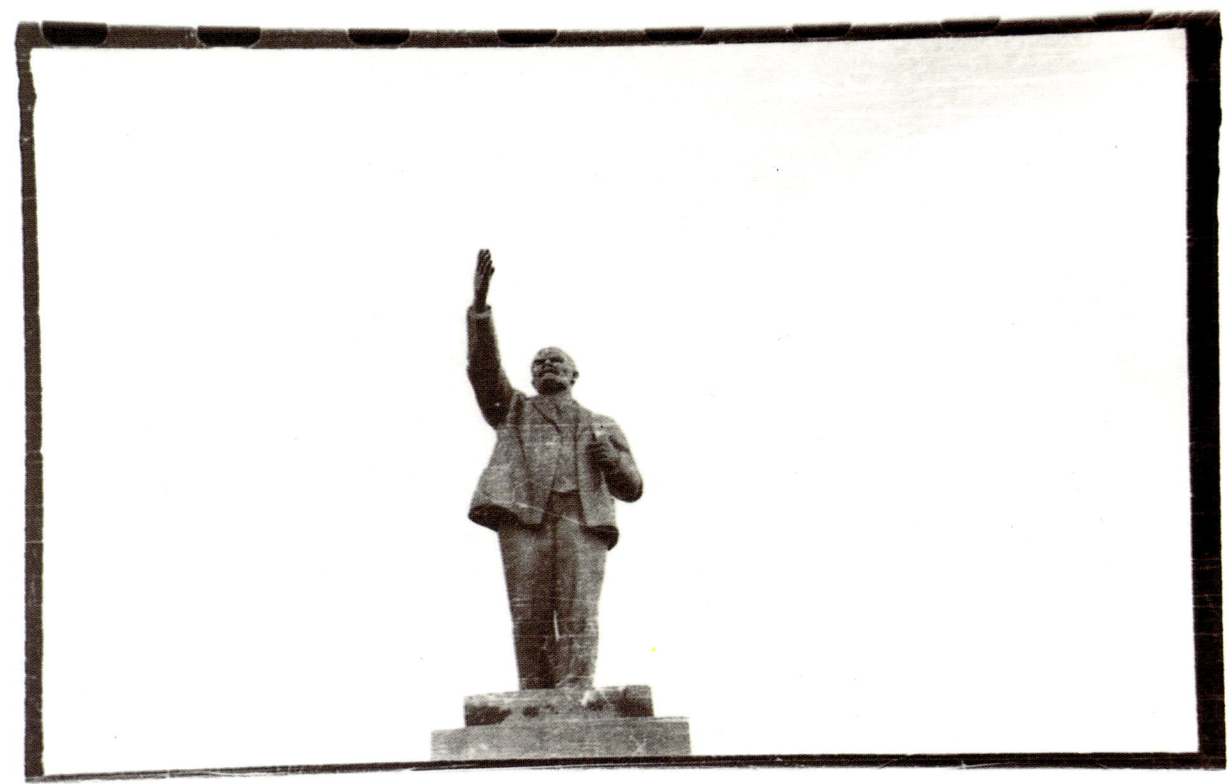

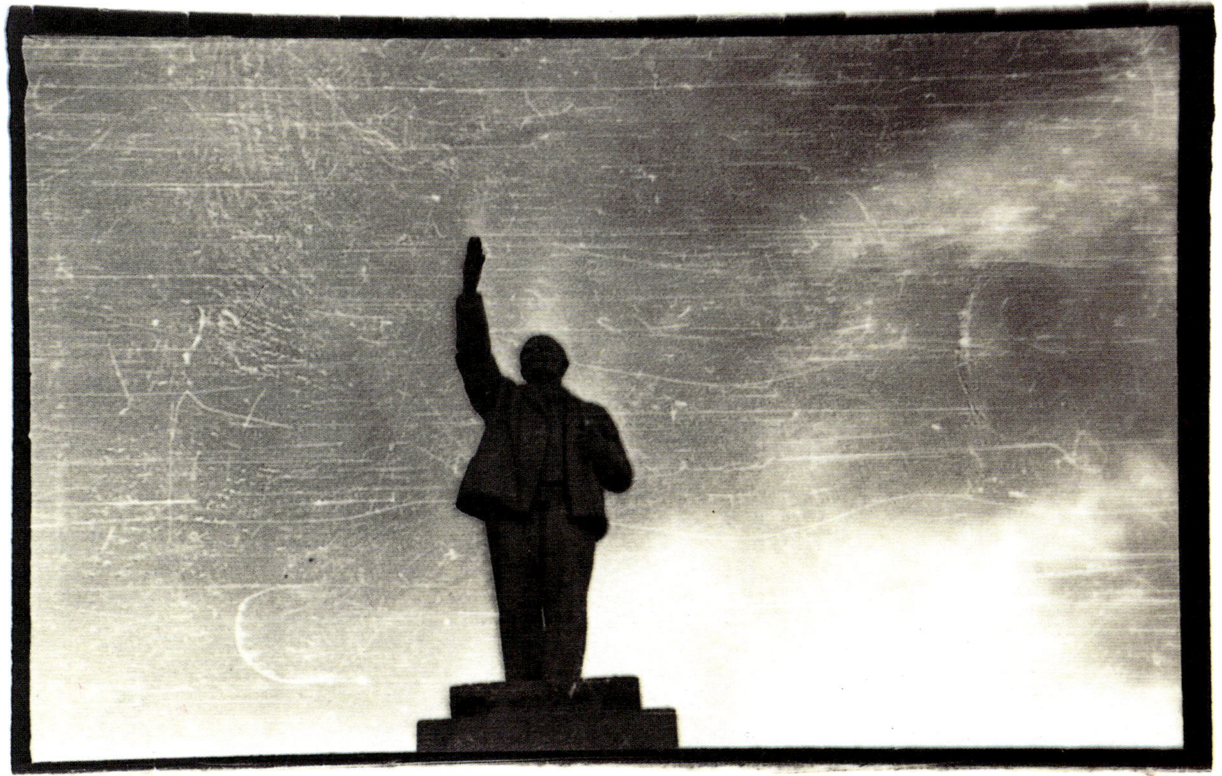

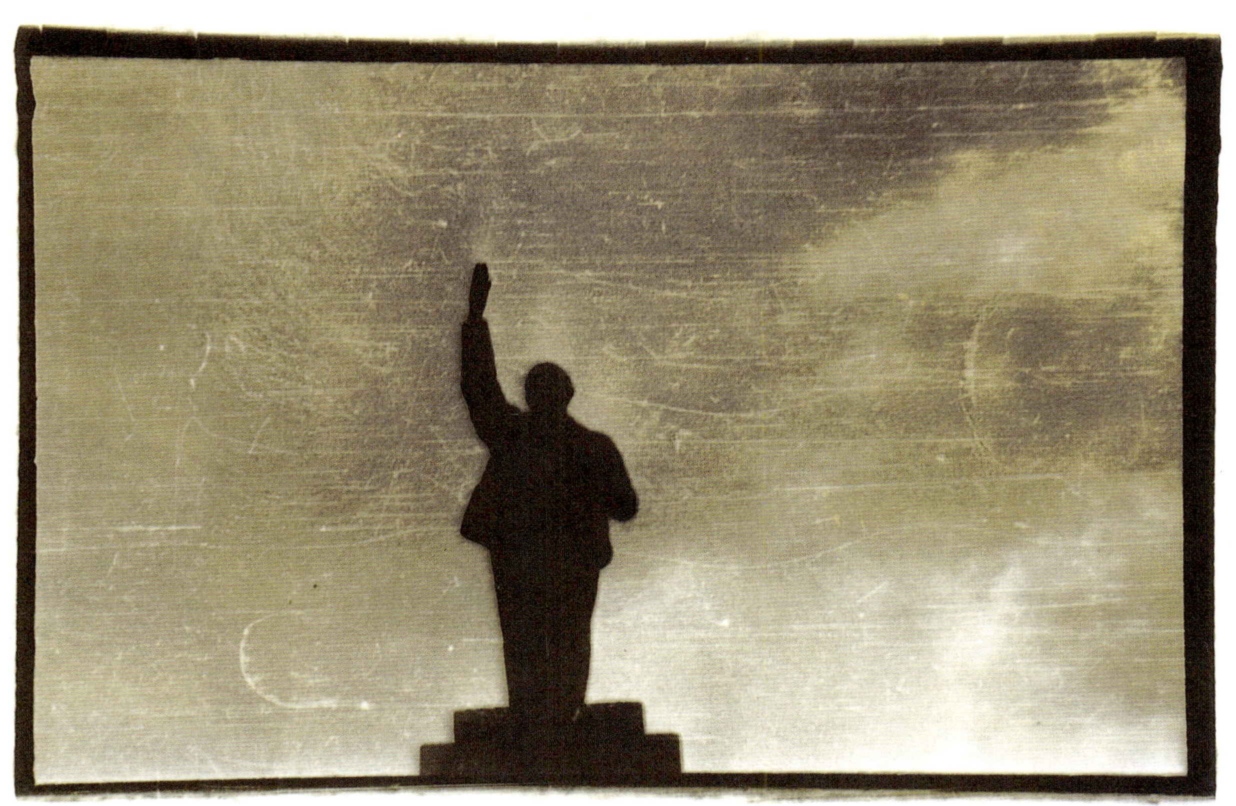

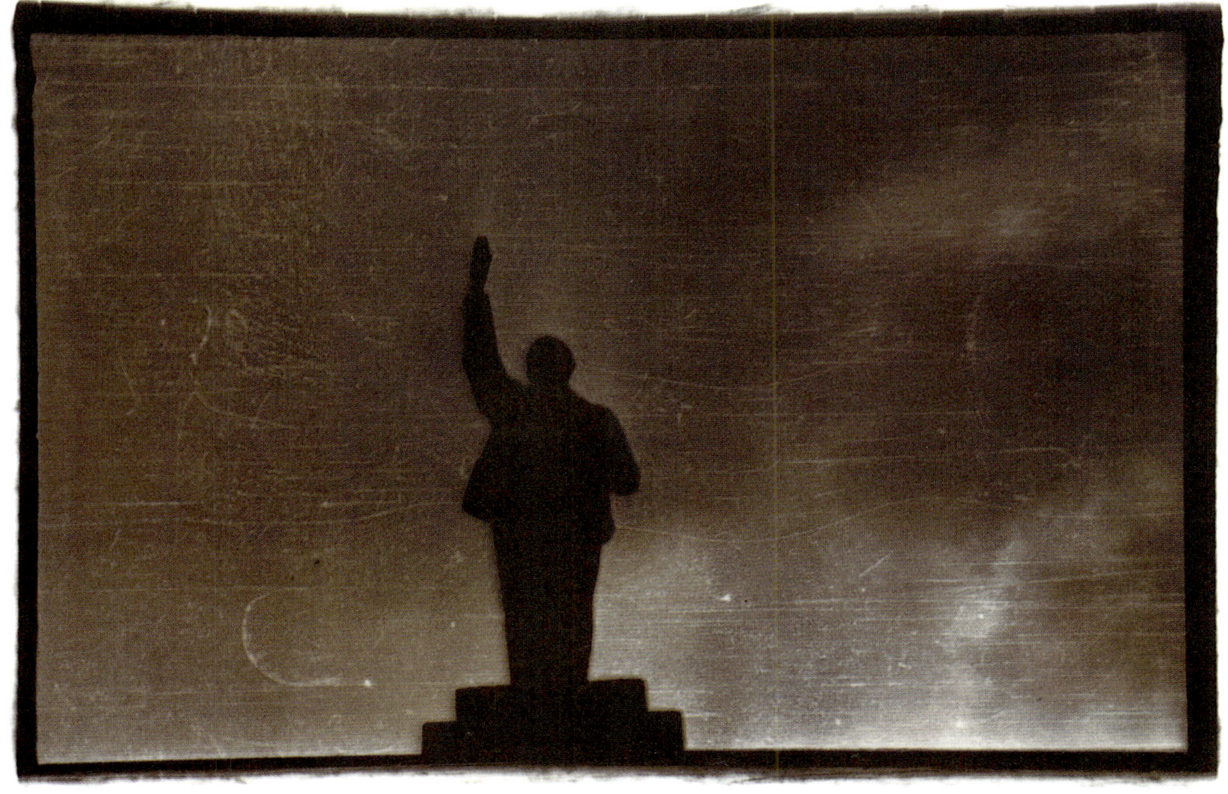

SERGEY KOZHEMYAKIN
****, 1990
6 × 9½″ (each)

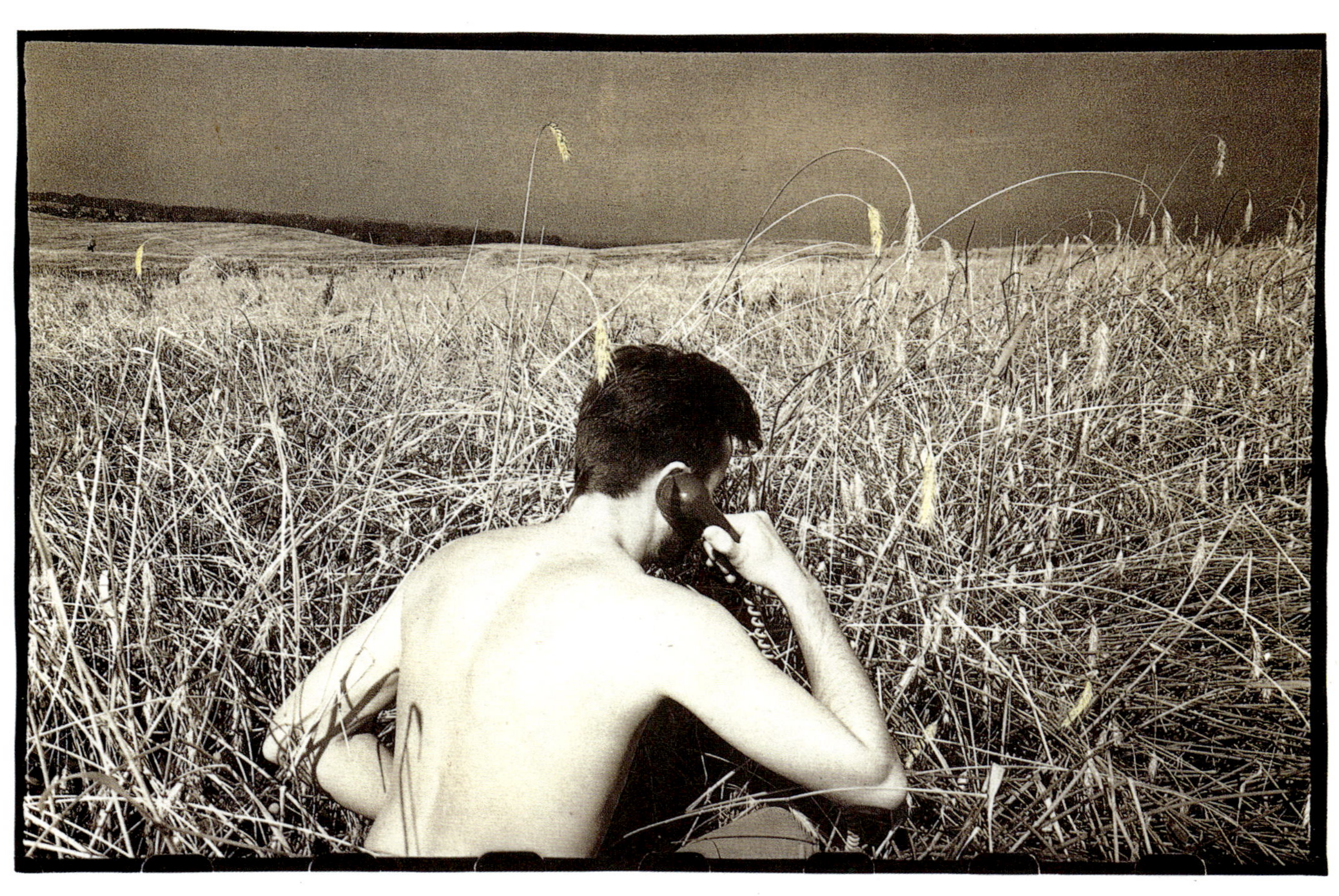

SERGEY KOZHEMYAKIN
STARTING POINT, 1990
6 × 9½″ (each)

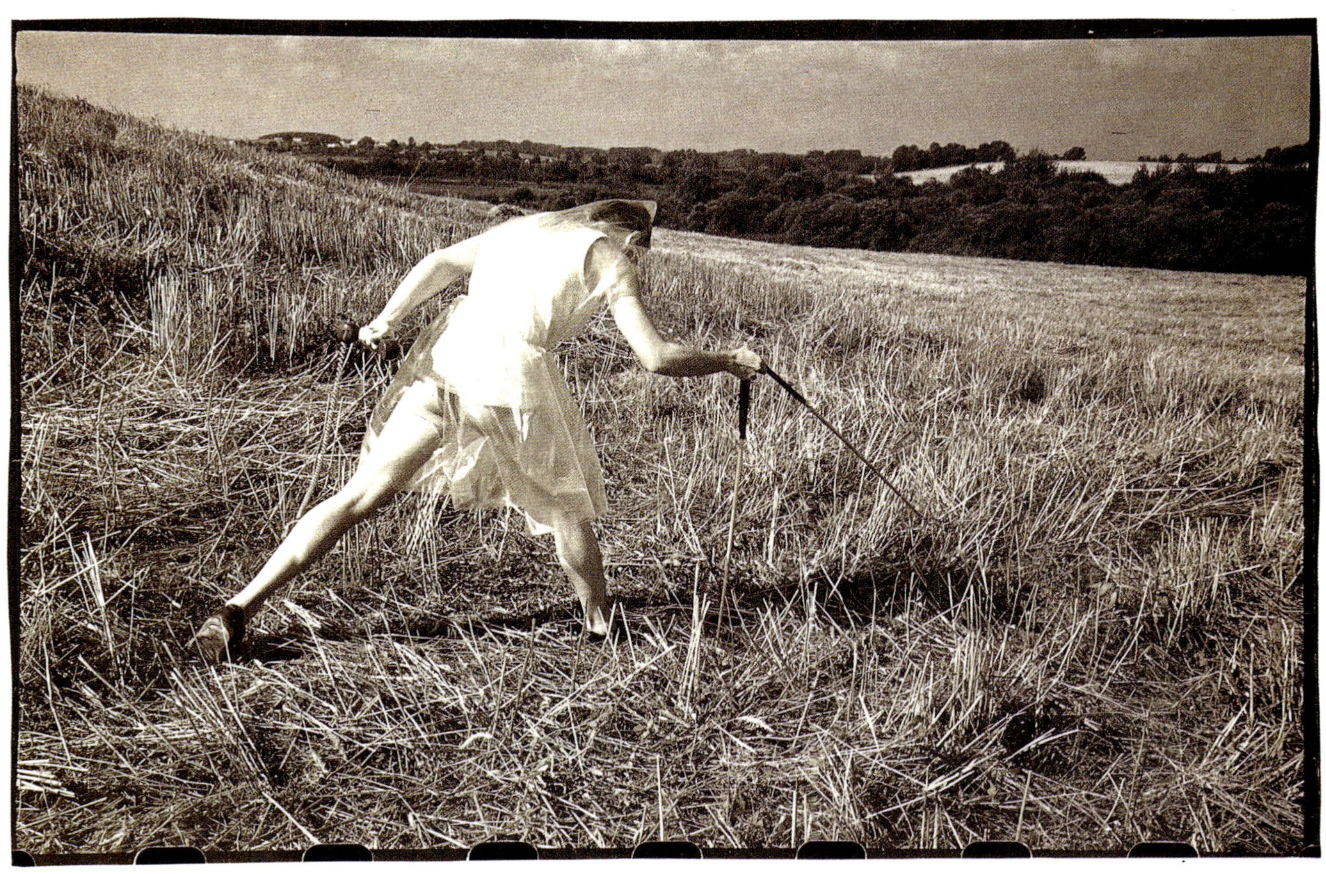

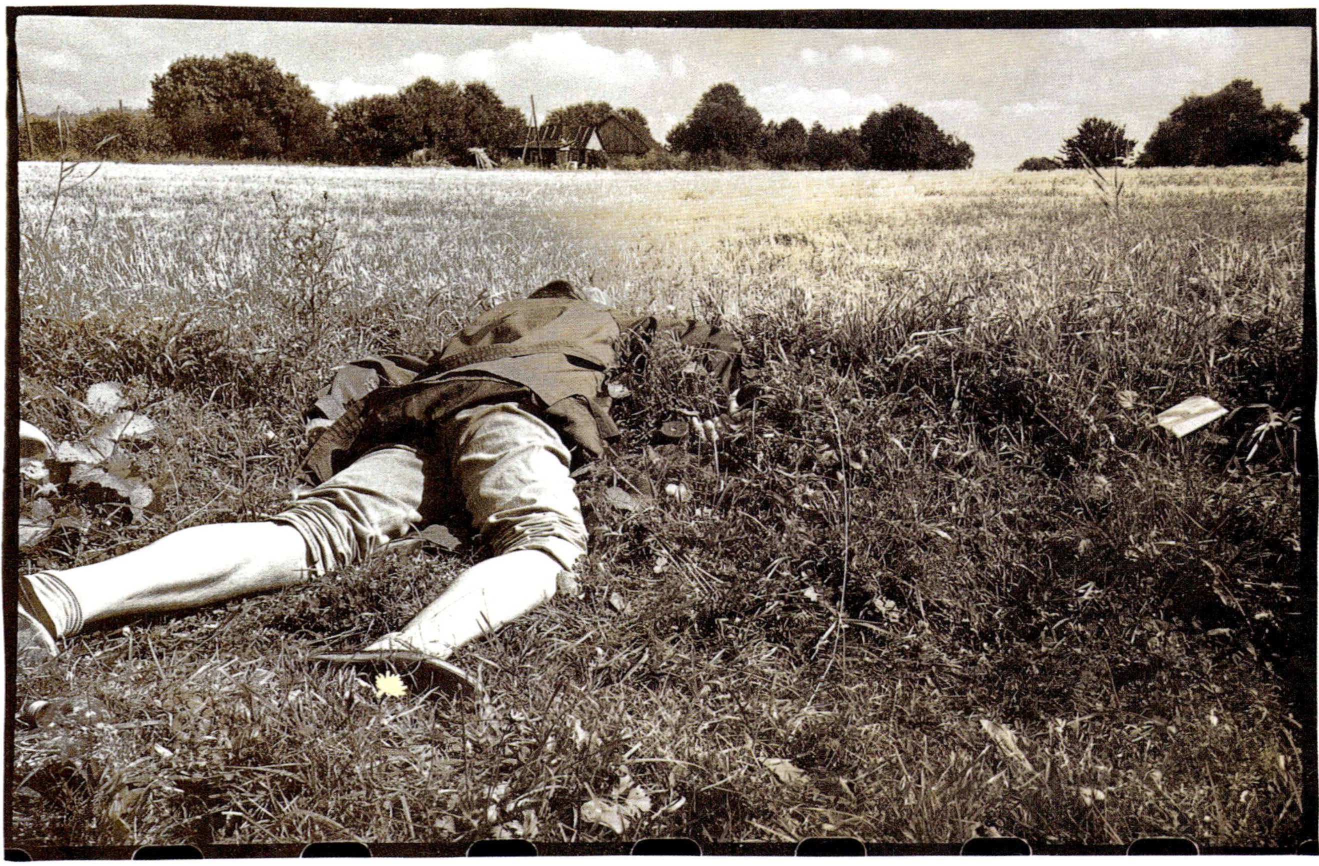

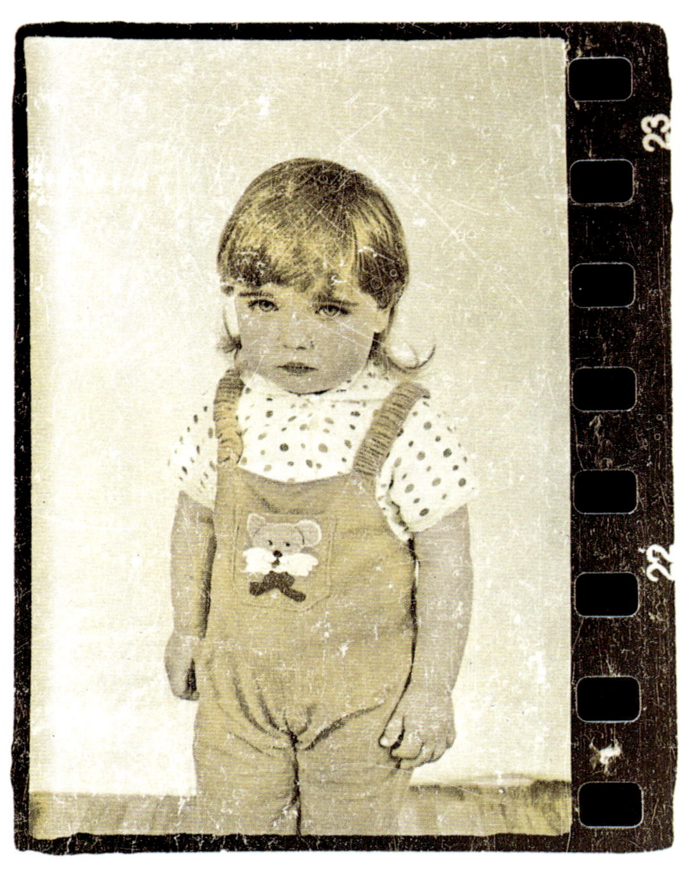
23
22

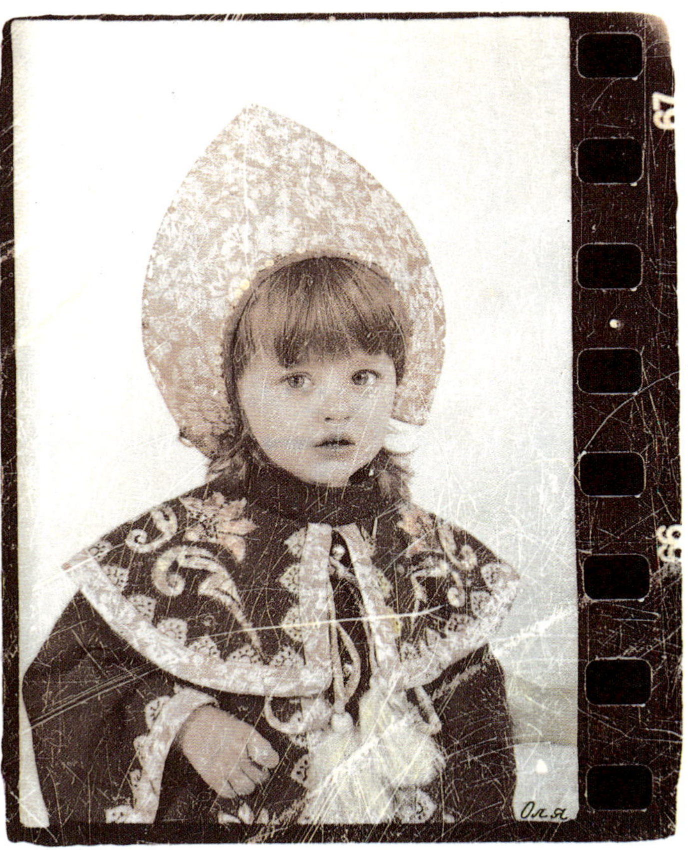
67
66
Оля

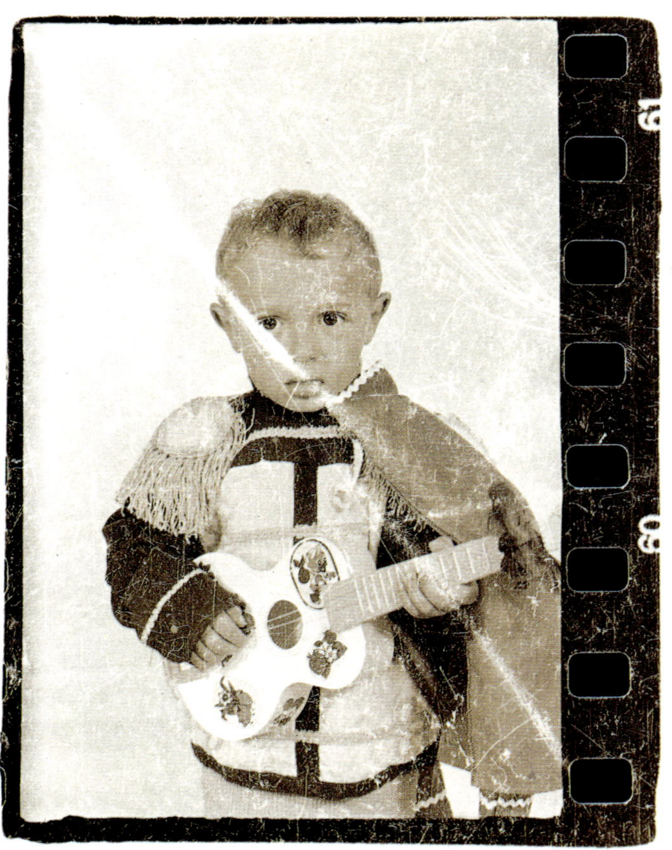
61
60

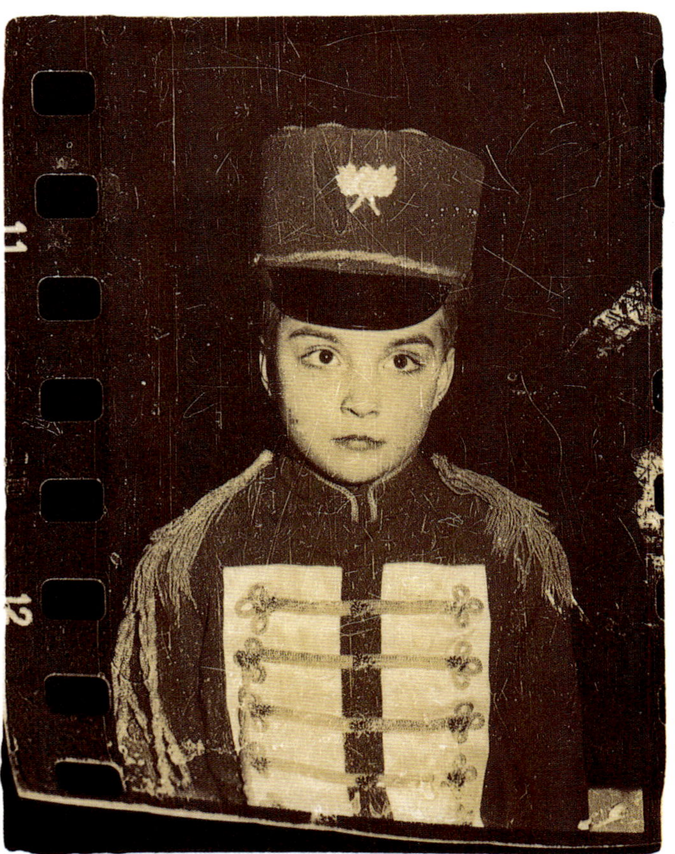
11
12

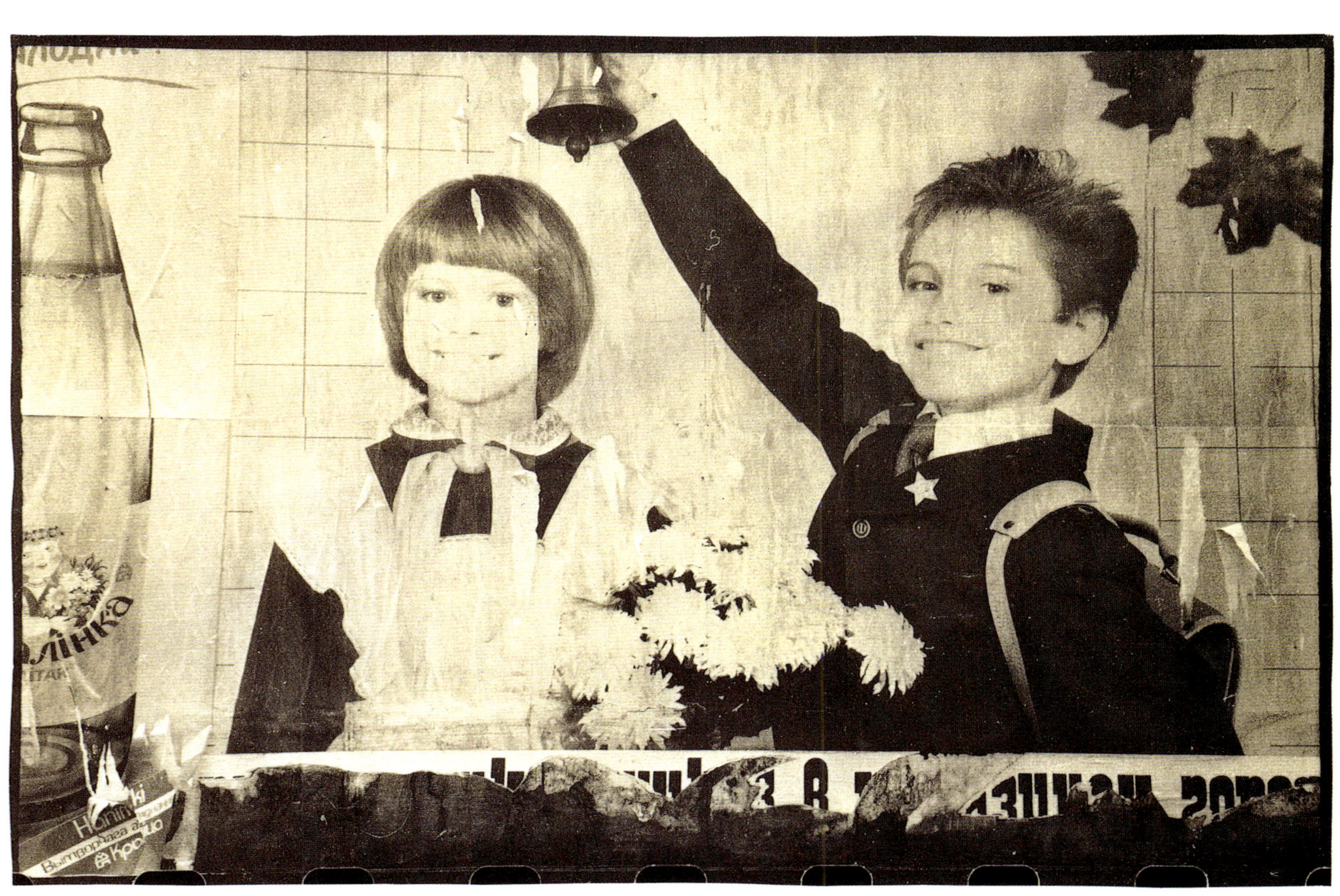

SERGEY KOZHEMYAKIN
from the series: A HOLIDAY, 1989
6 × 9½″

SERGEY KOZHEMYAKIN
CHILDREN'S ALBUM, 1989 (each)
Clockwise from top left: 8½ × 6½″, 7½ × 6″,
8½ × 6½″, 8½ × 6½″

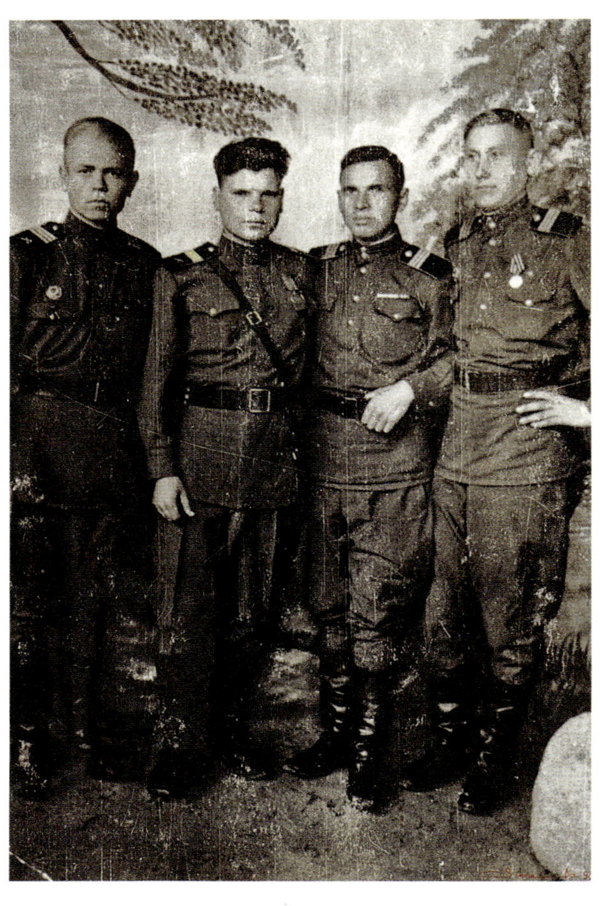

Opposite:
SERGEY KOZHEMYAKIN
THE ELDER BROTHER, ODESSA, 1967, from the series: FAMILY ALBUM, 1990
11 × 7″

SERGEY KOZHEMYAKIN
FATHER, KRUPKI(?), 194(?), from the series: FAMILY ALBUM, 1990
11 × 7″

SERGEY KOZHEMYAKIN
NIECE MARINA, ROVNO, 1981, from the series: FAMILY ALBUM, 1990
7 × 11″

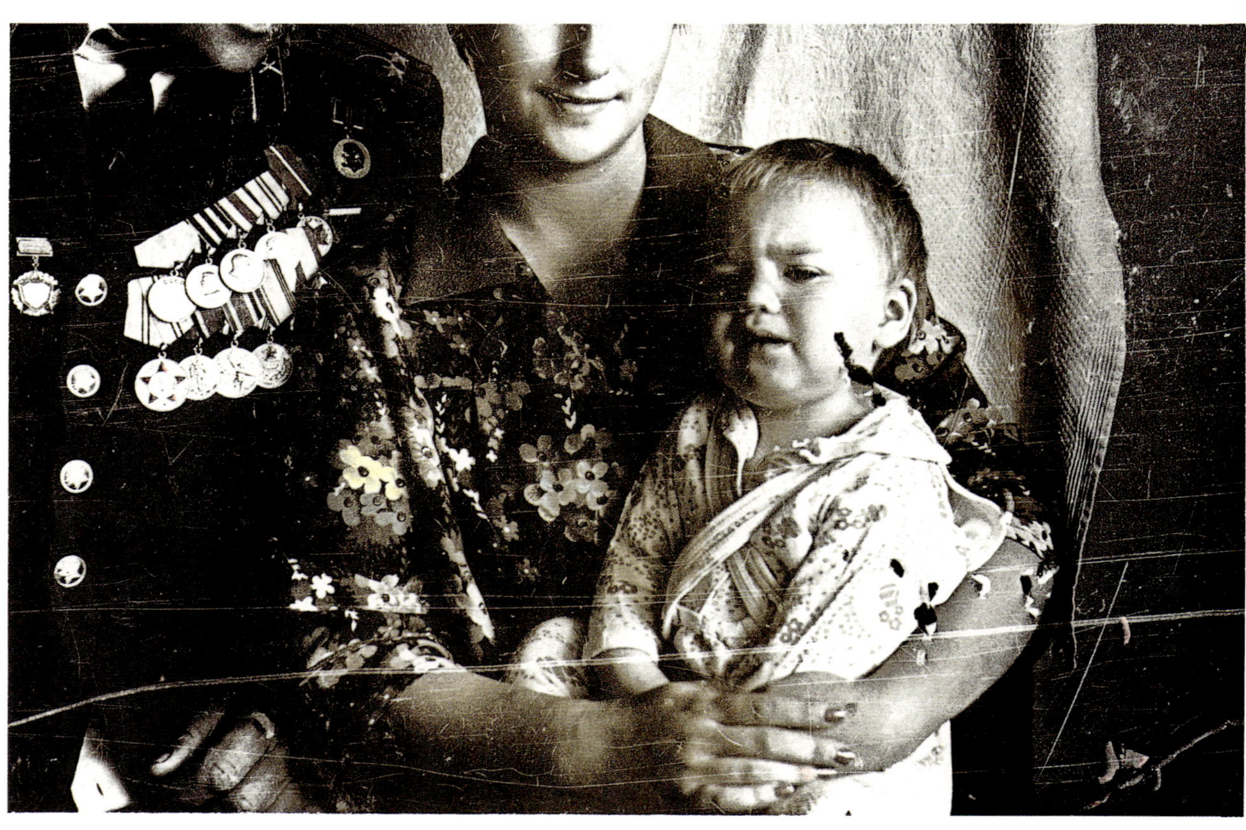

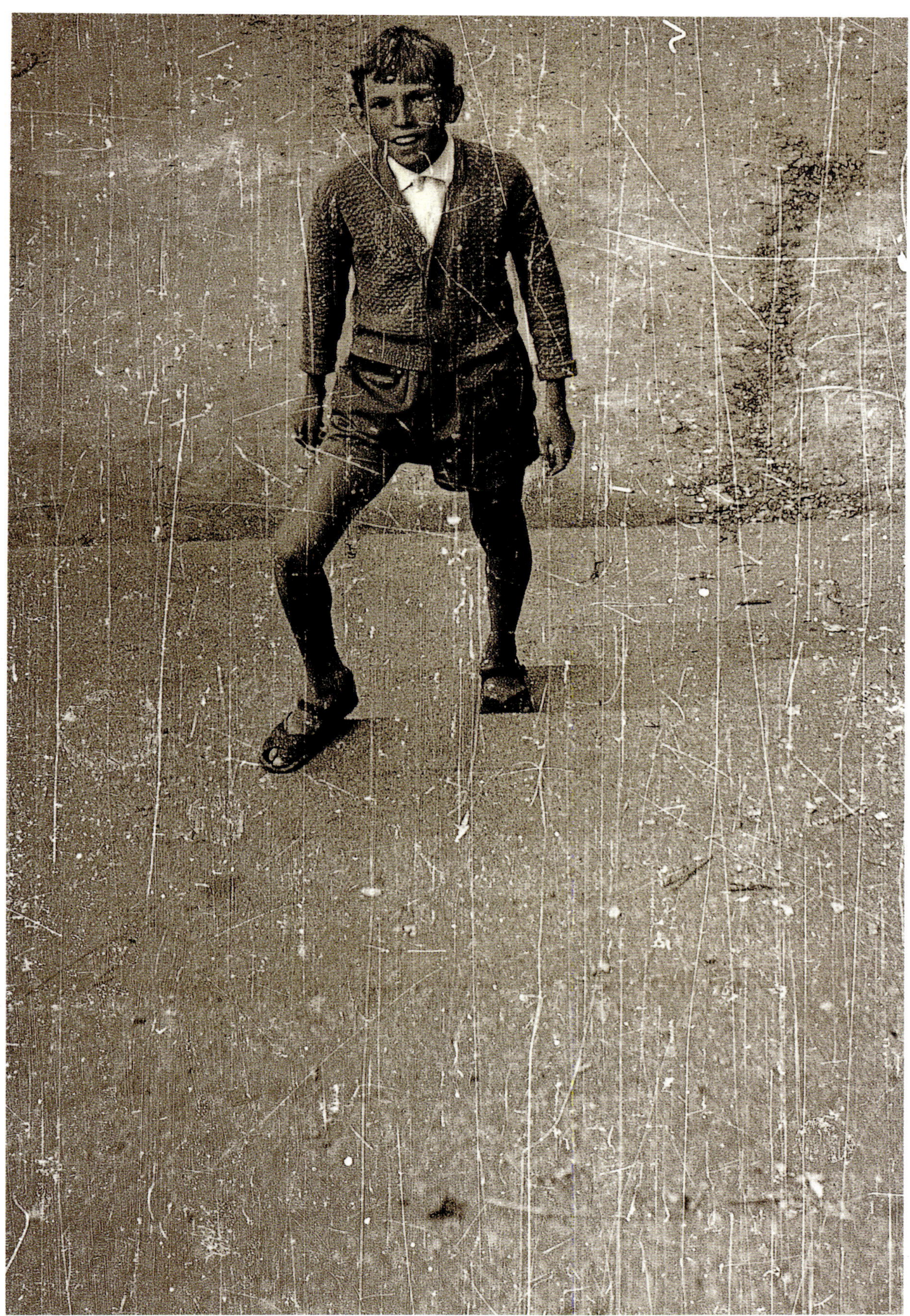

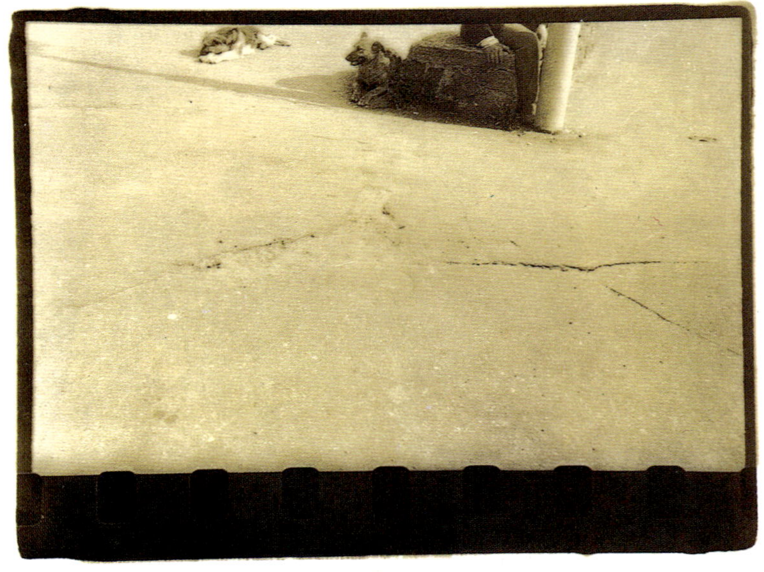

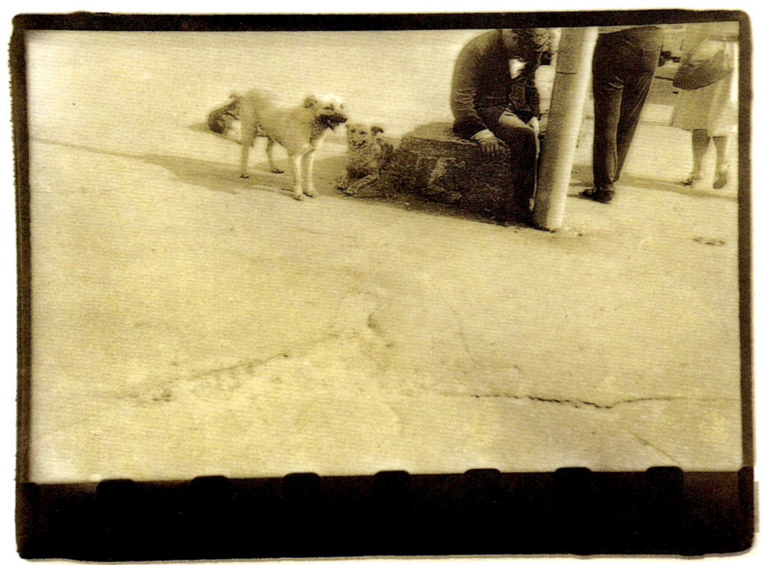

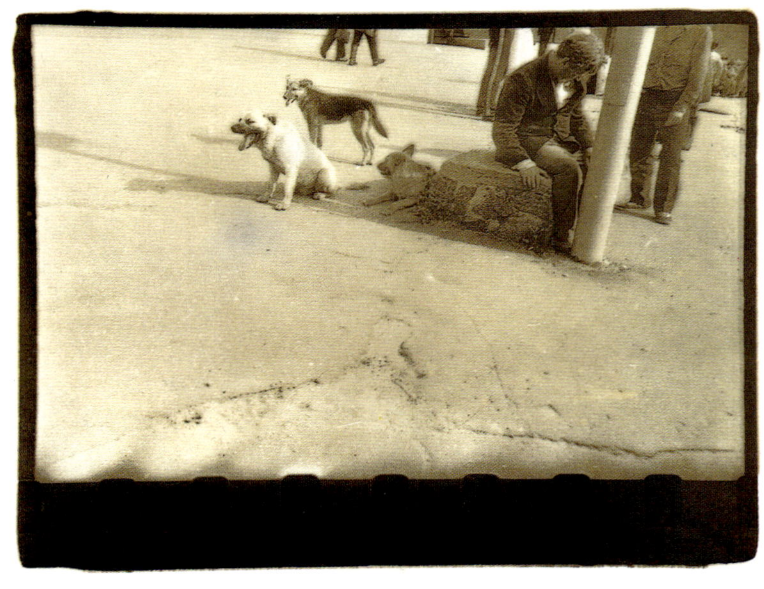

Opposite, top:
SERGEY KOVALYOV
A YARD, 1990
6 × 9″

Opposite, bottom:
SERGEY KOVALYOV
A BRIDGE, 1990
5 × 7″

SERGEY KOZHEMYAKIN
MOVEMENTS 1, 2, 3, 1990
7 × 9″ (each)

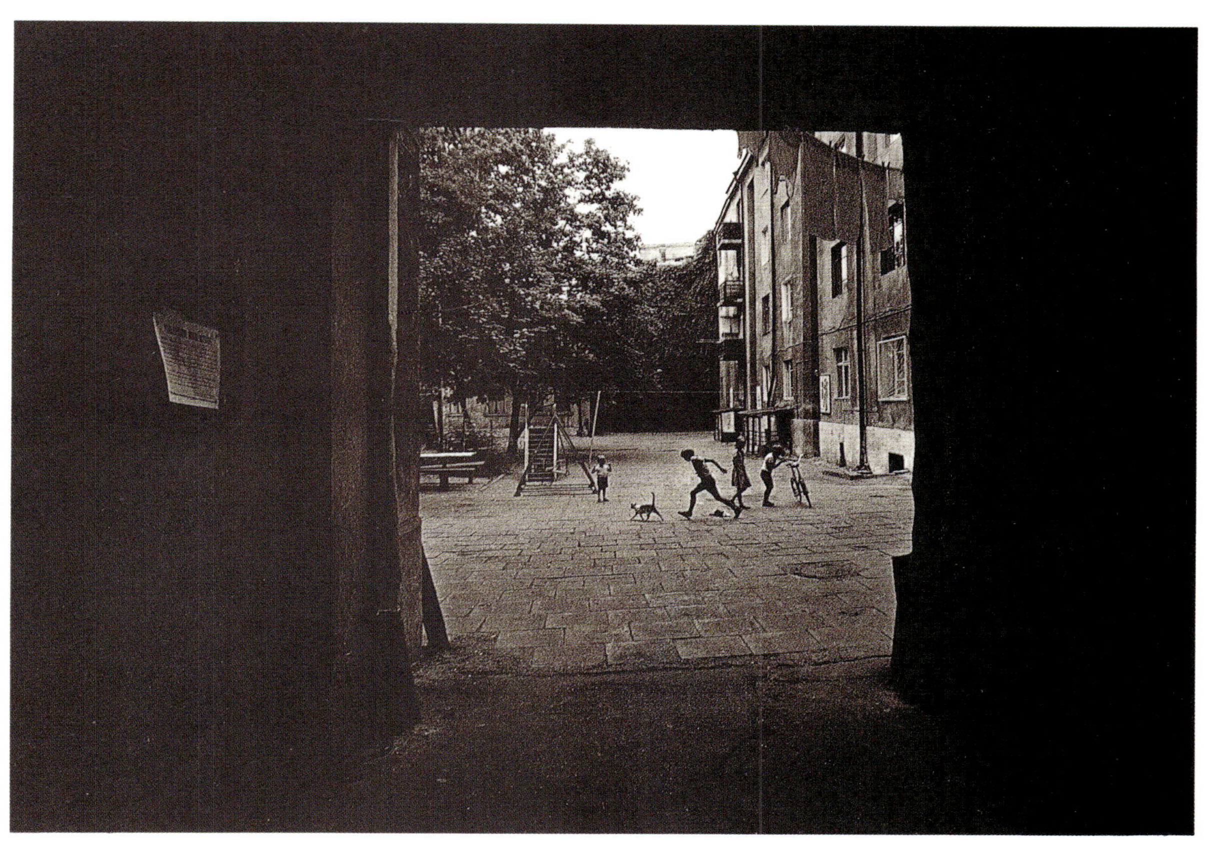

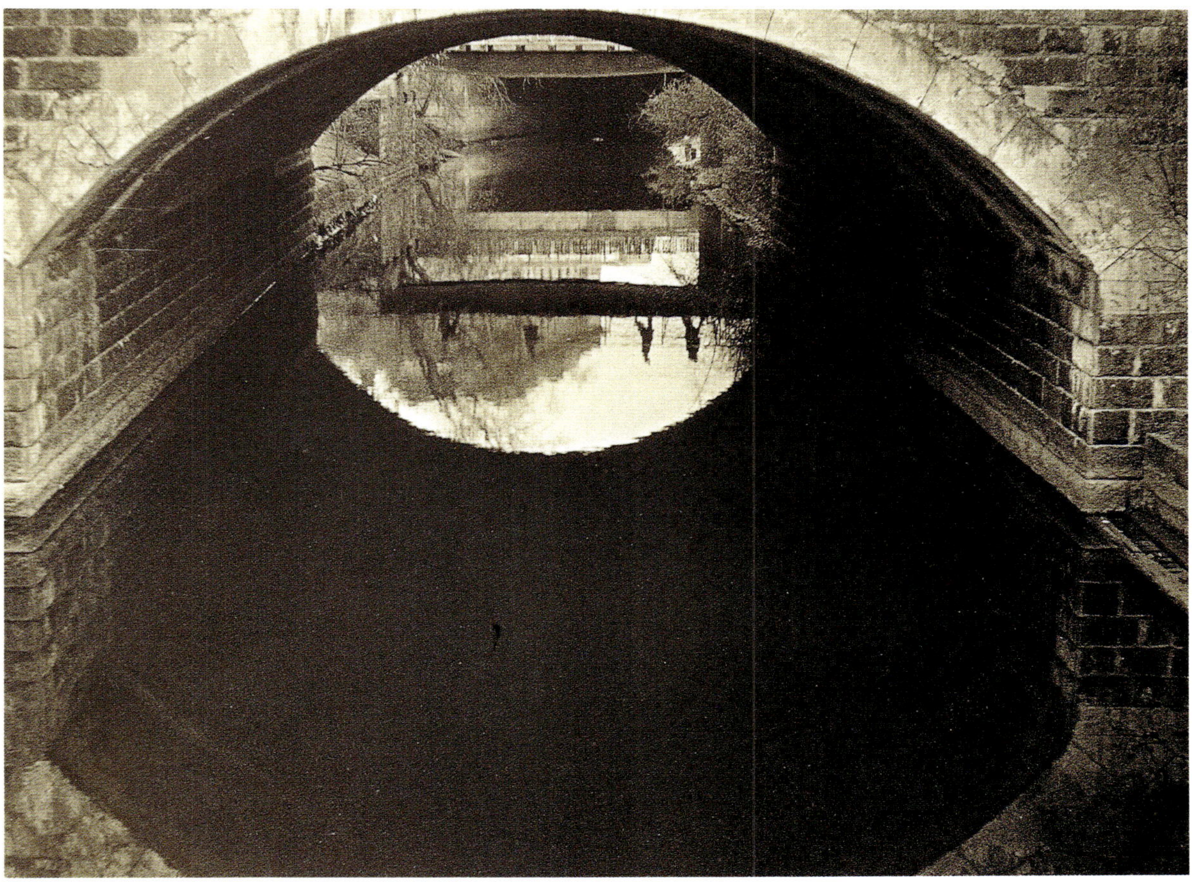

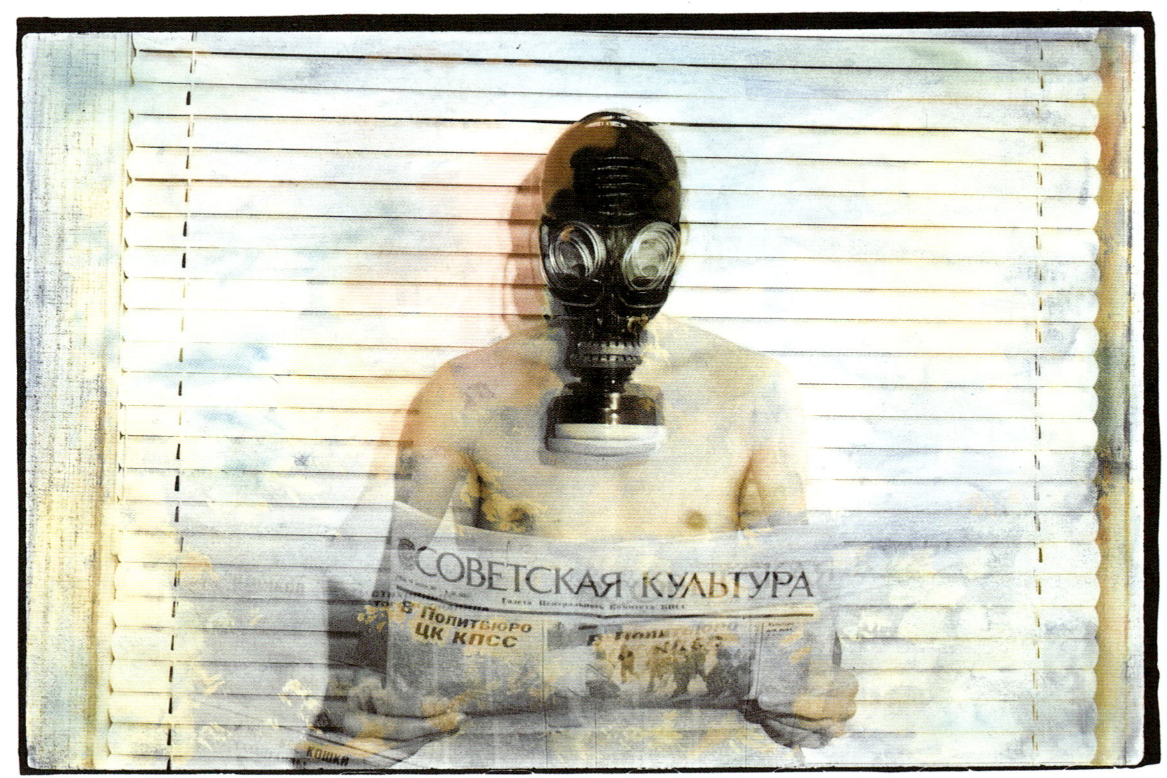

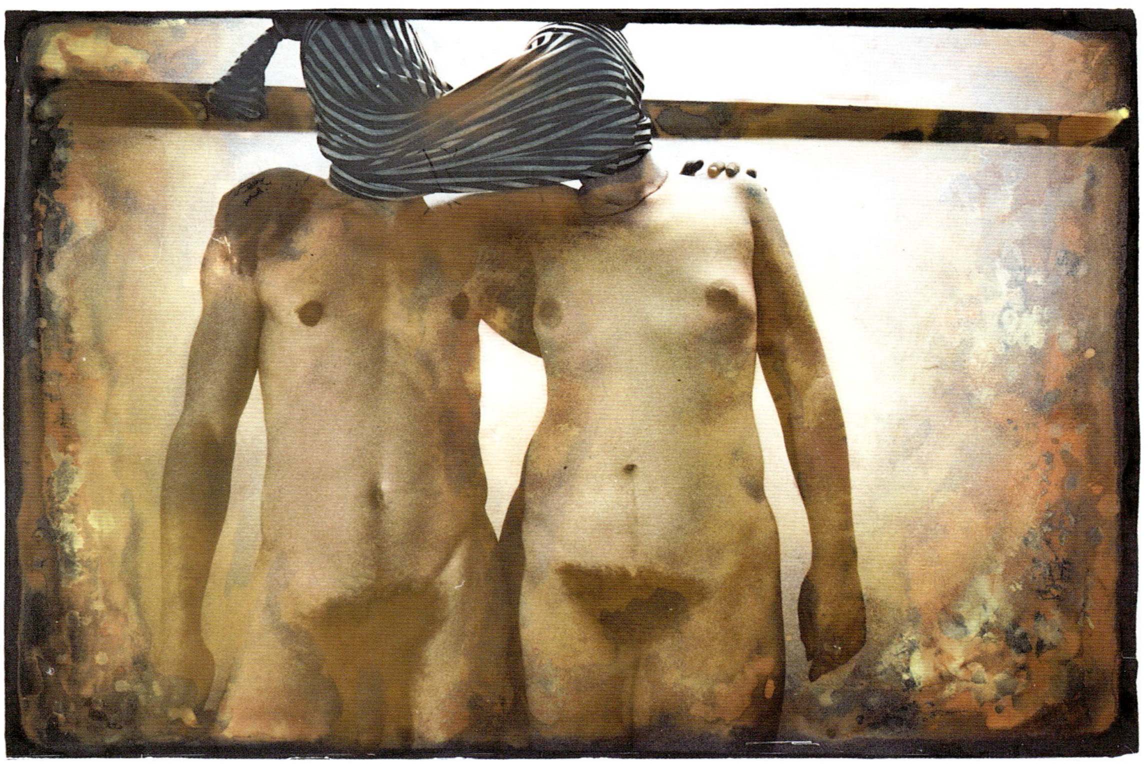

Top:
VLADZIMIR P. PARFIANOK
BEING A PATRON, from the series:
PERSONA NON GRATA, 1988
"Soviet culture"
6½ × 10″

Bottom:
VLADZIMIR P. PARFIANOK
MALES AND FEMALES, from the series:
PERSONA NON GRATA, 1988
6½ × 10″

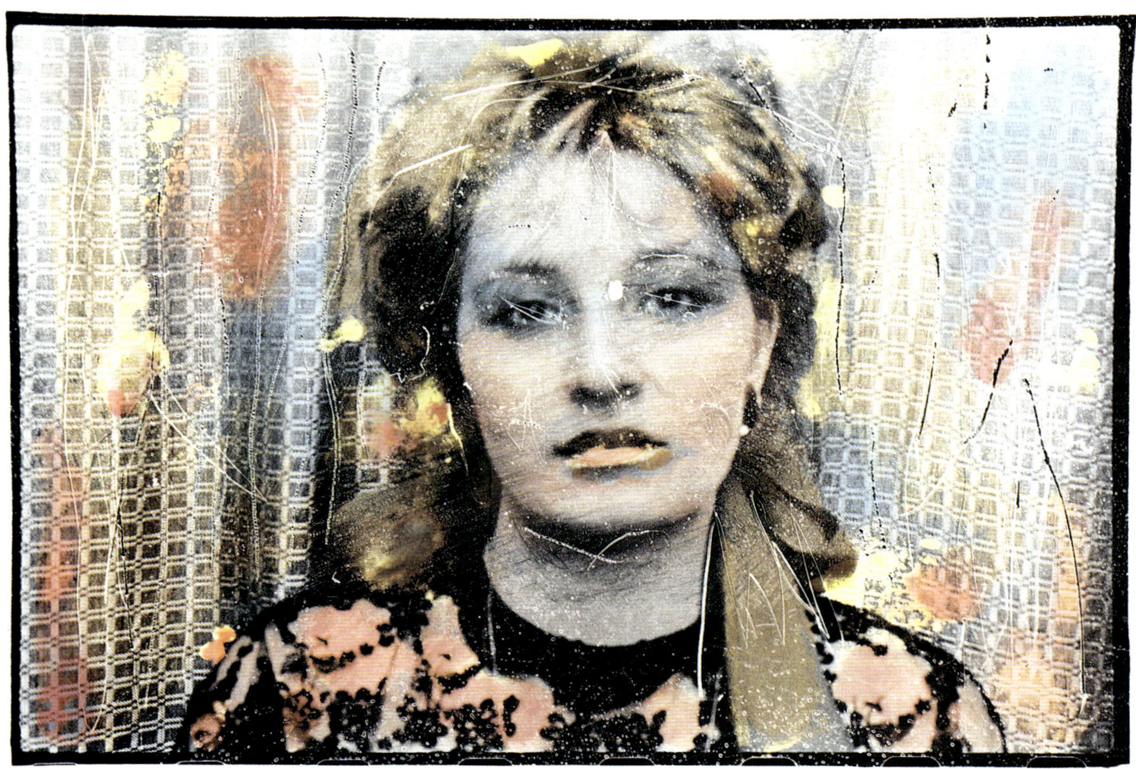

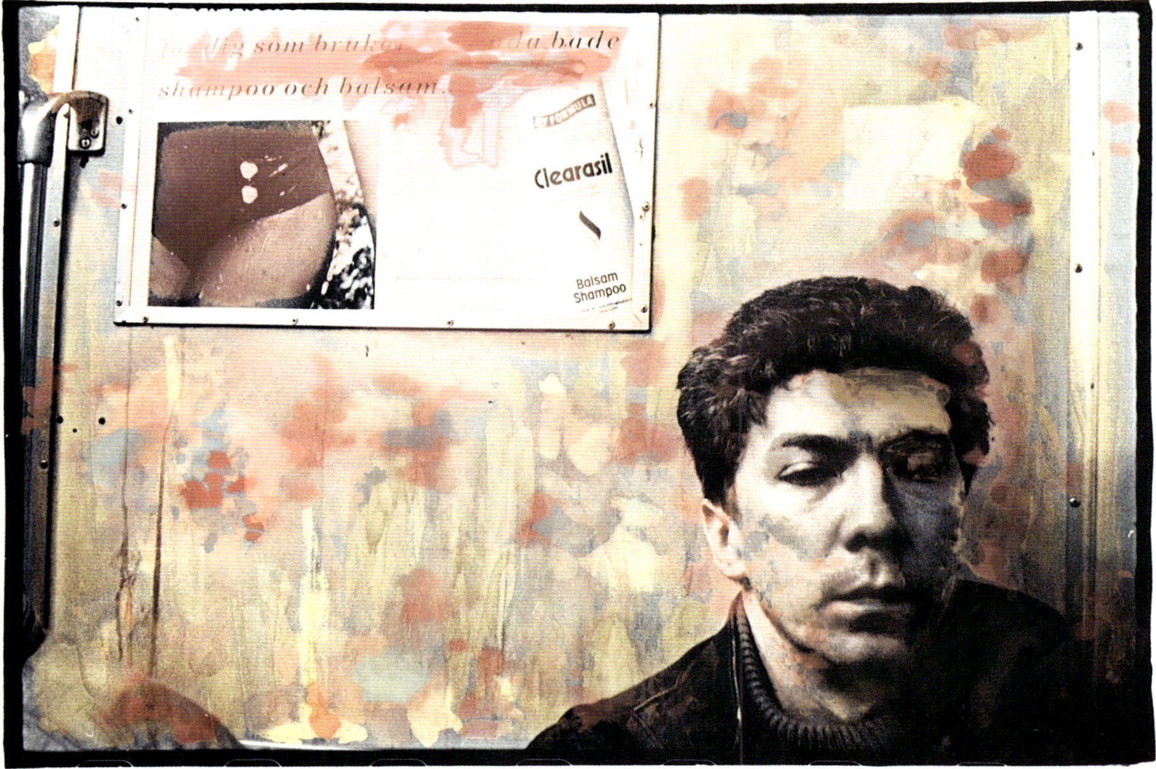

Top:
VLADZIMIR P. PARFIANOK
LONELY GIRL, from the series:
PERSONA NON GRATA, 1989/90
6½ × 9½″

Bottom:
VLADZIMIR P. PARFIANOK
TOURIST BEYOND THE CULTIVATED FIELD,
from the series: PERSONA NON GRATA,
1989/90
6½ × 10″

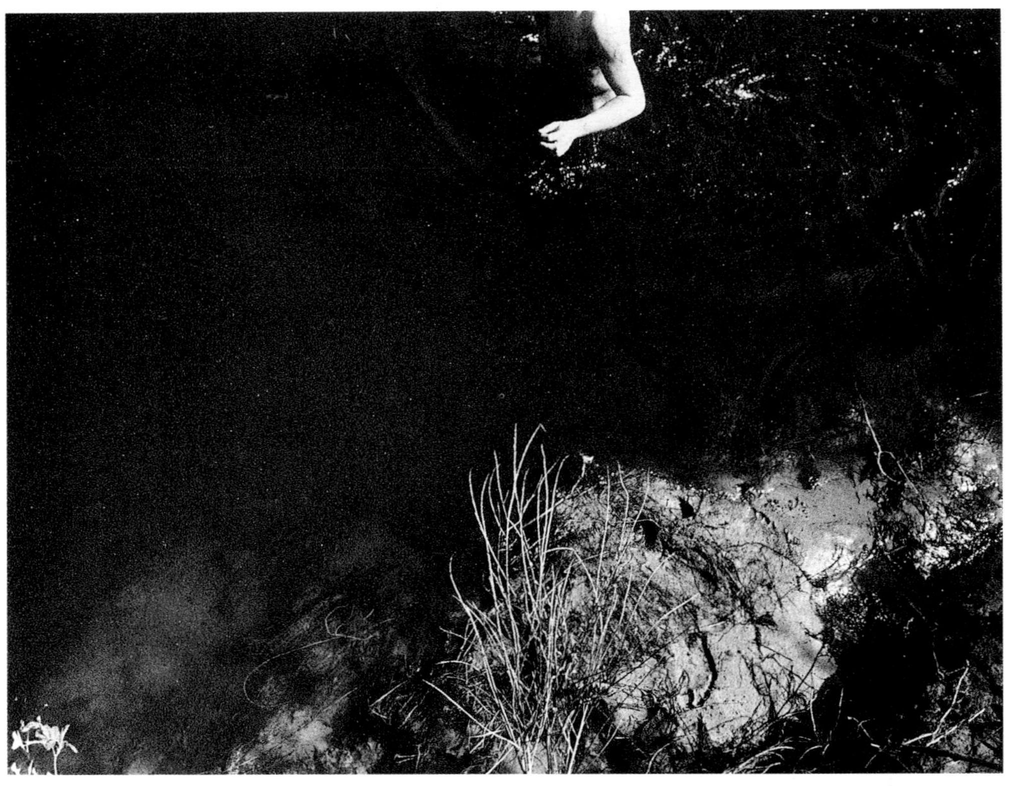

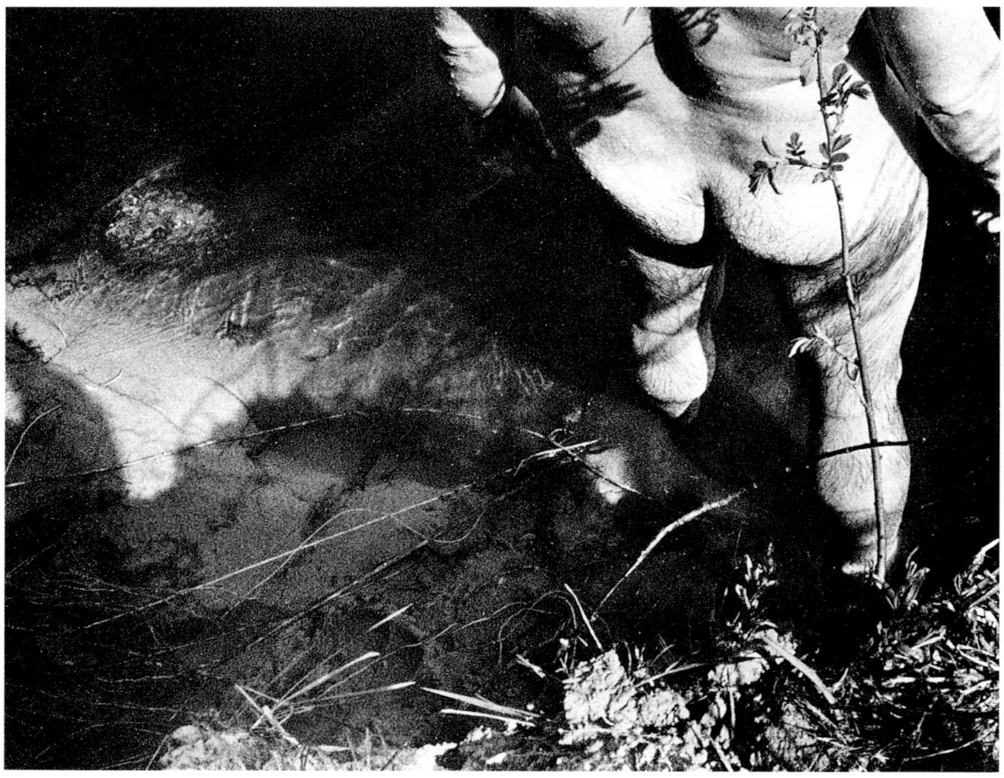

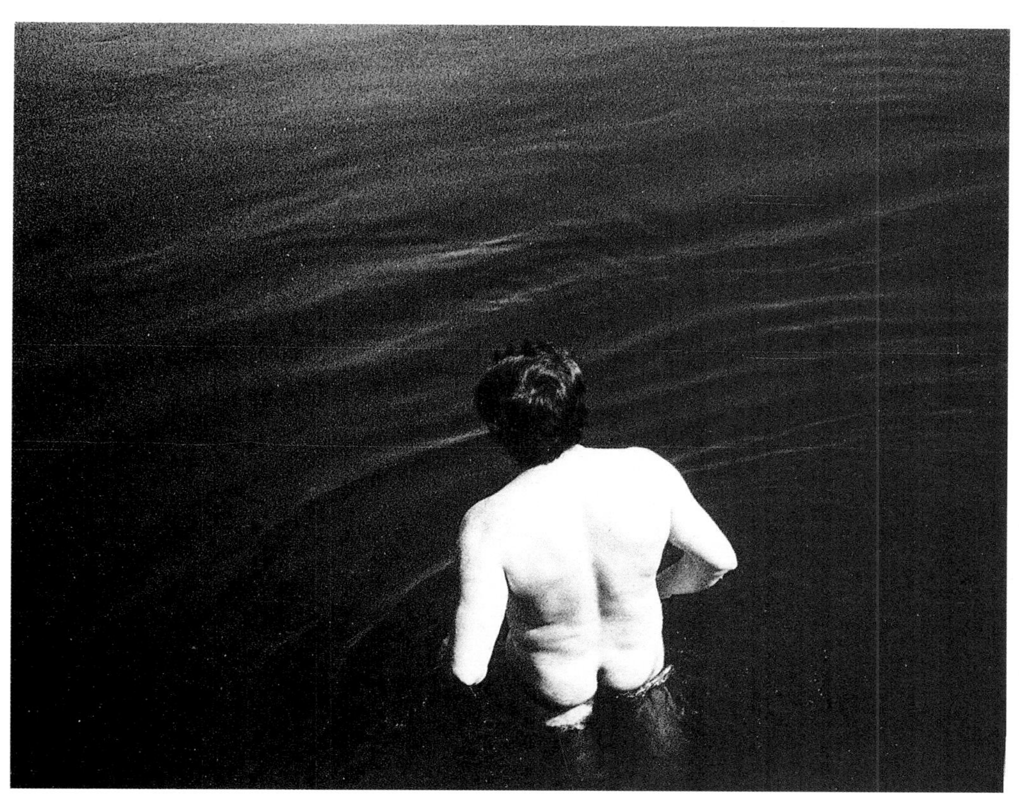

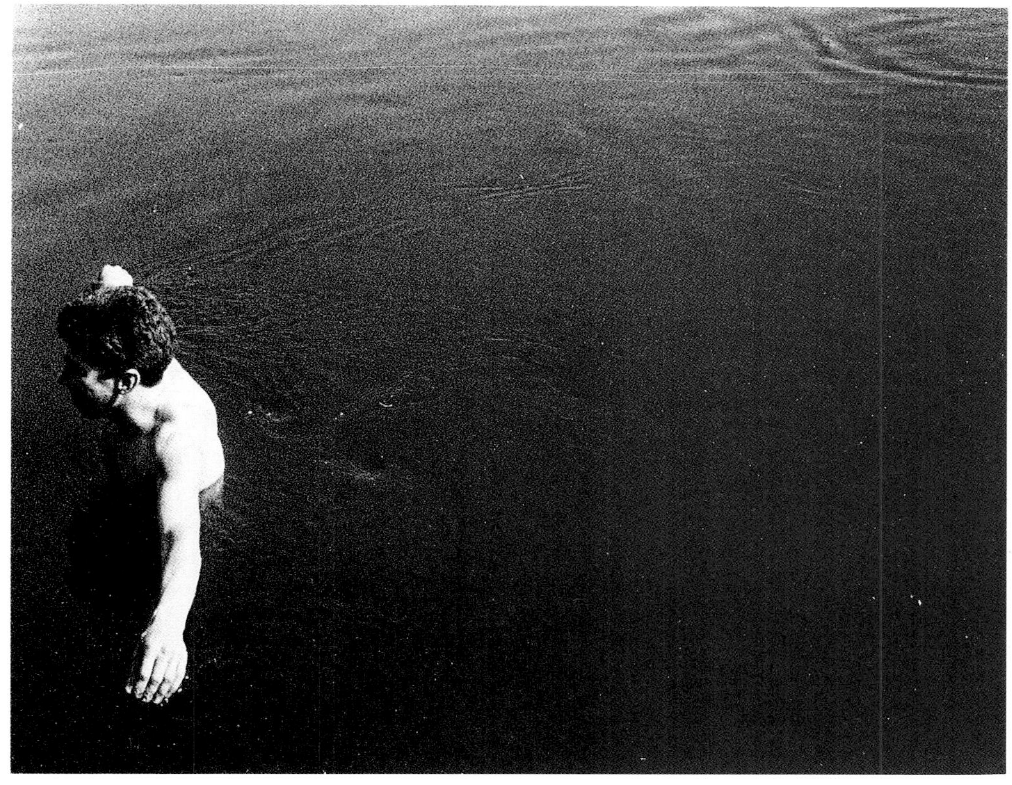

VLADZIMIR P. PARFIANOK
BATHING, 1989
6 × 7½" (each)

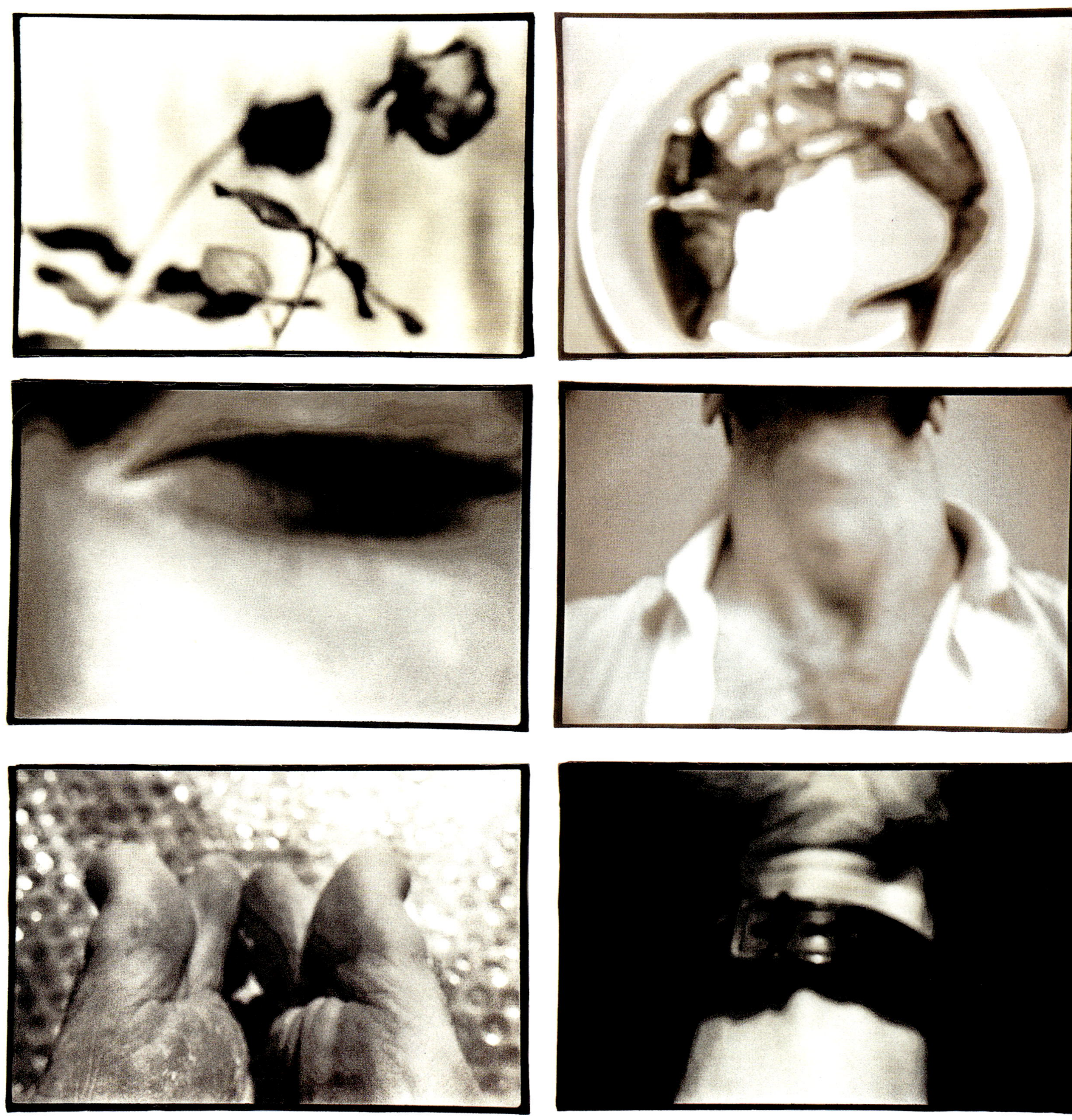

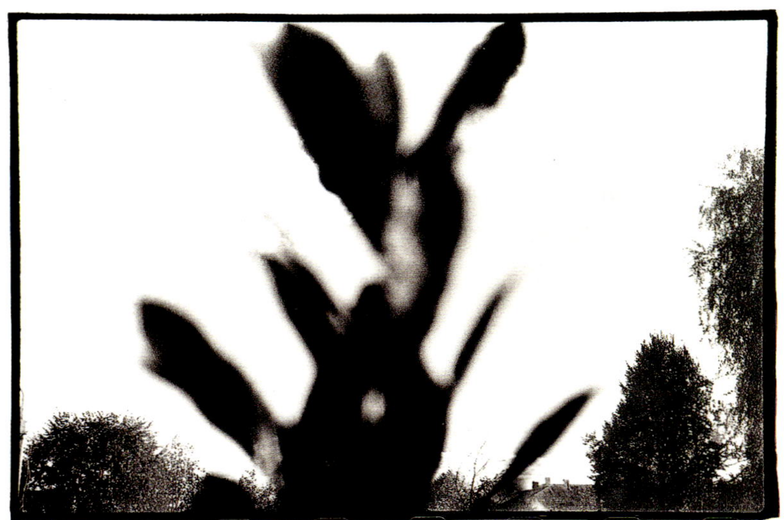

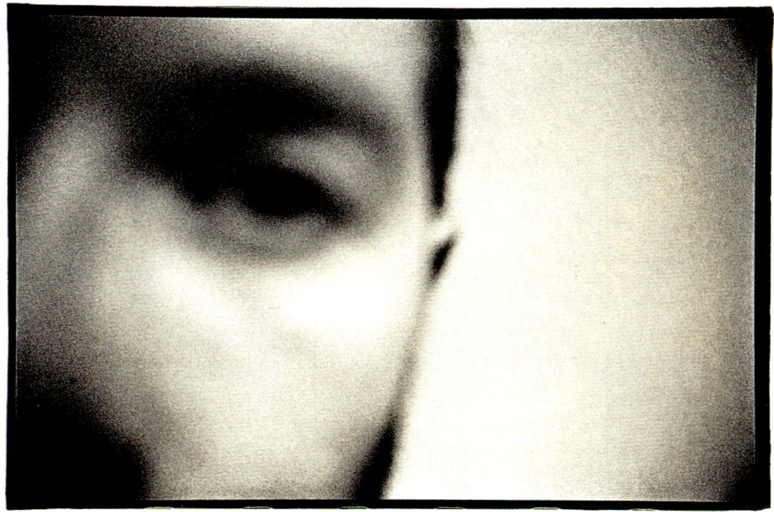

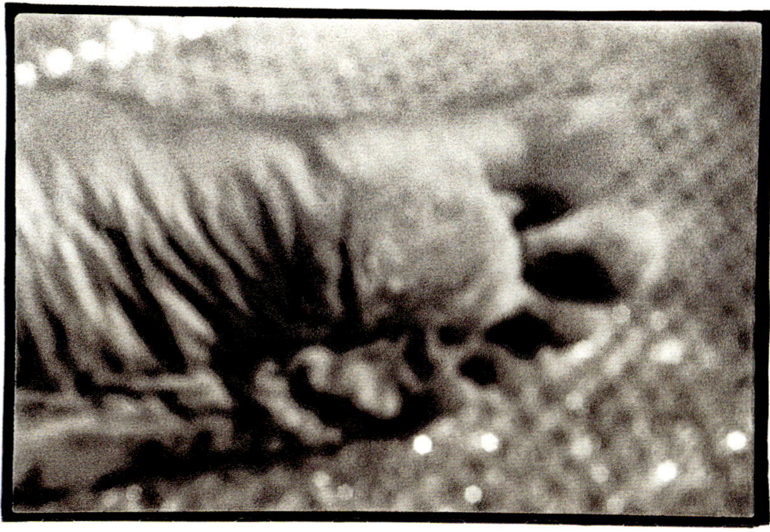

VLADZIMIR P. PARFIANOK
UNTITLED, 1990
9½ × 14″ (each)

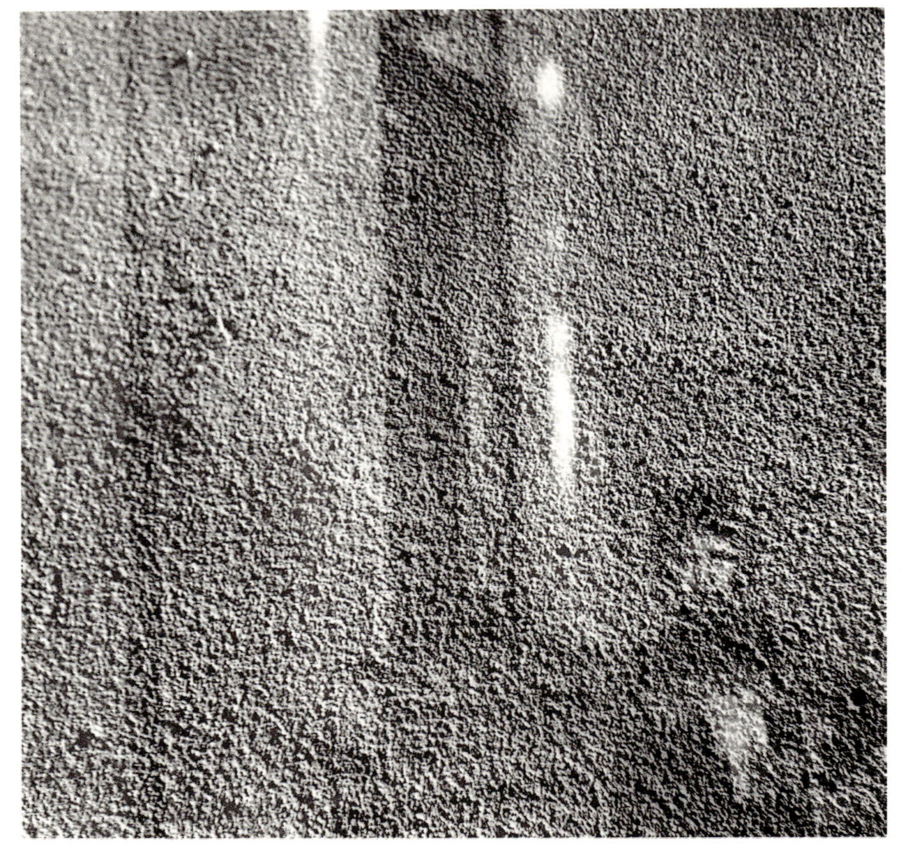

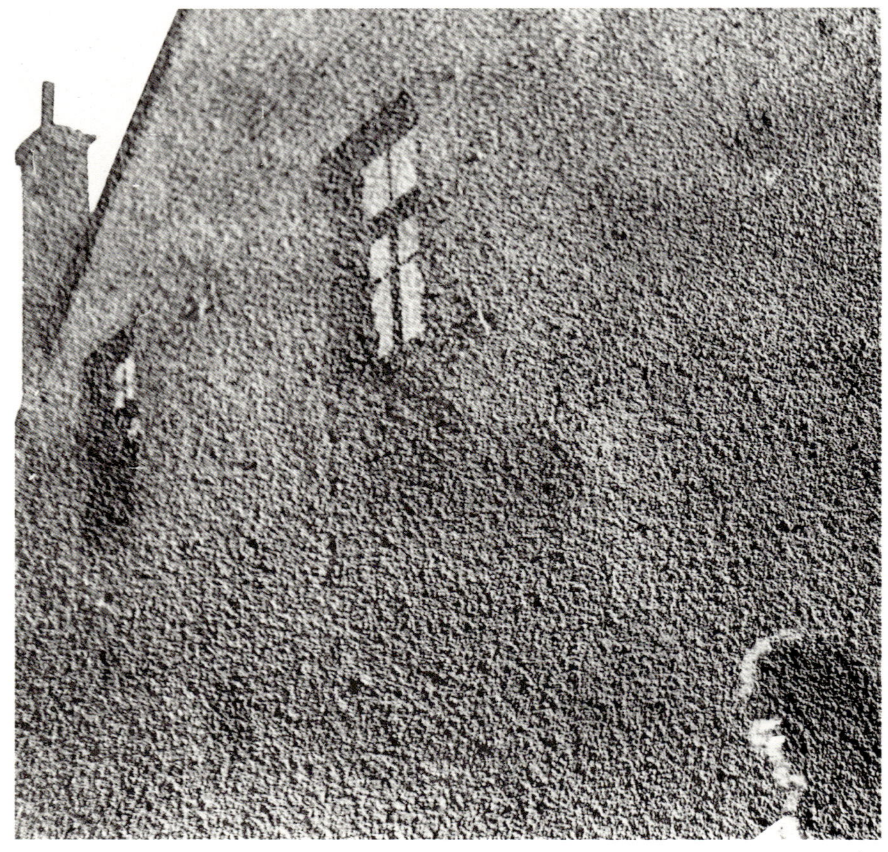

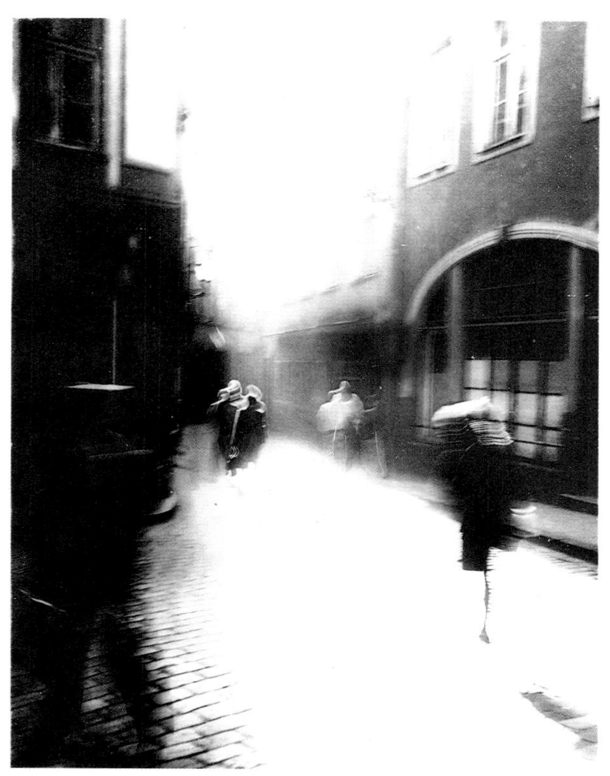

Opposite:
GENNADY RODIKOV
from the series: WALLS, 1990
7 × 7″ (each)

GENNADY RODIKOV
from the series: CITIZENS, 1990
Left: 9 × 7″, below: 7 × 9″

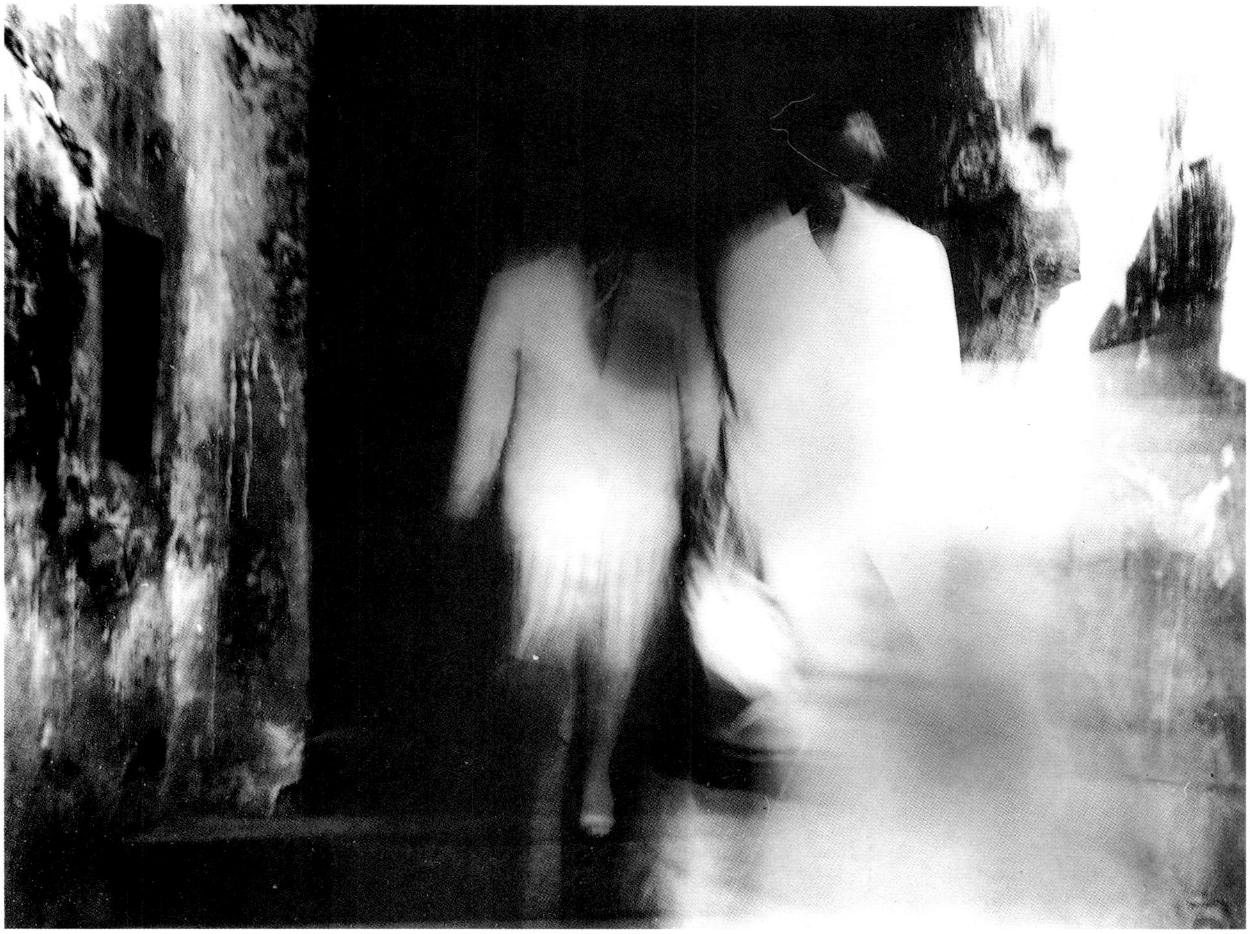

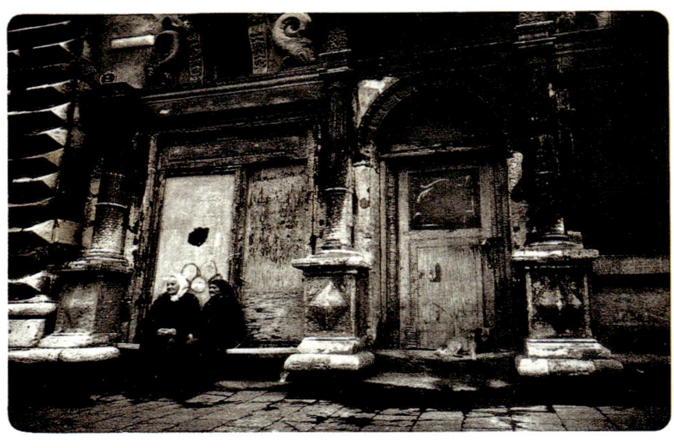

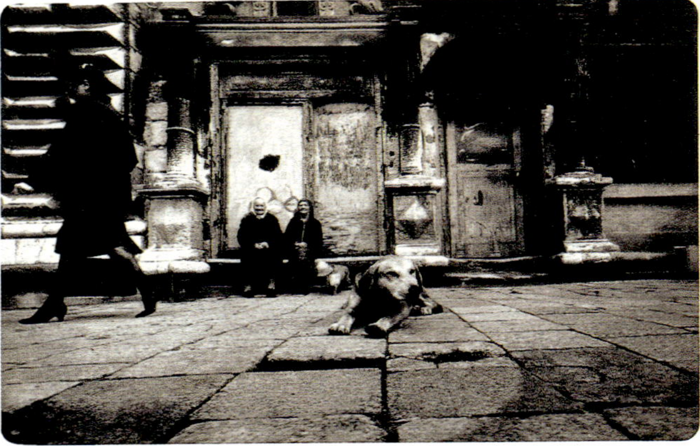

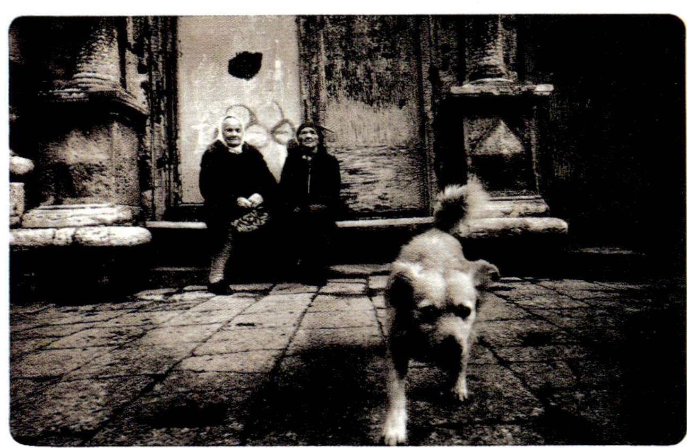

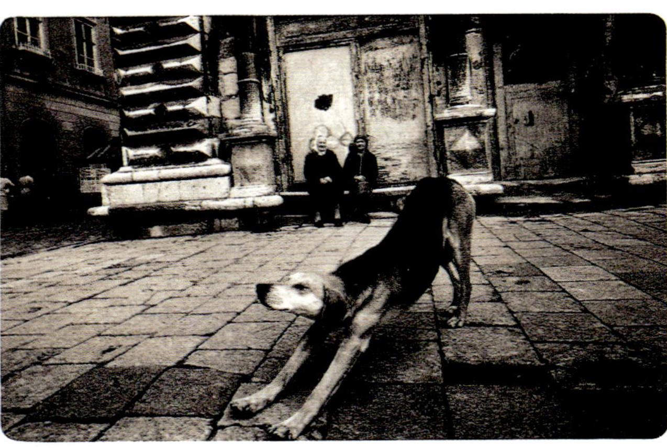

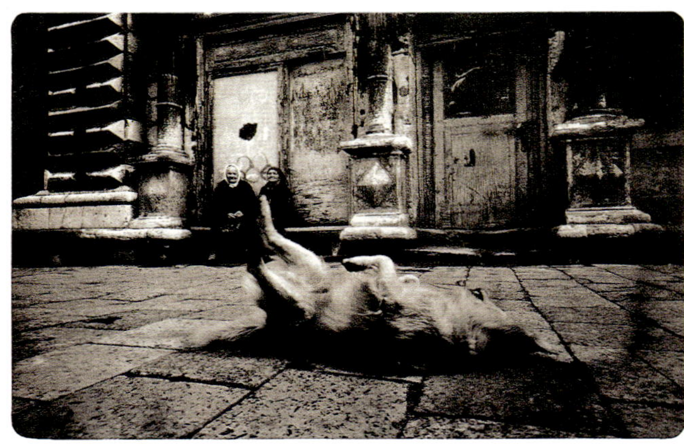

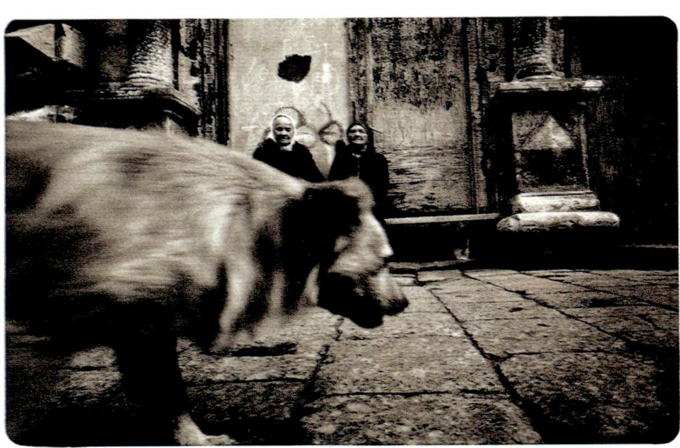

VALERY D. LOBKO
from the series: REST, 1989
7 × 11" (each)

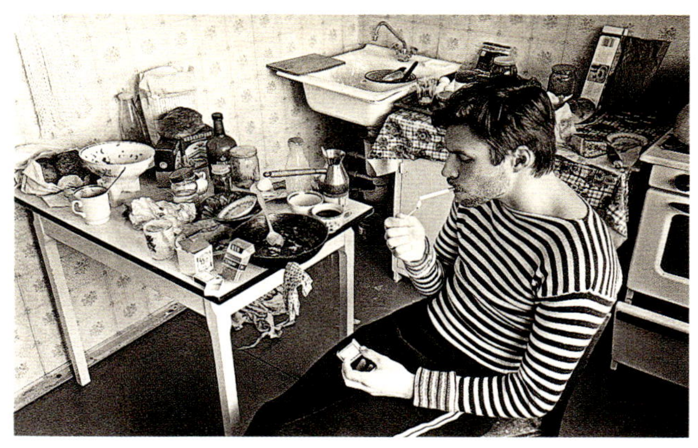

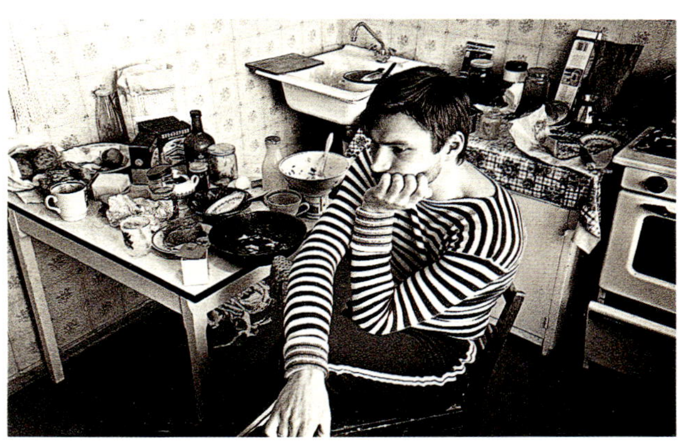

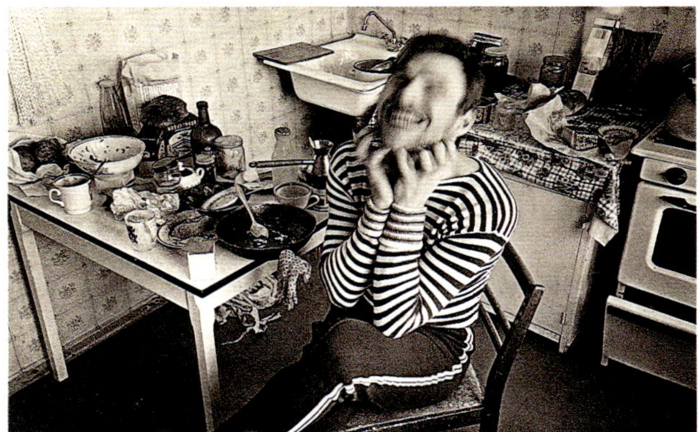

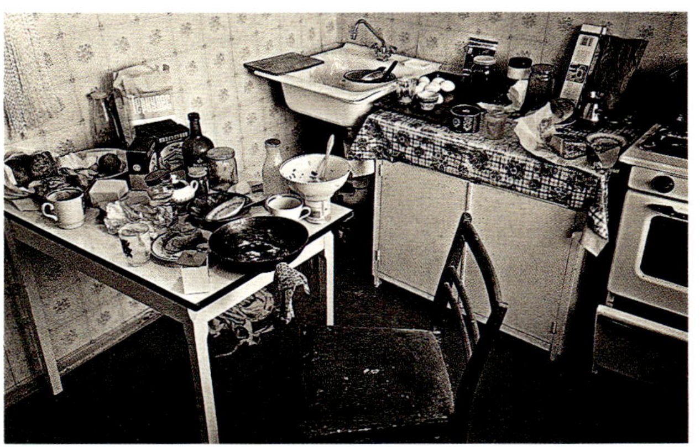

SERGEI SUKOVITZIN
from the series: SPIRITUAL APOCALYPSE,
1990
7 × 11″ (each)

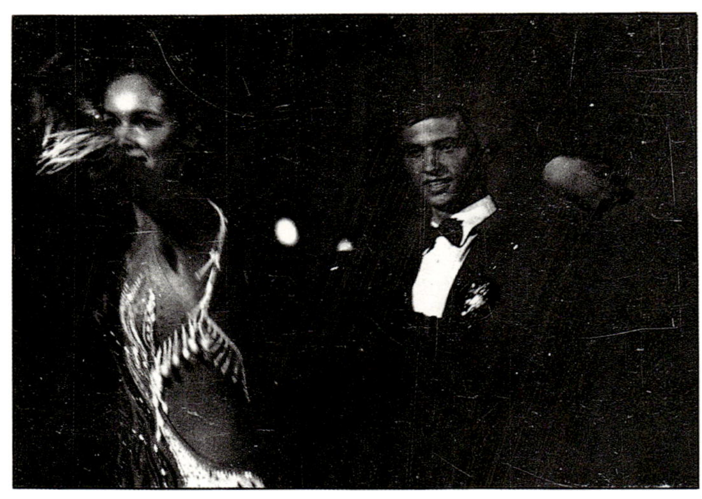

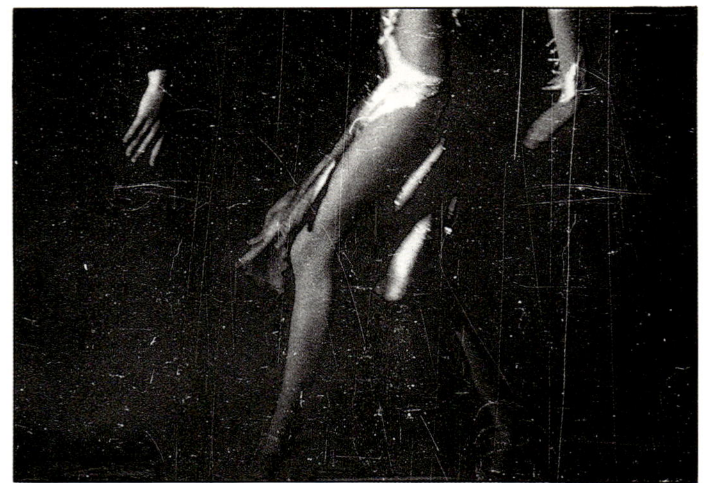

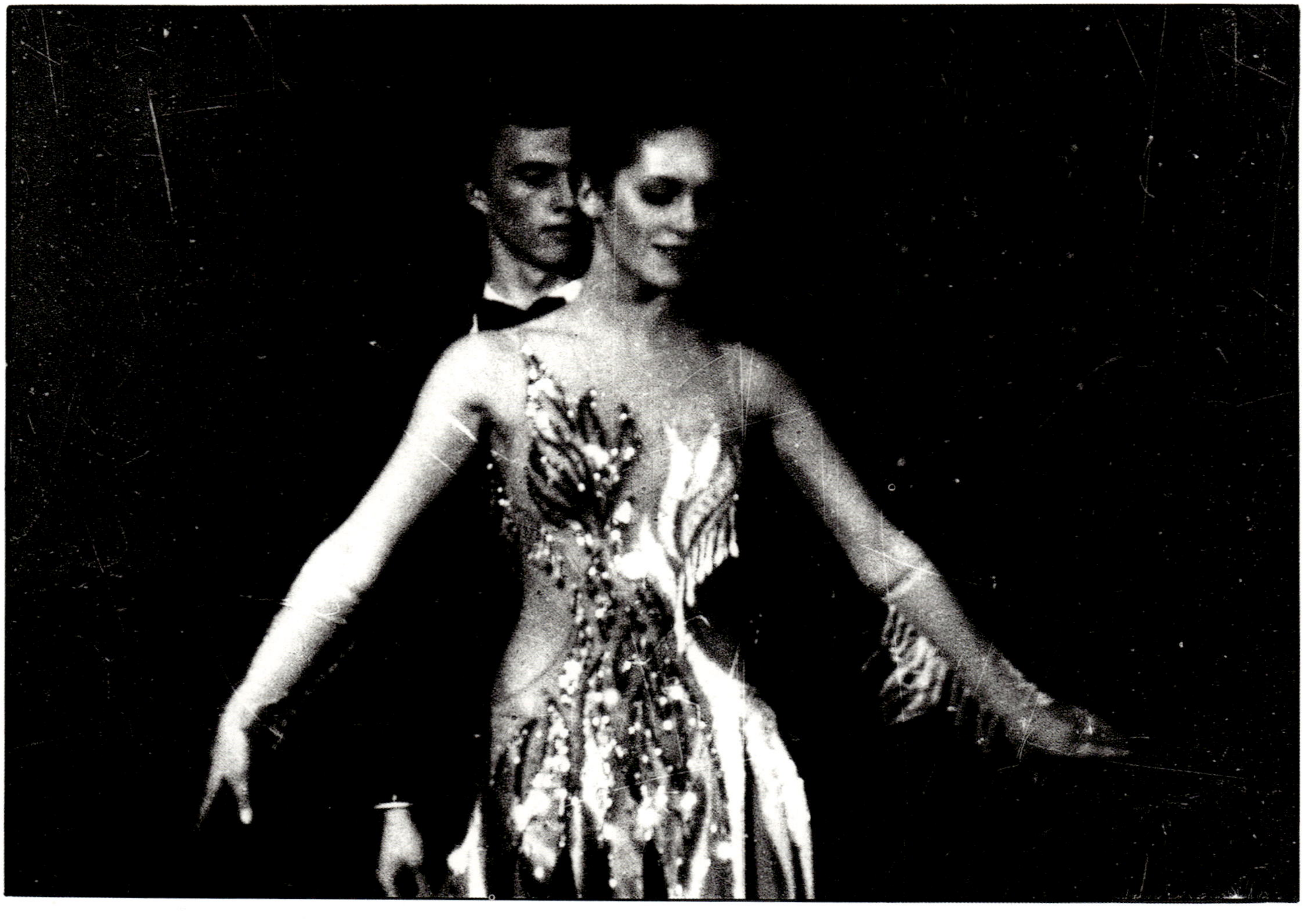

ALEXEY PAVLUTS
DANCE, 1990
4½ × 6″ (each)

Opposite:
ALEKSEY ILYIN
EMISSION 1, and EMISSION 2, 1990
4 × 6″ (each)

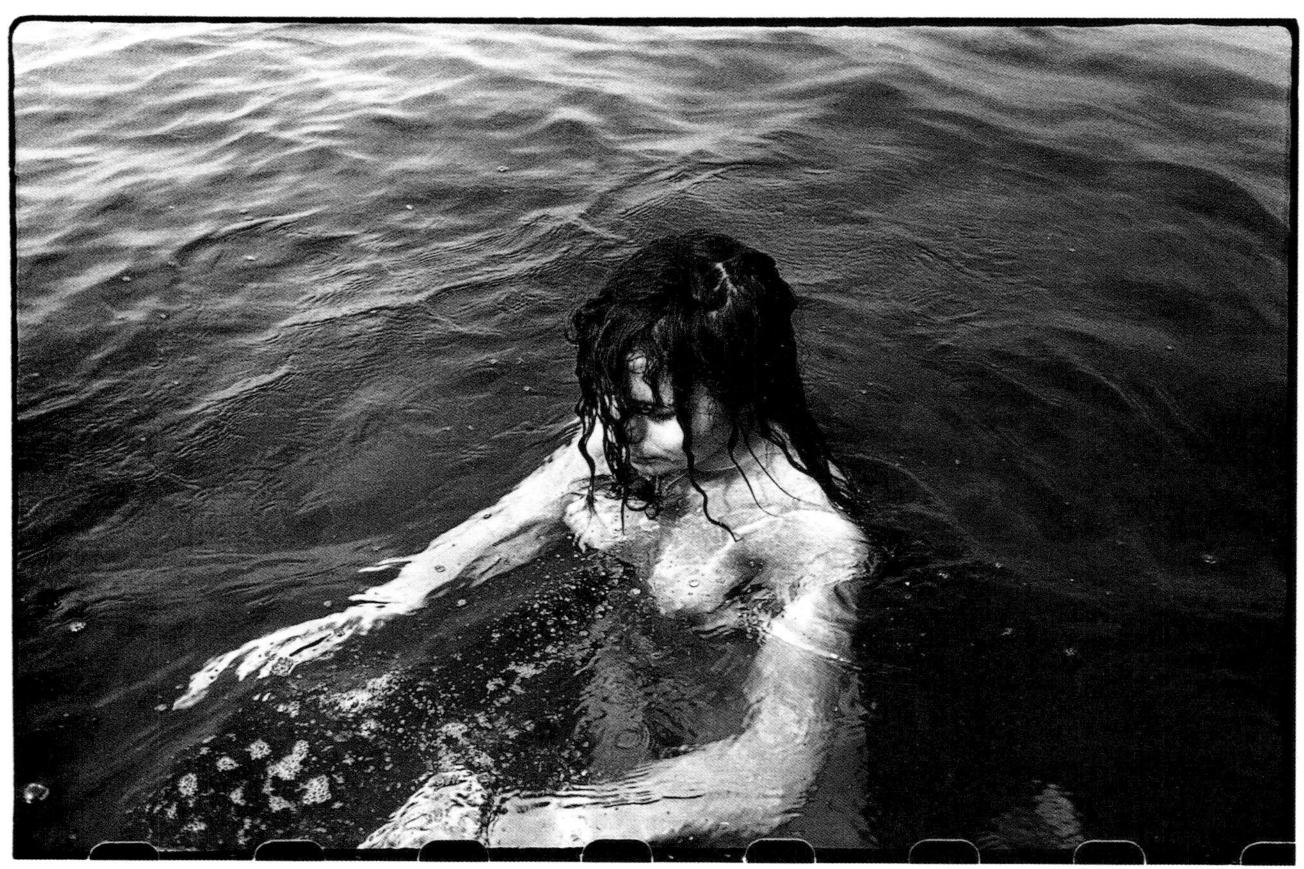

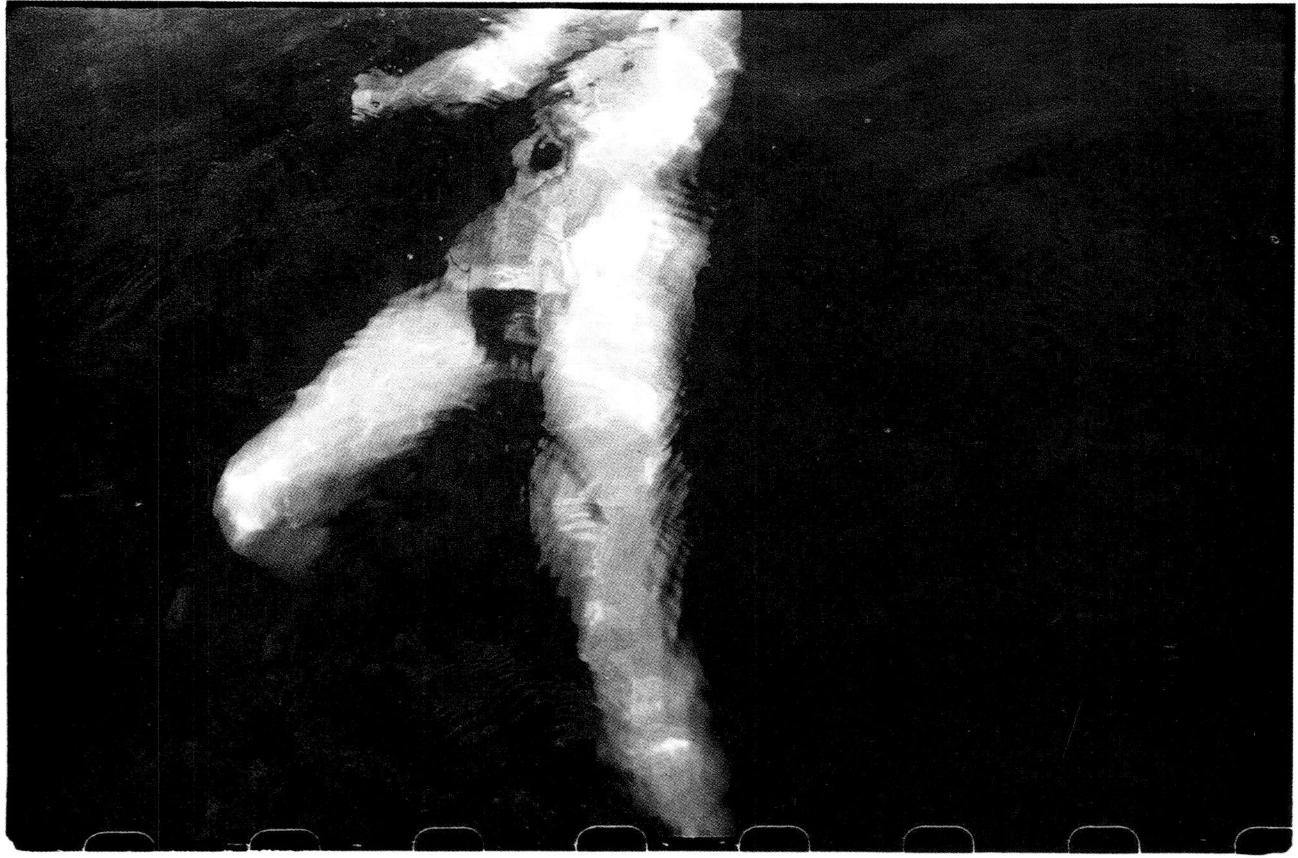

YURY MATVEEV • ANDREY CHEGIN • DMITRY SHNEYERSON • TAK • LUDMILA FEDORENKO • VALENTIN SIMANKOV • VALERY POTAPOV • ALEXANDER IGNATJEV

LENINGRAD

In the spring of 1990 the Photo Gallery inaugurated its newly renovated exhibition space in Leningrad with a presentation of the work of the seven founding members that best exemplified their shared influences. Appropriately, this first exhibit focused on the artistic sensibilities that personified the group as a whole, recognizing the importance of the entire group effort in creating the gallery, an undertaking unprecedented in contemporary Leningrad.

Photo Gallery exists due to the new, positive attitude toward entrepreneurial initiative in the Soviet Union. The artists and their consultants combined efforts to obtain financing, locate and renovate space, program exhibitions, and create and execute a promotional plan. In a country with few if any patrons of photography, the Photo Gallery represents hope for artists in search of a support system.

YURY MATVEEV
SOUR CREAM, 1990
8 × 9″

YURY MATVEEV
SUGAR, 1990
8 × 9″

YURY MATVEEV
TEA, 1990
8 × 9″

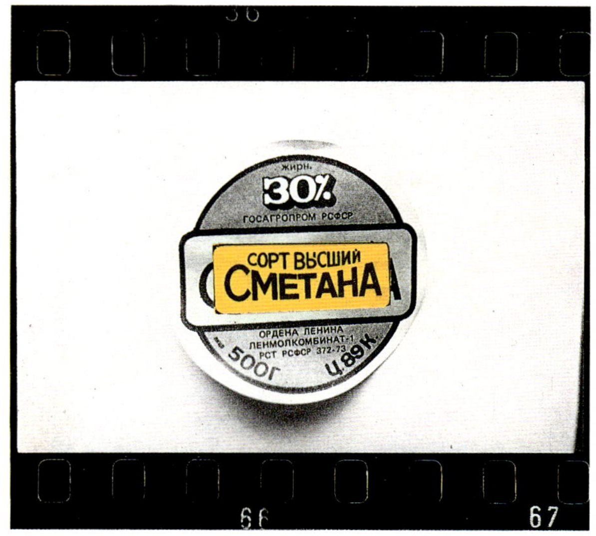
жирн.
30%
ГОСАГРОПРОМ РСФСР
СОРТ ВЫСШИЙ
СМЕТАНА
ОРДЕНА ЛЕНИНА
ЛЕНМОЛКОМБИНАТ-1
РСТ РСФСР 372-73
500г
Ц.89К.
66
67

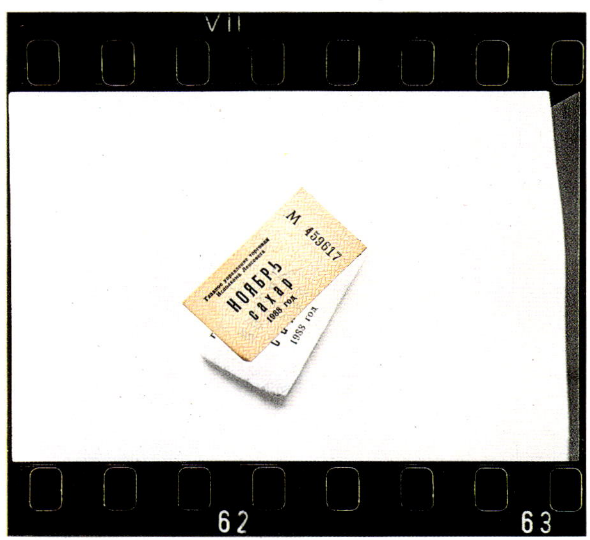
М 459617
НОЯБРЬ
сахар
1988 год
62
63

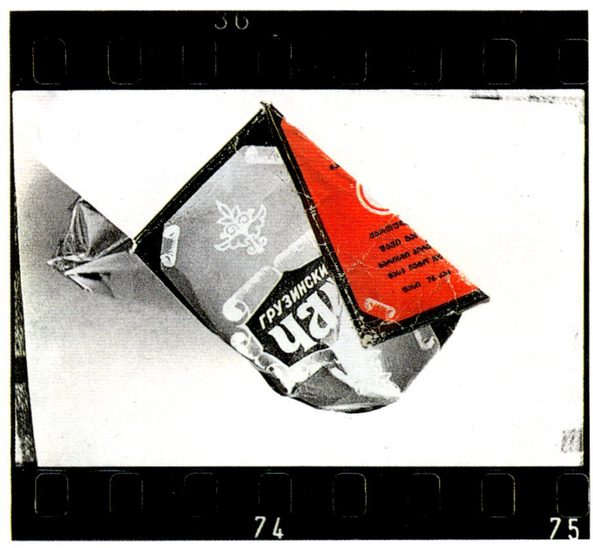
ГРУЗИНСКИ
74
75

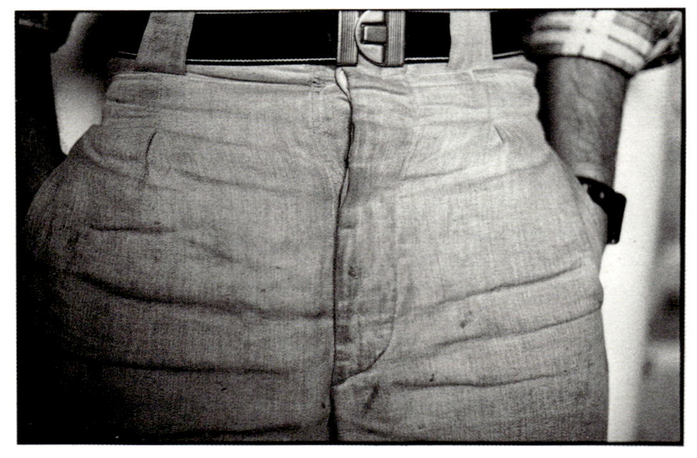

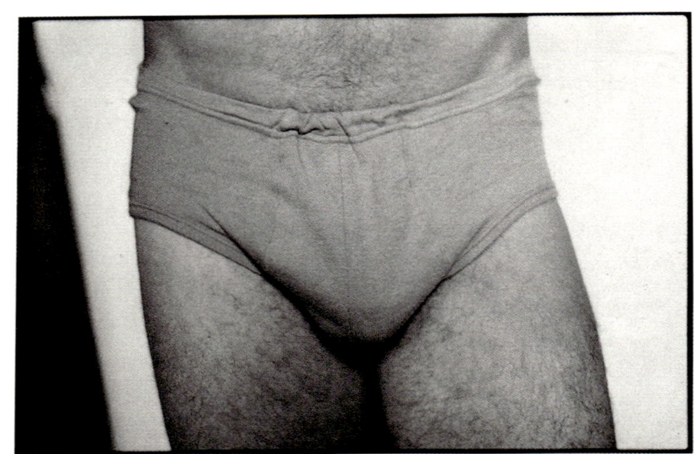

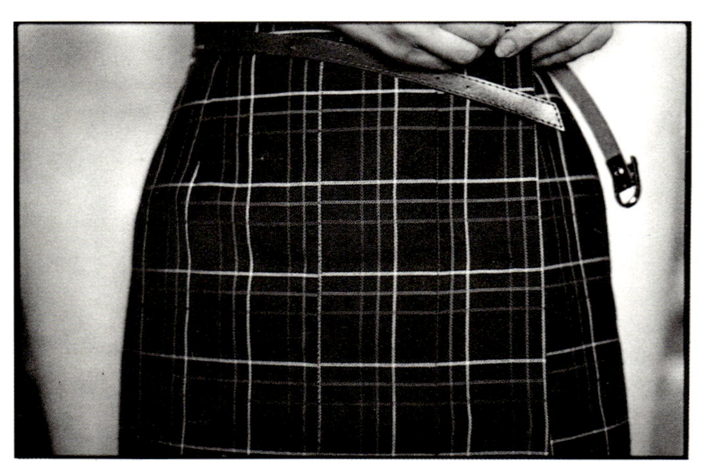

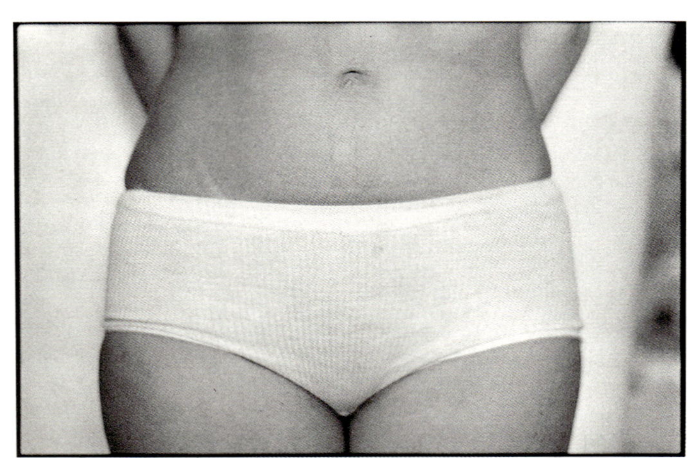

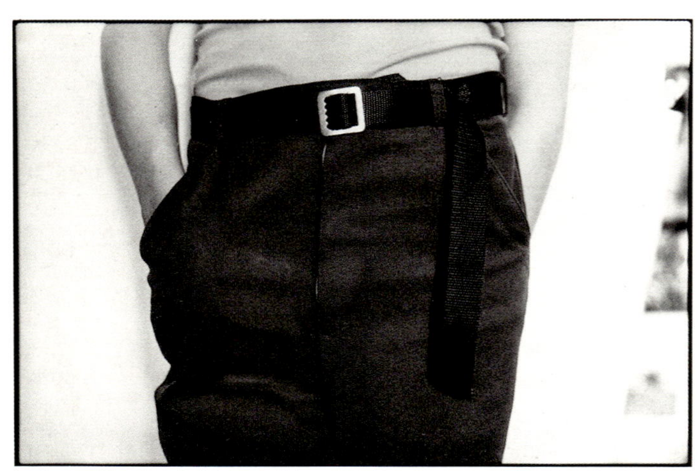

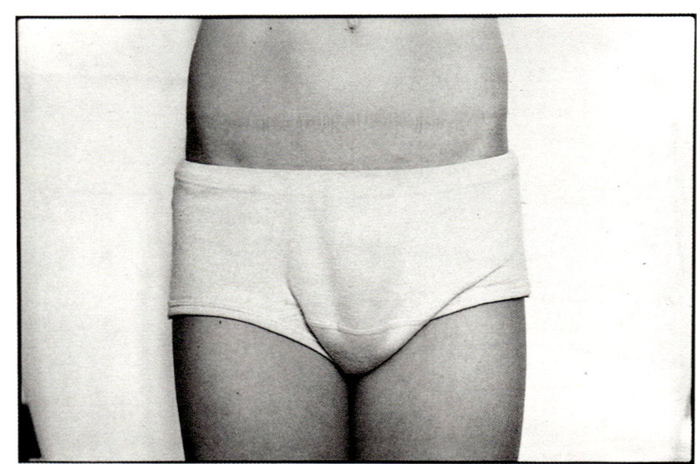

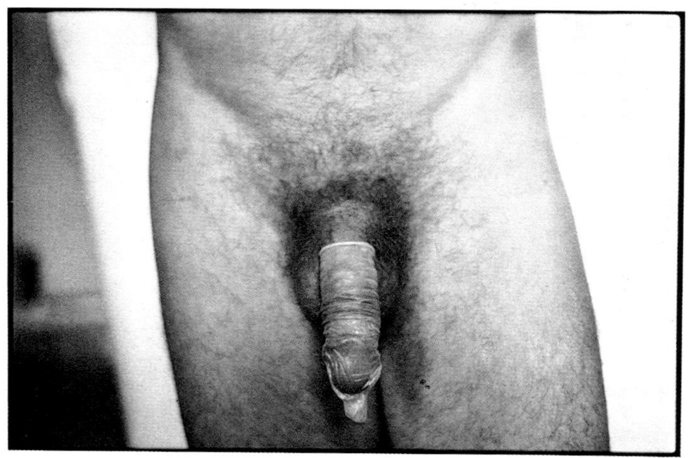

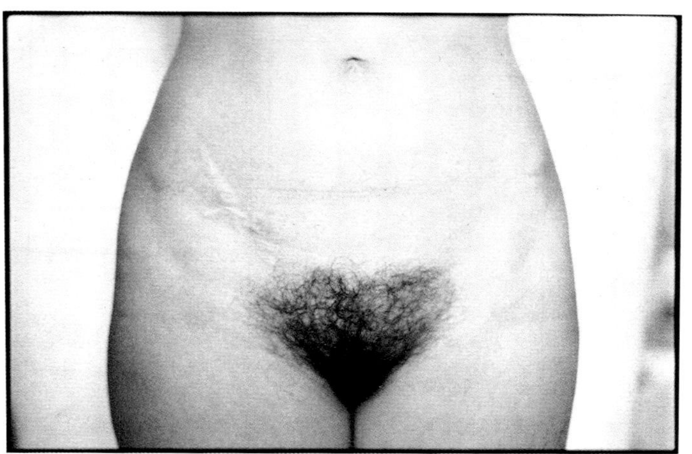

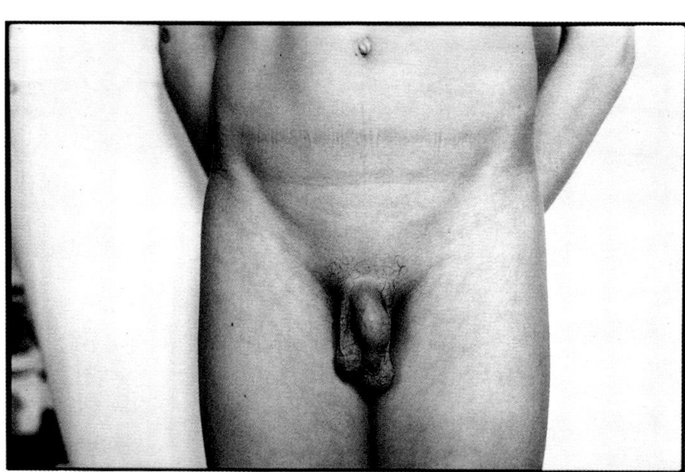

YURY MATVEEV
FATHER, MOTHER, AND SON, from the series:
FAMILY, 1989
7 × 11" (each)

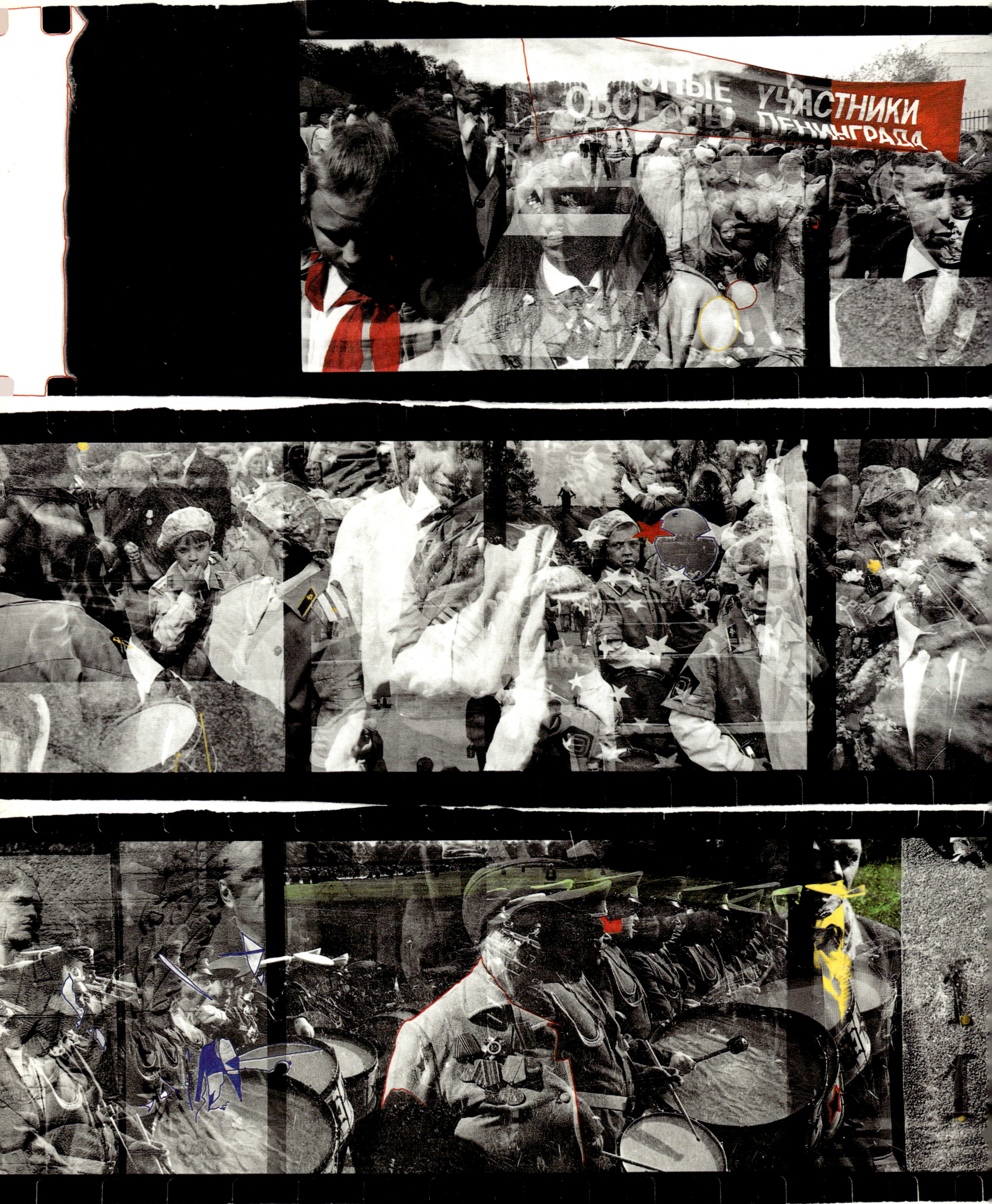
УЧАСТНИКИ
ЛЕНИНГРАДА

ANDREY CHEGIN
MAY 9, VICTORY DAY, 1990
6 × 15½" (each)

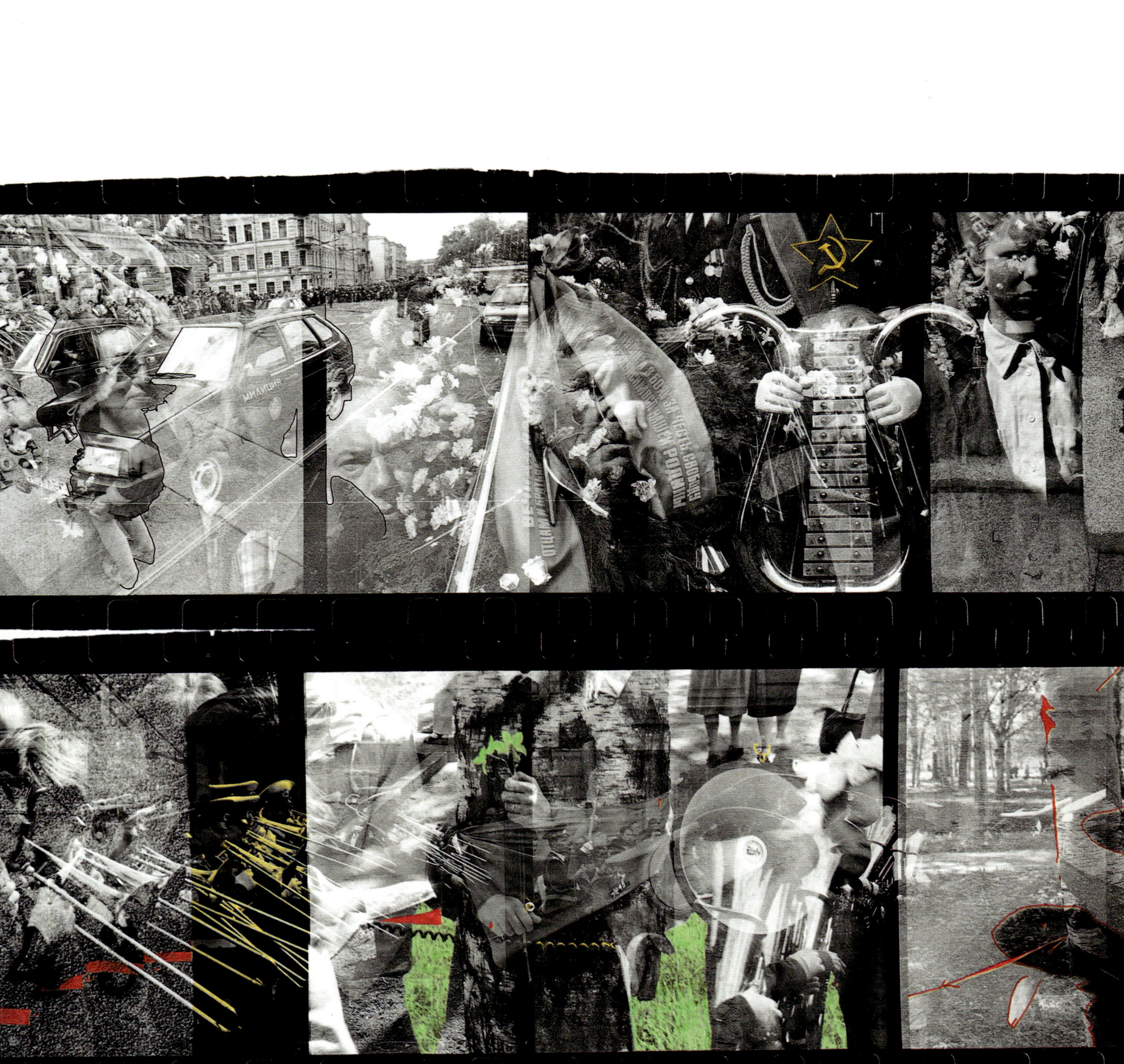

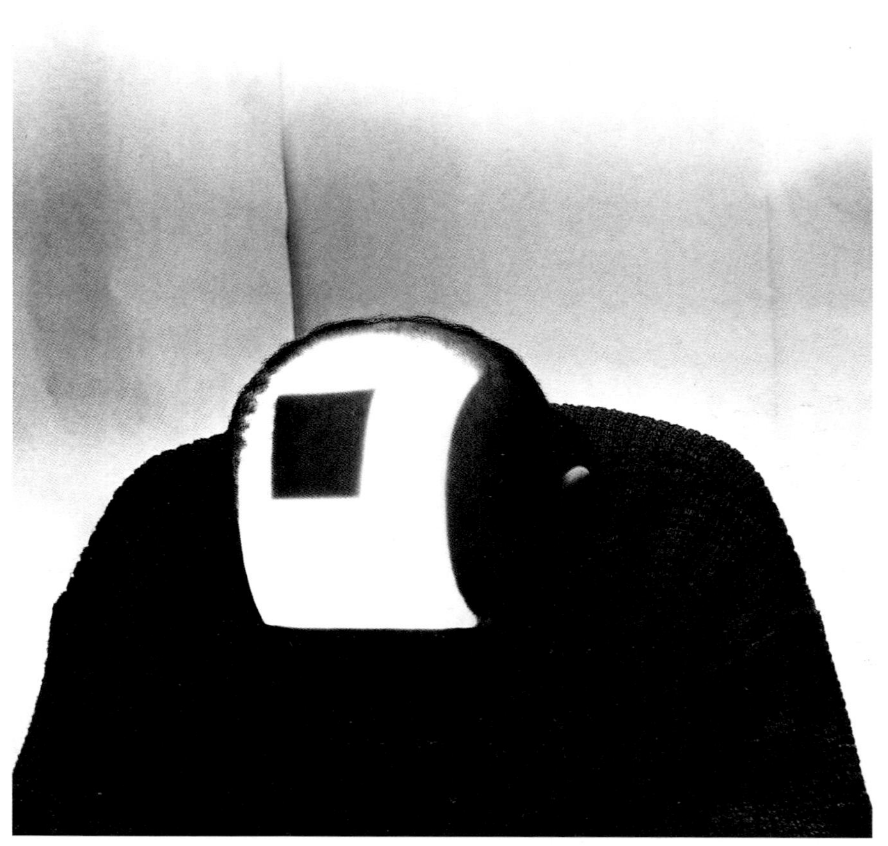

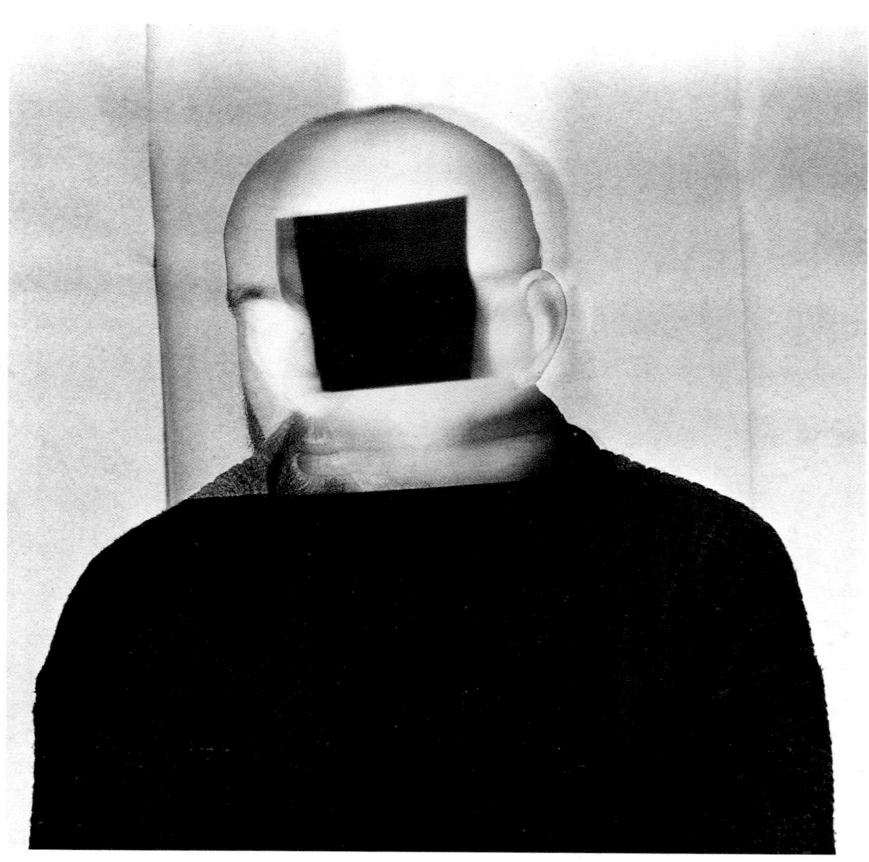

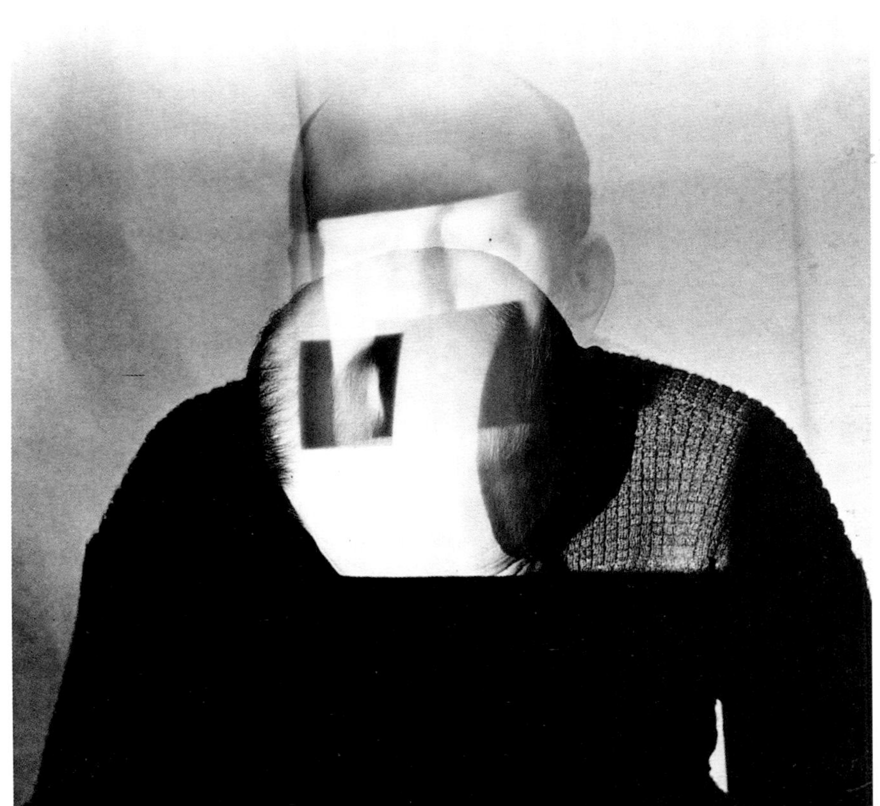

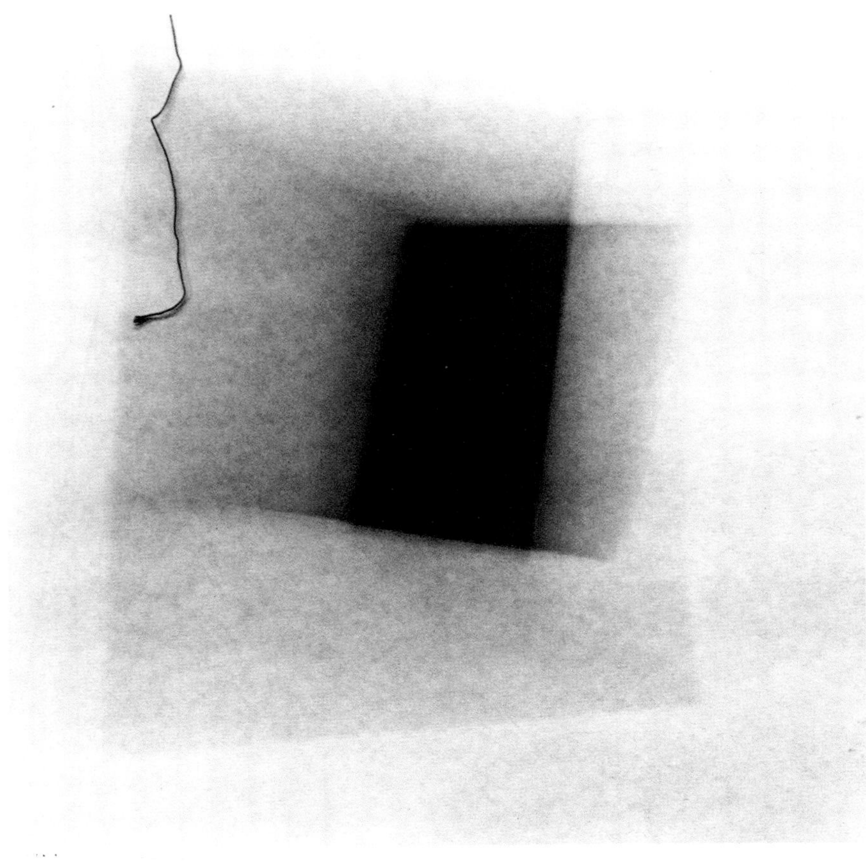

ANDREY CHEGIN
BLACK SQUARE, 1988
9 × 9″ (each)

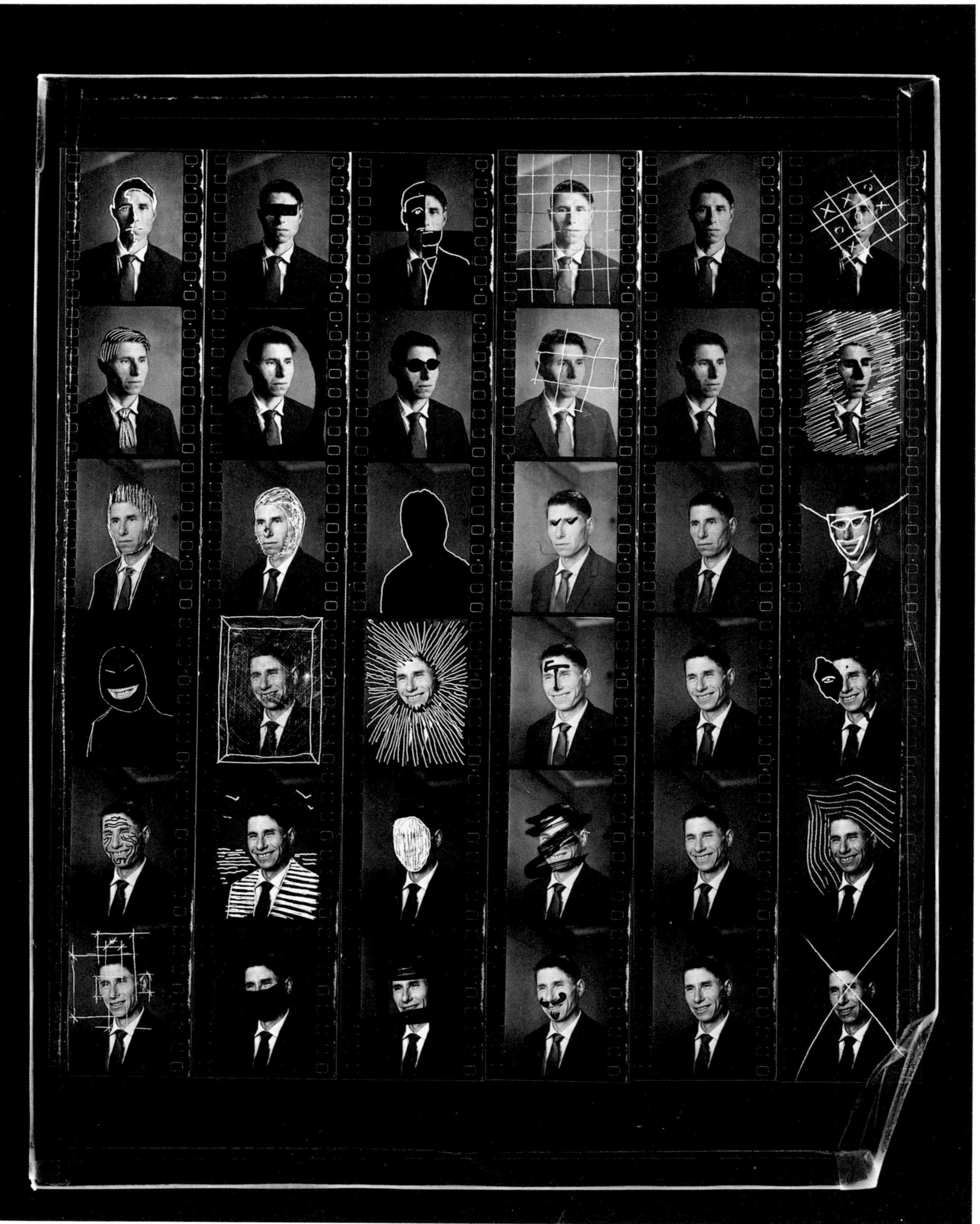

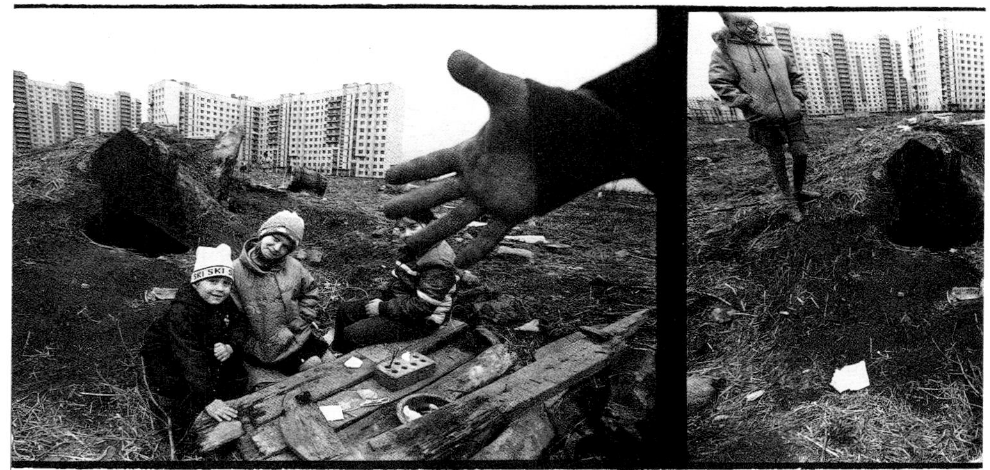

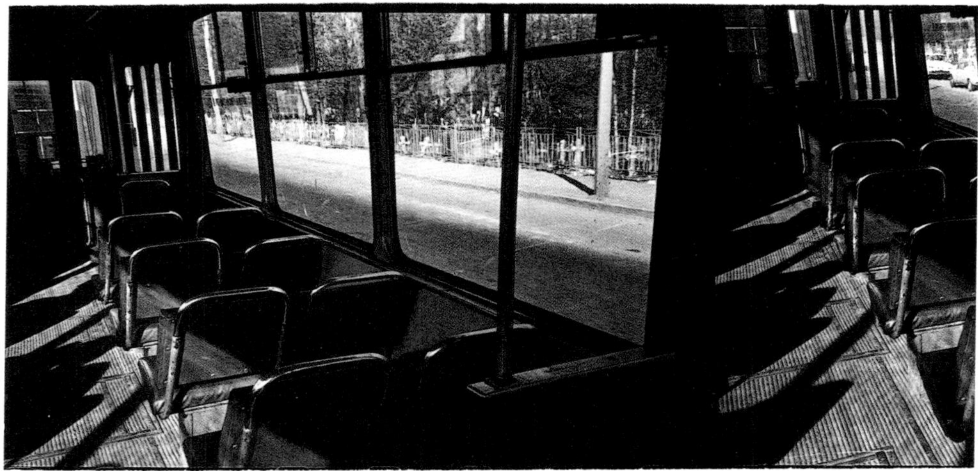

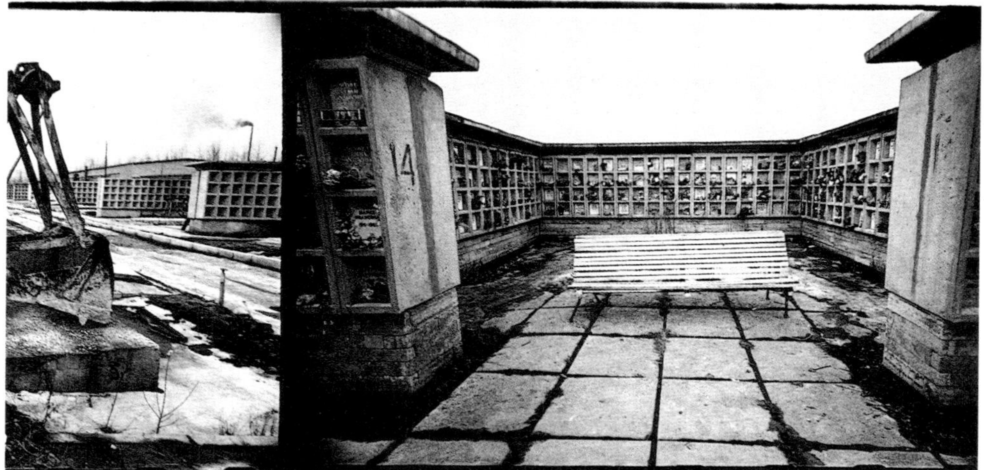

DMITRY SHNEYERSON
NEW BUILT HOUSES, 1990
7½ × 15½″

DMITRY SHNEYERSON
CEMETERY, 1990
7½ × 15½″

DMITRY SHNEYERSON
A BENCH, 1990
7½ × 15½″

ANDREY CHEGIN
PORTRAIT, 1990
11½ × 9″

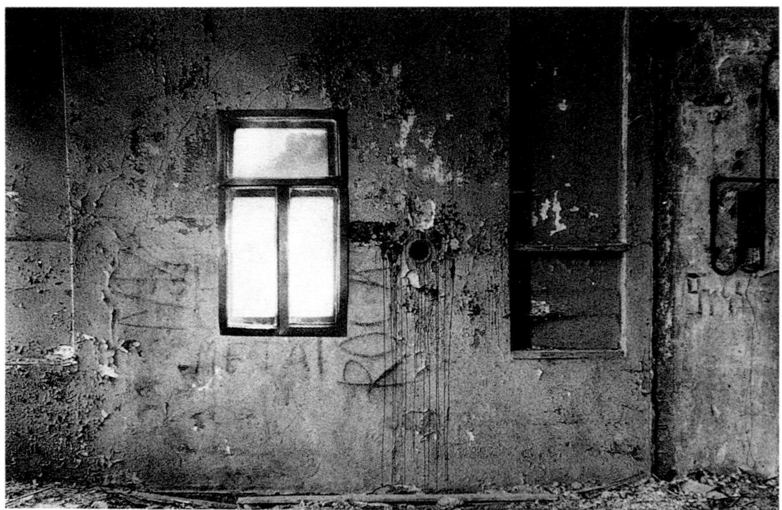

„Но едва желание наше исполняется, мы на миг словно бы перестаем существовать..."

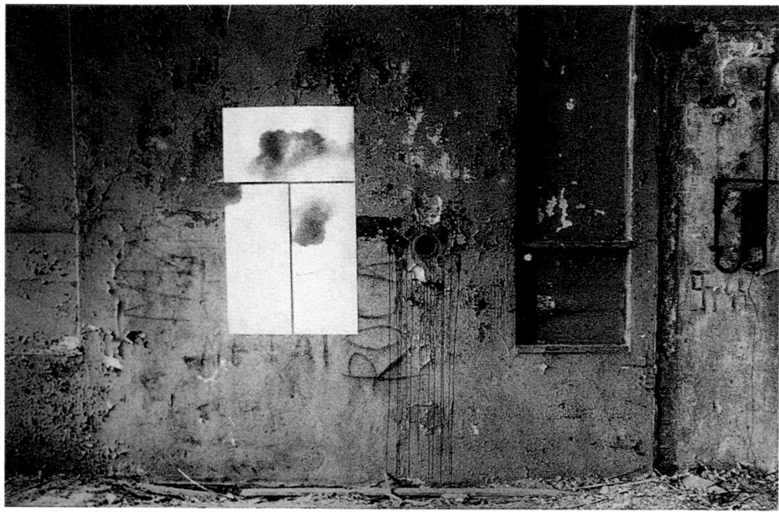

„...бы перестаем существовать... Или это и есть мы – то, чего после пробуждения – нет..."

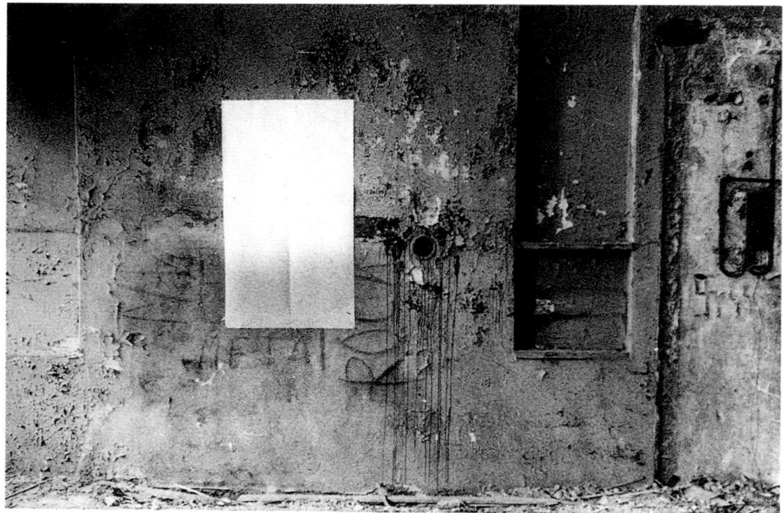

И эта линия цвета тени, линия, о которой известно всё

Opposite, top:
LUDMILA FEDORENKO
UNTITLED, 1987
5 × 9″

Opposite, bottom:
VALENTIN SIMANKOV
from the series: A VISIT TO CHURCH, 1989
8½ × 12″

TAK
from the series: AFTER THE LIFE, c.1989
Top: "Once our desire is fulfilled we at this very moment seem to be stopping." Middle: "We cease to exist or we is precisely what doesn't exist when we wake up." Bottom: "And this line is the line between light and shadow, the line by which one knows everything."
12 × 15½″ (each)

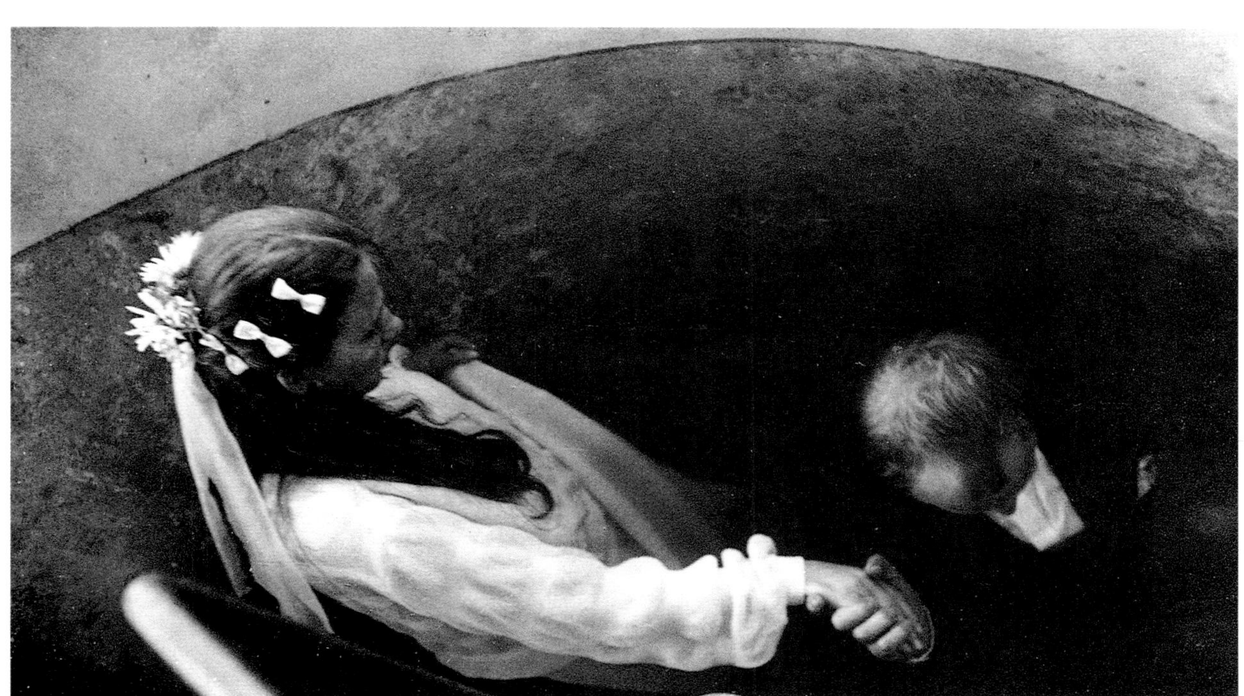

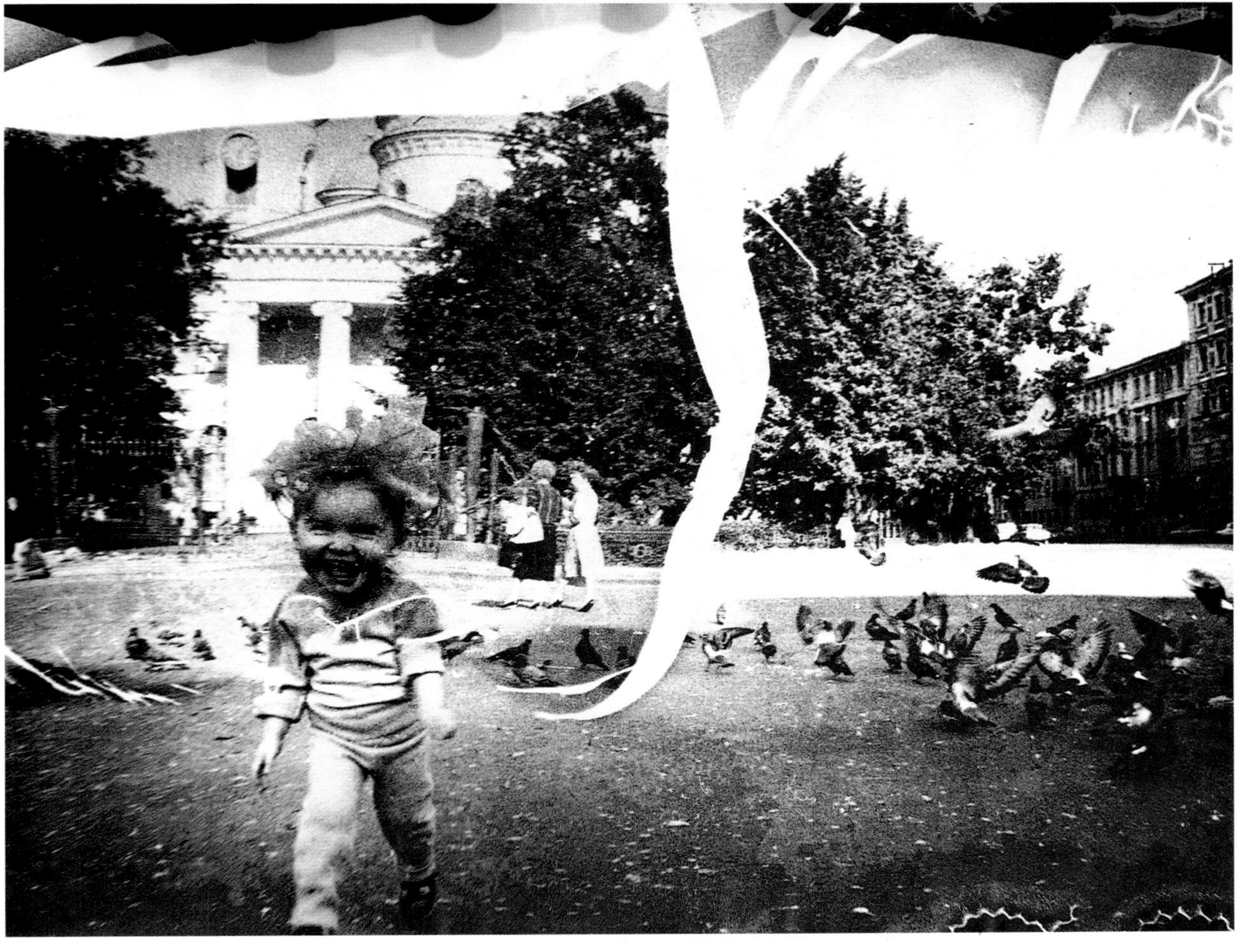

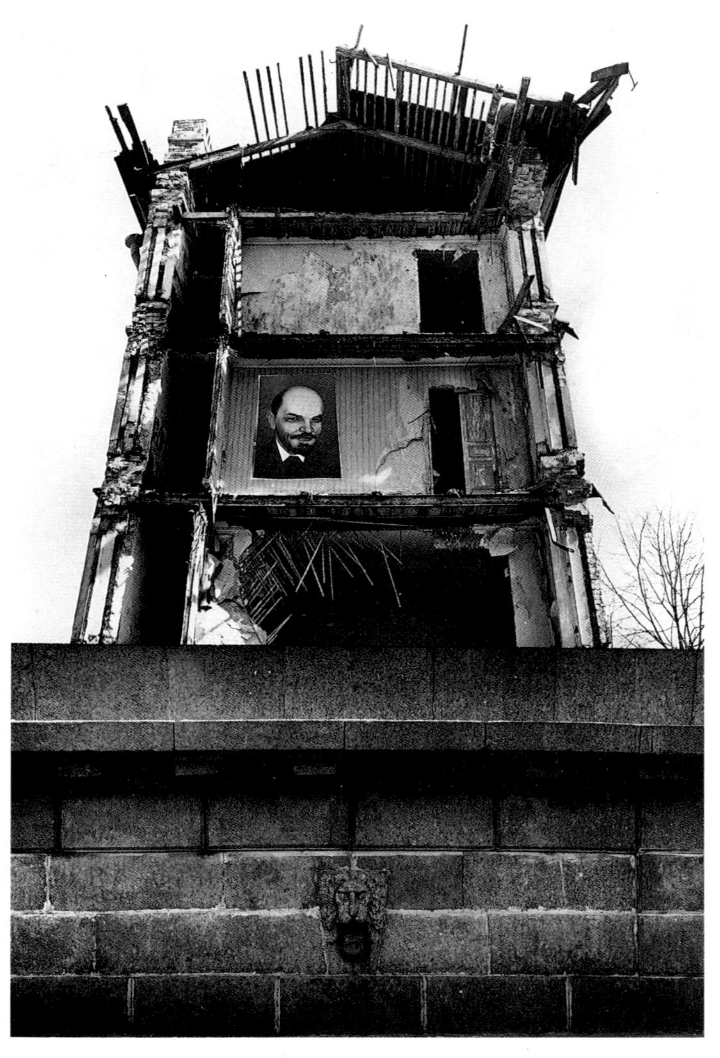

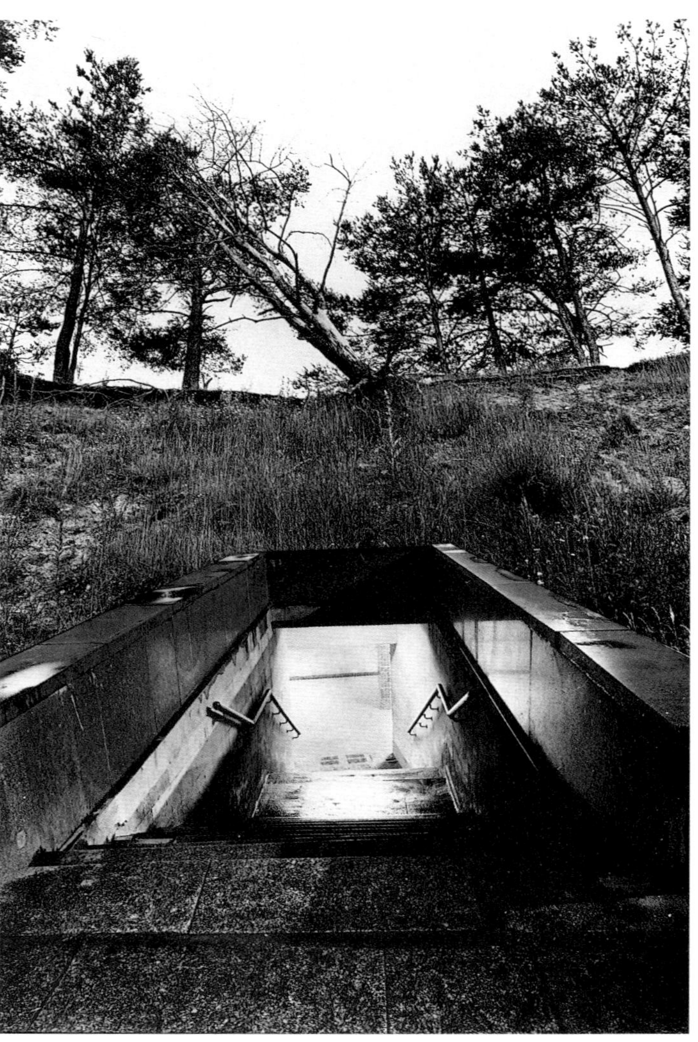

VALERY POTAPOV
ARCHITECTURE WITH A PORTRAIT, 1989
10 × 7″

VALERY POTAPOV
GROWING INTO 1, 1989
10½ × 7″

VALERY POTAPOV
GROWING INTO 2, 1989
10½ × 11″

VALERY POTAPOV
GATES, 1989
10½ × 11″

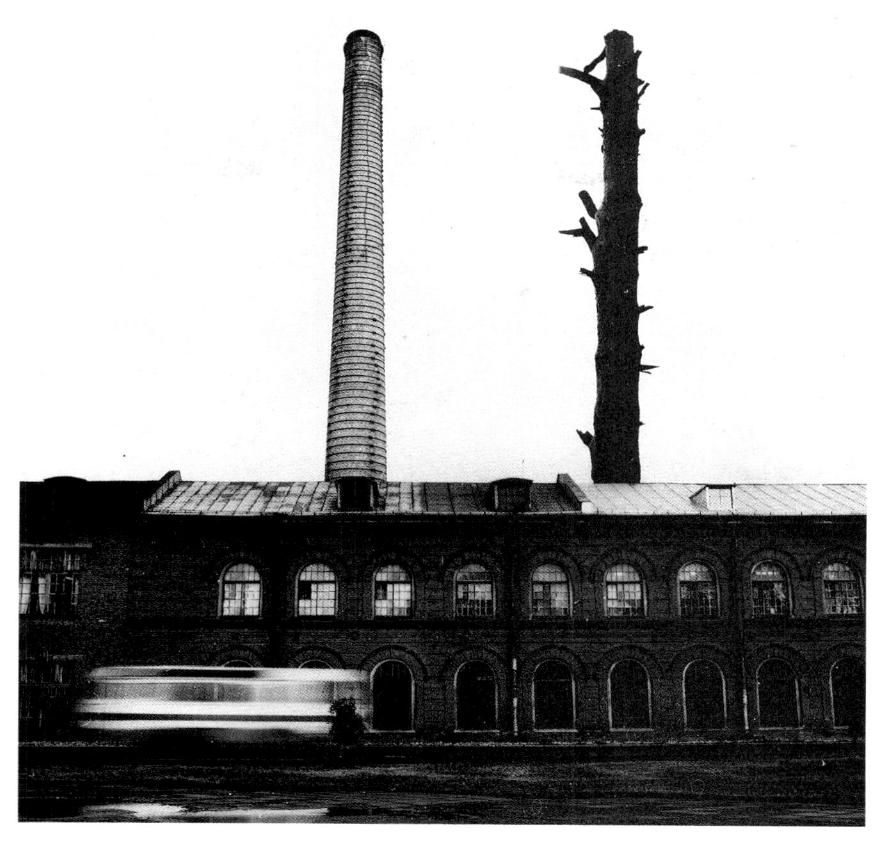

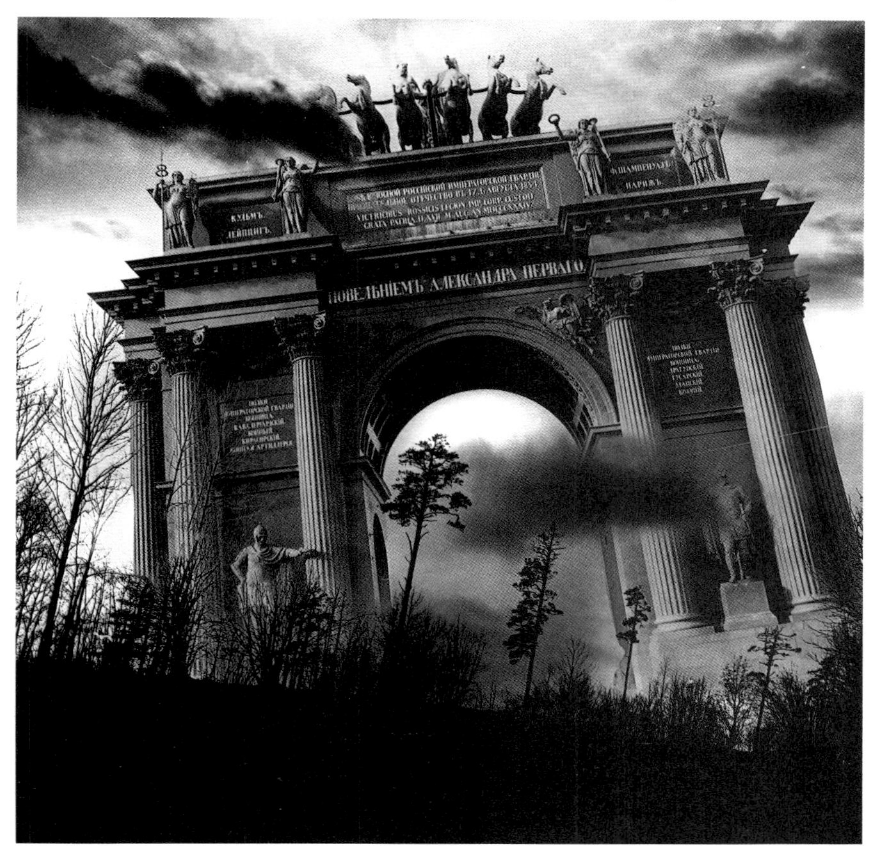
КУЛЬМЪ.
ЛЕЙПЦИГЪ.
VICTRICIBUS ROSSICIS LEGION. IMP. CORP. CUSTOD.
ПАРИЖЪ
ПОВЕЛѢНIЕМЪ АЛЕКСАНДРА ПЕРВАГО

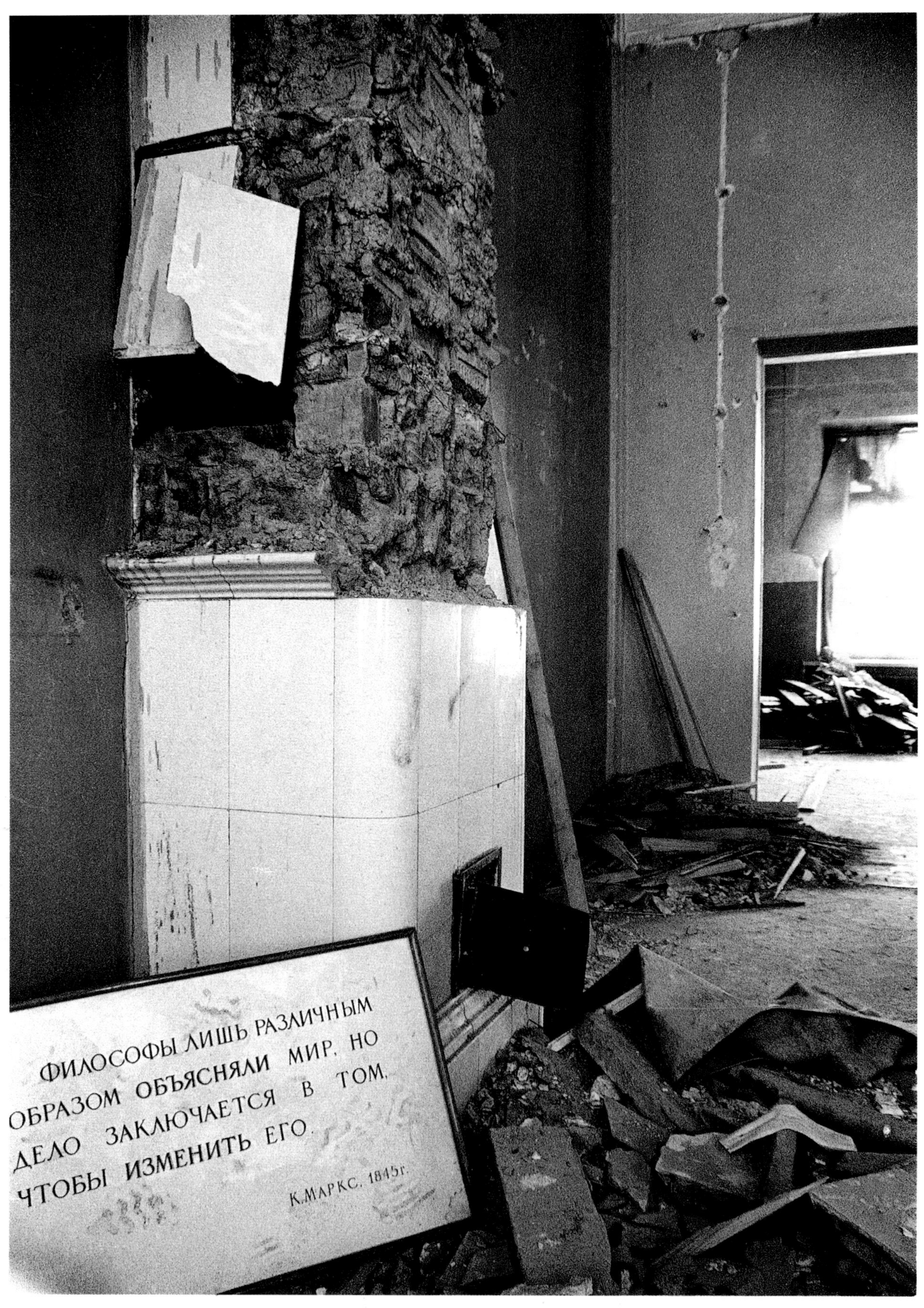
ФИЛОСОФЫ ЛИШЬ РАЗЛИЧНЫМ
ОБРАЗОМ ОБЪЯСНЯЛИ МИР, НО
ДЕЛО ЗАКЛЮЧАЕТСЯ В ТОМ,
ЧТОБЫ ИЗМЕНИТЬ ЕГО.
К.МАРКС. 1845г.

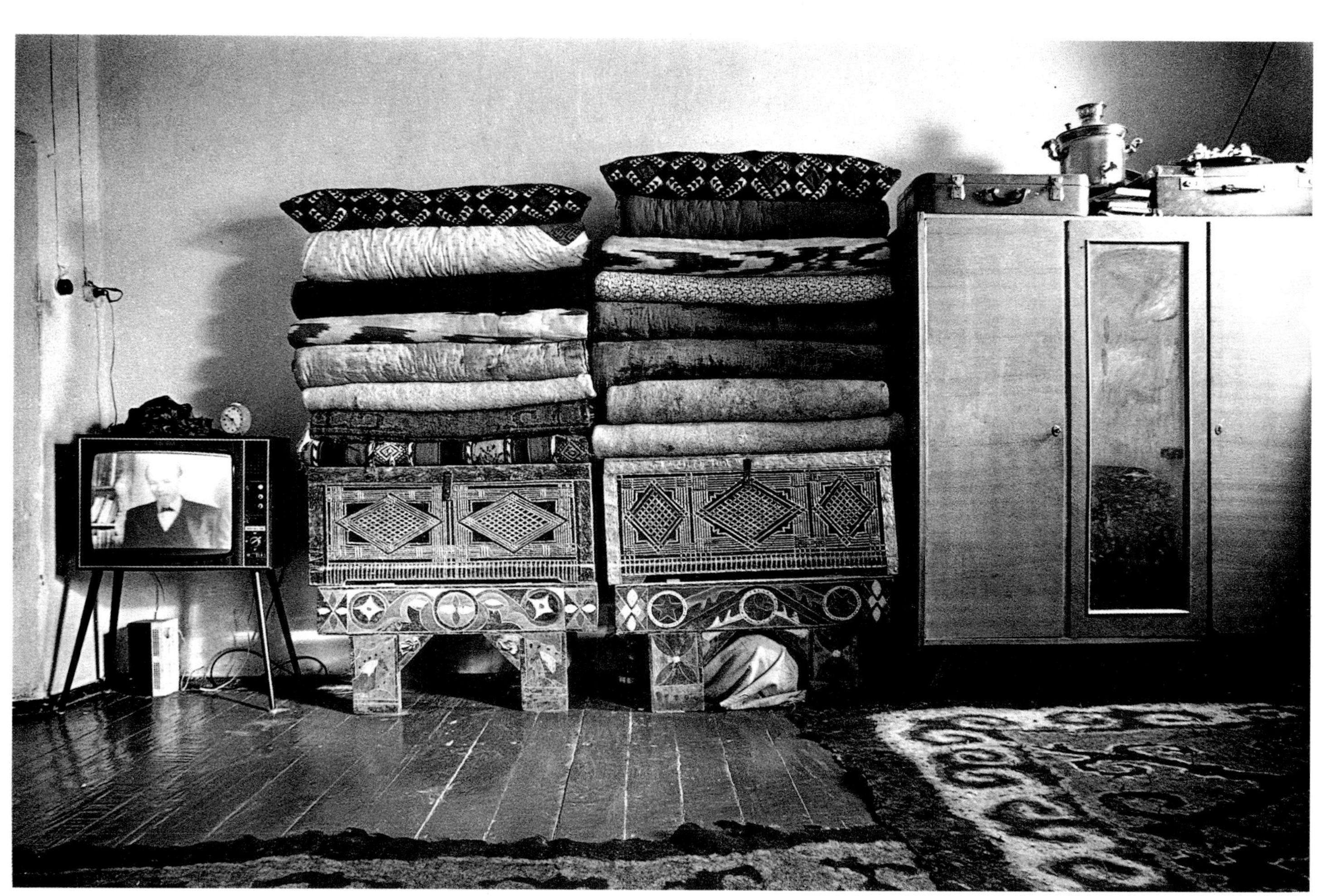

ALEXANDER IGNATJEV
from the series: KAZAKHSTAN AND KIRGIZIA,
1985
10 × 15″

ALEXANDER IGNATJEV
AN OFFICE IN BETWEEN TENANTS,
1988/89
"Philosophers have simply been explaining the world in all different ways, but the real issue is how to change it."
KARL MARX, 1845
15 × 10″

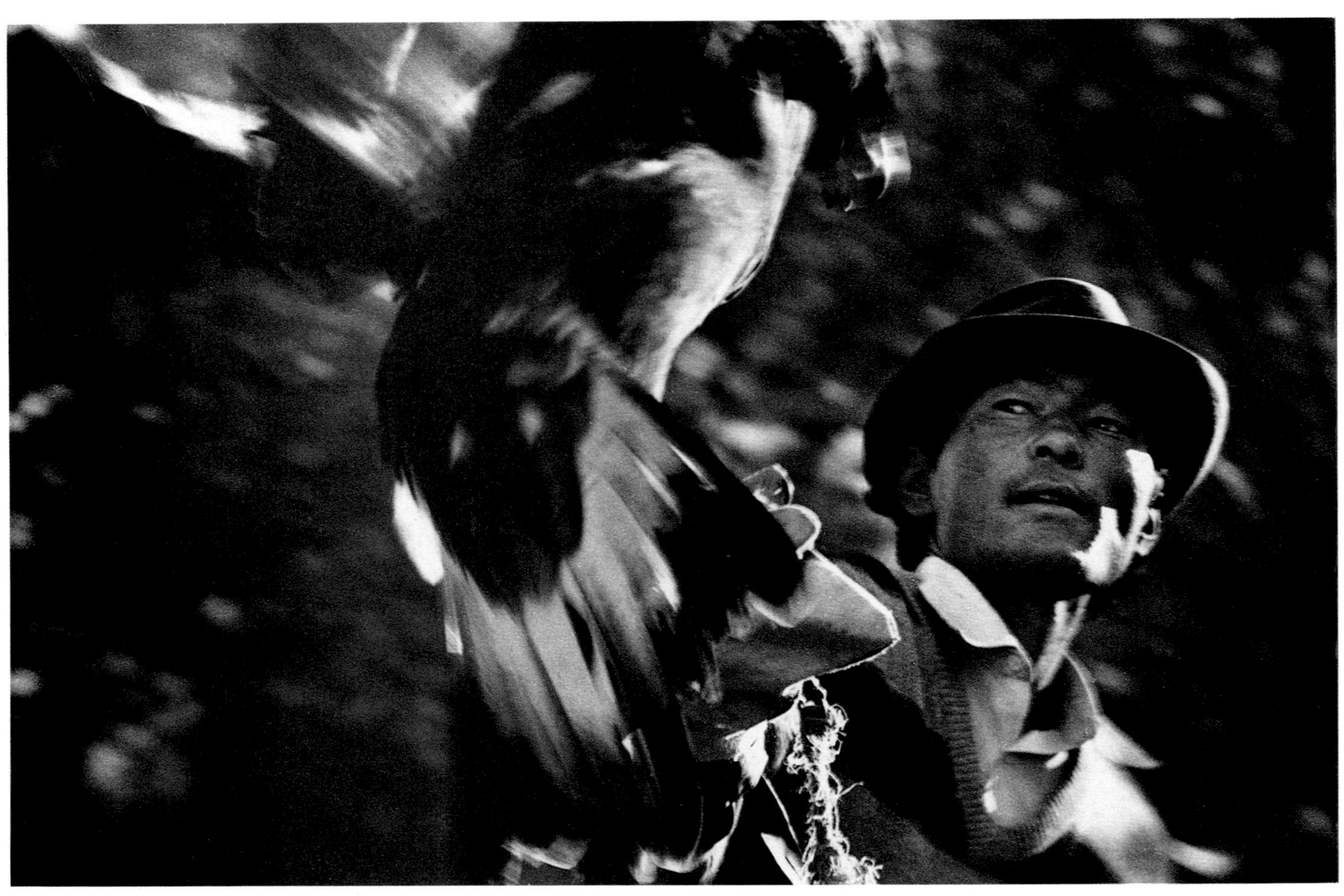

ALEXANDER IGNATJEV
from the series: KAZAKHSTAN AND KIRGIZIA, 1985
10 × 15″

ALEXANDER IGNATJEV
AN OFFICE IN BETWEEN TENANTS, 1988/89
"Lenin is always with us."
15 × 10″

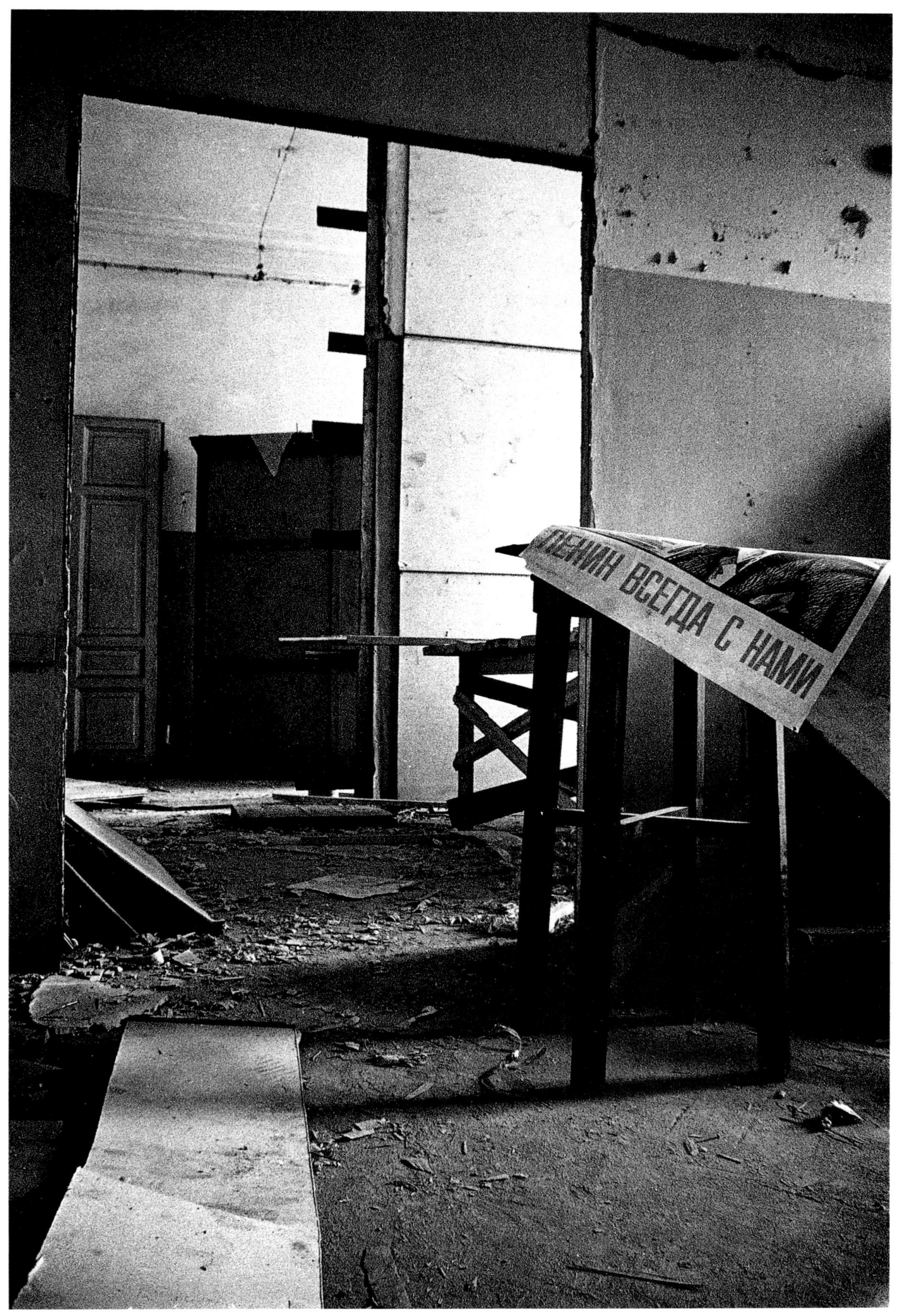
ЛЕНИН ВСЕГДА С НАМИ

SERGEY LEONTIEV • VLADIMIR KUPREJANOV • ALEXANDER SLIUSSAREV • TANIA LIEBERMAN • IGOR MOUKHIN • VLADISLAV EFIMOV • ALEXEY SHULGIN

MOSCOW

The most prominent group of photographers in Moscow is known as Immediate Photography, a loose affiliation maintained over several years by approximately ten photographers and extending beyond Moscow to include an association with Boris Mikhailov from Kharkov in the Ukraine. One of the advantages offered the photographers by working in Moscow is advanced integration with the Western art world. All have exhibited abroad and most have had the opportunity to travel to Western Europe or the United States.

Intellectual stimulation and shared resources serve as the *raison d'être* for the group more than does a unified artistic focus. Indeed, the artistic emphases within the group span conceptual photography to photo documentation. The artists are the most sophisticated of the young Soviet photographers in the presentation and articulation of their artistic process. But the fact that they are pioneering relationships between Soviet photographers and the West demands they balance the effects of exposure with the artistic act of creation, an age-old task fraught with obstacles. How these artists realize their potential in the midst of opportunity will have a pronounced impact on their Soviet peers.

Pages 143–47:
SERGEY LEONTIEV
from the series: STUDY IN HARD PHOTOGRAPHY, 1988
22 × 23″ (each)

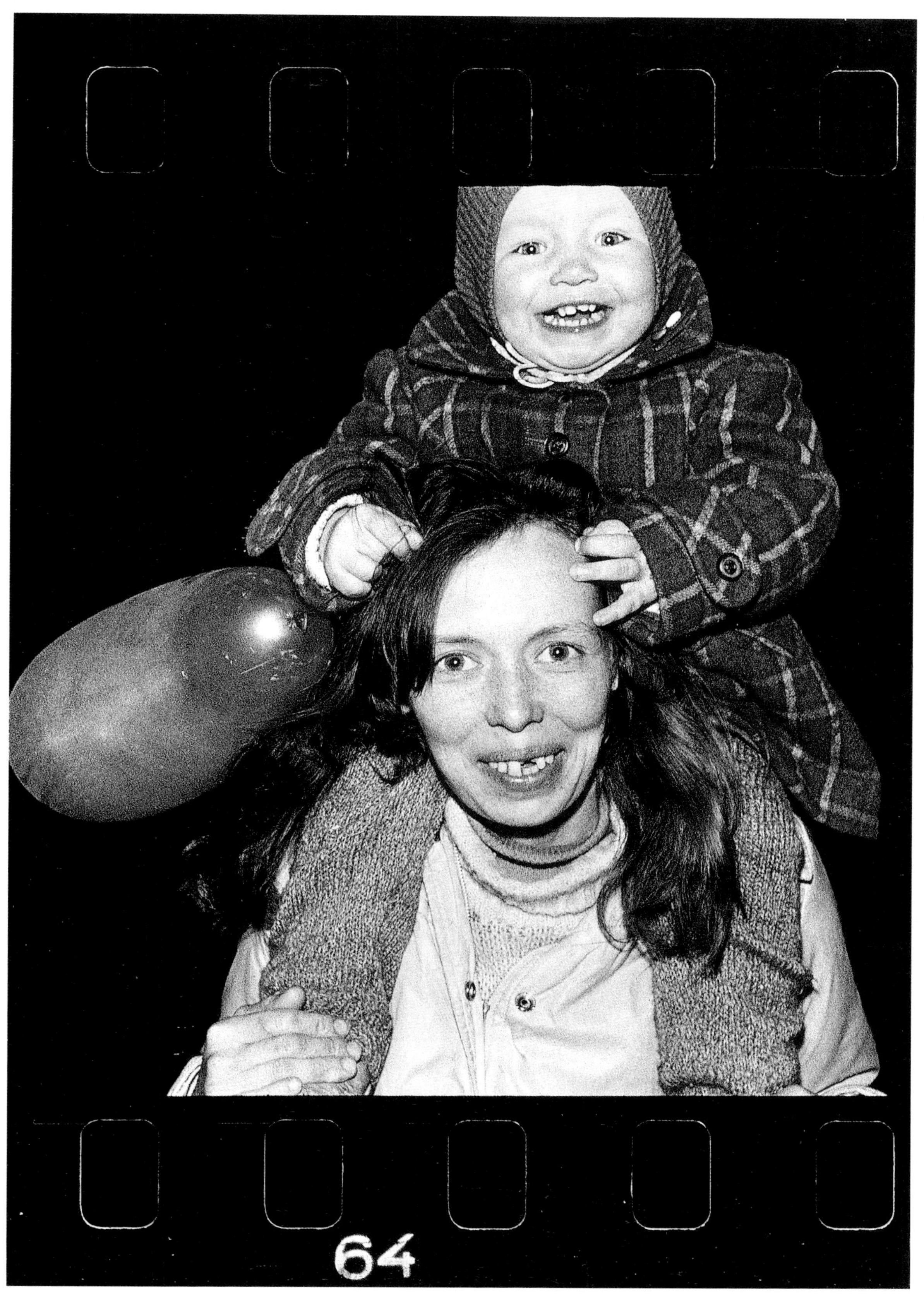
64

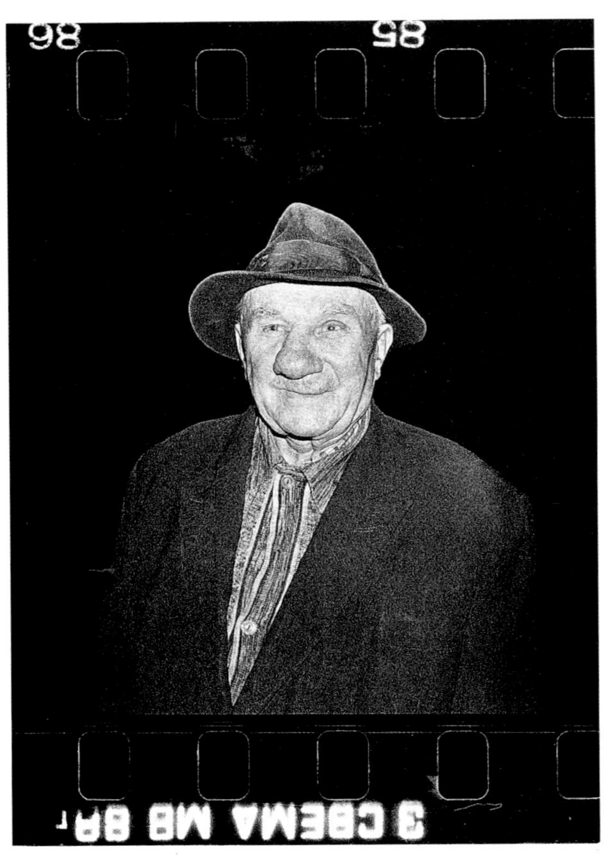

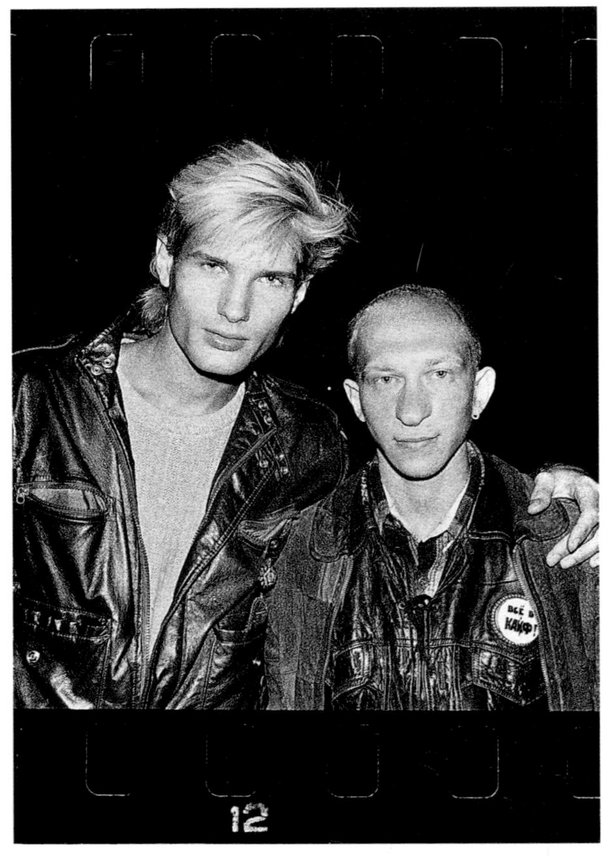

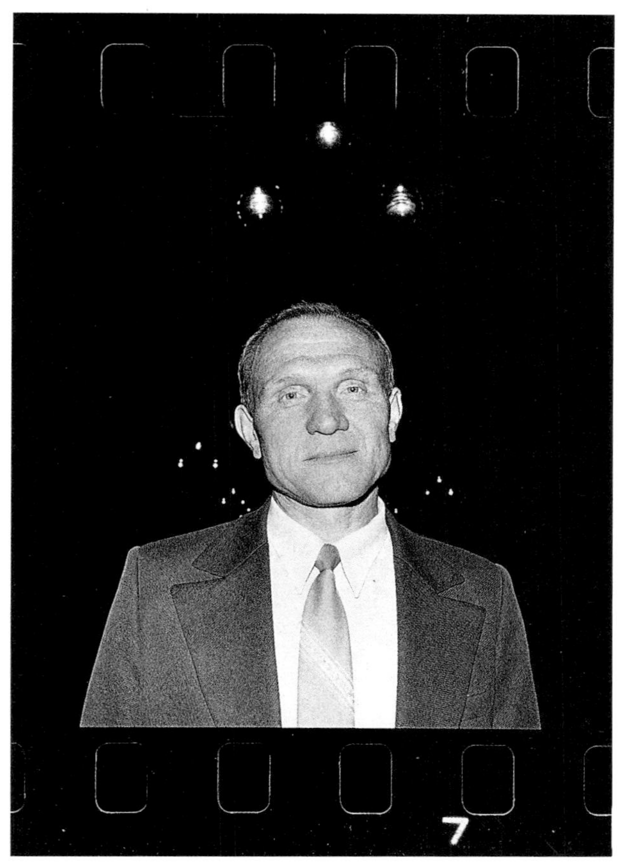
7

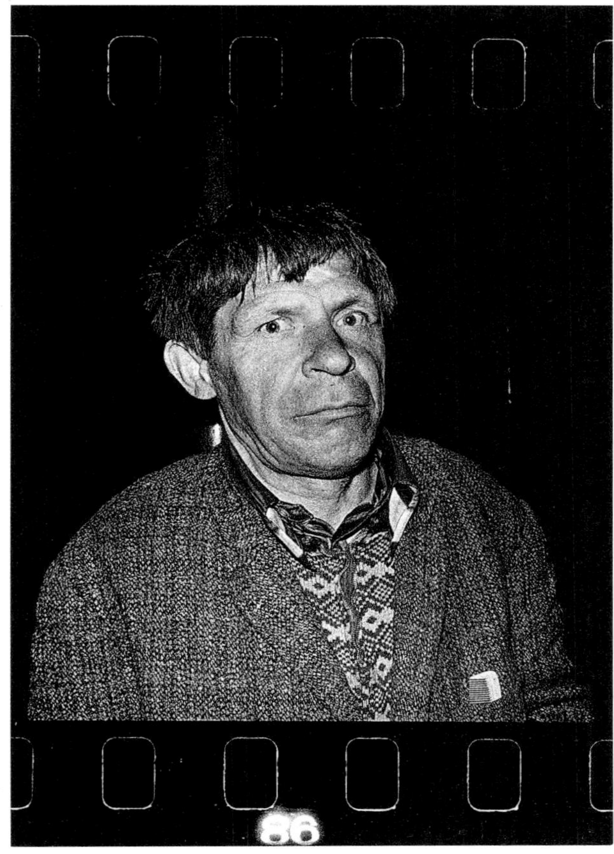
86

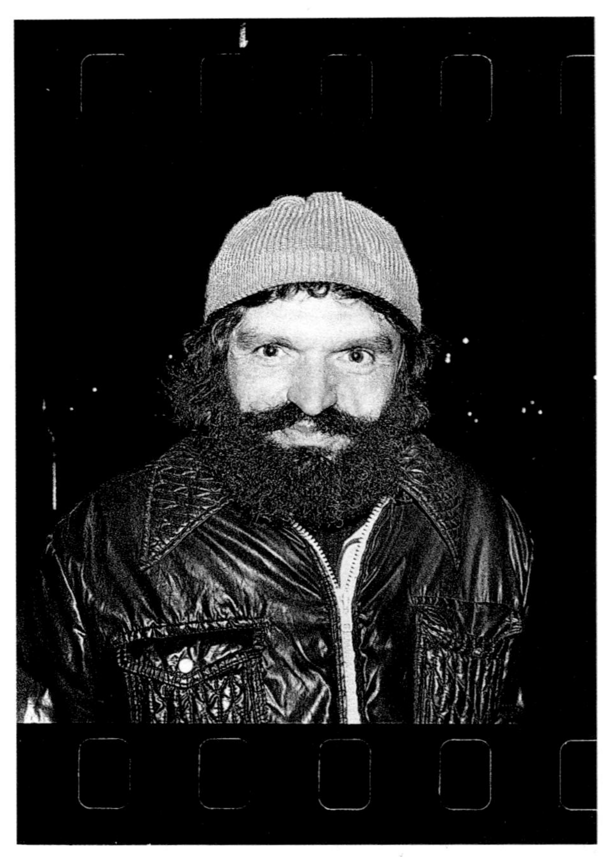

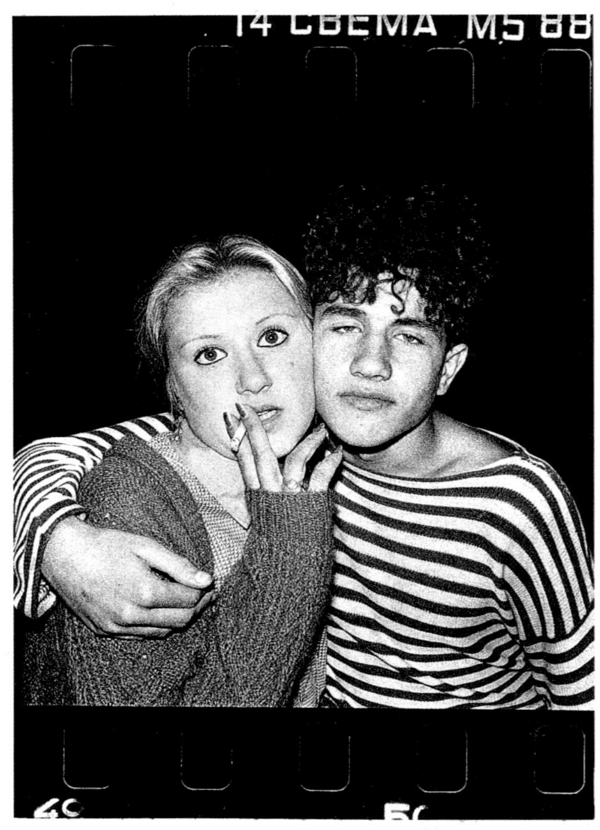
14 СВЕМА М5 88

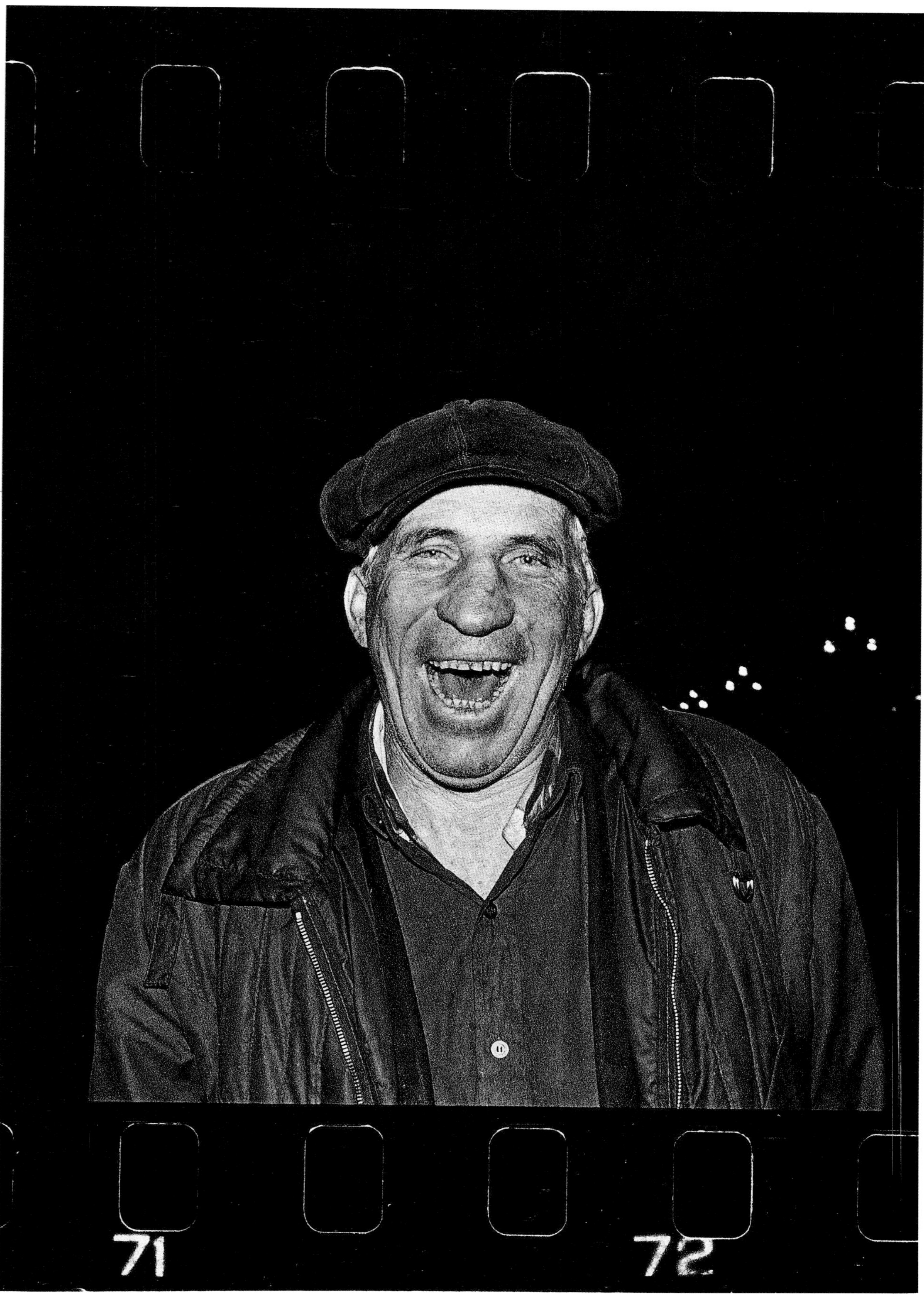
71
72

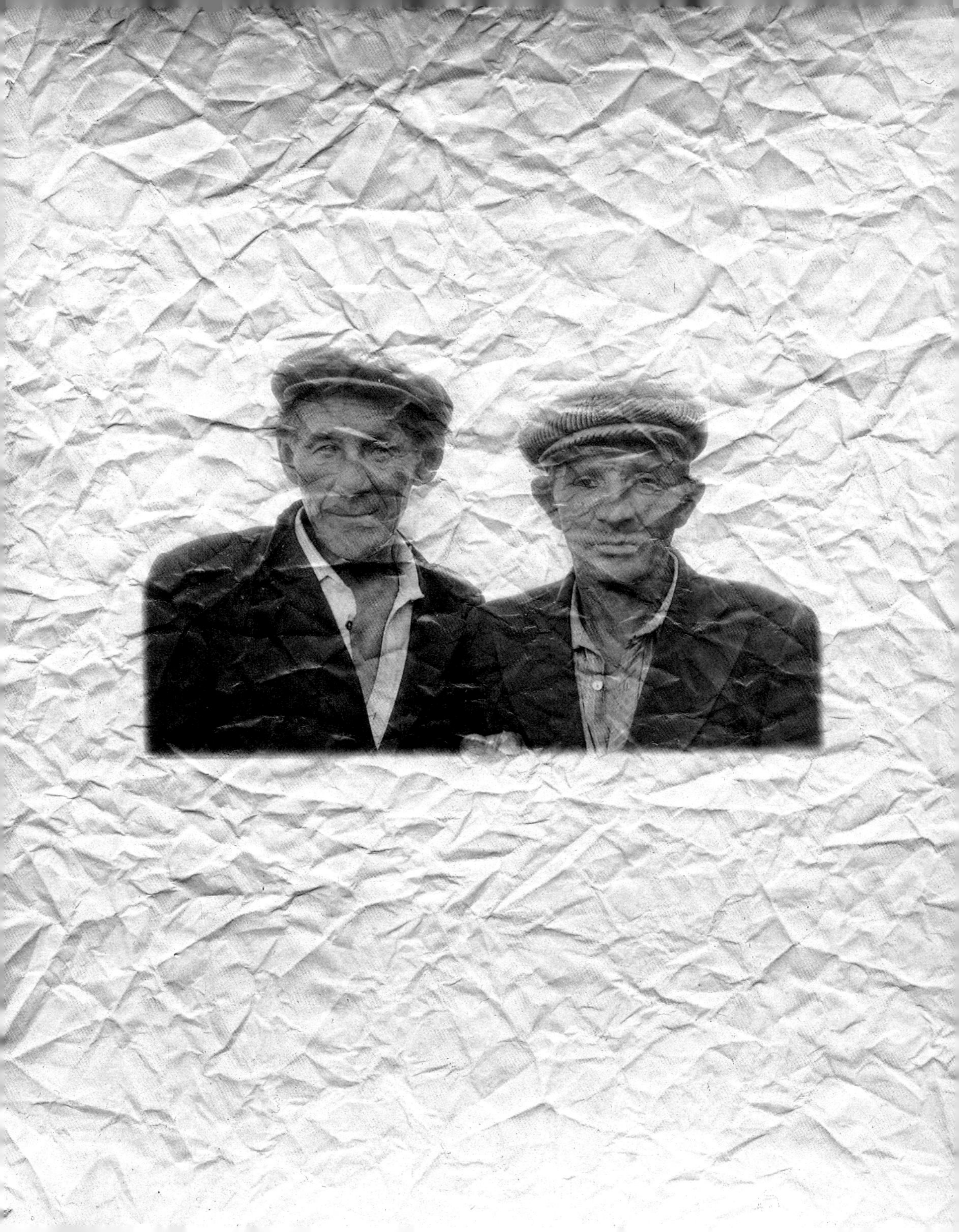

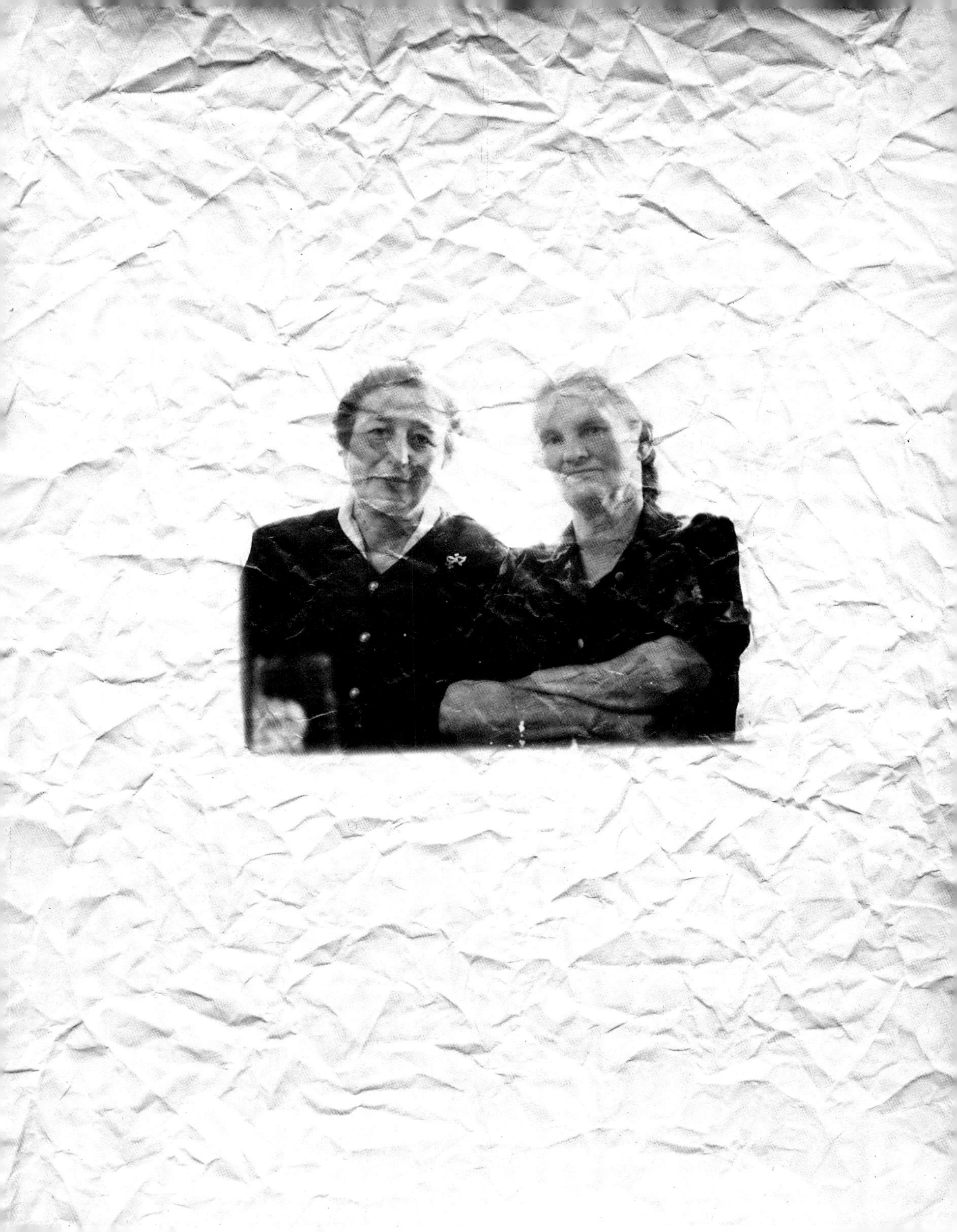

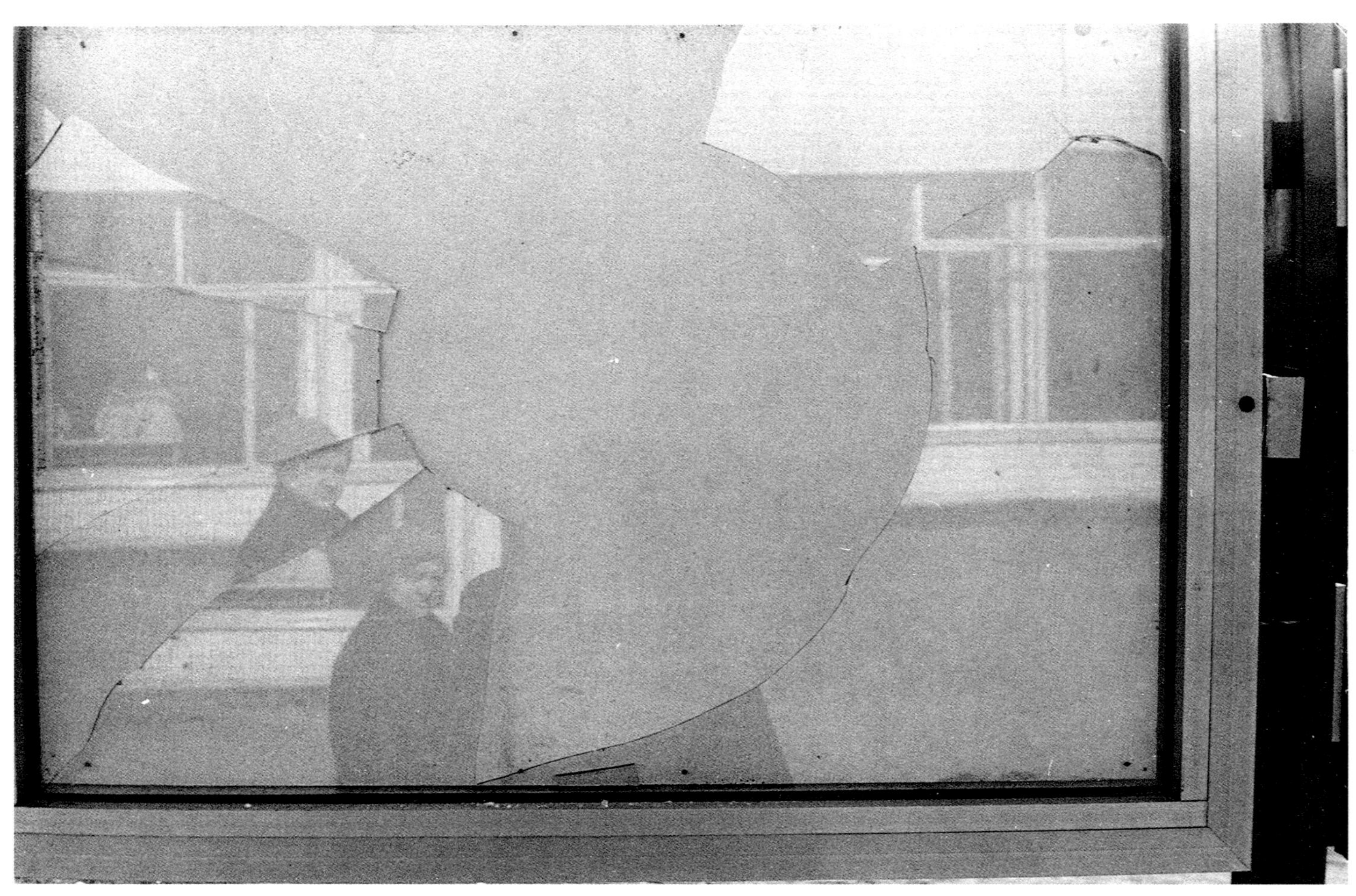

ALEXANDER SLIUSSAREV
from an untitled series, 1989
4½ × 7″

Preceding pages:
VLADIMIR KUPREJANOV
from the series: MIDDLE RUSSIAN LANDSCAPE
#3, 1989
15 × 11½″ (each)

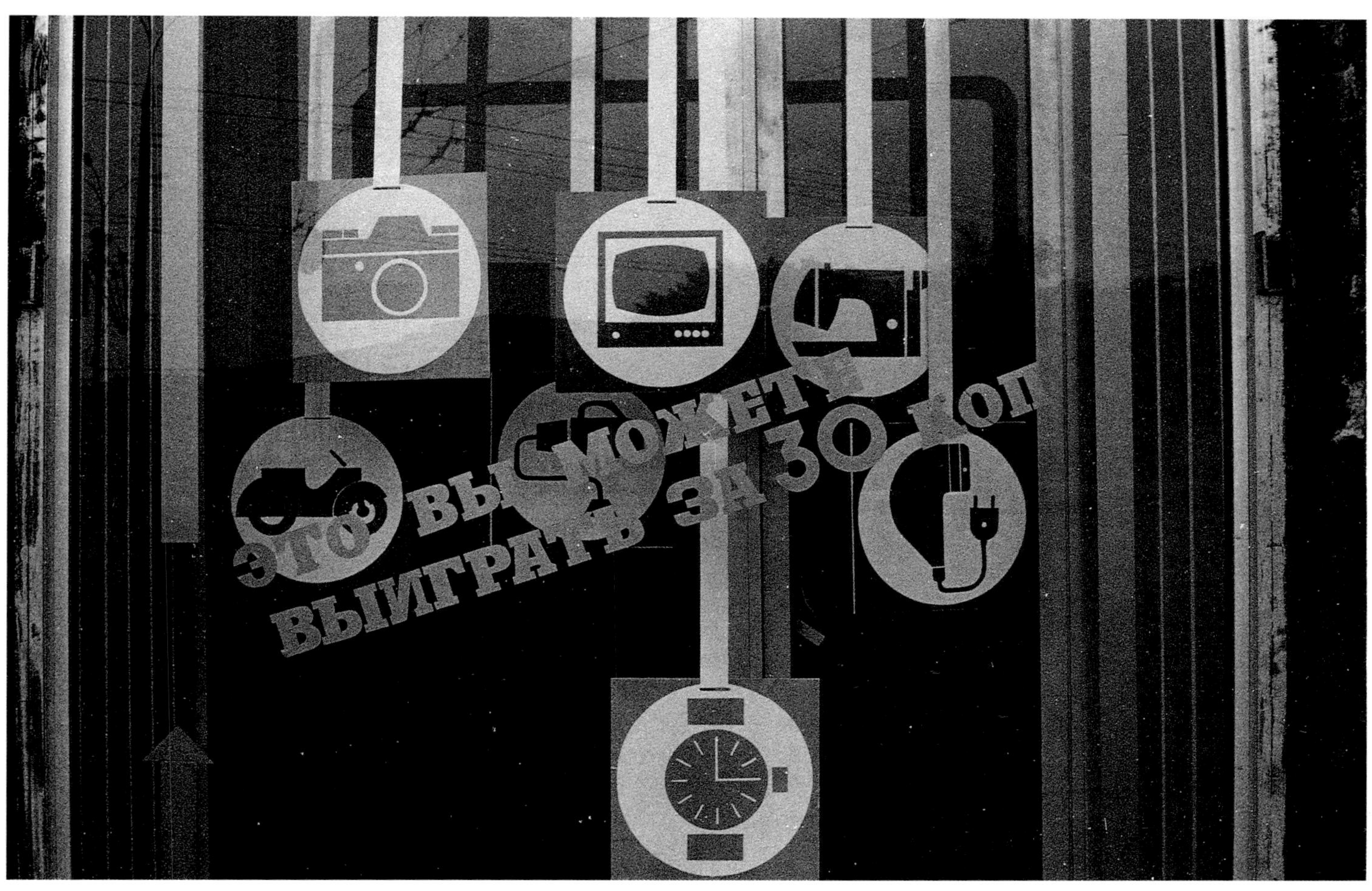

ALEXANDER SLIUSSAREV
from an untitled series, 1989
"For 30 kopeks you might win"
5 × 7½"

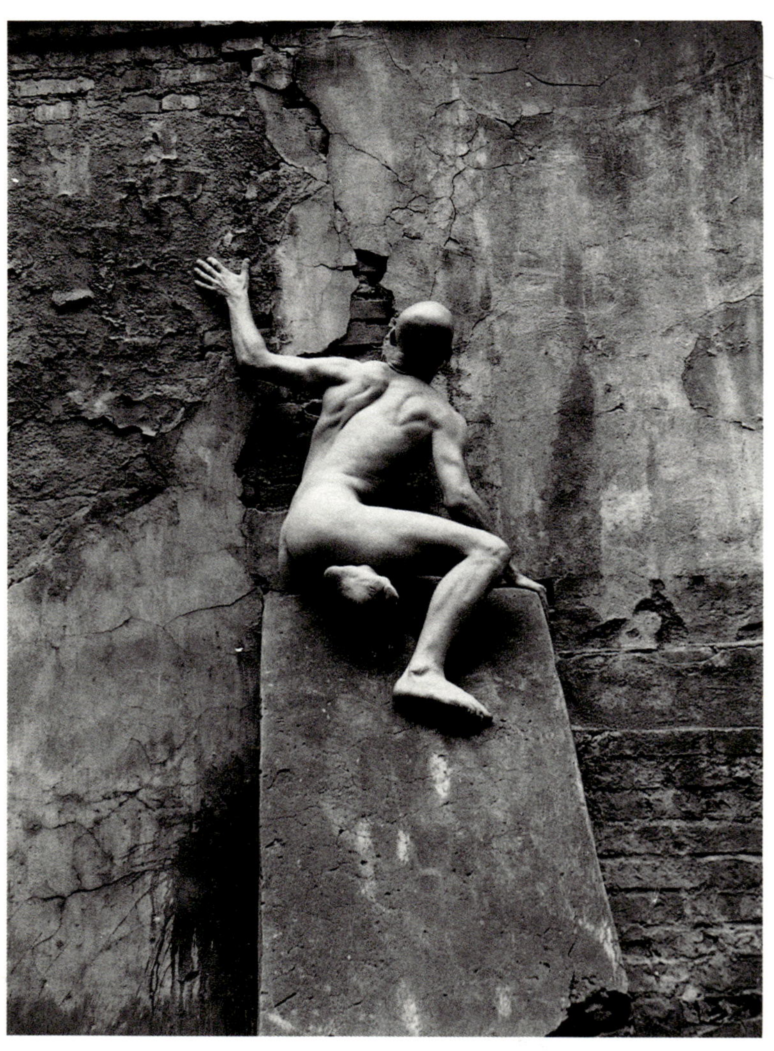

TANIA LIEBERMAN
from an untitled series, 1989
7 × 5″

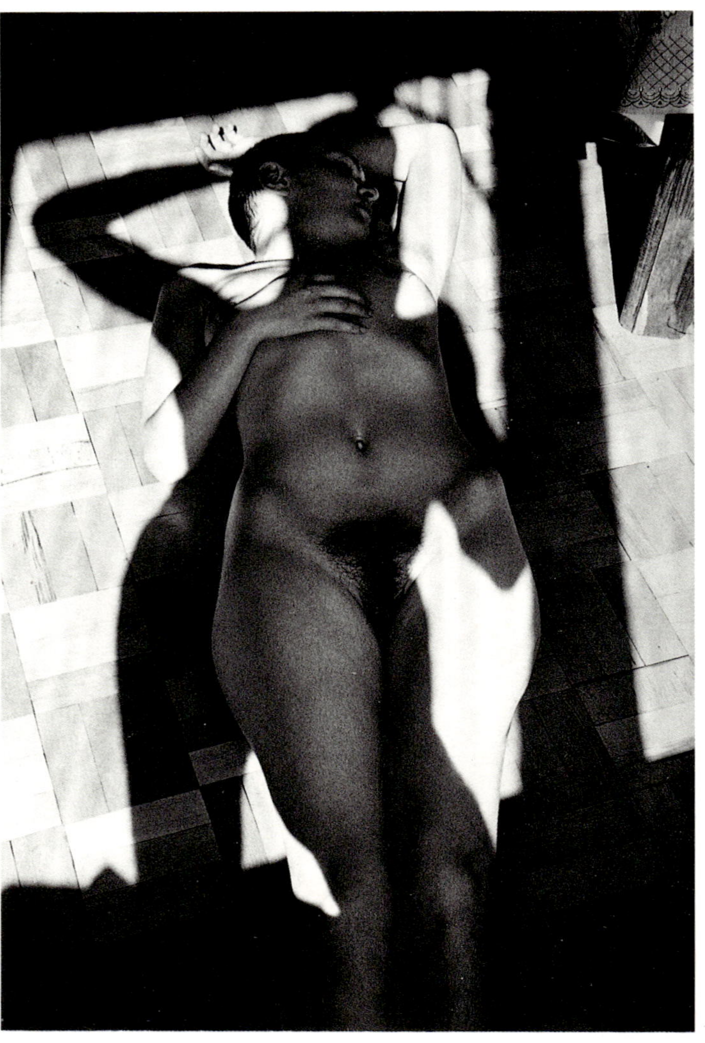

IGOR MOUKHIN and TANIA LIEBERMAN
WE, 1990
8 × 5″

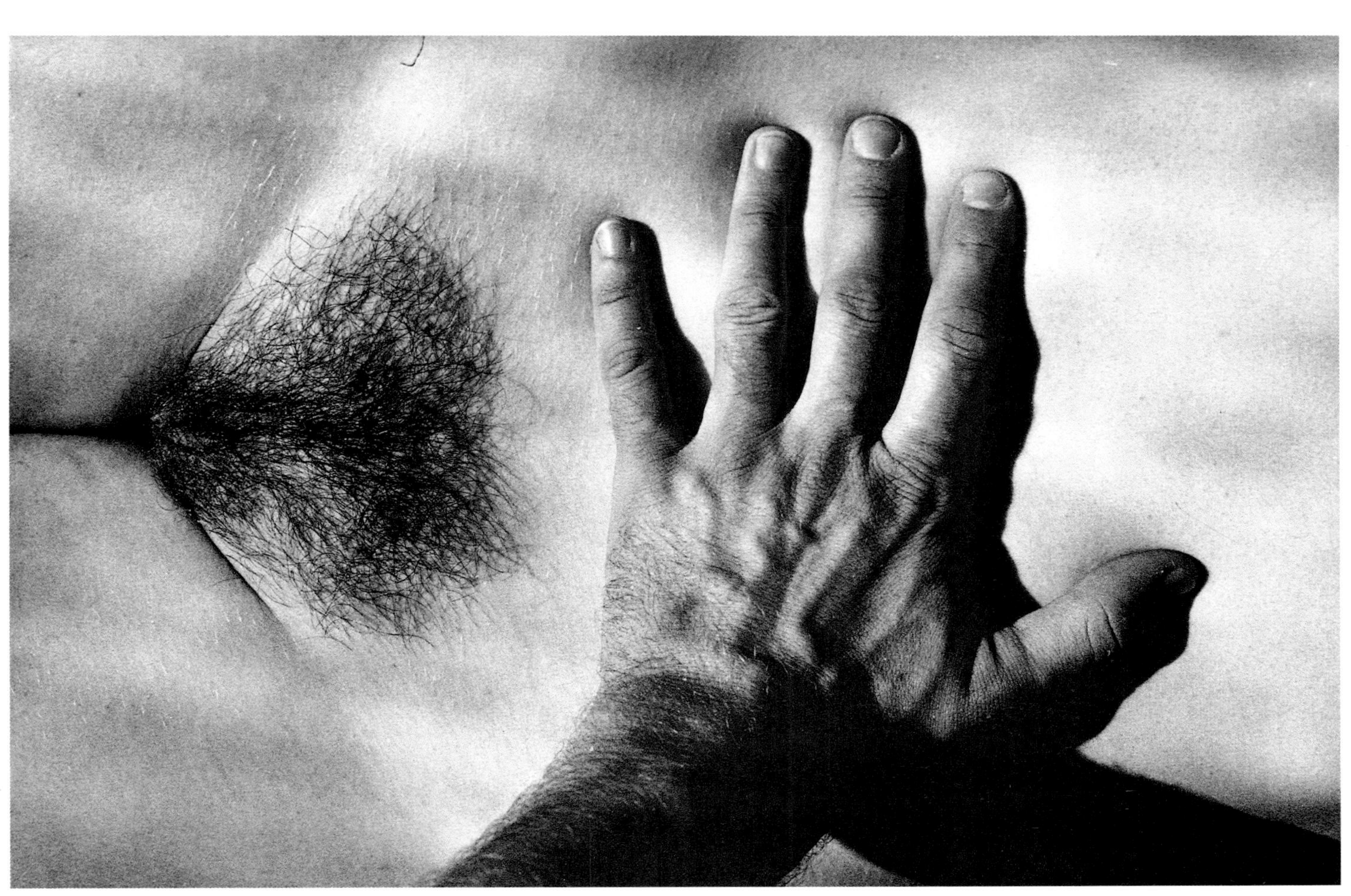

IGOR MOUKHIN and TANIA LIEBERMAN
WE, 1990
5 × 8″

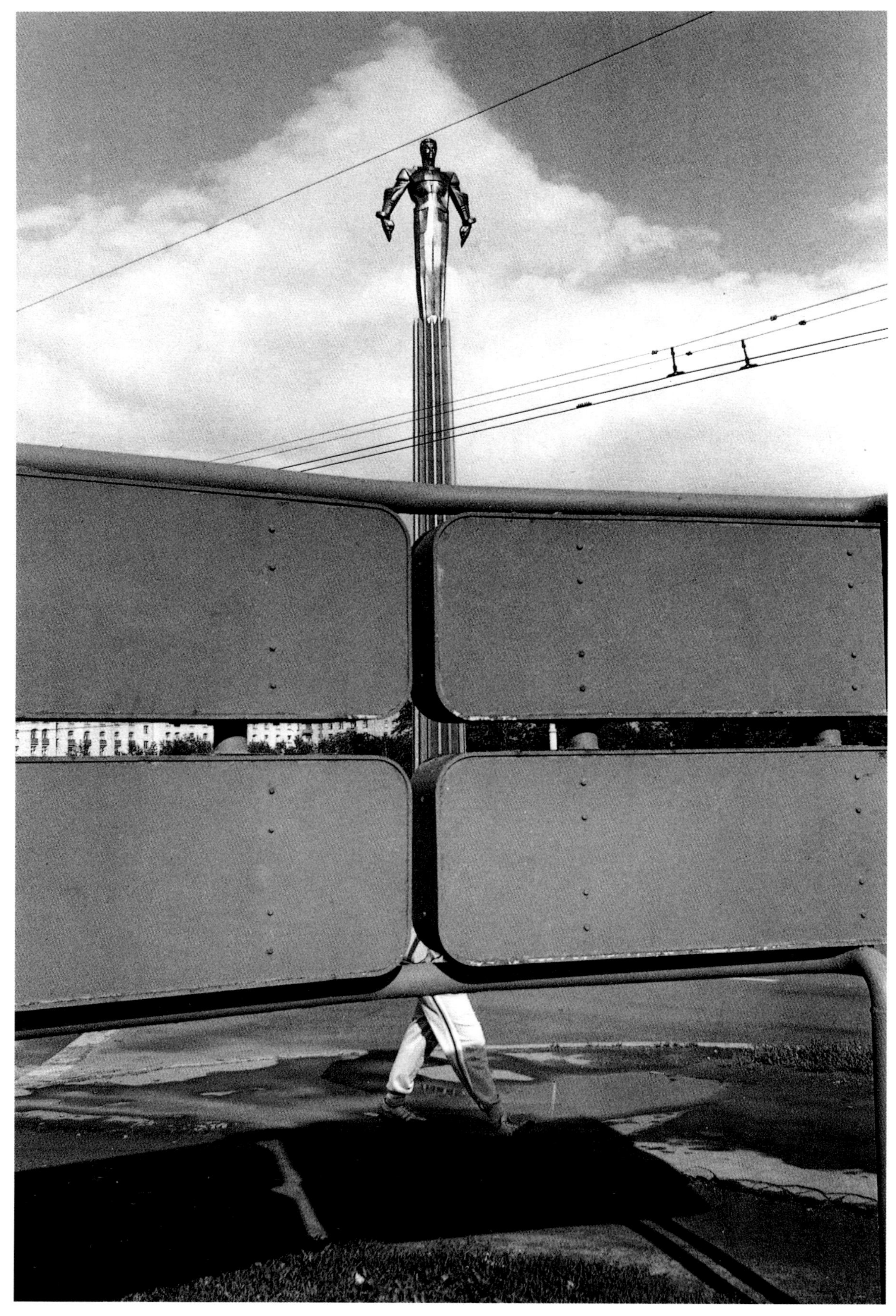

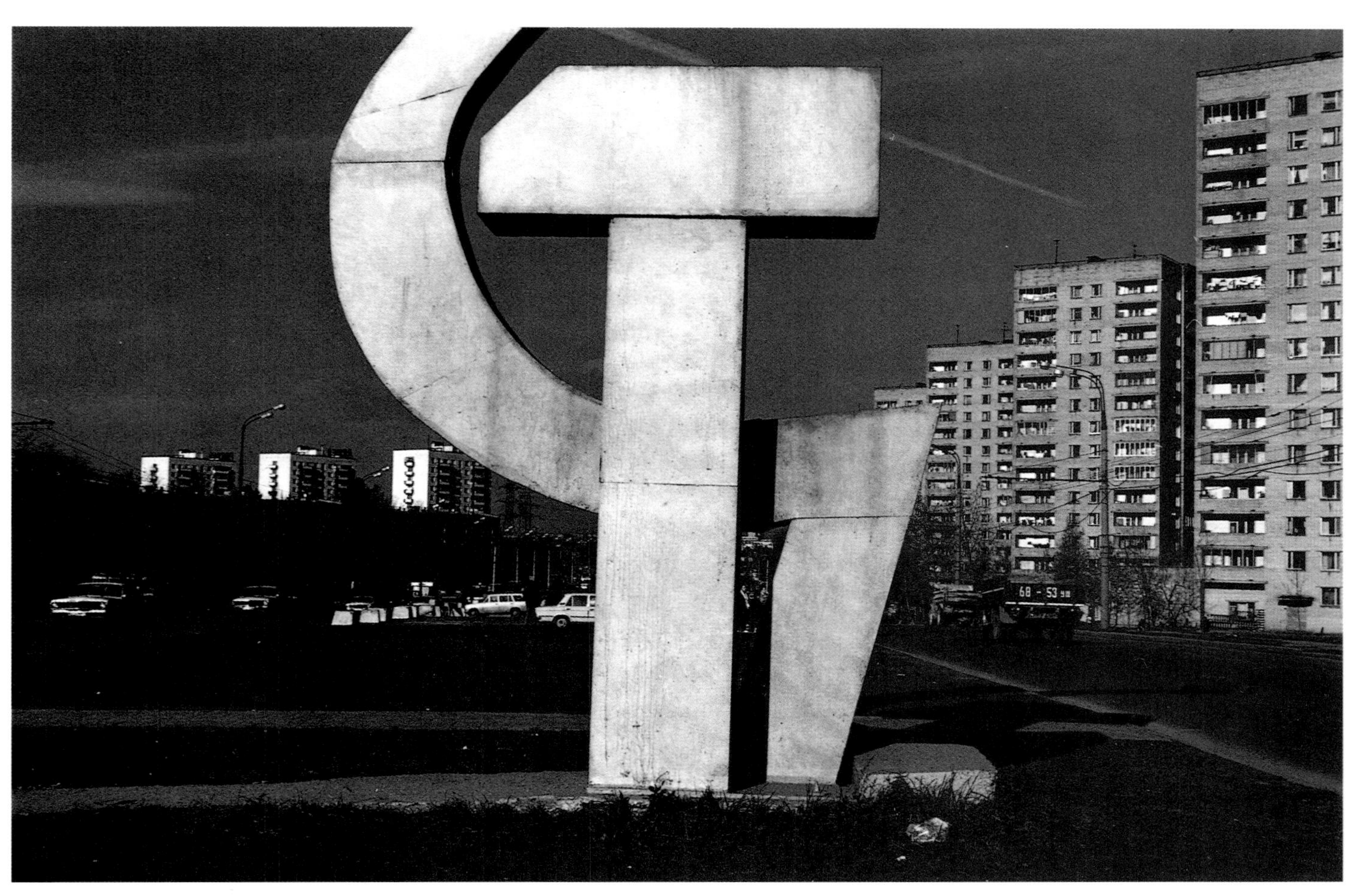

IGOR MOUKHIN
RESEARCH INVESTIGATION OF SOVIET
MONUMENTAL ARTS, 1989
4½ × 6½″

IGOR MOUKHIN
RESEARCH INVESTIGATION OF SOVIET
MONUMENTAL ARTS, 1990
6½ × 4″

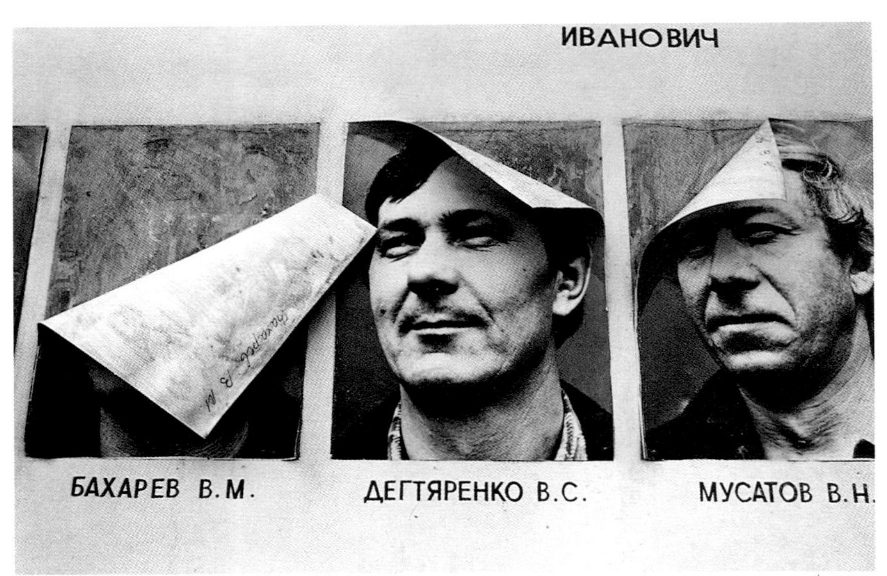
ИВАНОВИЧ
БАХАРЕВ В.М.
ДЕГТЯРЕНКО В.С.
МУСАТОВ В.Н.

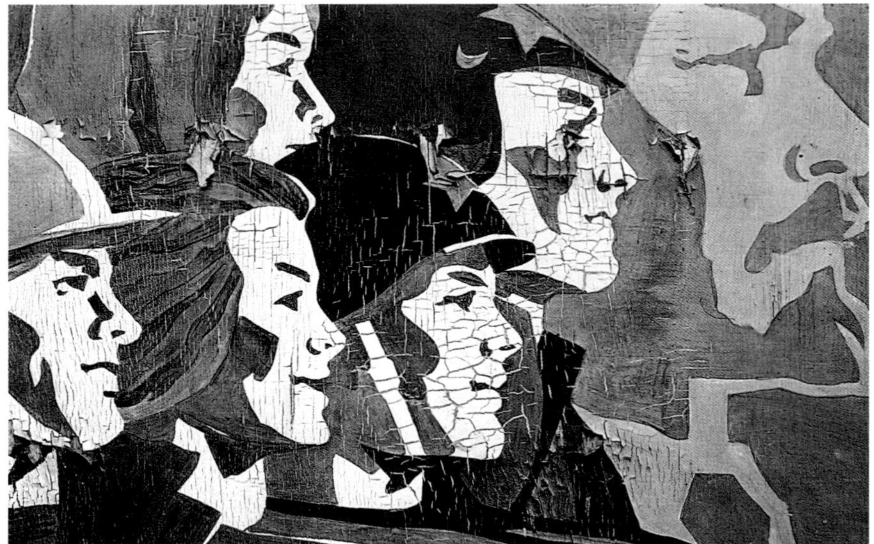

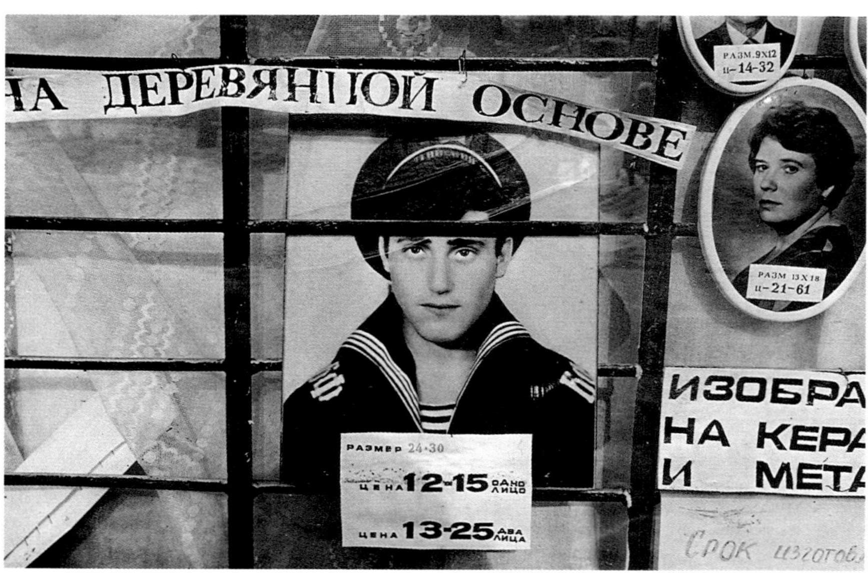
НА ДЕРЕВЯННОЙ ОСНОВЕ
РАЗМ.9Х12
Ц-14-32
РАЗМ 13Х18
Ц-21-61
ИЗОБРА
НА КЕРА
И МЕТА
РАЗМЕР 24-30
ЦЕНА 12-15 ОДНО ЛИЦО
ЦЕНА 13-25 ДВА ЛИЦА
Срок изготов

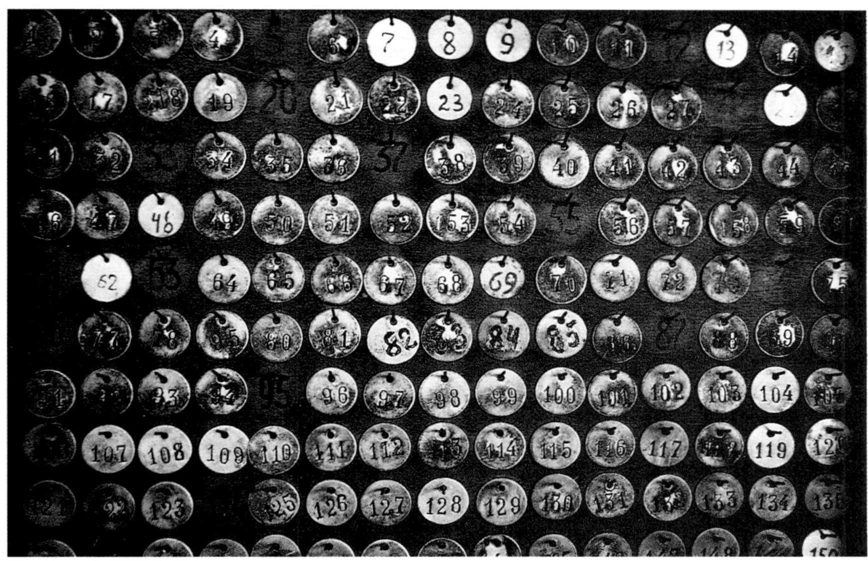

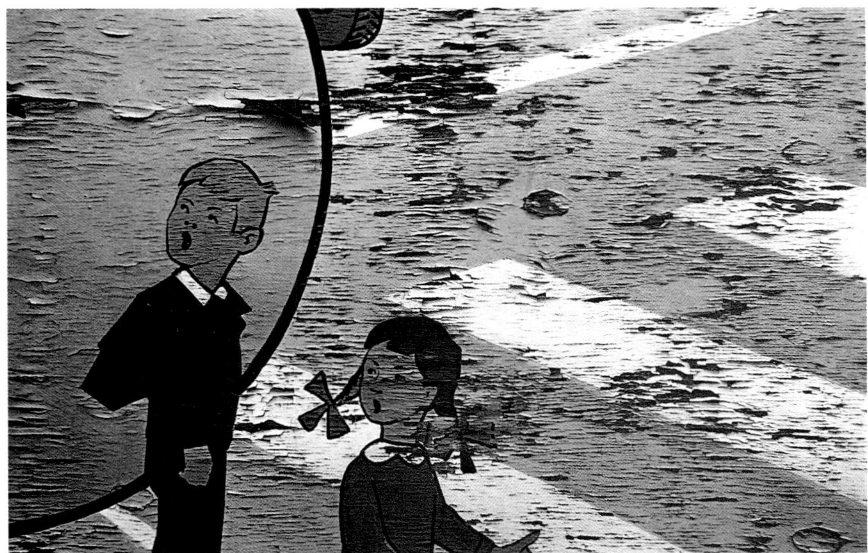

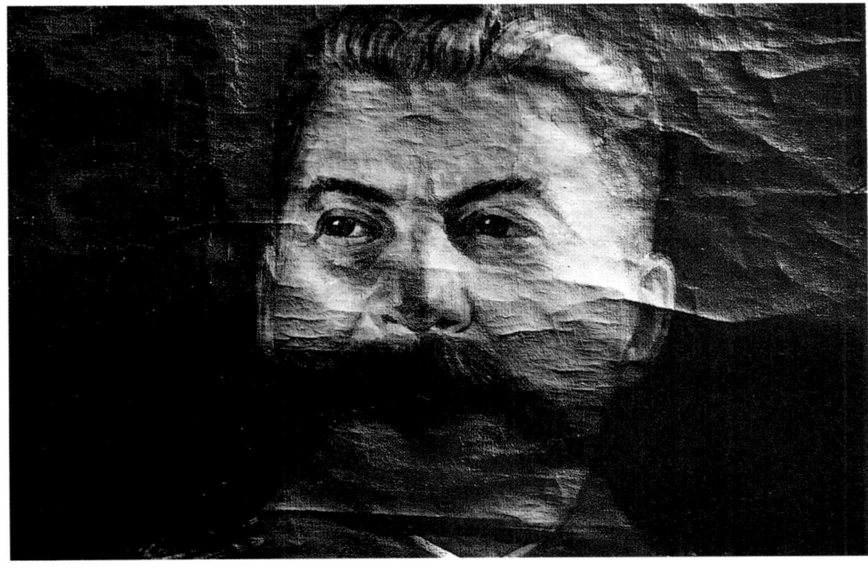

IGOR MOUKHIN
from the series:
FRAGMENTS, 1988–89
5 × 8″ (each)

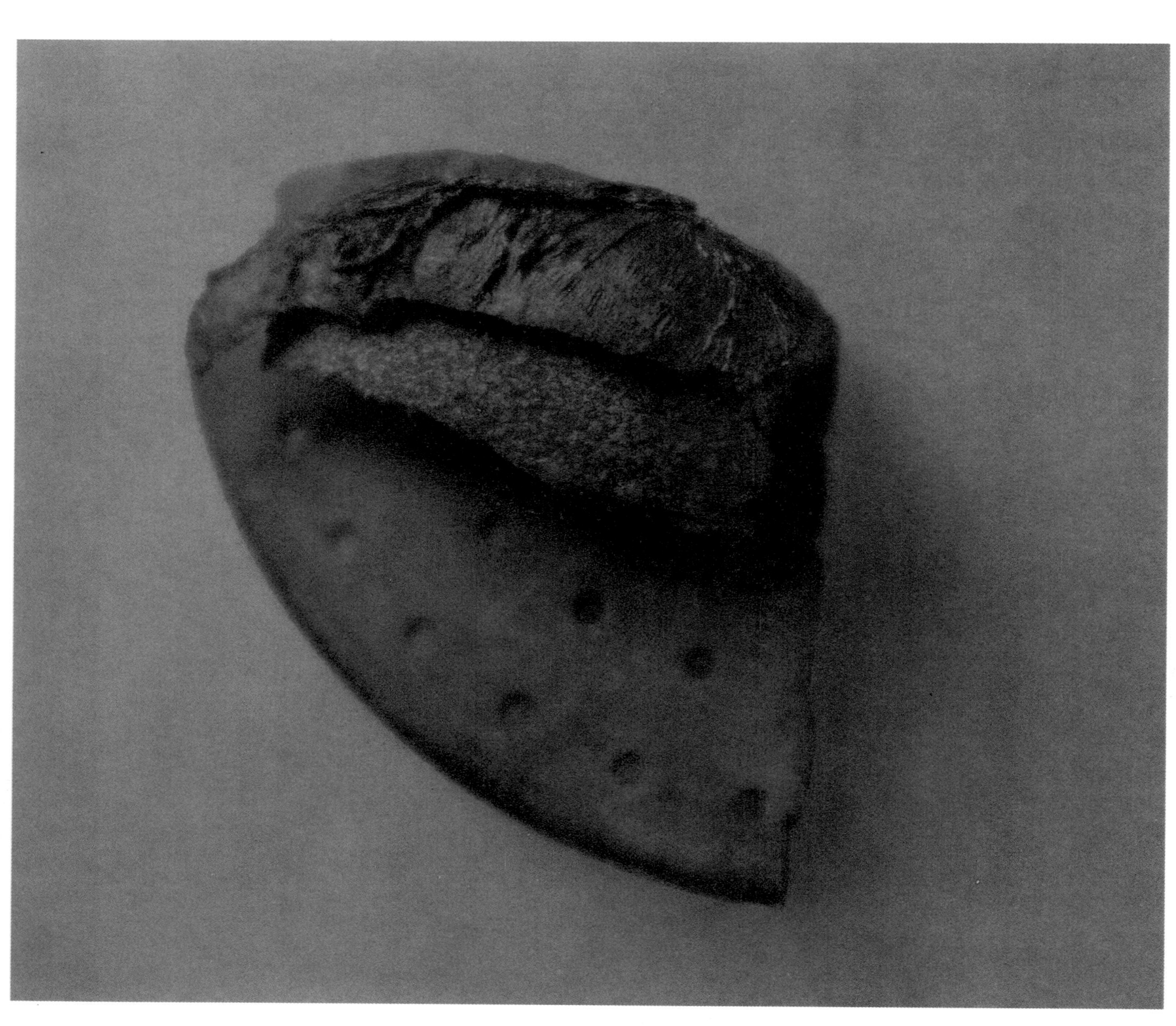

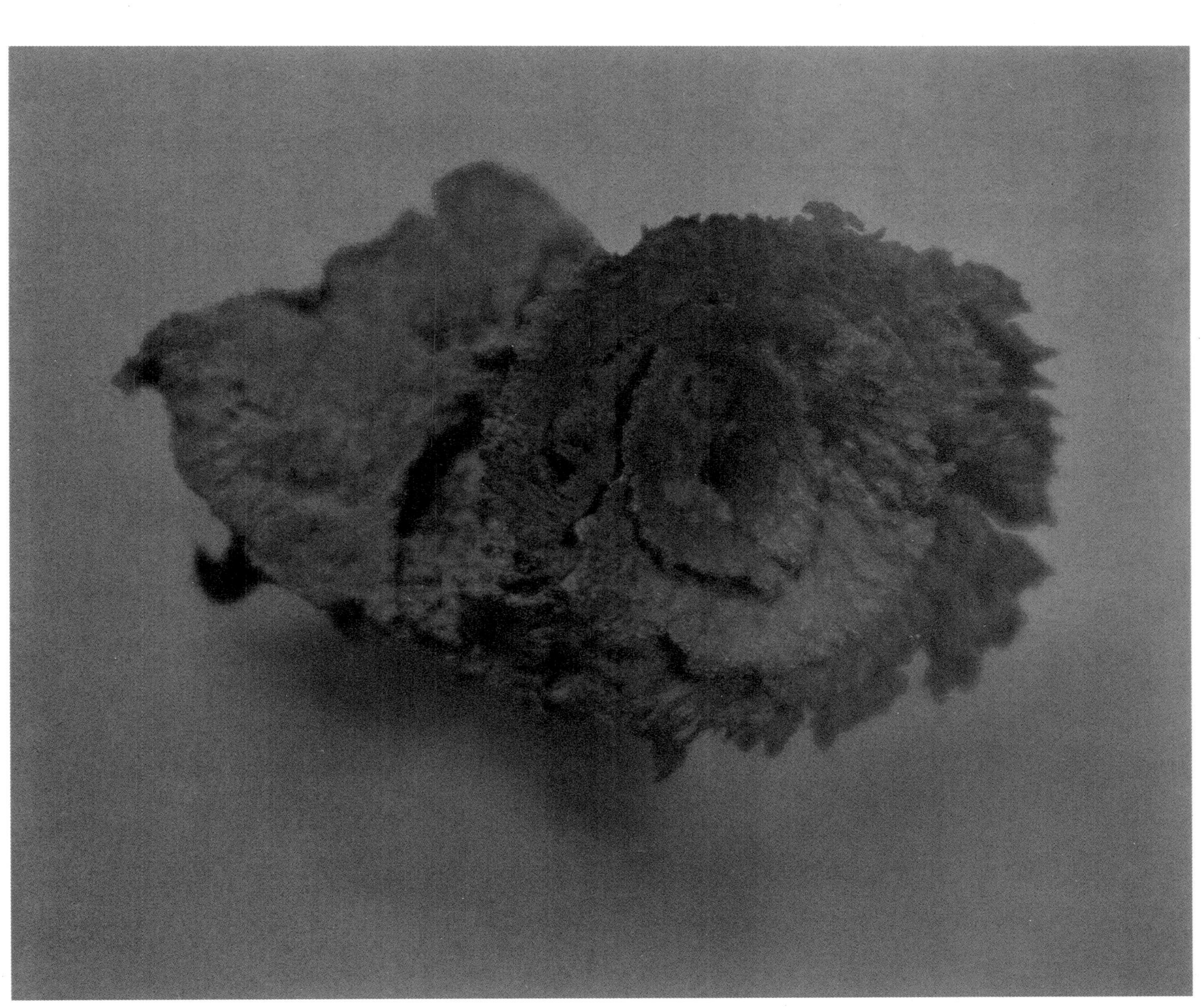

VLADISLAV EFIMOV
UNTITLED, 1989
6½ × 8″ (each)

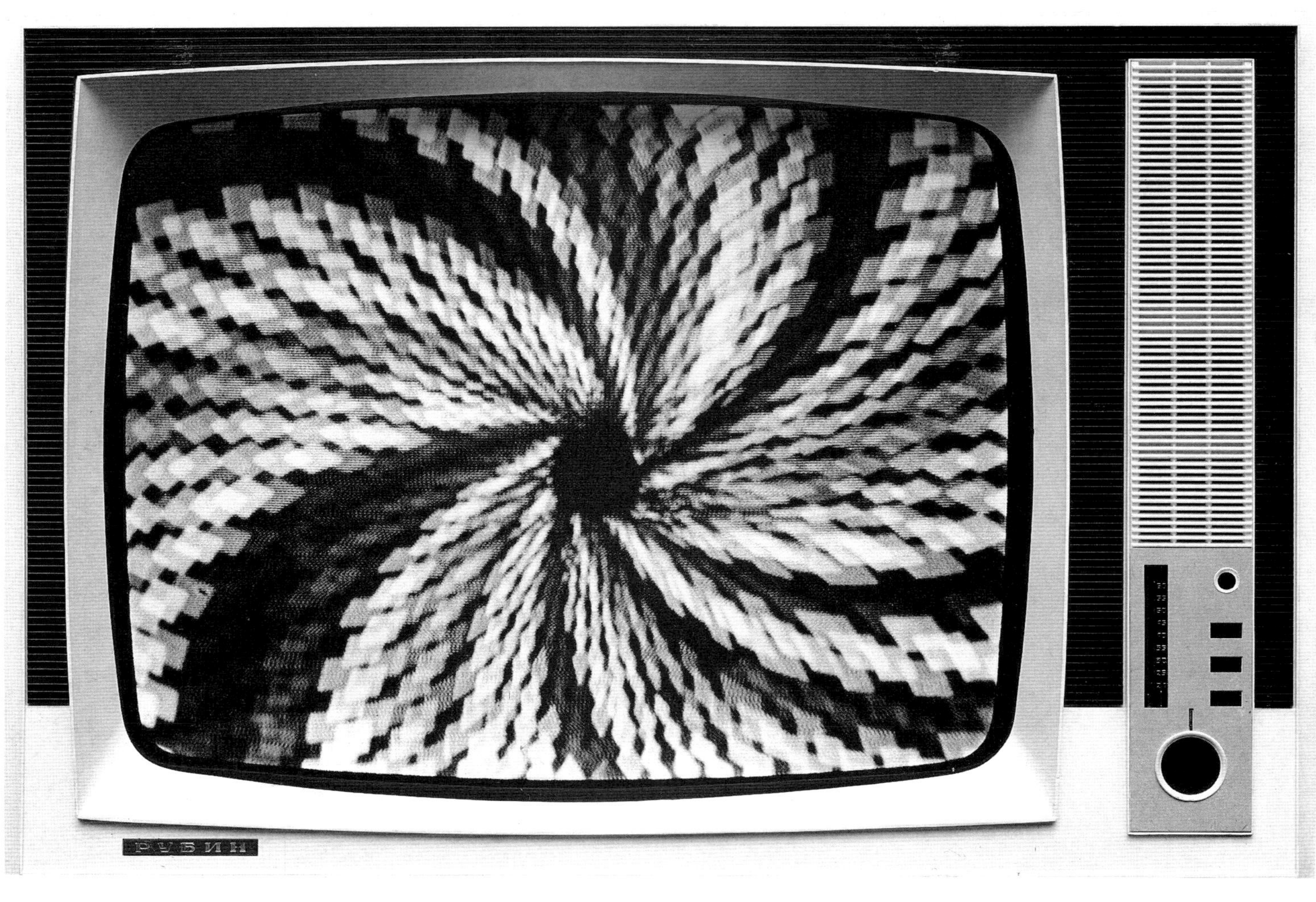
РУБИН

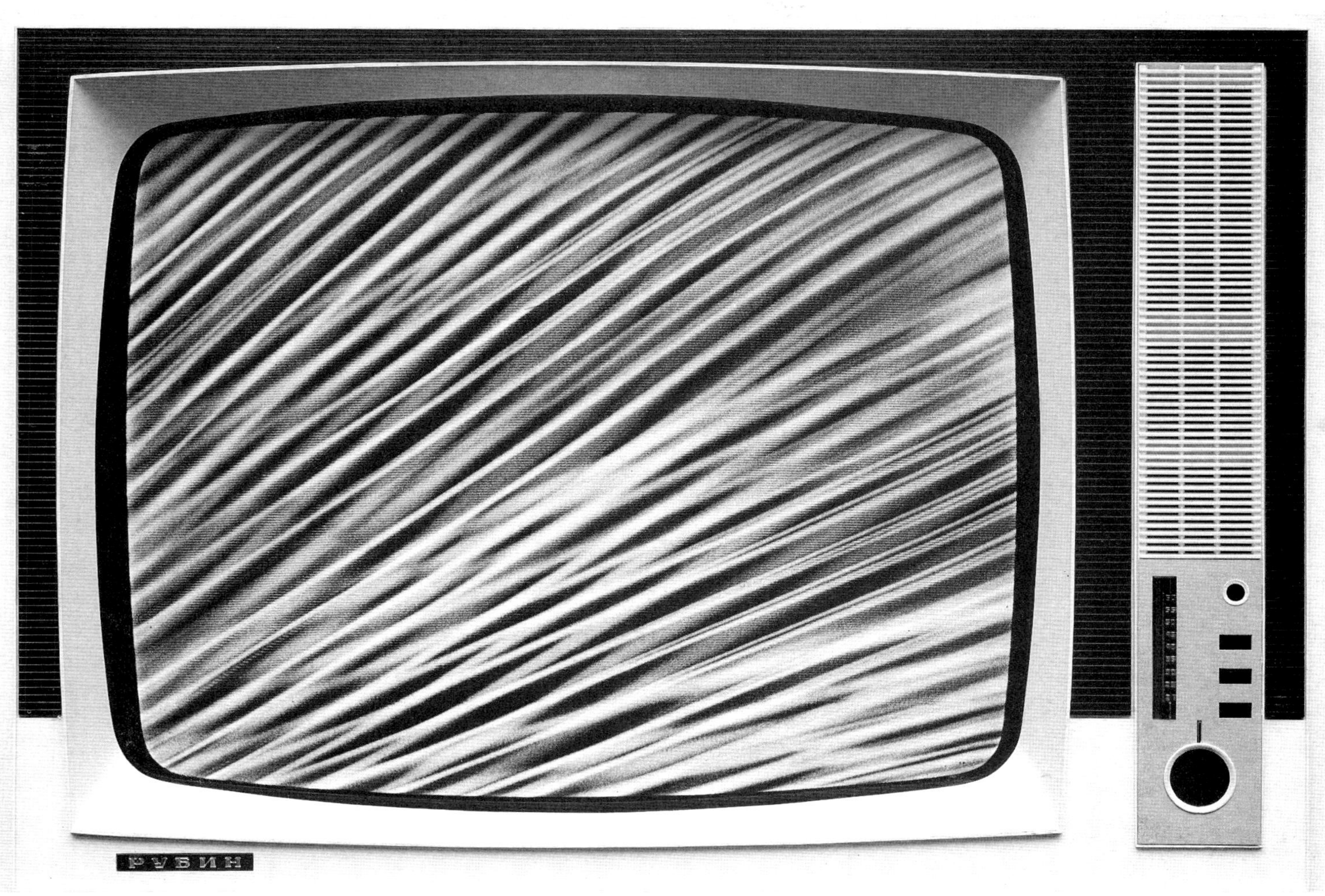

ALEXEY SHULGIN
from the series: TV SET, 1989
19¾ × 27½″ (each)

BORIS MIKHAILOV • VASSILY KRAVCHUK • TATIANA DANILOVA • VALERY STIGNEEV • VICTOR SHUROV • LUDMILA IVANOVA • EDWARD STRANADKO • VICTORIA STRANADKO • LEV MELIHOV • IGOR STOMACHIN • MARIA SNIGIREVSKAYA • VLADISLAV MIKHAILOV • NICHOLAI BACHAREV • BORIS SMELOV • VLADIMIR FILONOV • SERGEY OSMACHKIN • PAVEL KISELEV • MIKHAIL LADEISHIKOV

INDEPENDENTS

Among the artists who work apart from active participation in a group, there are individual relationships that encourage creativity and exchange. Boris Mikhailov, for instance, is loosely affiliated with the Moscow group; father and daughter Boris Smelov and Maria Snigirevskaya also enjoy a mentor-student relationship; Lev Melihov and Vassily Kravchuk share materials and a love of portraiture as well as friendship. These independent photographers often draw inspiration from life in communities: small towns, rural areas, religious and civic fellowships, as well as from other artists. Their work frequently focuses on the shared lives within the community and the community's ties to its rich, cultural traditions.

A vital dynamic exists in the Soviet Union among various circles of artists and independents as they explore their relationships abroad as well as resources at home. The independent artists play a pivotal role connecting communities of artists and providing alternative perspectives and fresh dialogue.

BORIS MIKHAILOV, KHARKOV
from the series: SOTS-ART, 1990/90
23½ × 18½"

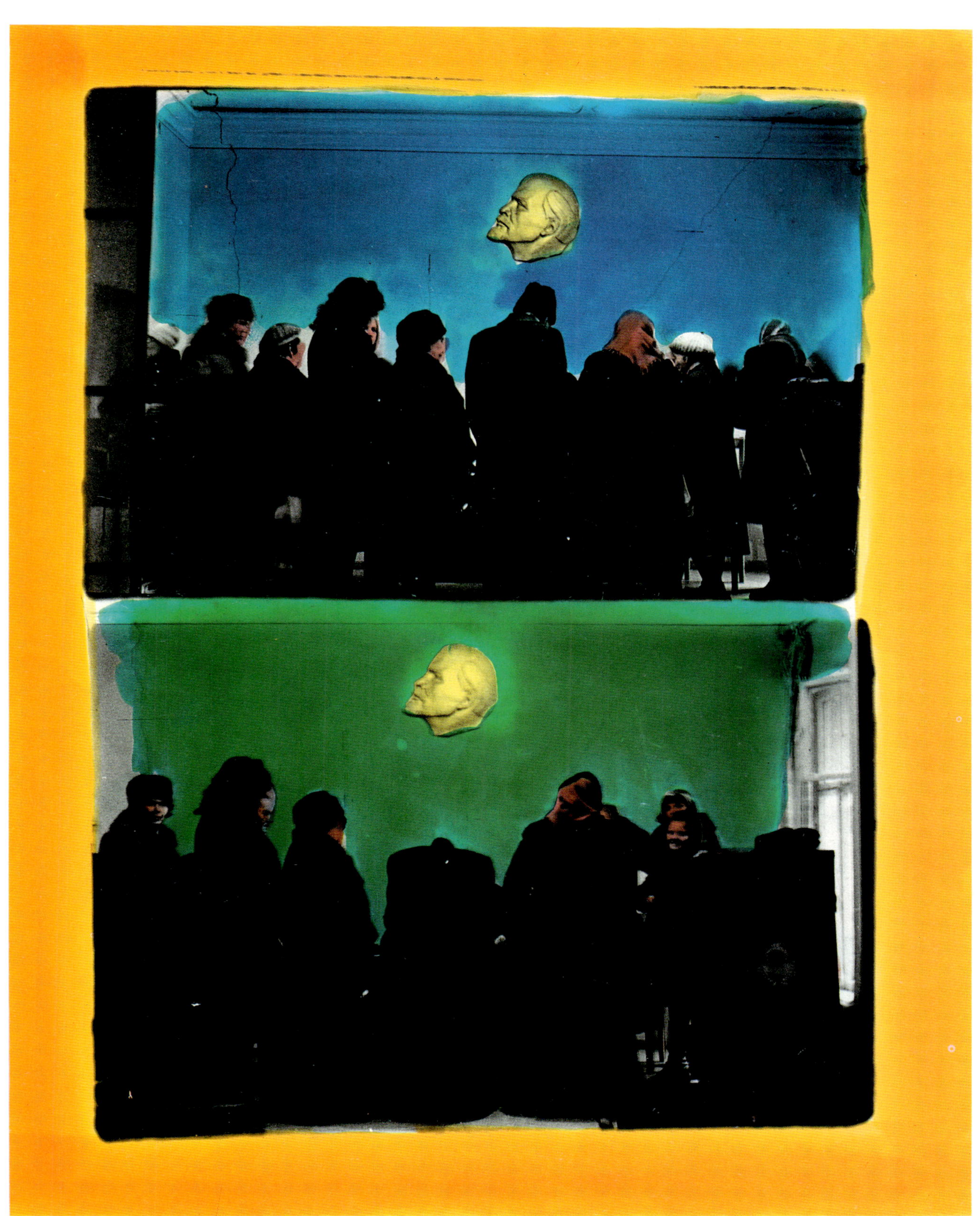

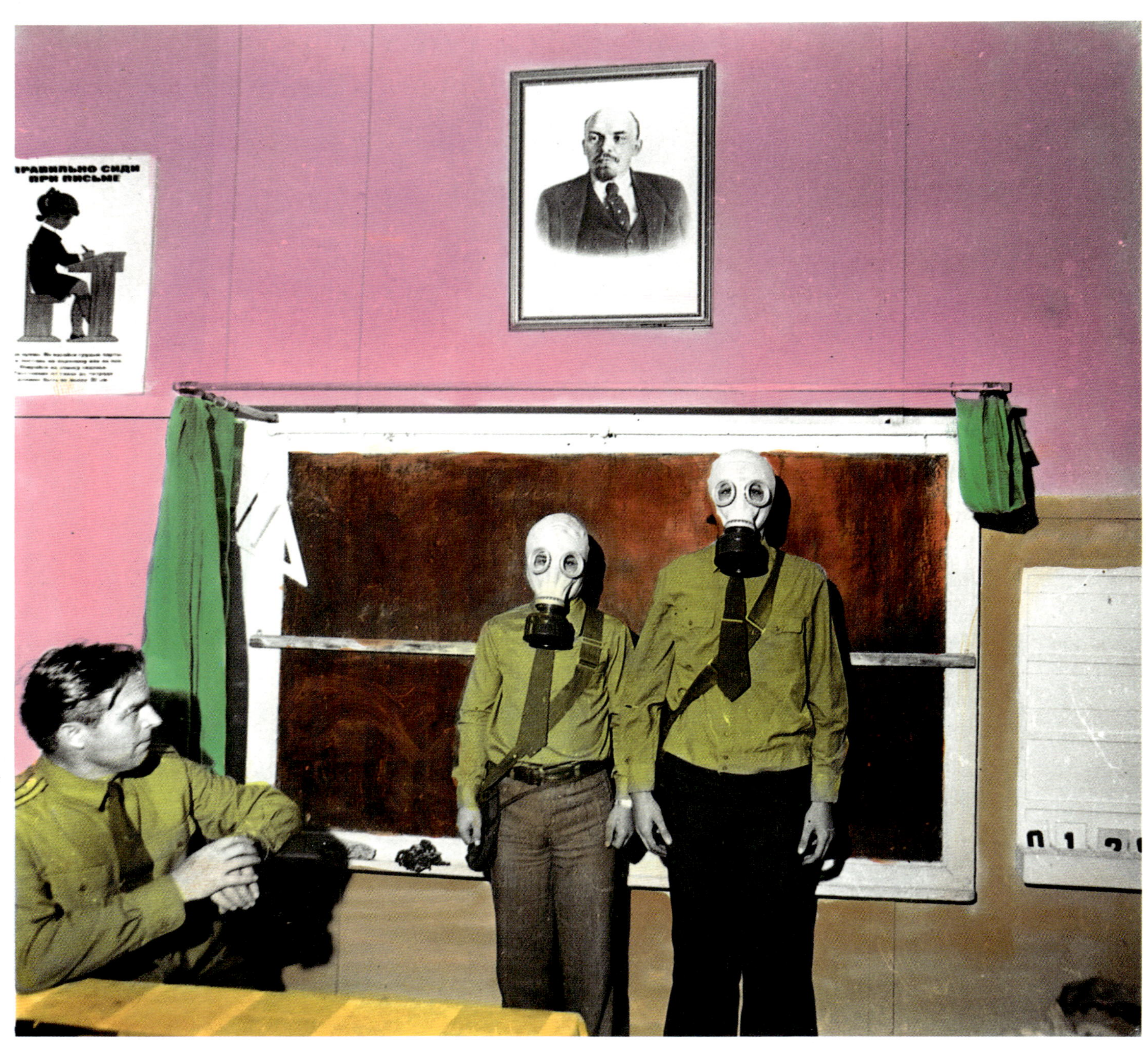

BORIS MIKHAILOV, KHARKOV
from the series: SOTS-ART, 1975/90
23½ × 31½"

BORIS MIKHAILOV, KHARKOV
from the series: SOTS-ART, 1987/89
23 × 18½"

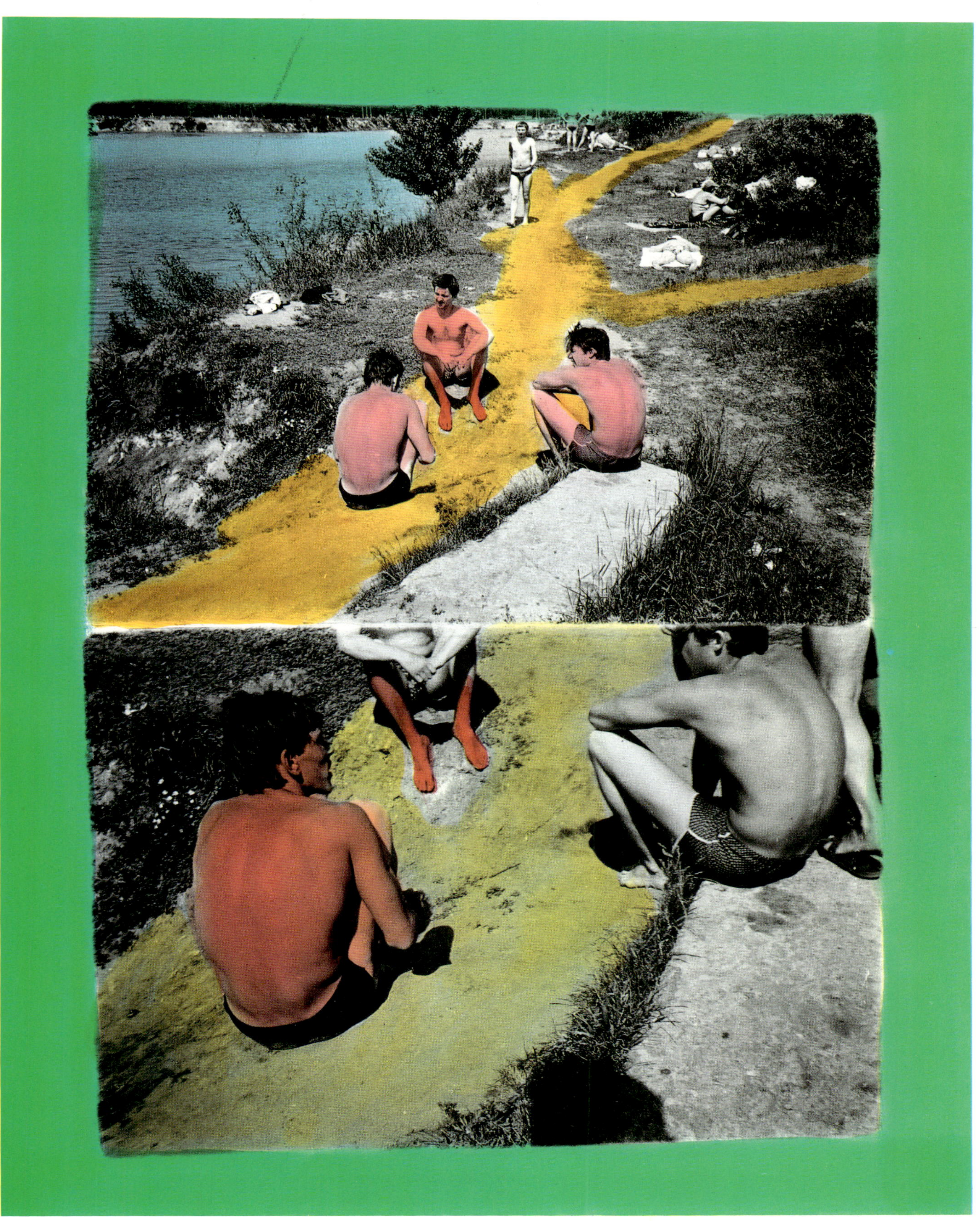

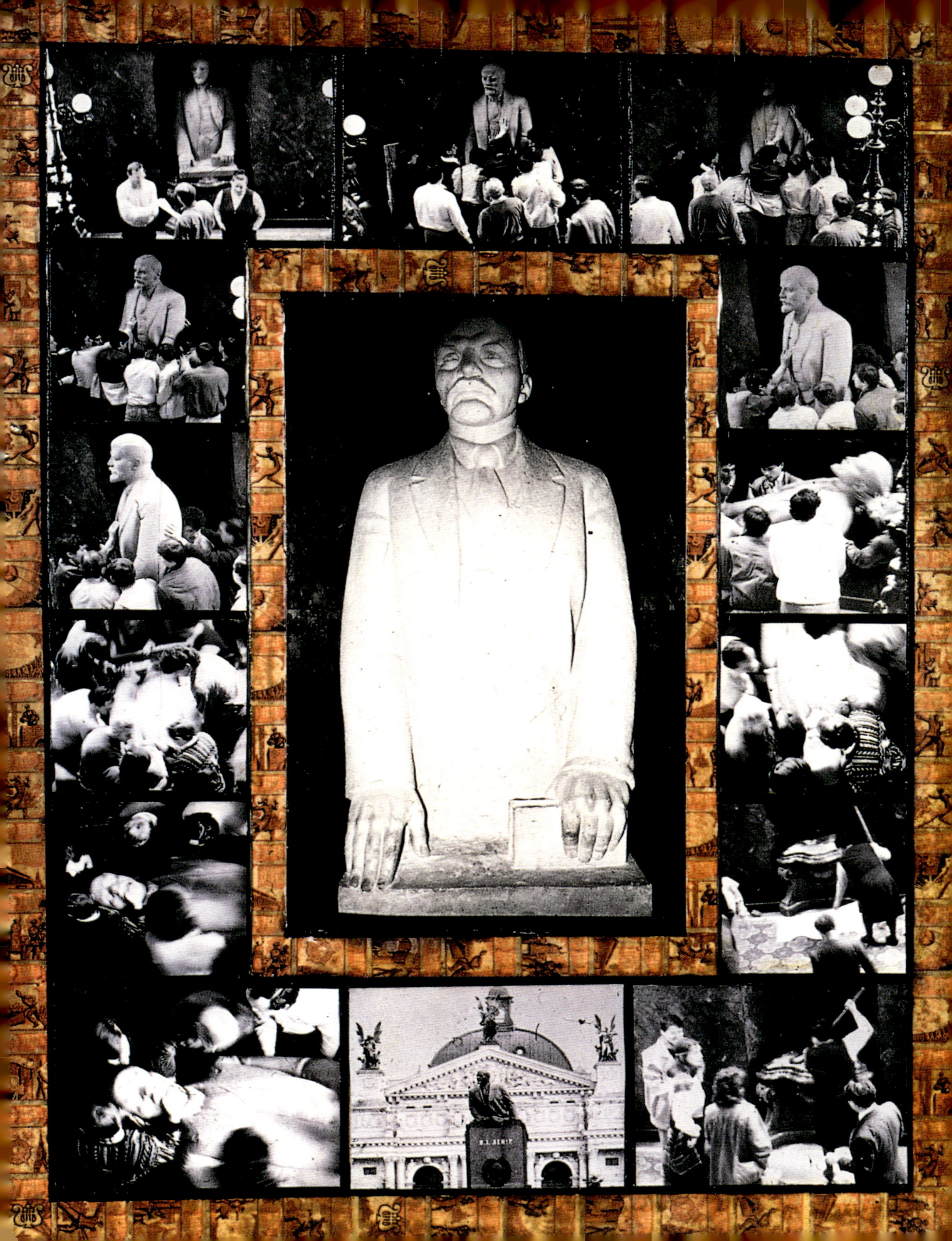

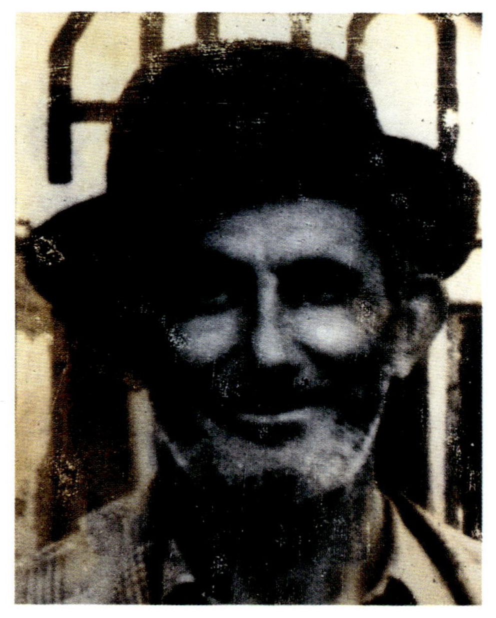

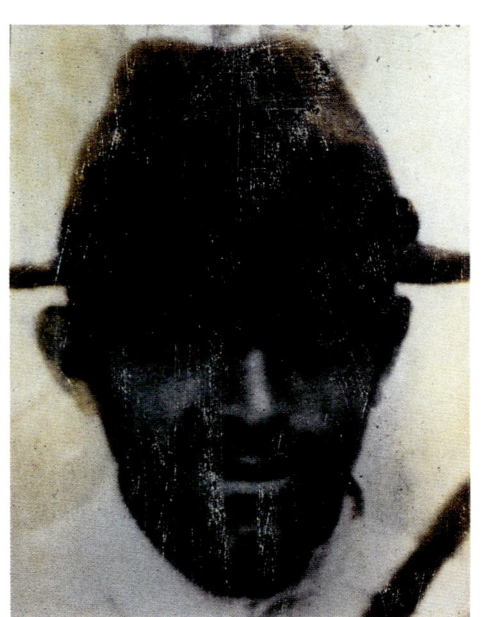

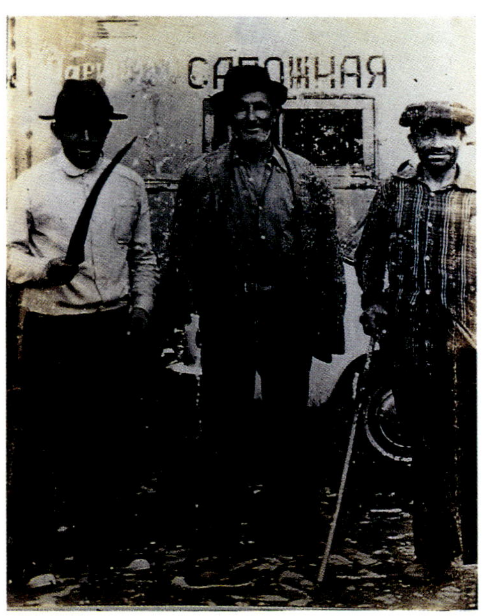

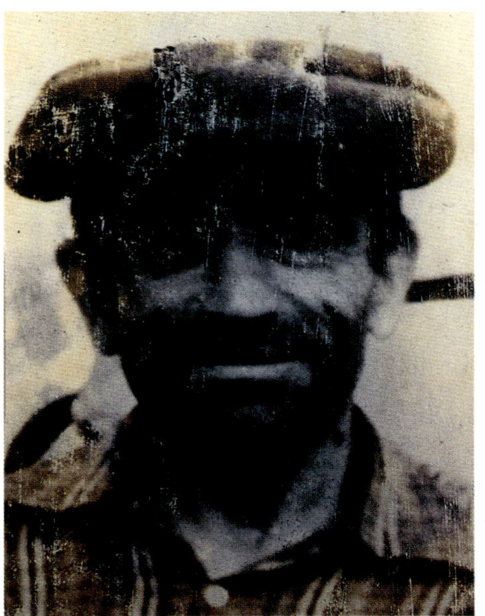

Opposite:
VASSILY KRAVCHUK, MOSCOW
LENIN, 1917–1990, 1990
31½ × 23½"

VASSILY KRAVCHUK, MOSCOW
KUBACHY, DAGESTAN, 1985/90
15½ × 12" (each)

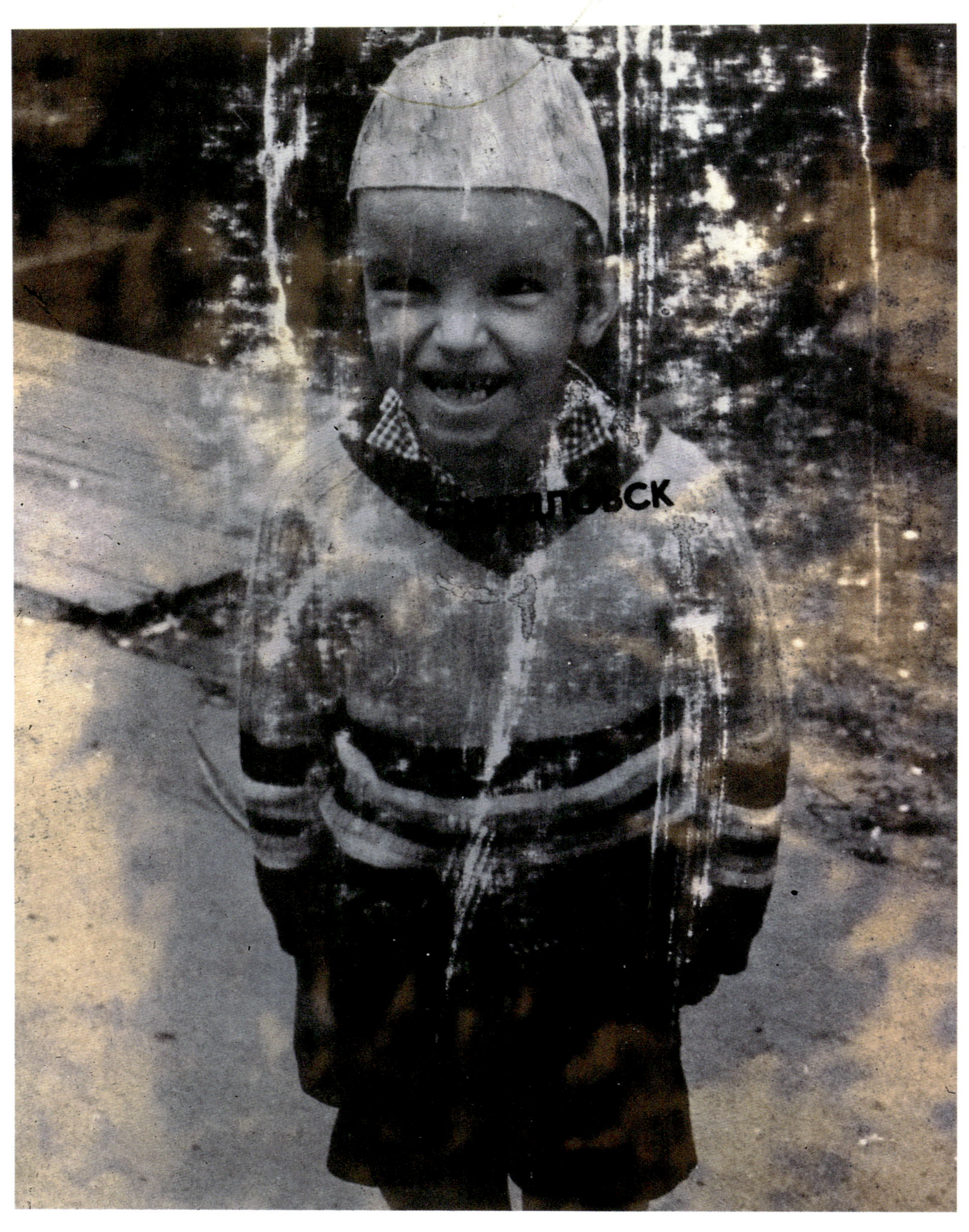

VASSILY KRAVCHUK, MOSCOW
SVERDLOVSK, BOY KIRIL, 1986/90
15½ × 12″ (each)

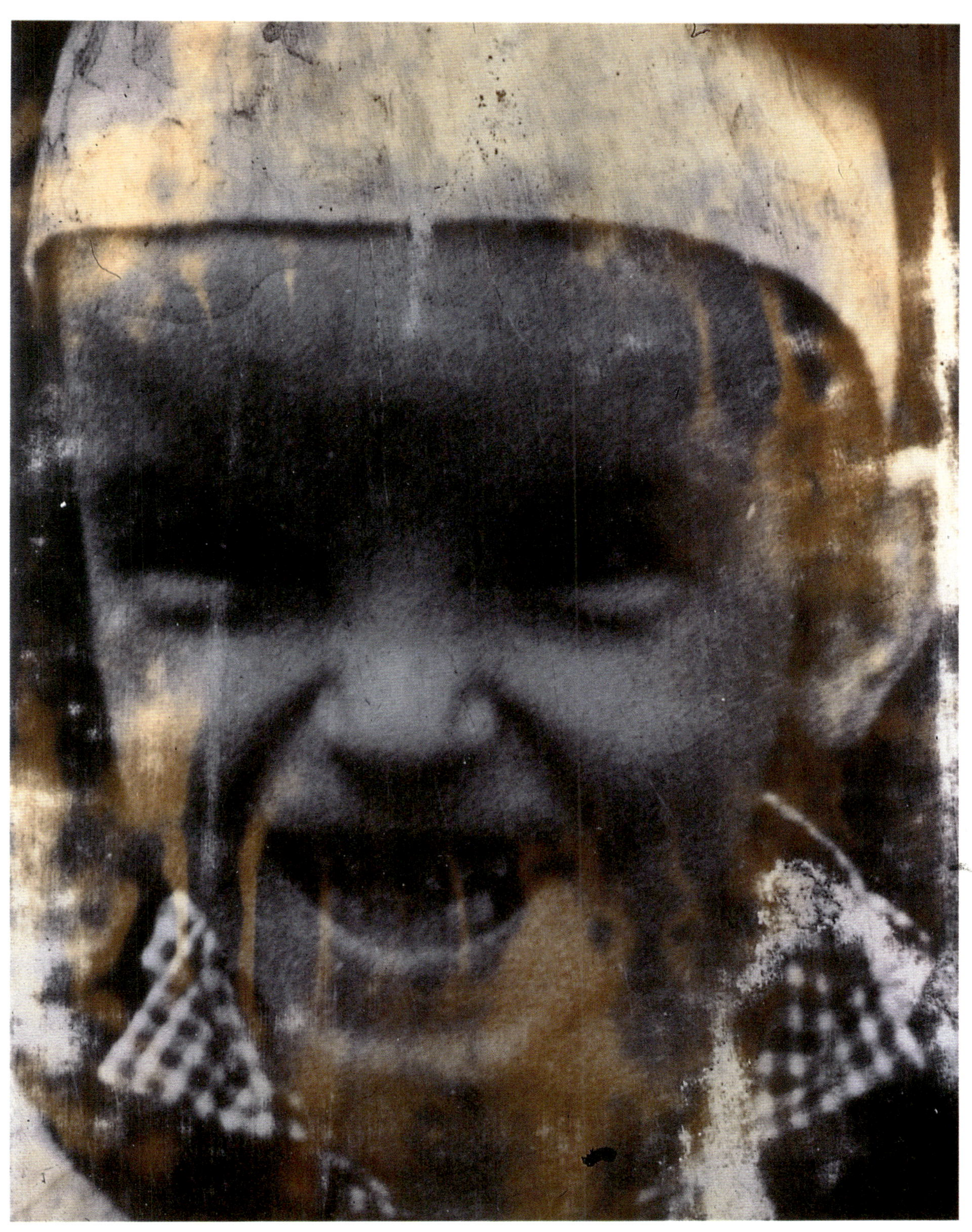

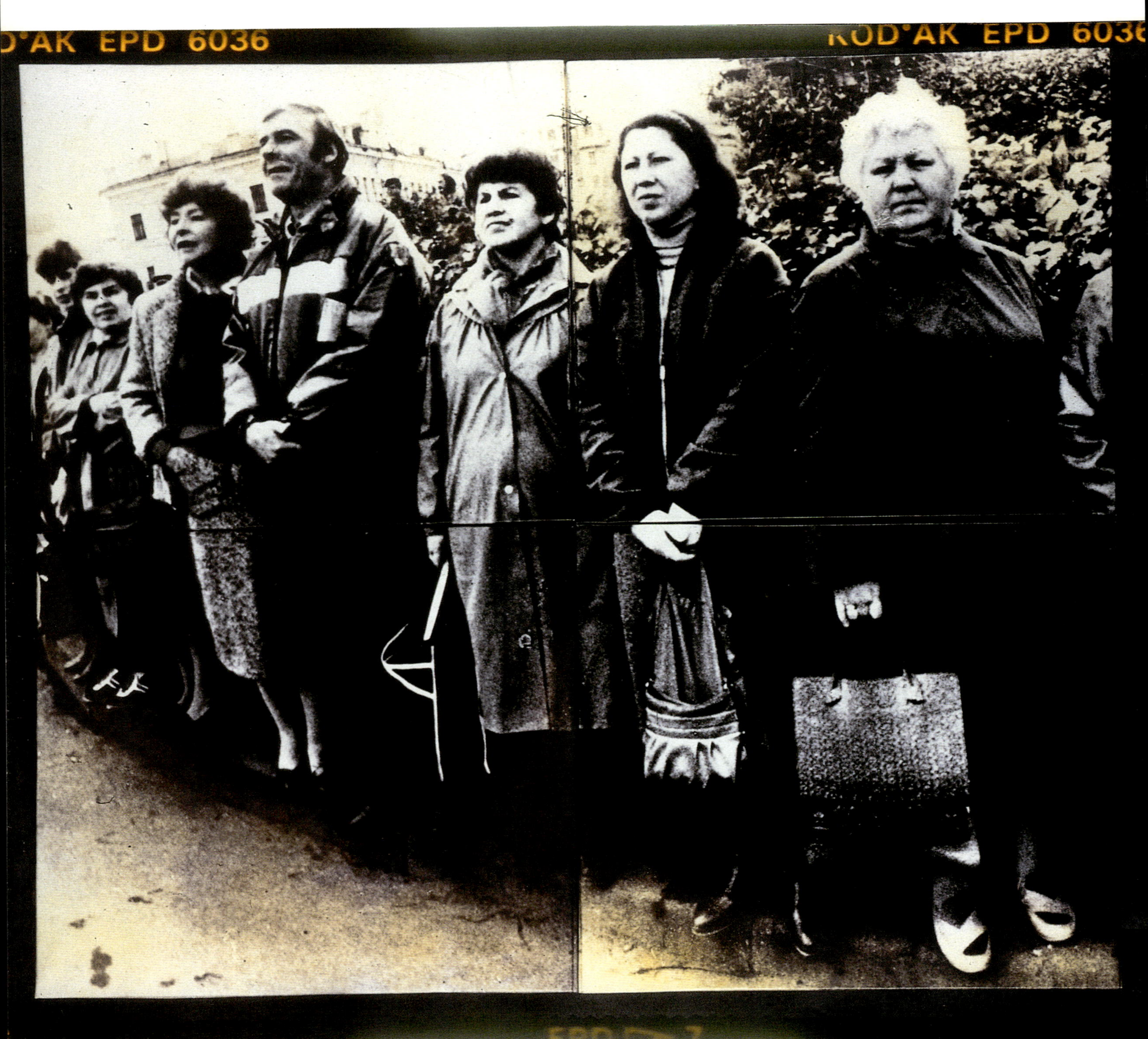
D'AK EPD 6036
KOD'AK EPD 6036

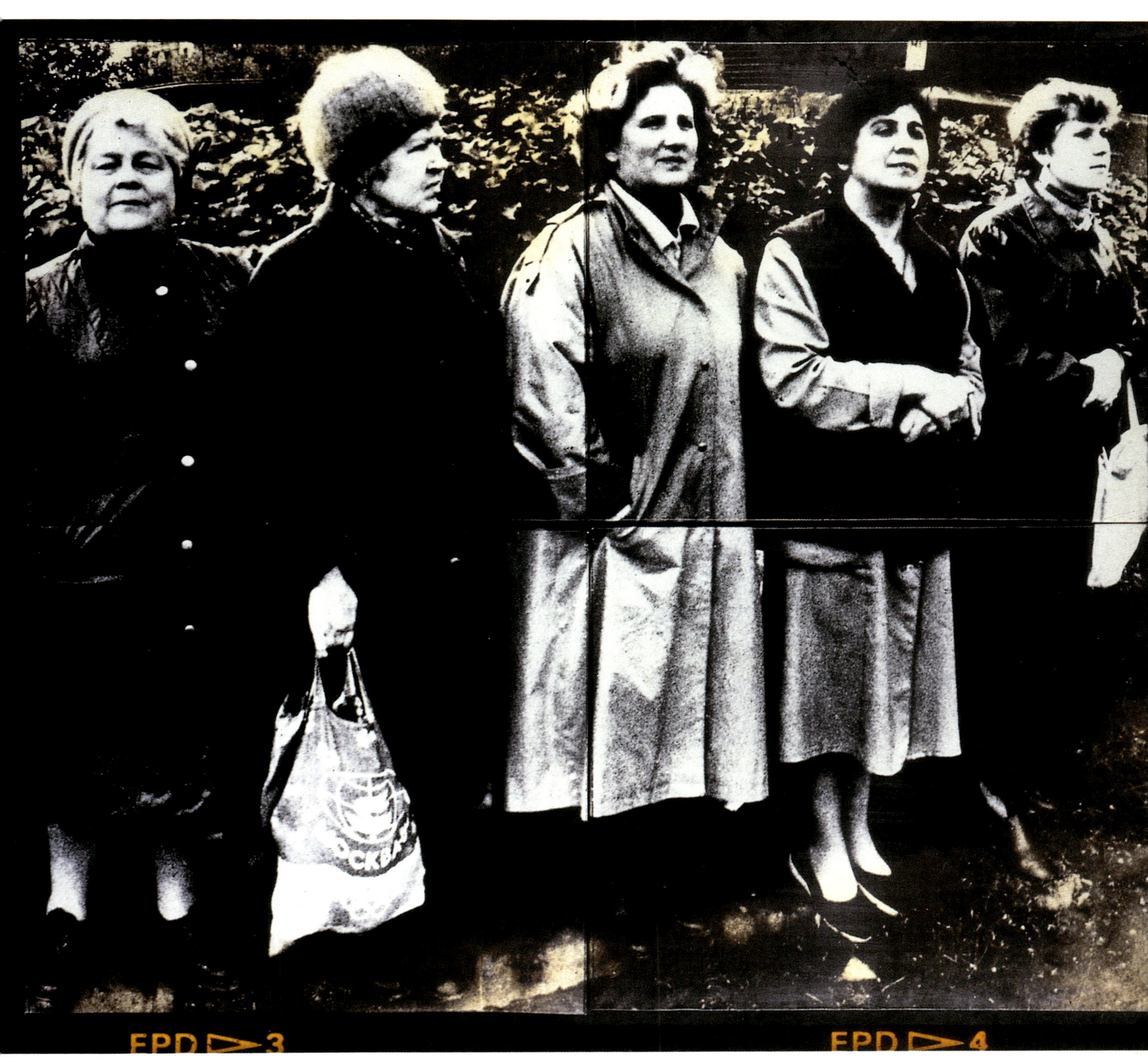

VASSILY KRAVCHUK, MOSCOW
MOSCOW DAY, 1987/90
39½ × 86½″

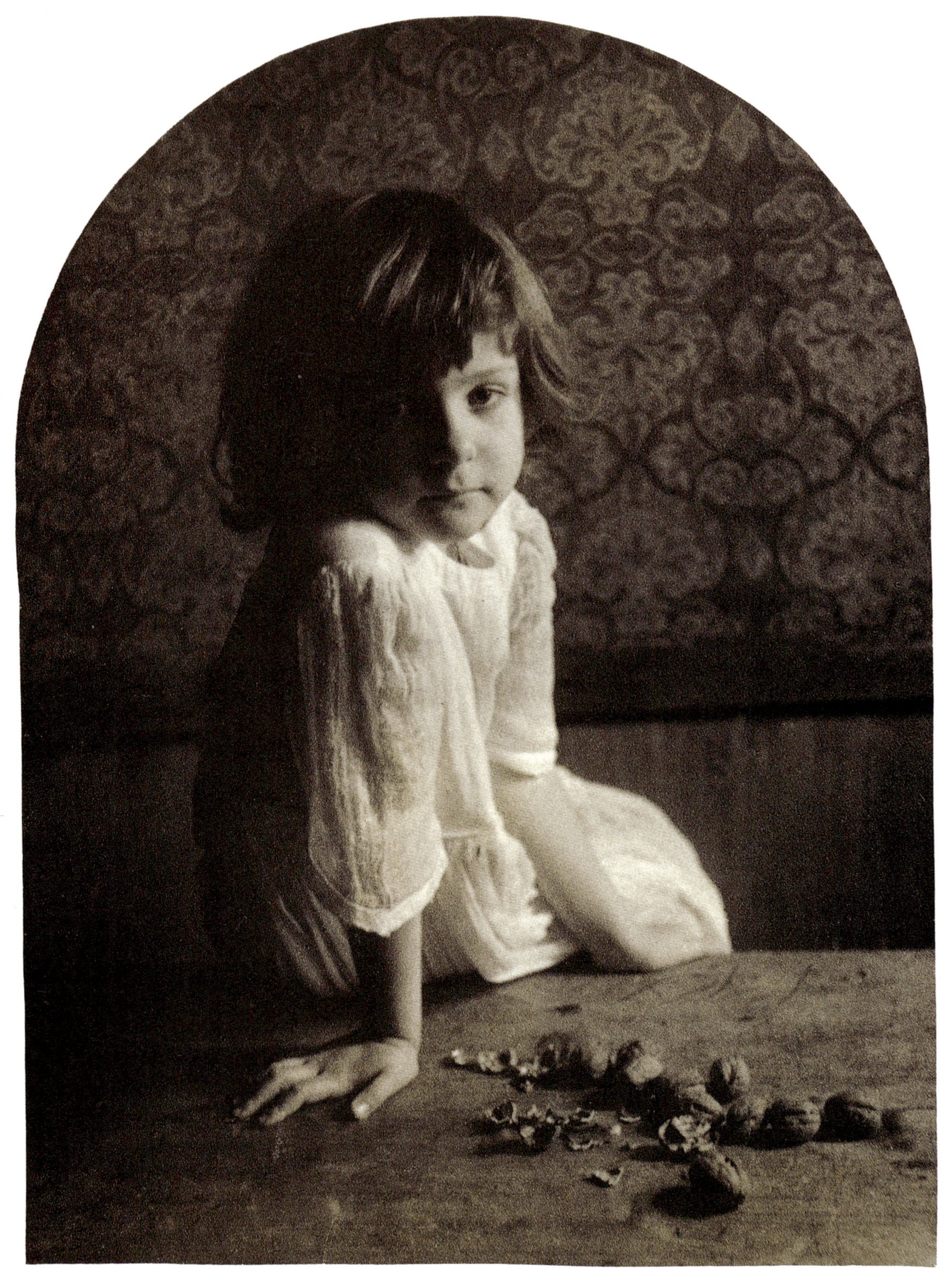

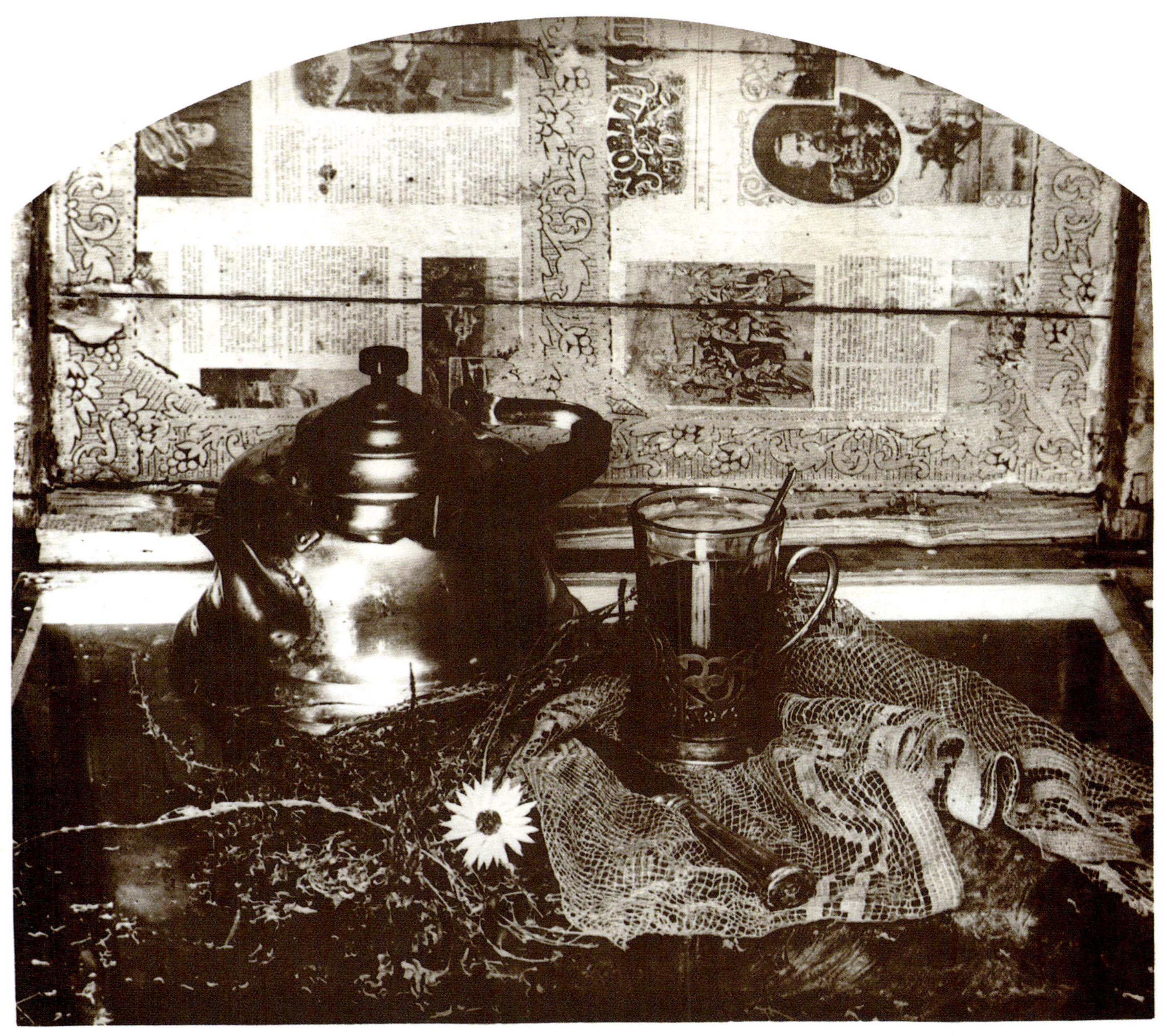

TATIANA DANILOVA, PSKOV
A TEAPOT AND A GLASS, 1990
6½ × 7″

TATIANA DANILOVA, PSKOV
A GIRL, 1990
7 × 5″

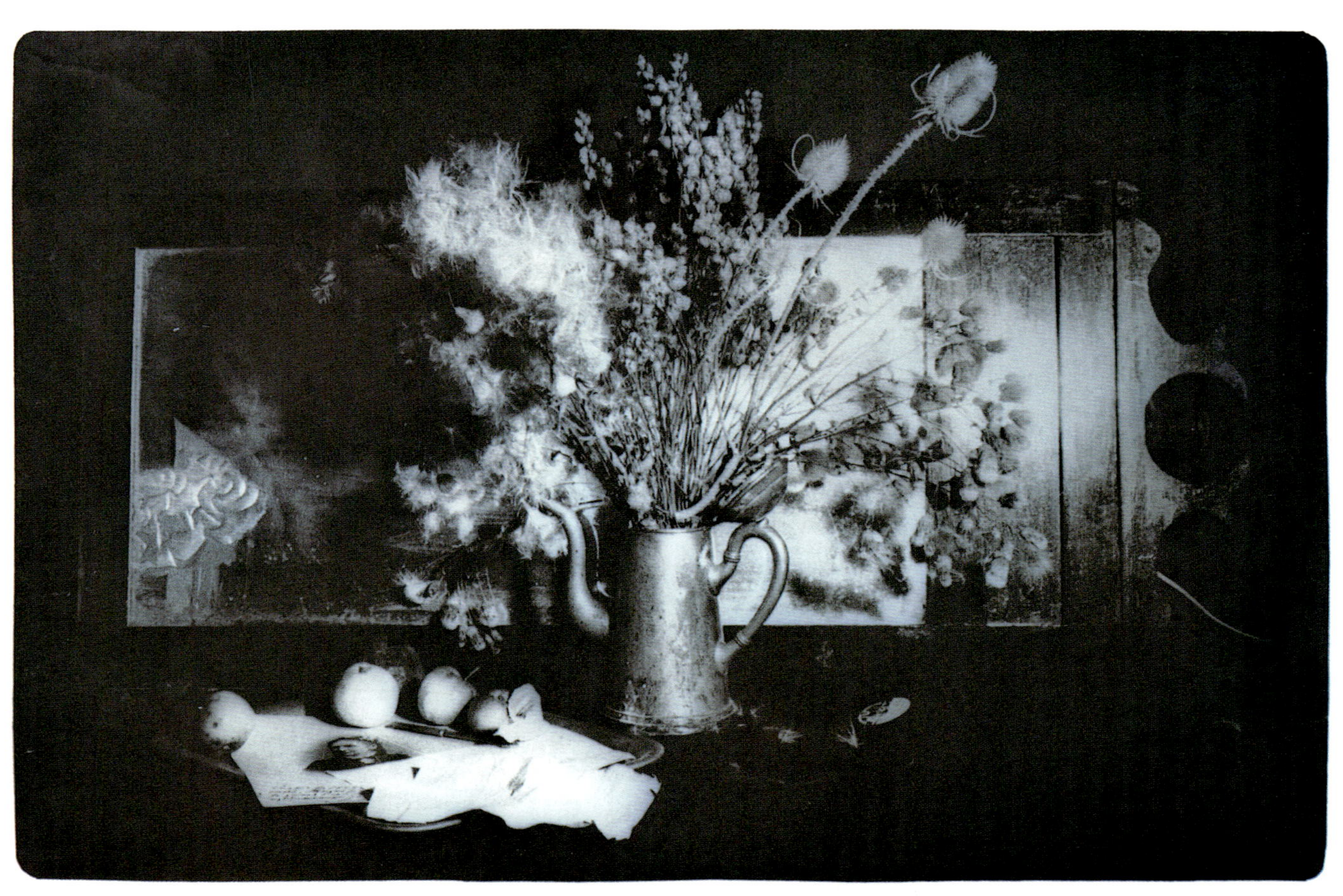

TATIANA DANILOVA, PSKOV
DRY BOUQUET, 1990
5 × 8″

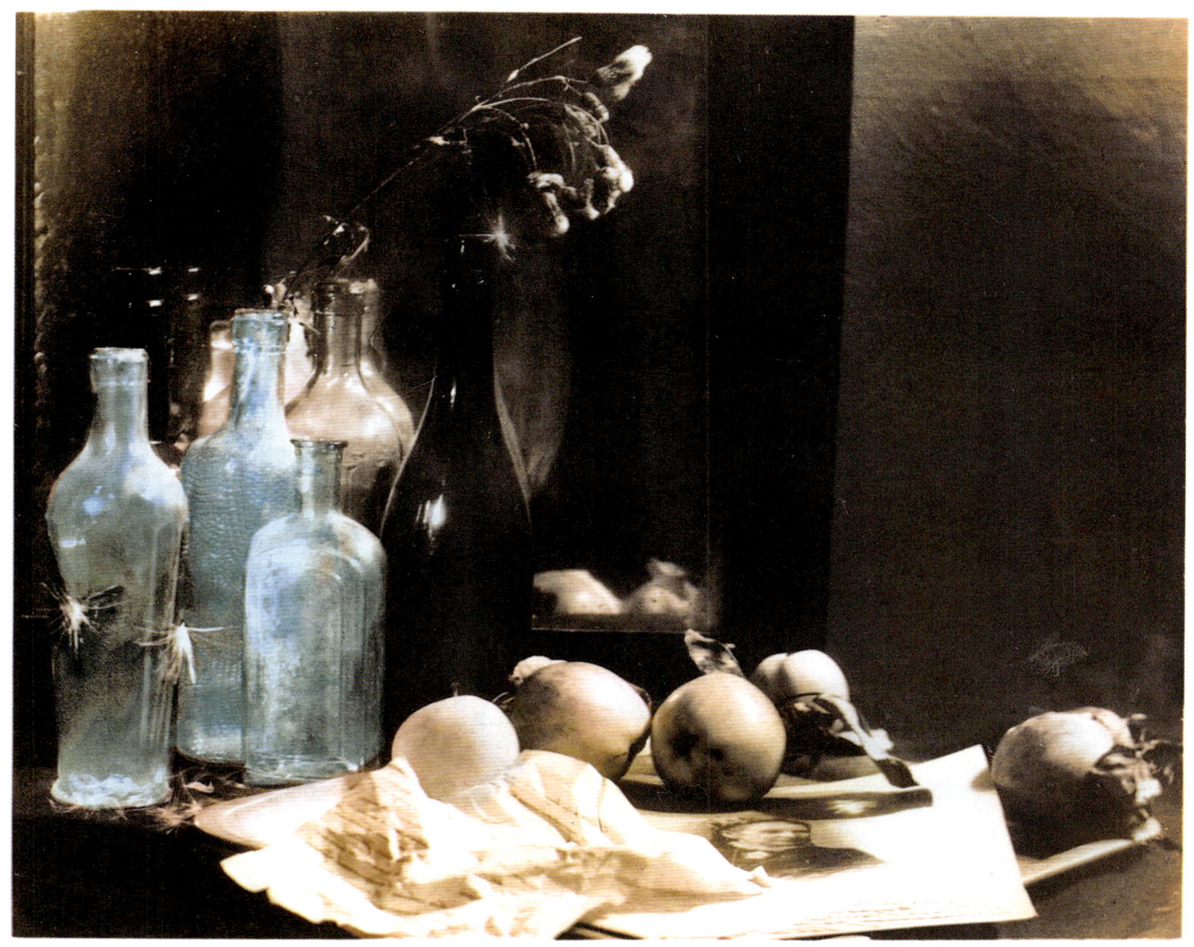

TATIANA DANILOVA, PSKOV
BLUE BOTTLES, 1990
4½ × 5½″

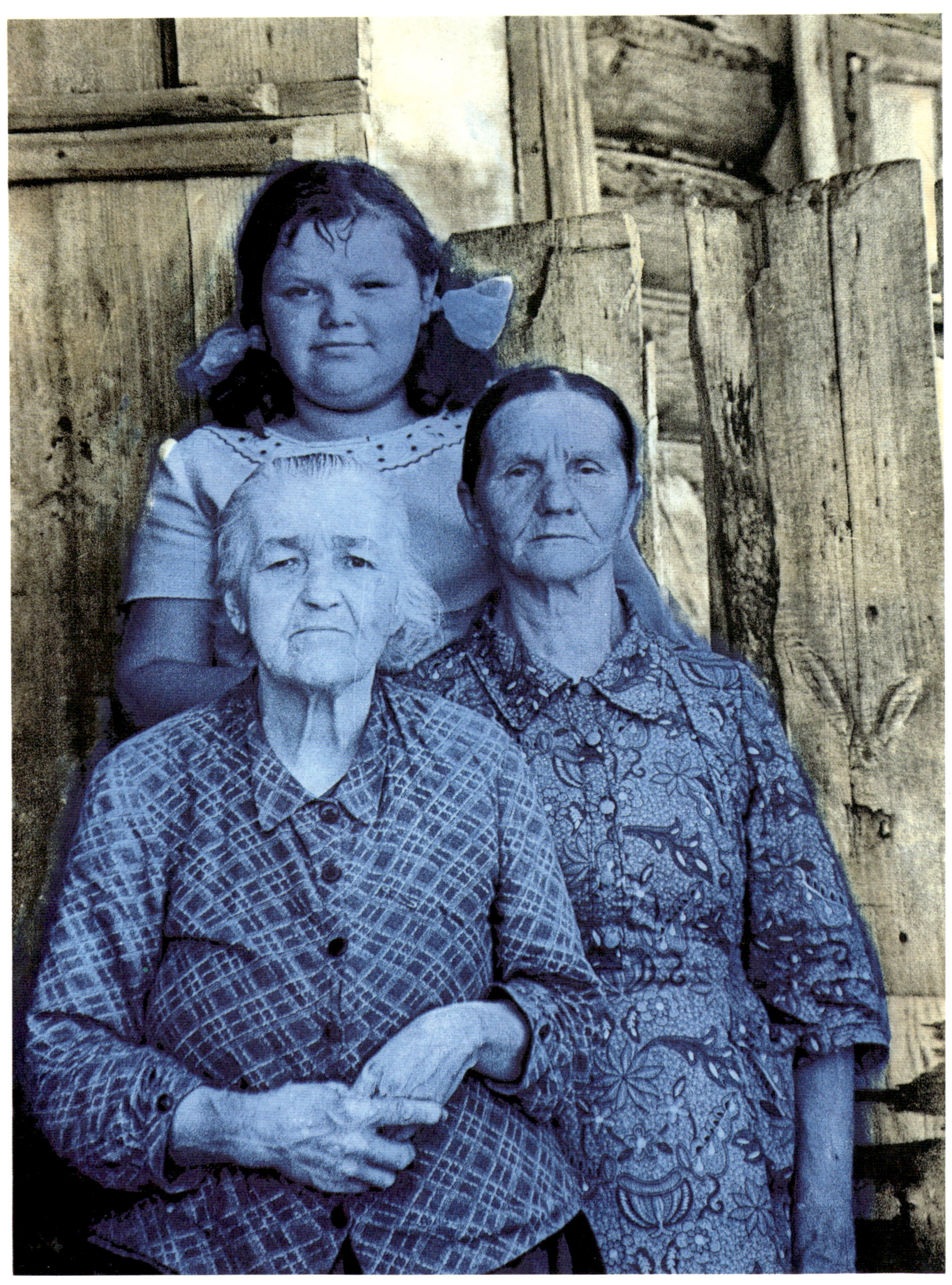

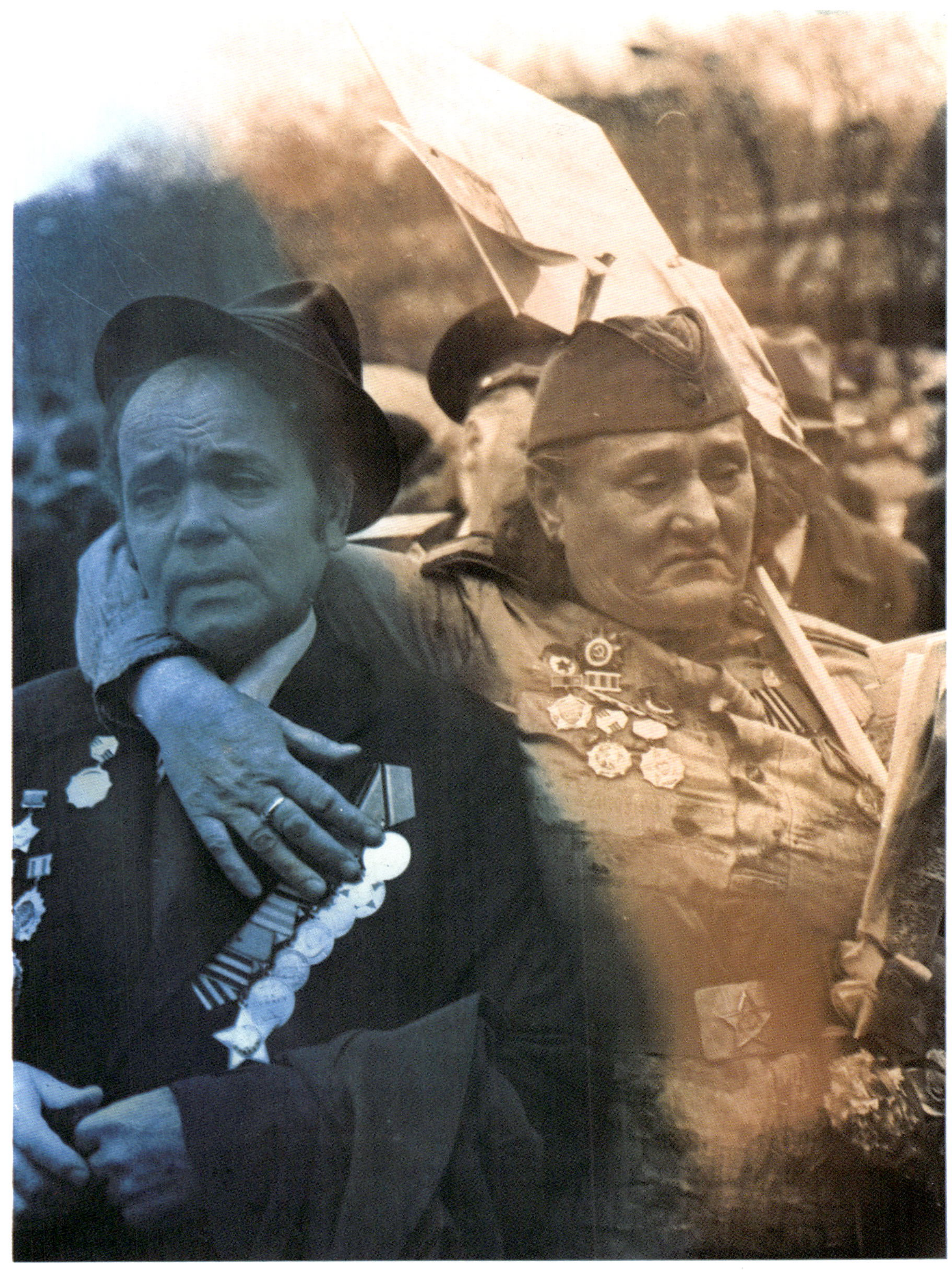

VALERY STIGNEEV, MOSCOW
VICTORY DAY, 1989
9½ × 7″

Opposite:
VALERY STIGNEEV, MOSCOW
THREE GENERATIONS, 1989
9½ × 7″

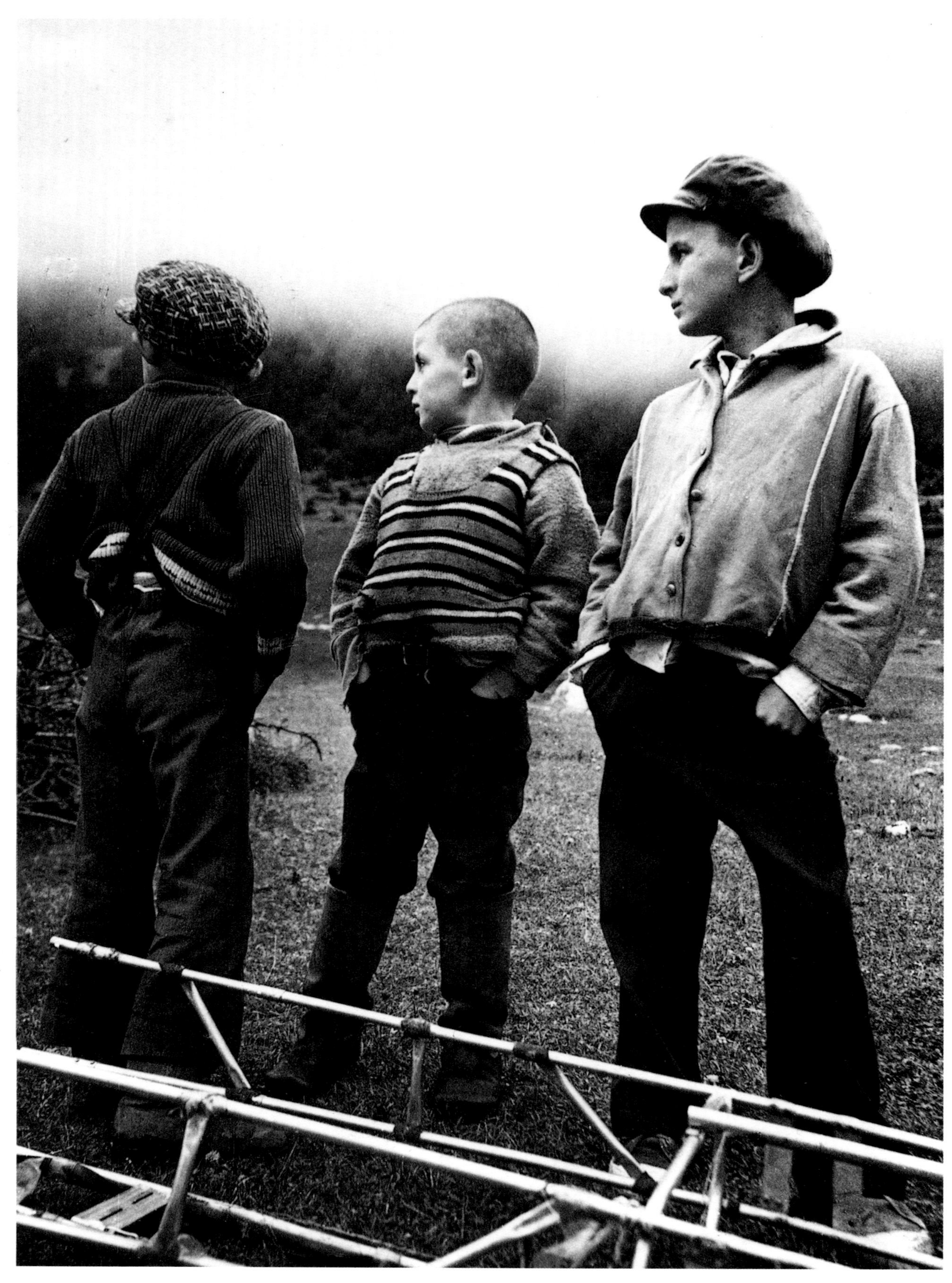

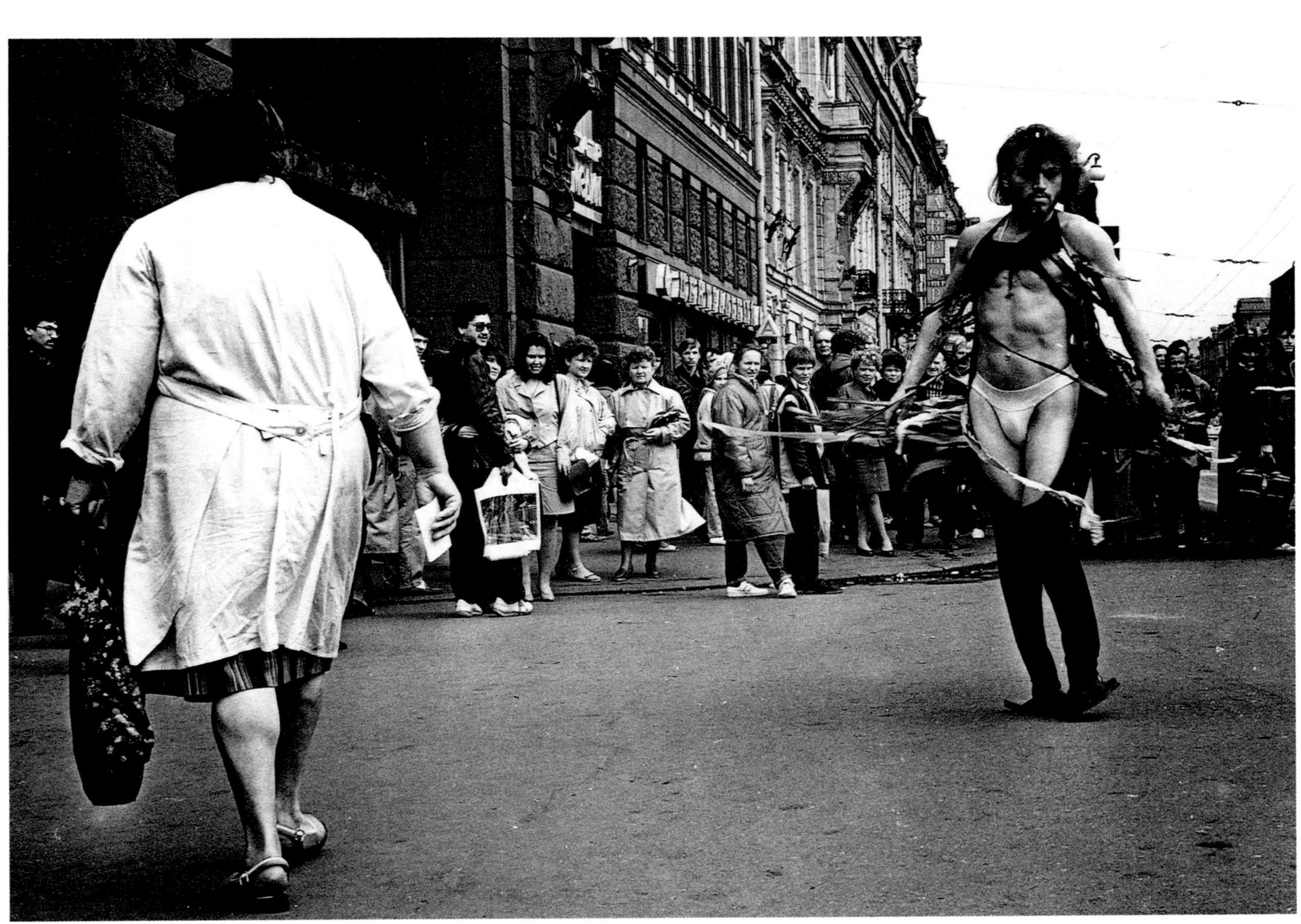

VICTOR SHUROV, LENINGRAD
IN THE STREET, 1990
3½ × 5″

VICTOR SHUROV, LENINGRAD
BOYS, 1990
7½ × 5″

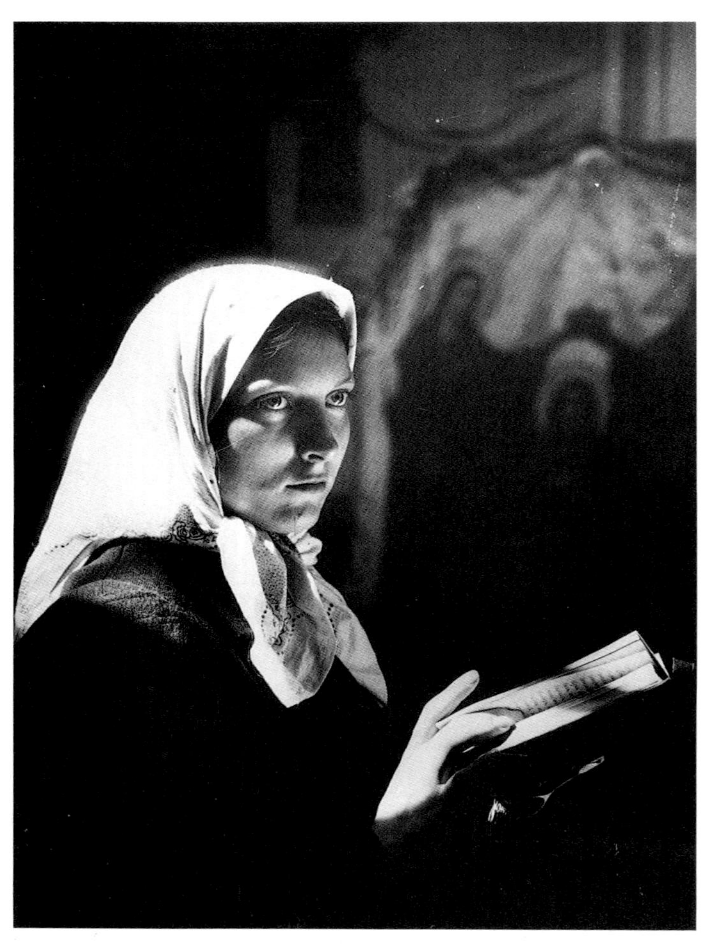

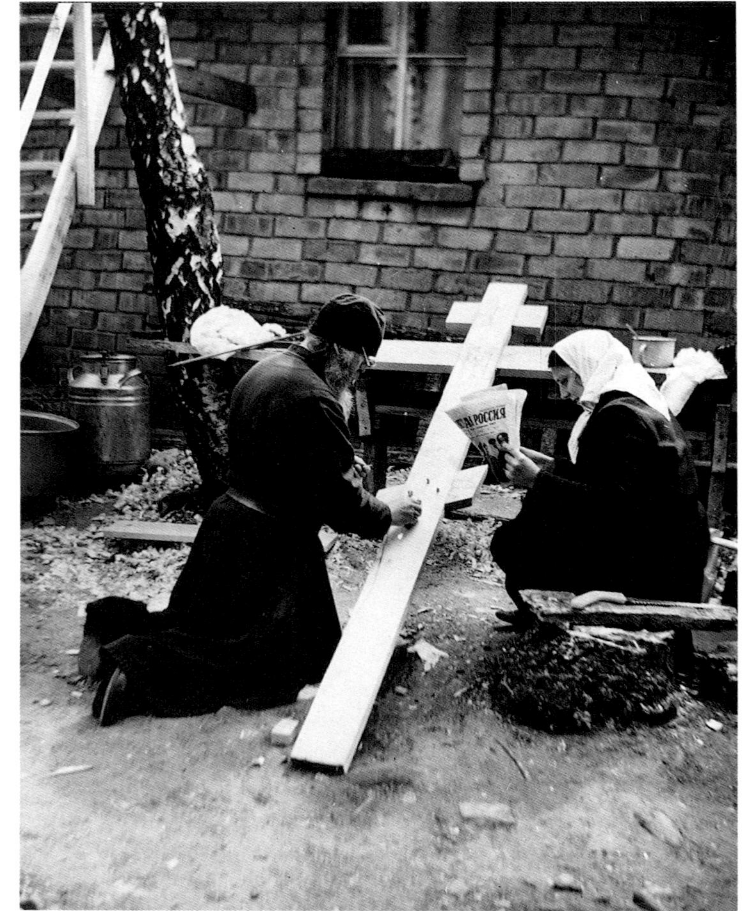
РОССИЯ

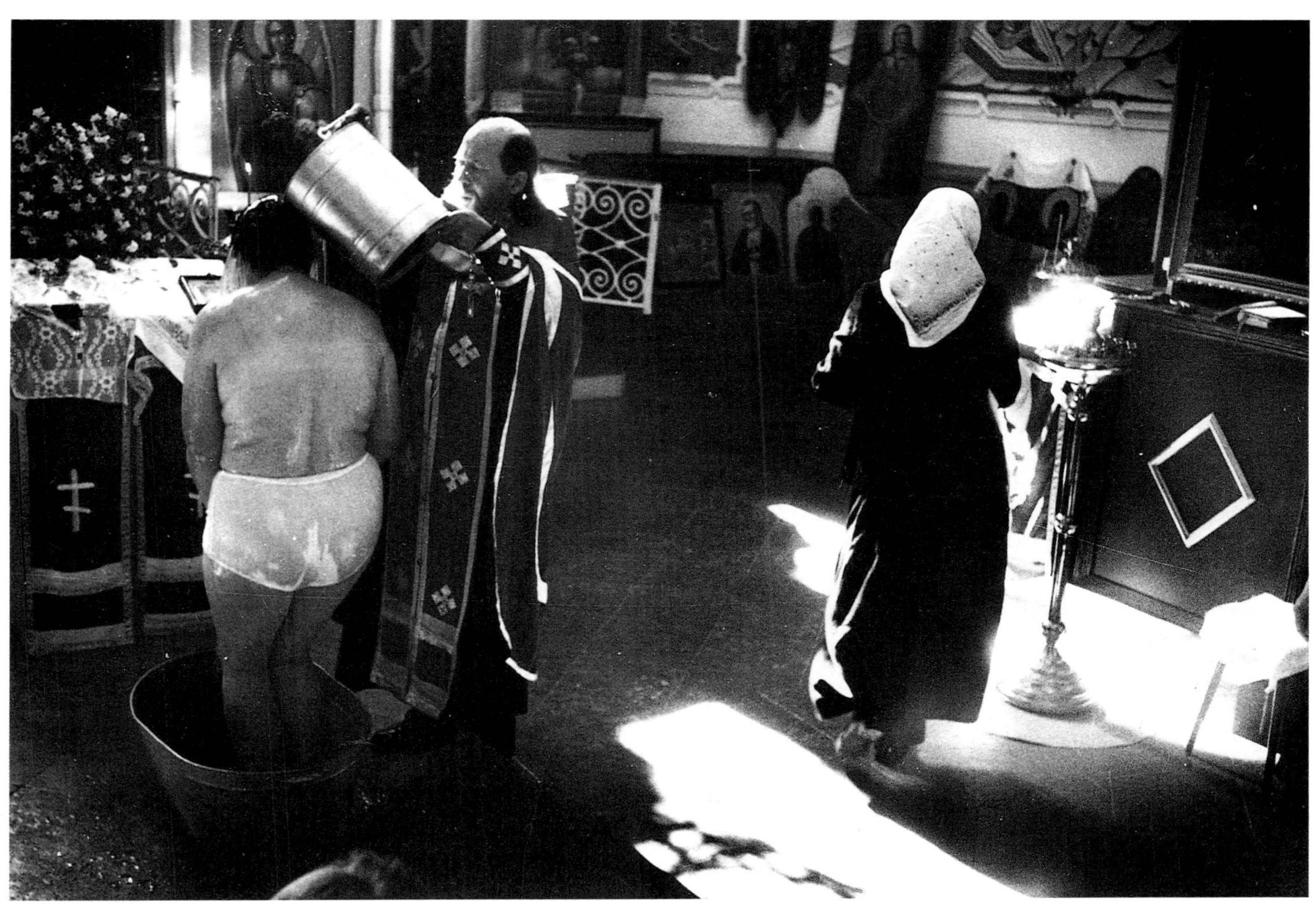

LUDMILA IVANOVA, LENINGRAD
from the series: THE CATHEDRAL, 1989
Left to right: 9½ × 7", 9 × 7", 6½ × 9½"

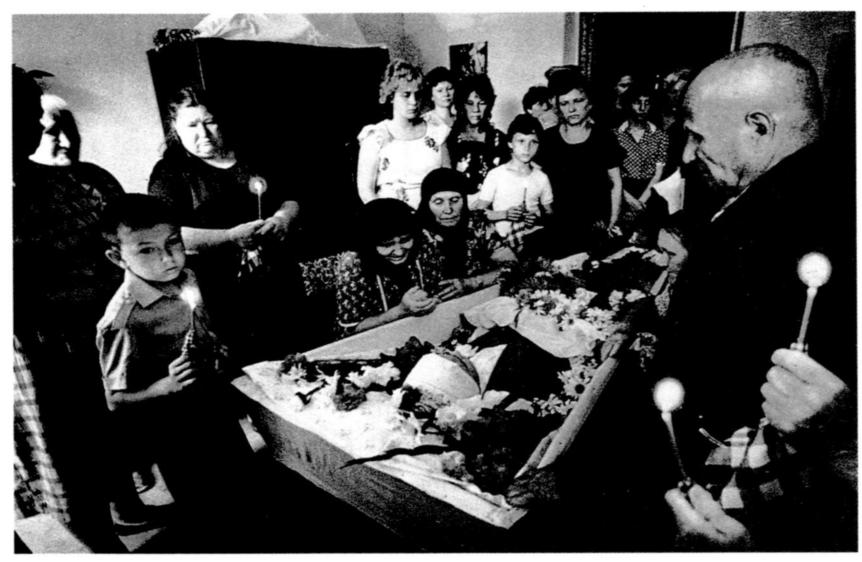

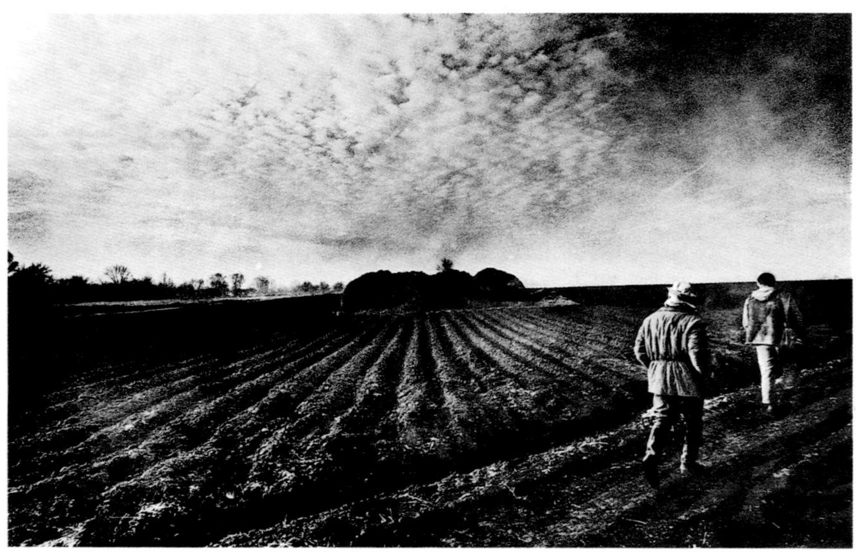

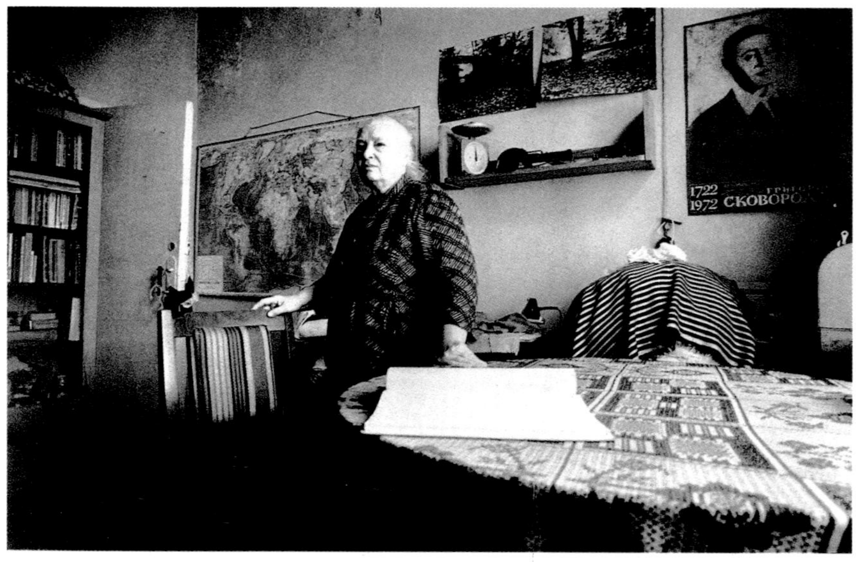

EDWARD STRANADKO, LENINGRAD
from the series:
UKRAINE AFTER CHERNOBYL, 1990
7 × 11″

EDWARD STRANADKO, LENINGRAD
from the series:
UKRAINE AFTER CHERNOBYL, 1987
7½ × 11½″

EDWARD STRANADKO, LENINGRAD
MY GRANNY—DESPOTIC WOMAN, 1988
7 × 11½″

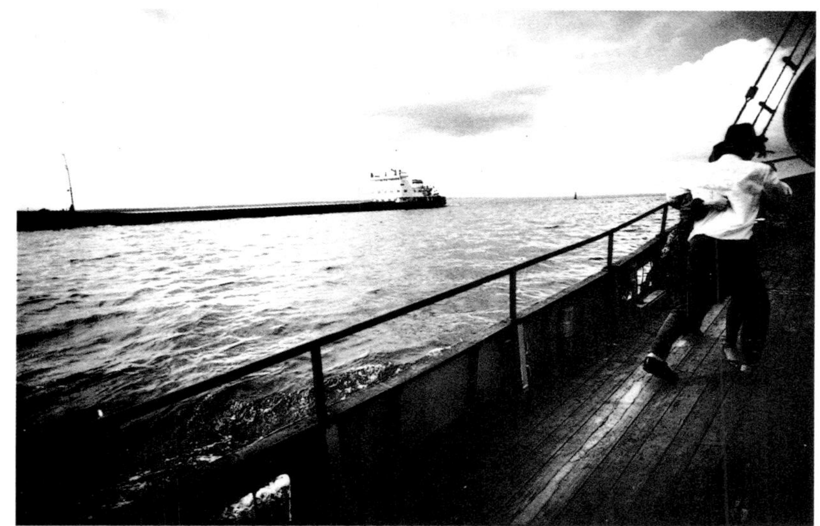

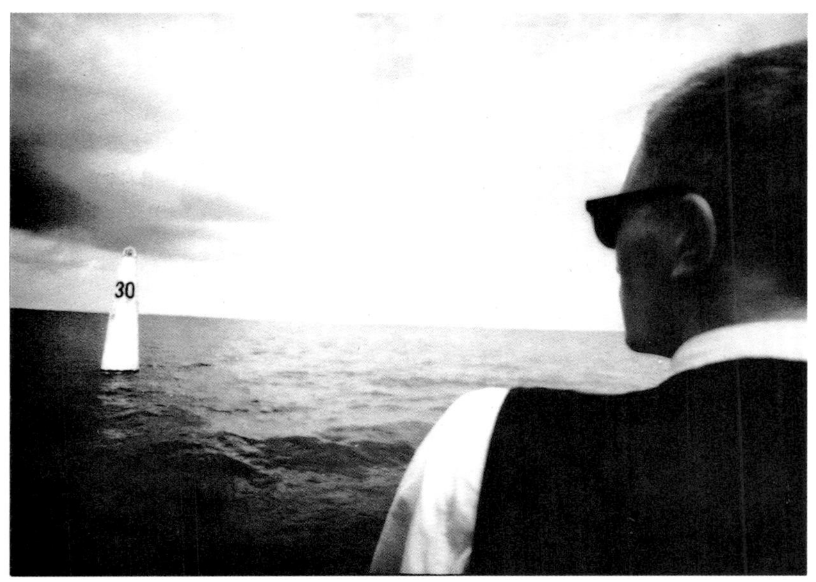

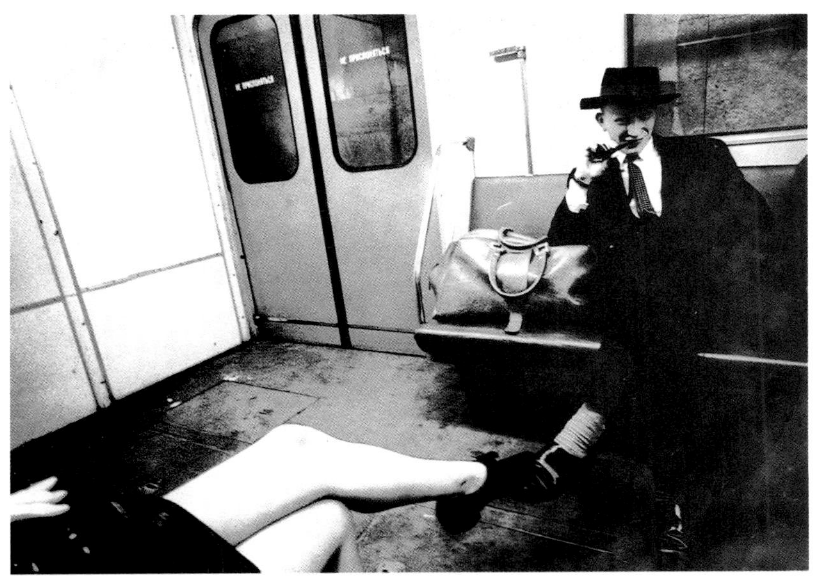

VICTORIA STRANADKO, LENINGRAD
TANGO, 1990
6 × 9″

VICTORIA STRANADKO, LENINGRAD
BALTIC SEA, 1990
6½ × 9″

VICTORIA STRANADKO, LENINGRAD
THE LENINGRAD METRO, 1990
6½ × 9″

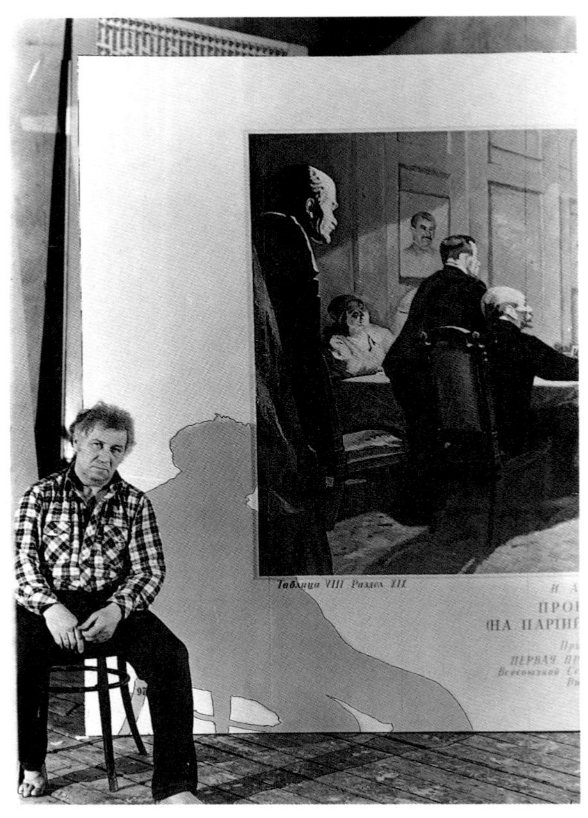
Таблица VIII Раздел. III

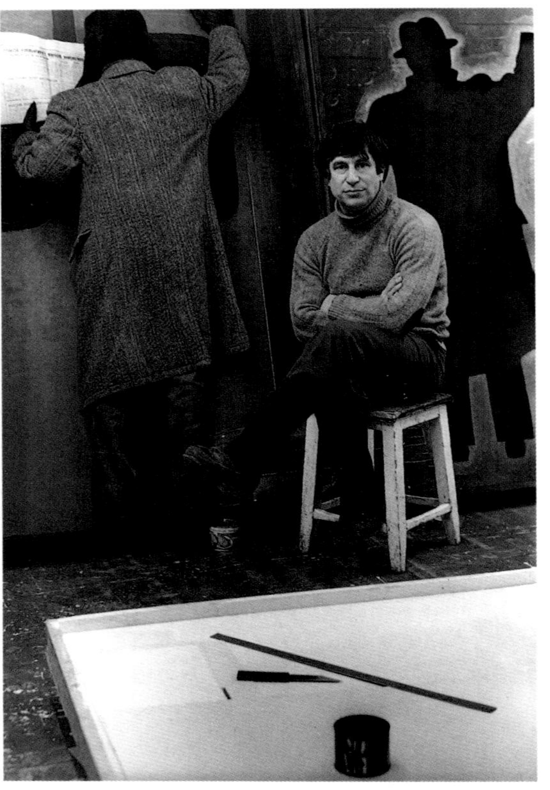

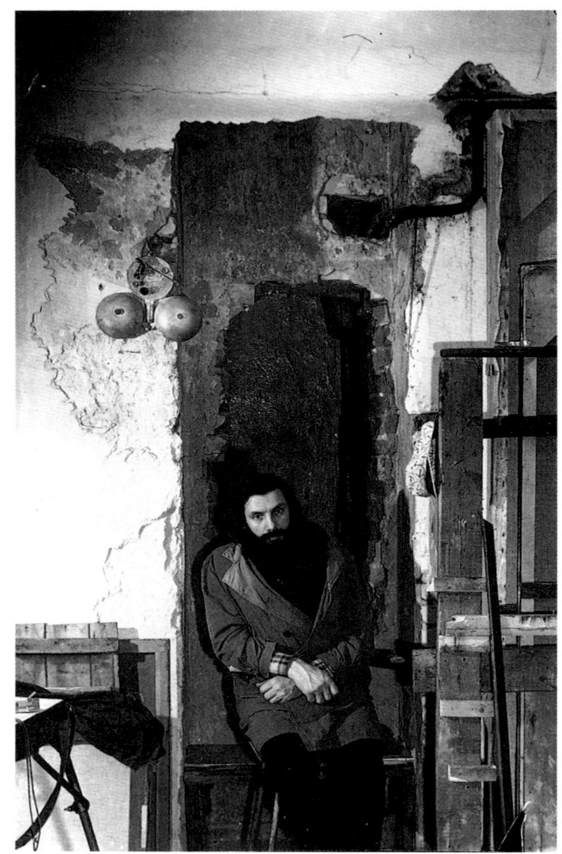

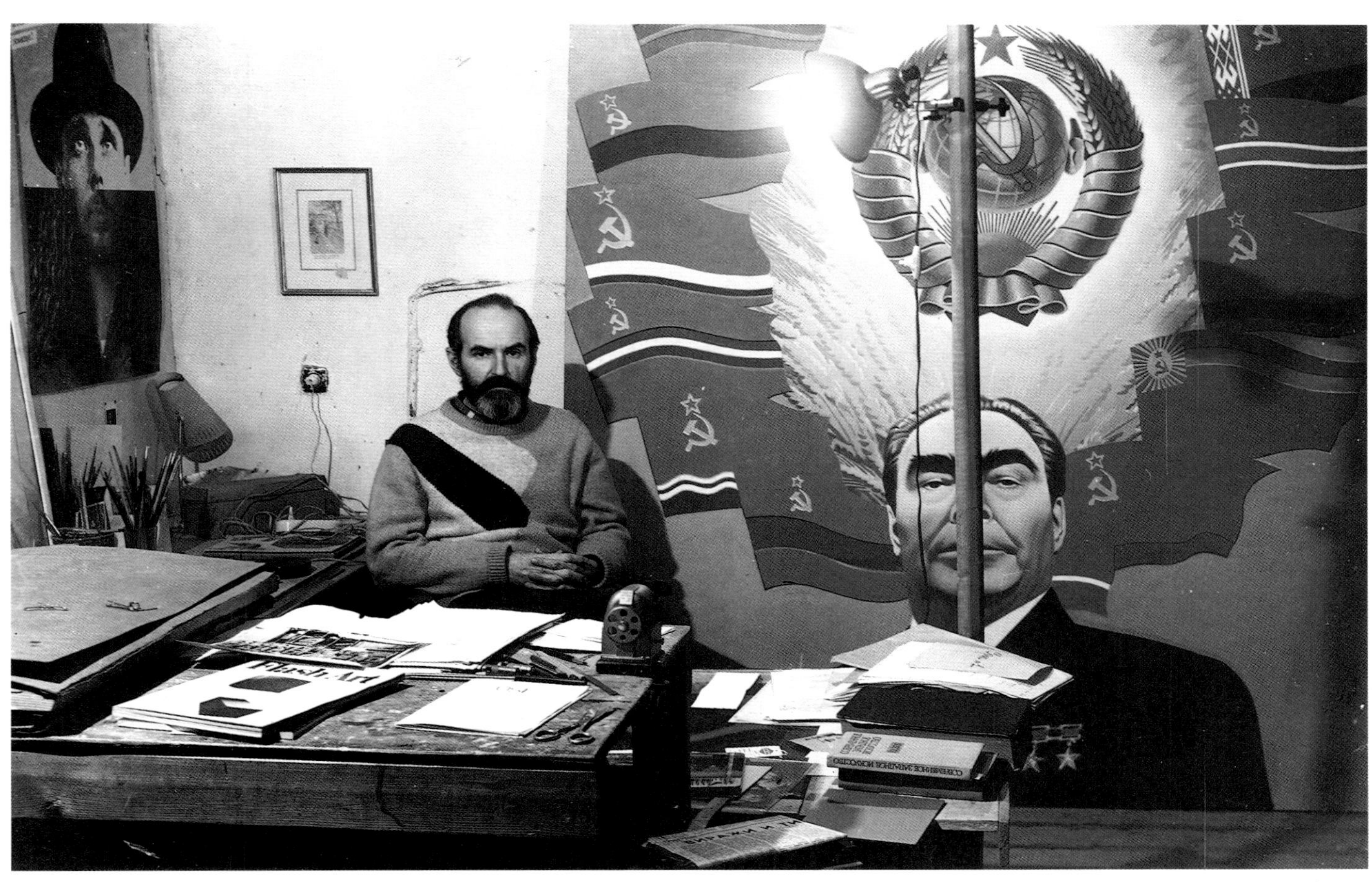

Top, left:
LEV MELIHOV, MOSCOW
ILYA KABAKOV, 1988
15½ × 11″

Top, right:
LEV MELIHOV, MOSCOW
VLADIMIR YANKILEVSKY, 1988
15½ × 11″

Bottom:
LEV MELIHOV, MOSCOW
ALEXI SUNDUKOV, 1987
17 × 11″

LEV MELIHOV, MOSCOW
ERIK BULATOV, 1986
11 × 17″

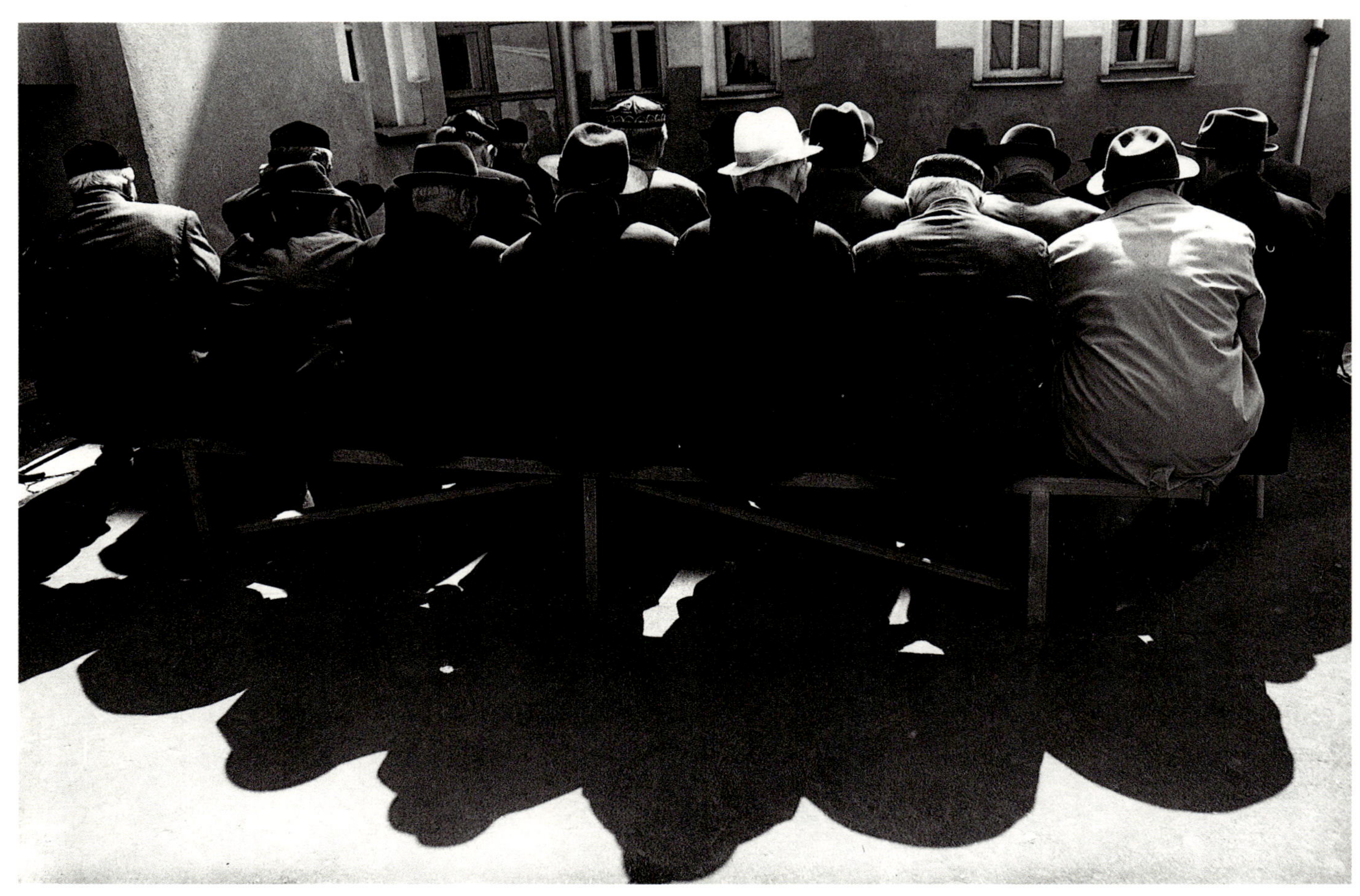

IGOR STOMACHIN, MOSCOW
MOSQUE, 1989
6½ × 9½″

IGOR STOMACHIN, MOSCOW
MOSQUE, 1989
9½ × 6½″

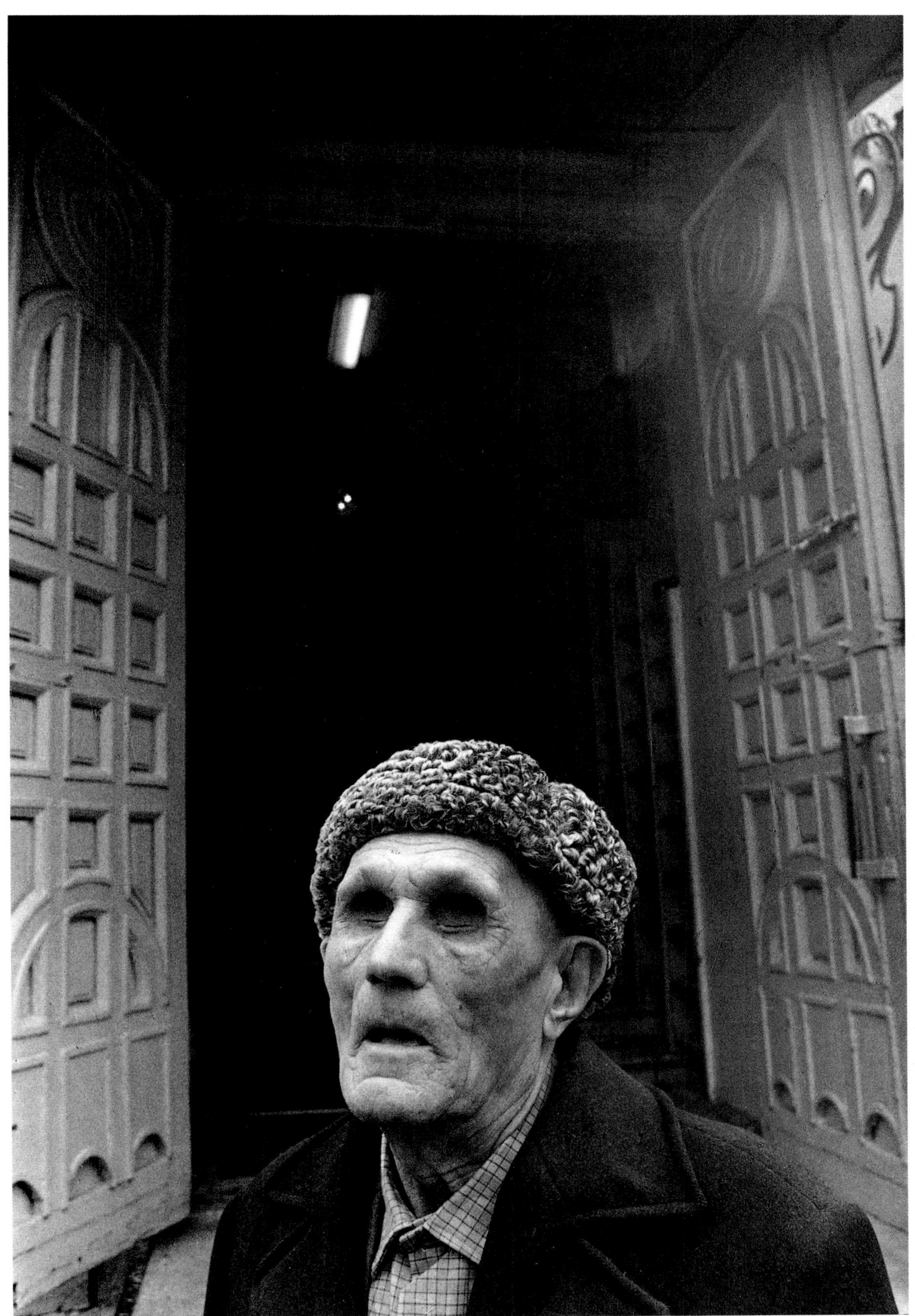

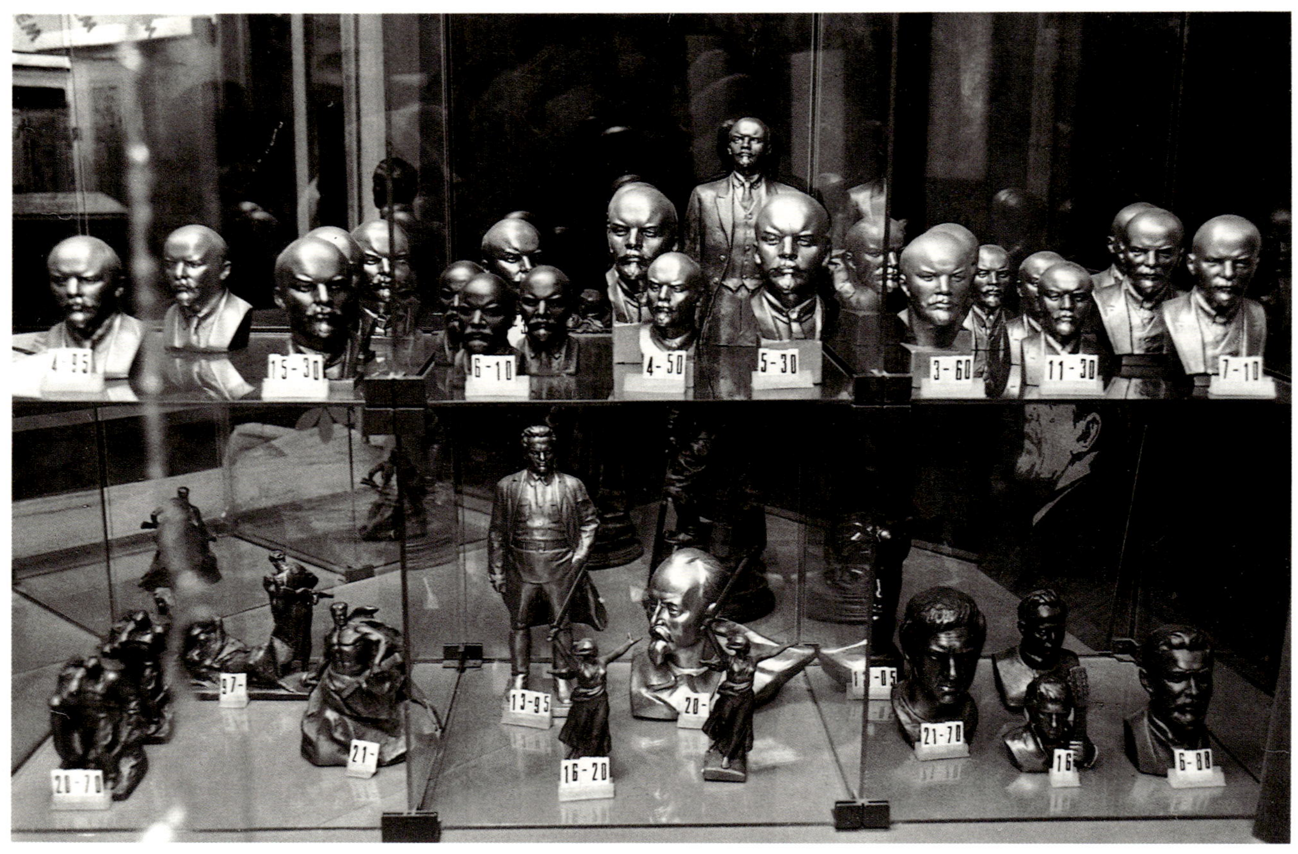

4-95
15-30
6-10
4-50
5-30
3-60
11-30
7-10
20-70
13-95
16-20
21-70
6-88

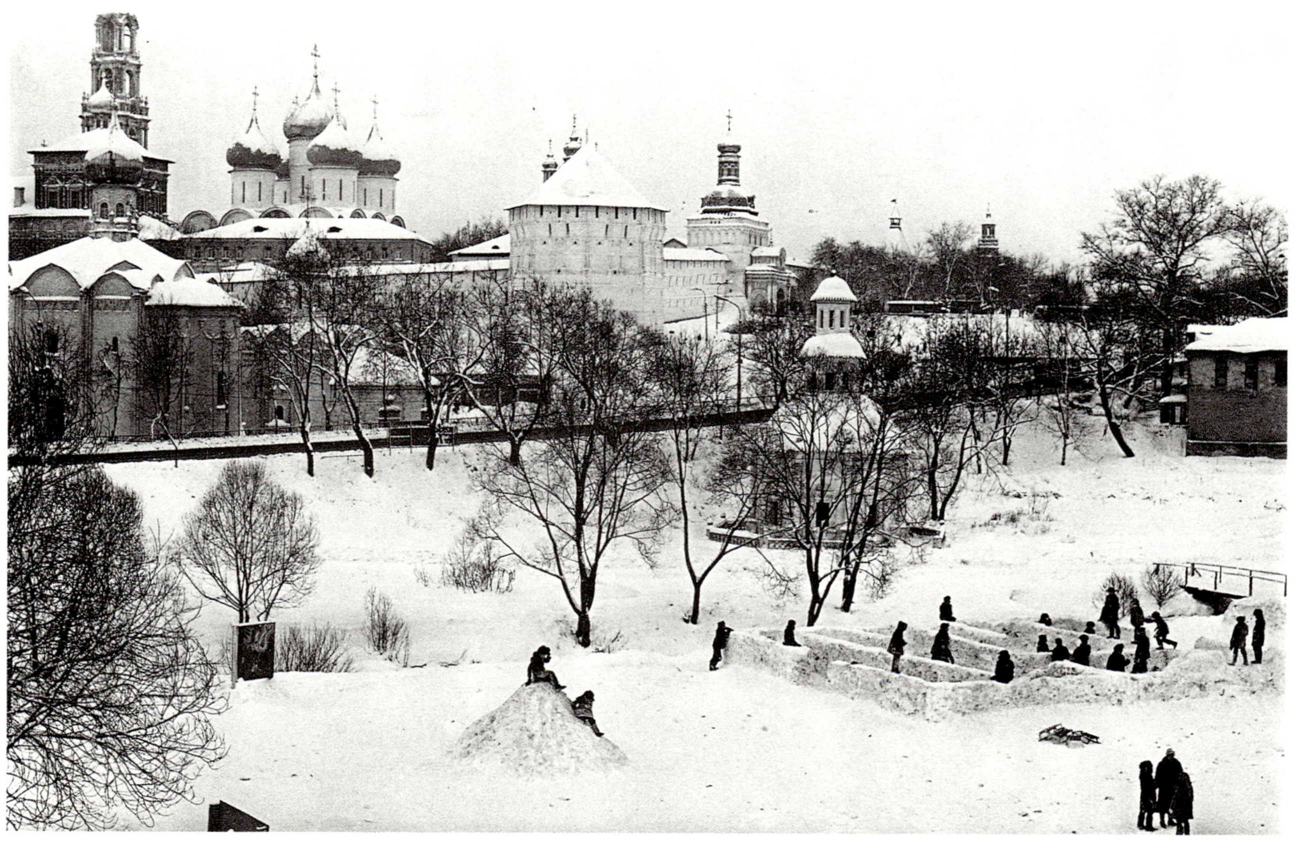

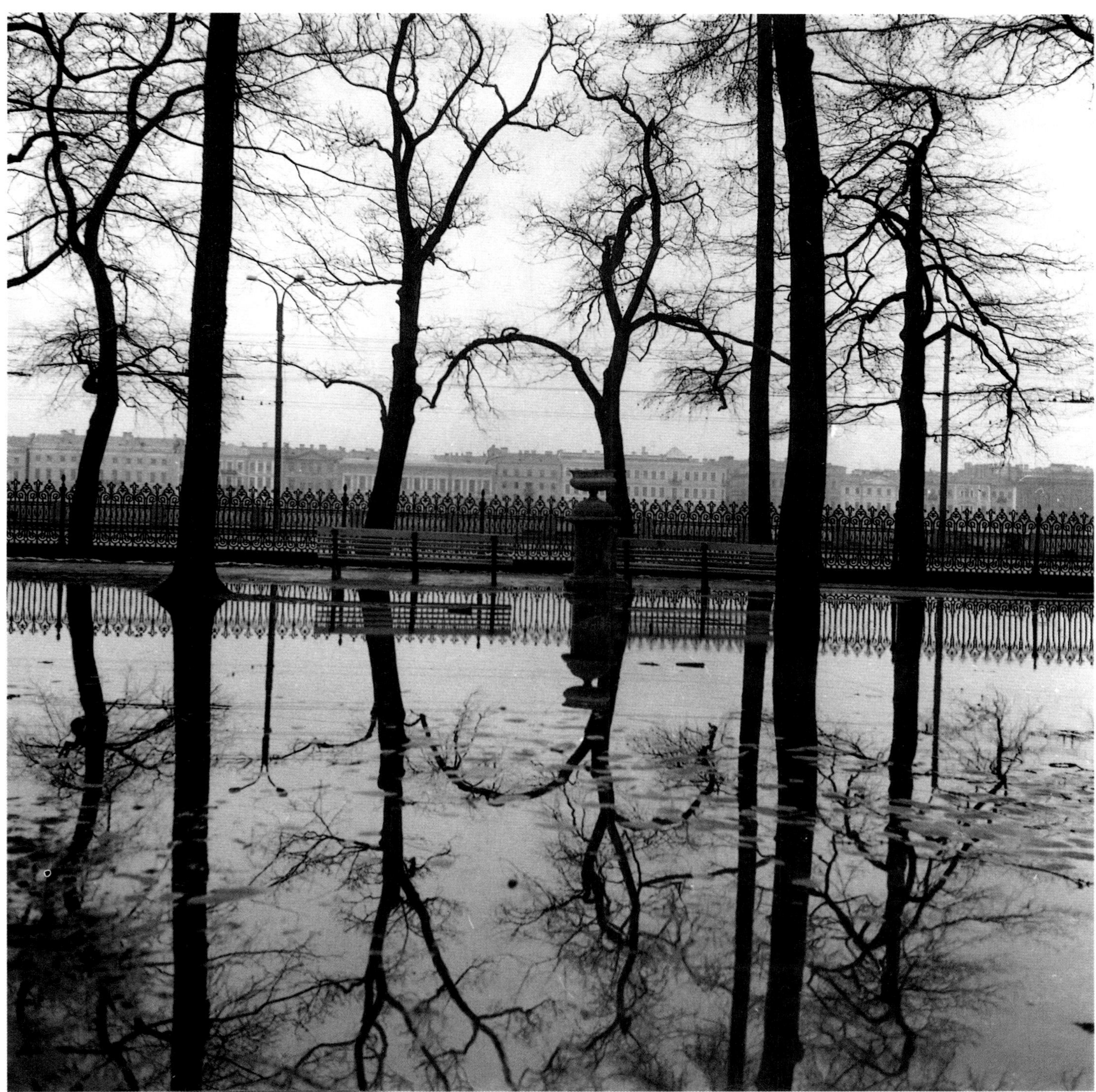

Top:
IGOR STOMACHIN, MOSCOW
GUM DEPARTMENT STORE, MOSCOW, 1990
6½ × 9½″

Bottom:
IGOR STOMACHIN, MOSCOW
ZAGORSK, 1986
6 × 9½″

MARIA SNIGIREVSKAYA, LENINGRAD
SPRING, 1987
11½ × 11½″

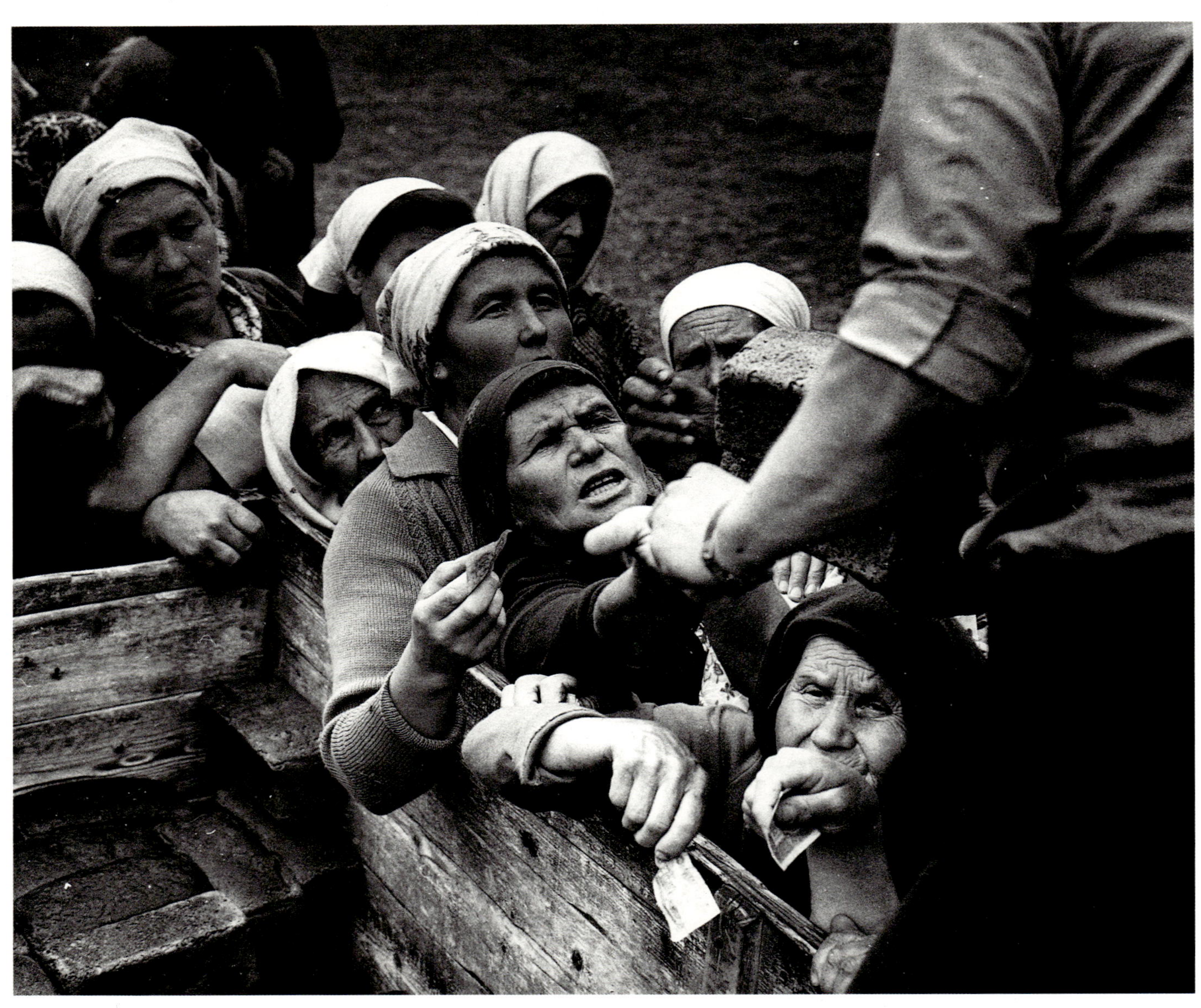

VLADISLAV MIKHAILOV, CHEBOKSARY
UNTITLED, 1988
10 × 11½″

VLADISLAV MIKHAILOV, CHEBOKSARY
UNTITLED, 1988
11½ × 10″

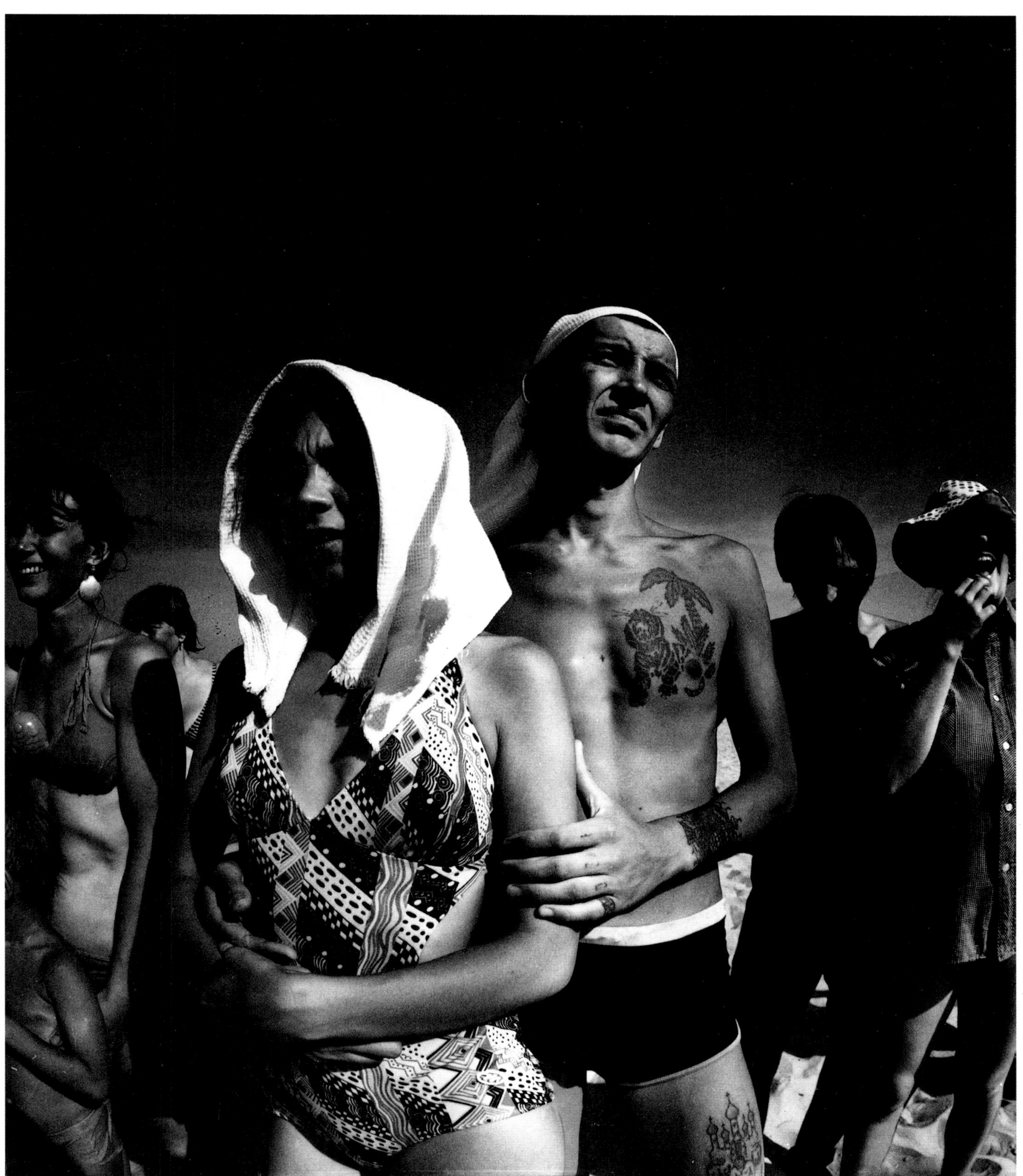

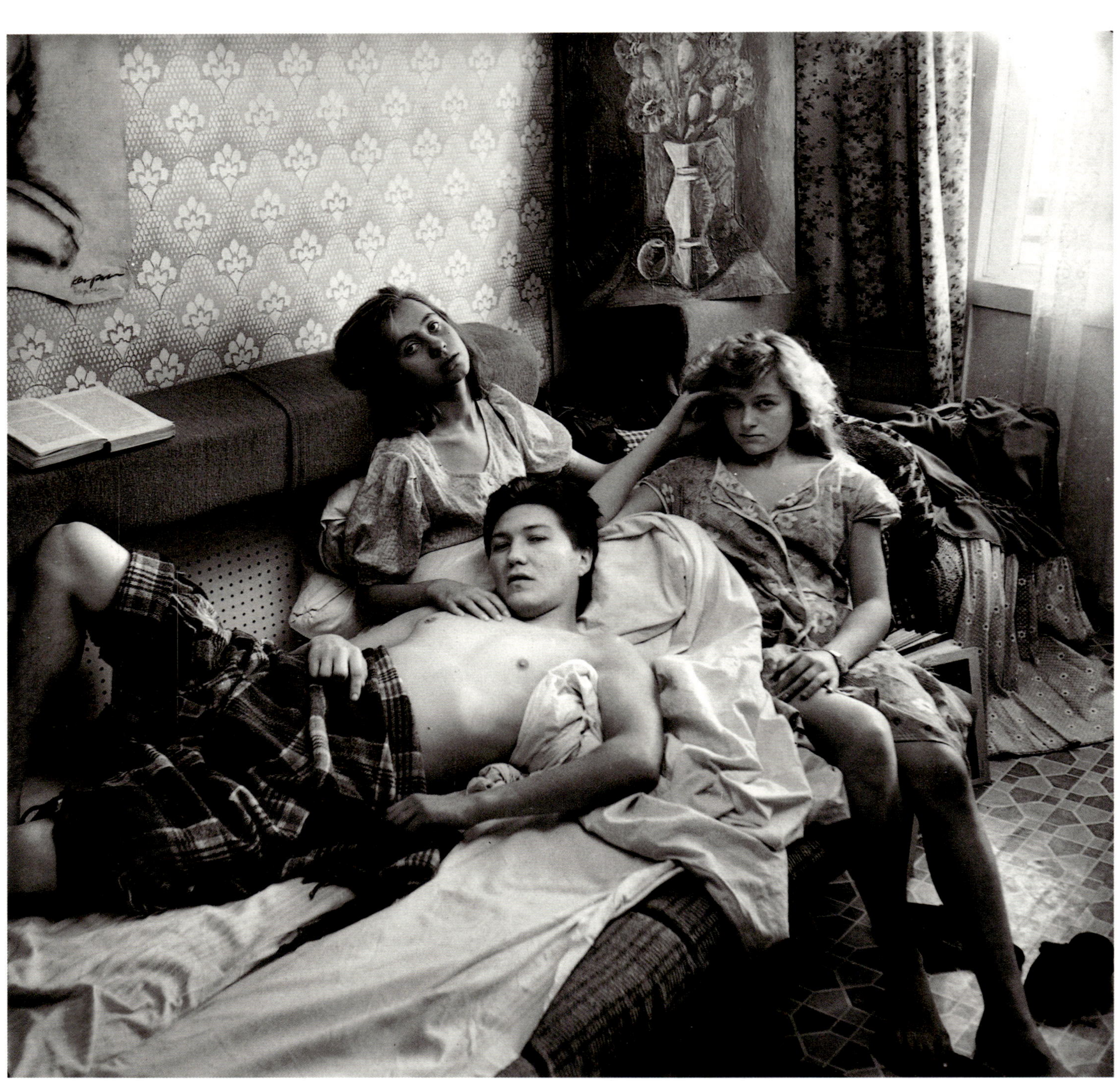

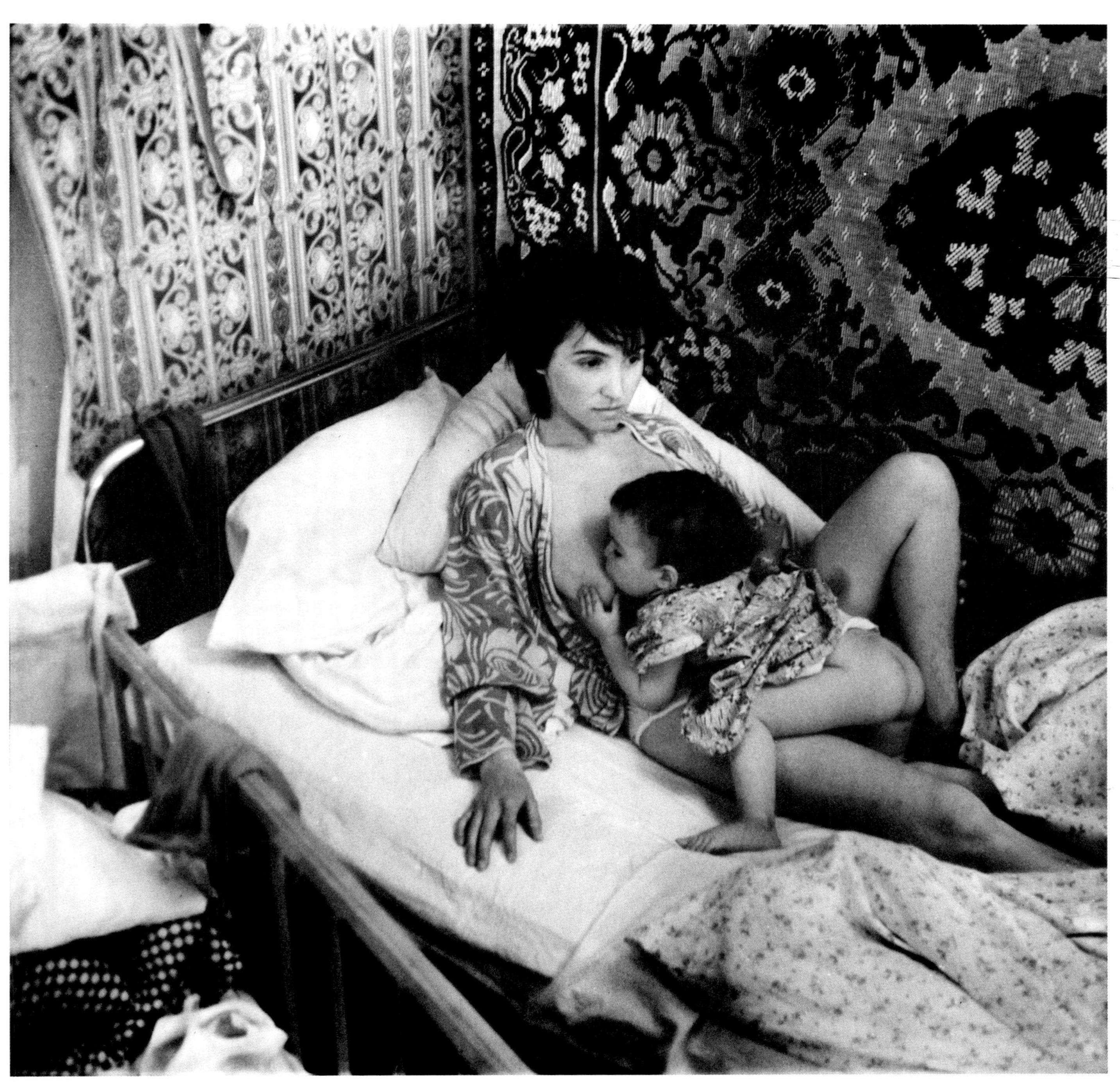

NICHOLAI BACHAREV, NOVOKUZNETSK
from the series:
OUR LIFE IS NOT A CASTLE, 1989
11 × 11½" (each)

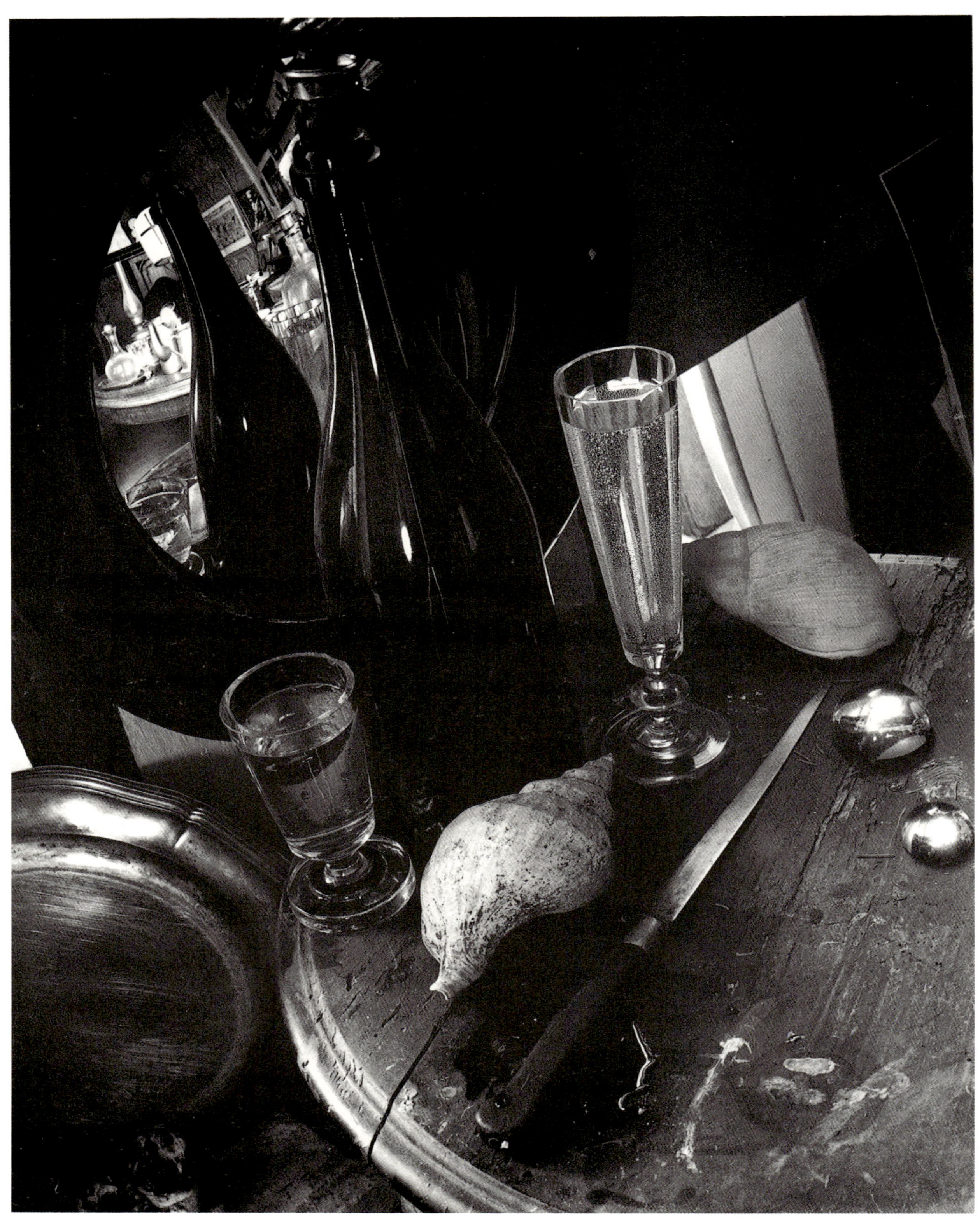

BORIS SMELOV, LENINGRAD
STILL LIFE WITH A MIRROR, 1990
8½ × 6½″

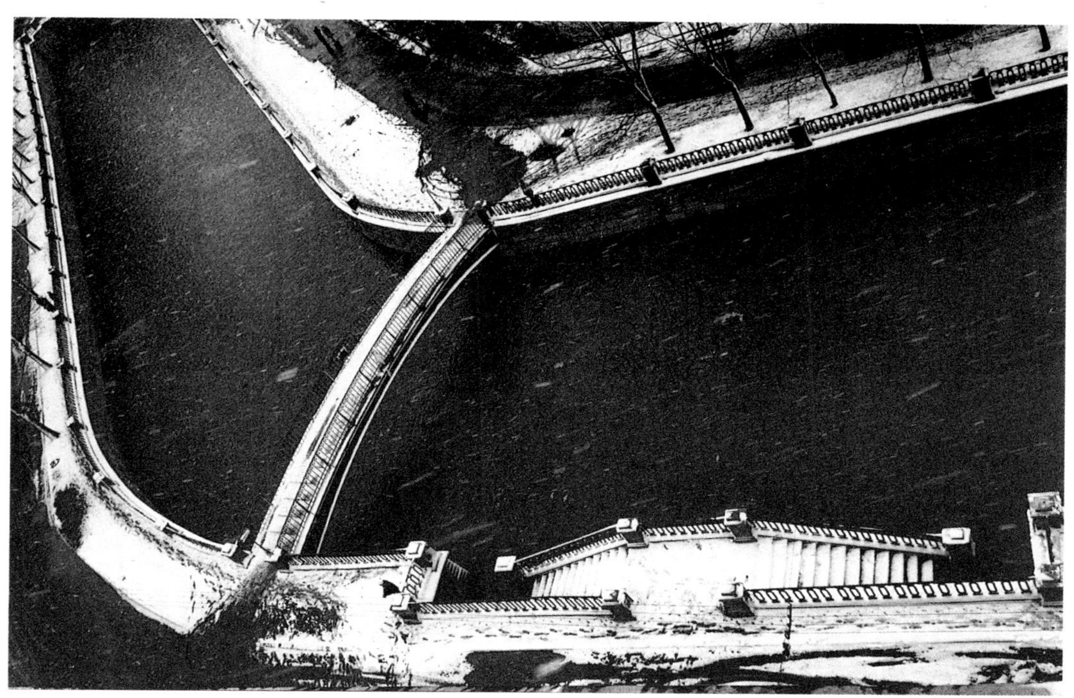

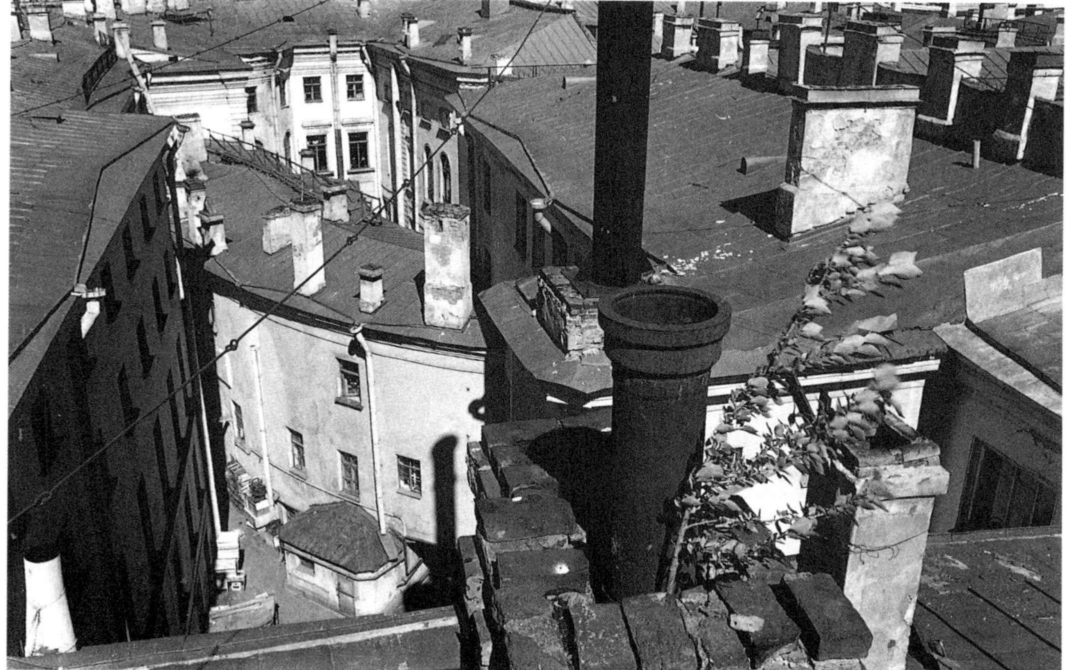

BORIS SMELOV, LENINGRAD
SENNOI BRIDGE, 1989
5½ × 8½″

BORIS SMELOV, LENINGRAD
HOUSE OF ART, 1989
5½ × 8½″

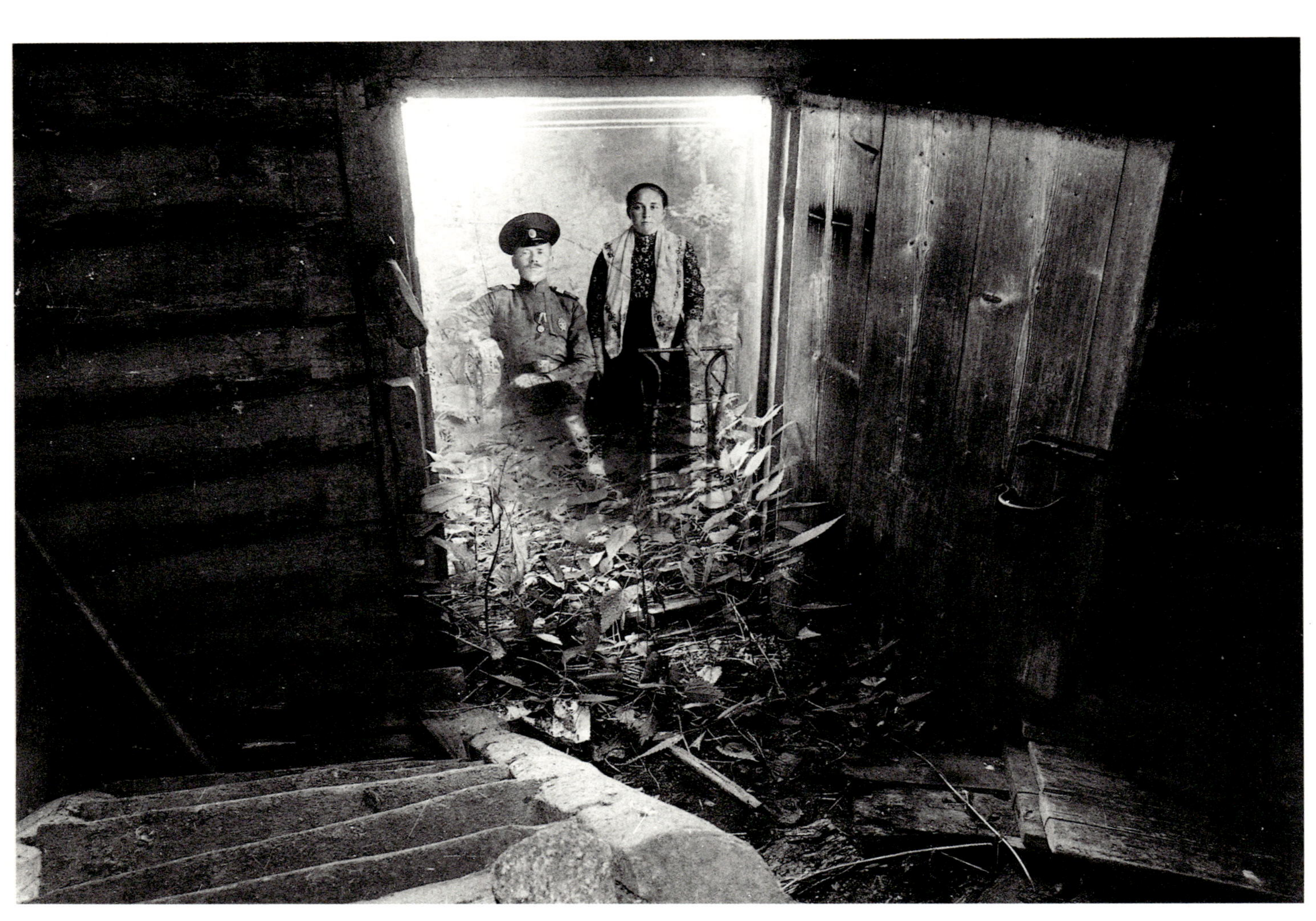

VLADIMIR FILONOV, ZAPOROZHYE
from the series: REMINISCENCES OF RUSSIAN PROVINCES, 1990
7½ × 11″, 10½ × 7½″

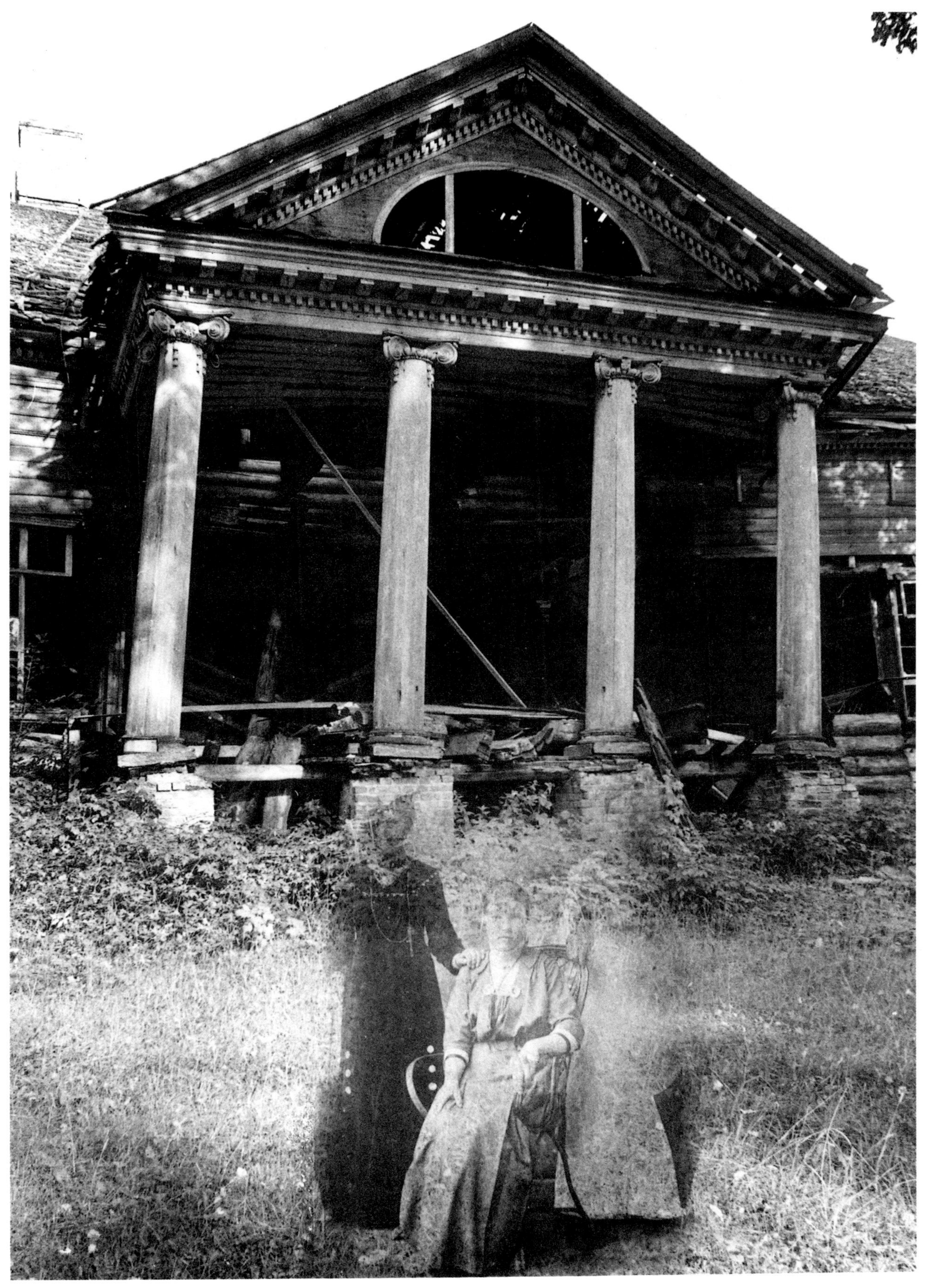

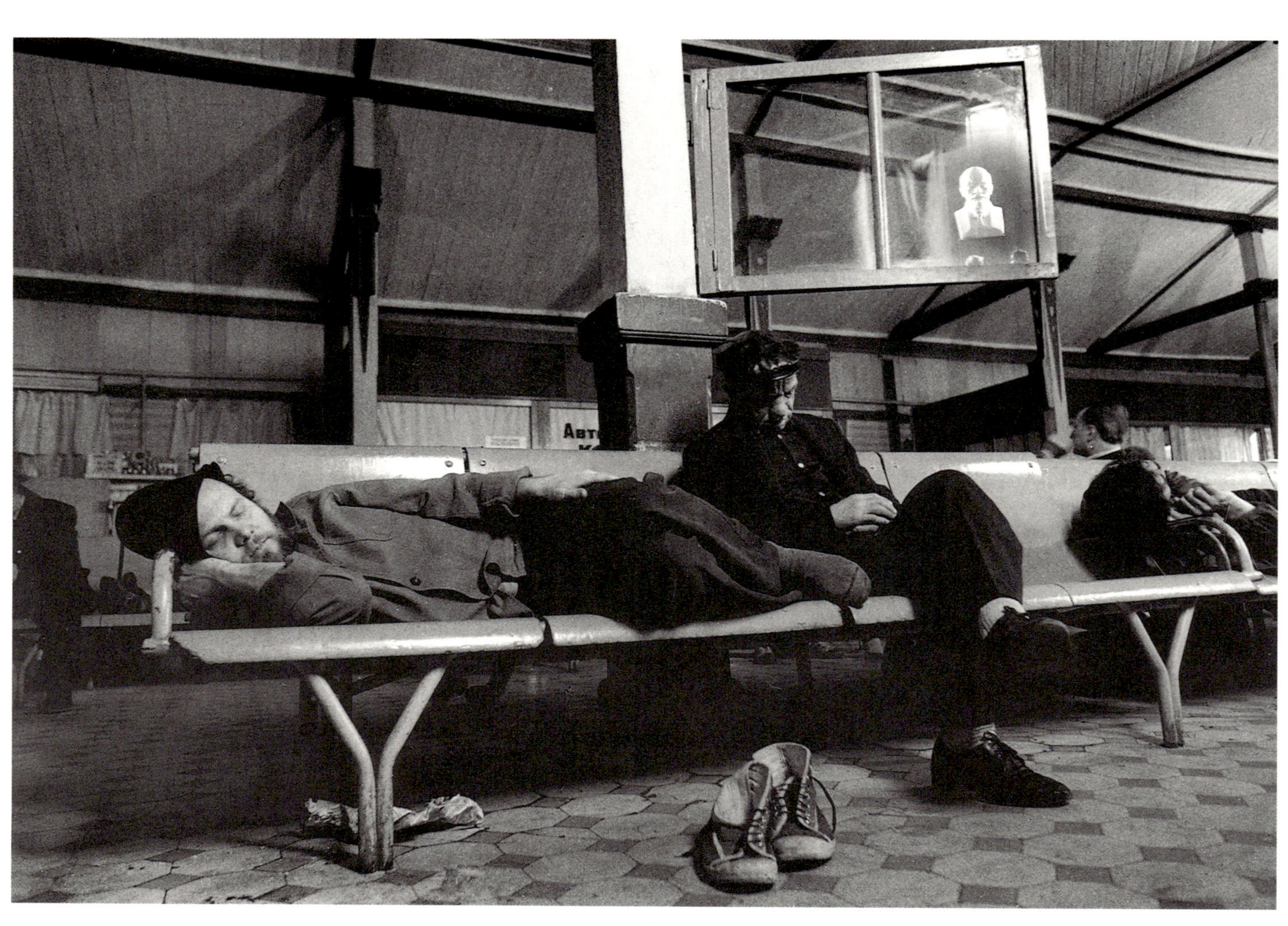

VLADIMIR FILONOV, ZAPOROZHYE
from the series: REMINISCENCES OF RUSSIAN PROVINCES, 1990
7½ × 10½", 10½ × 7½"

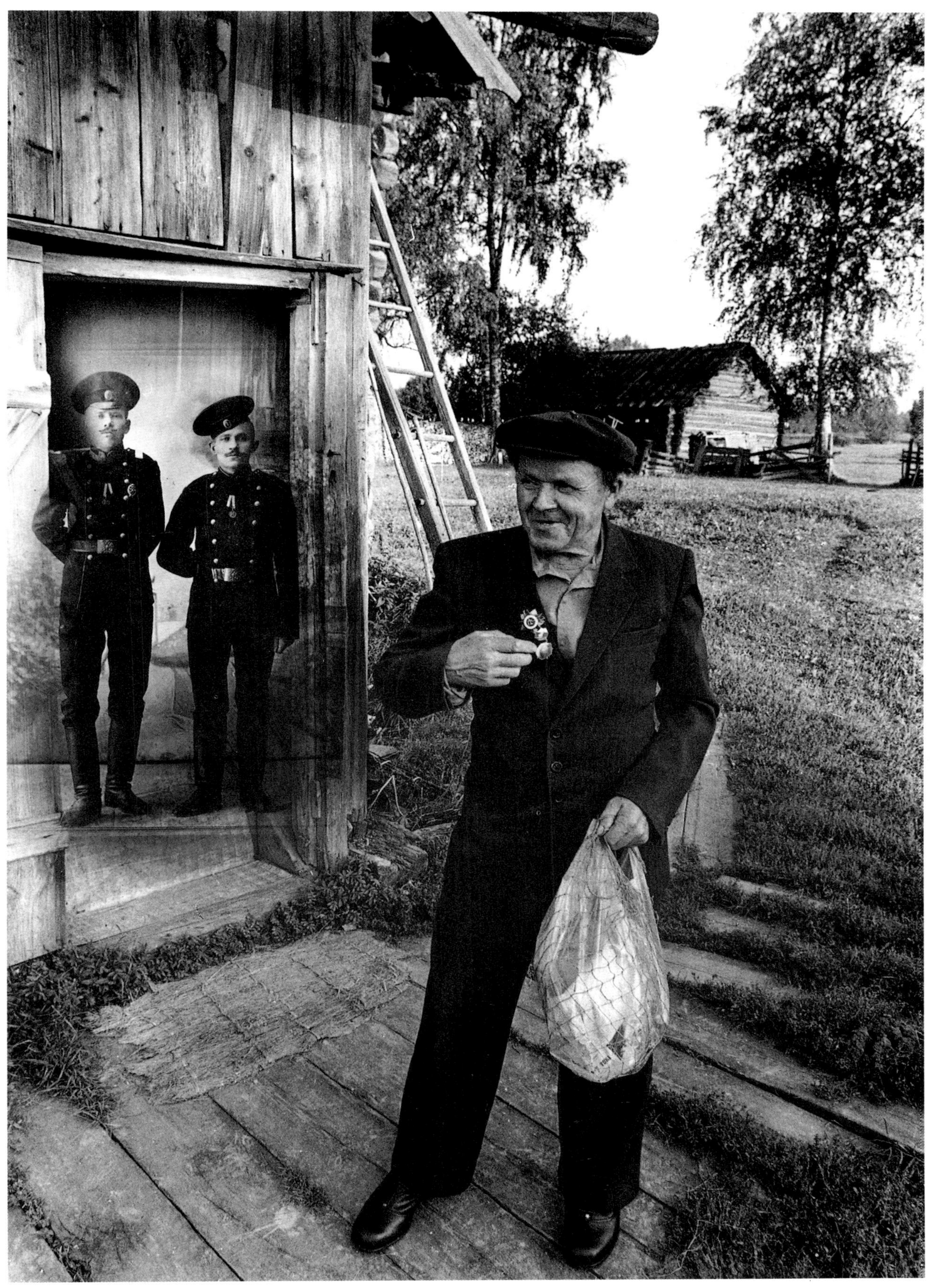

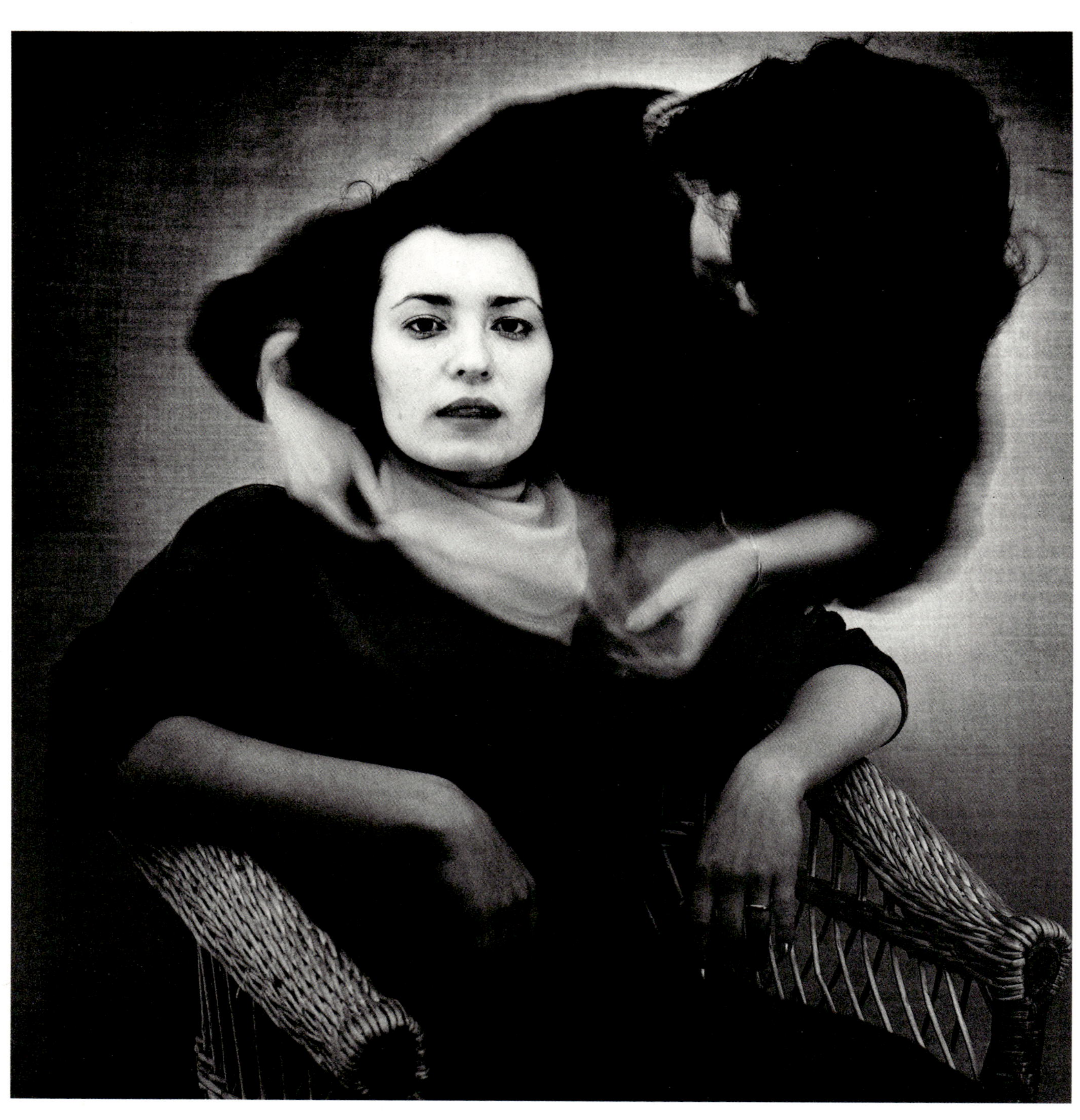

SERGEY OSMACHKIN, KUIBYSHEV
A MASK, 1988
11 × 10½″

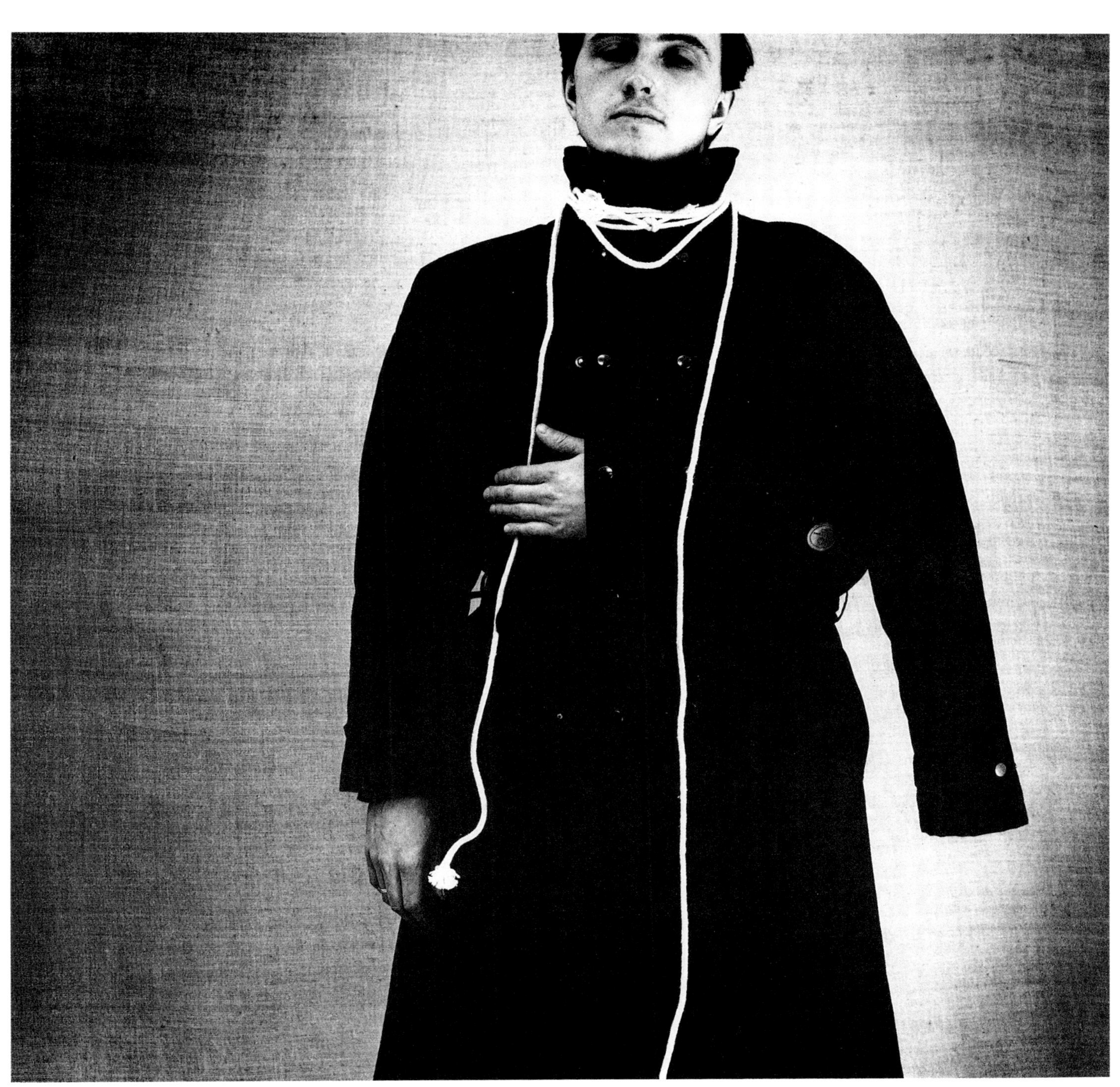

SERGEY OSMACHKIN, KUIBYSHEV
THE HERO OF MY NIGHT DREAMS, 1988
11 × 11″

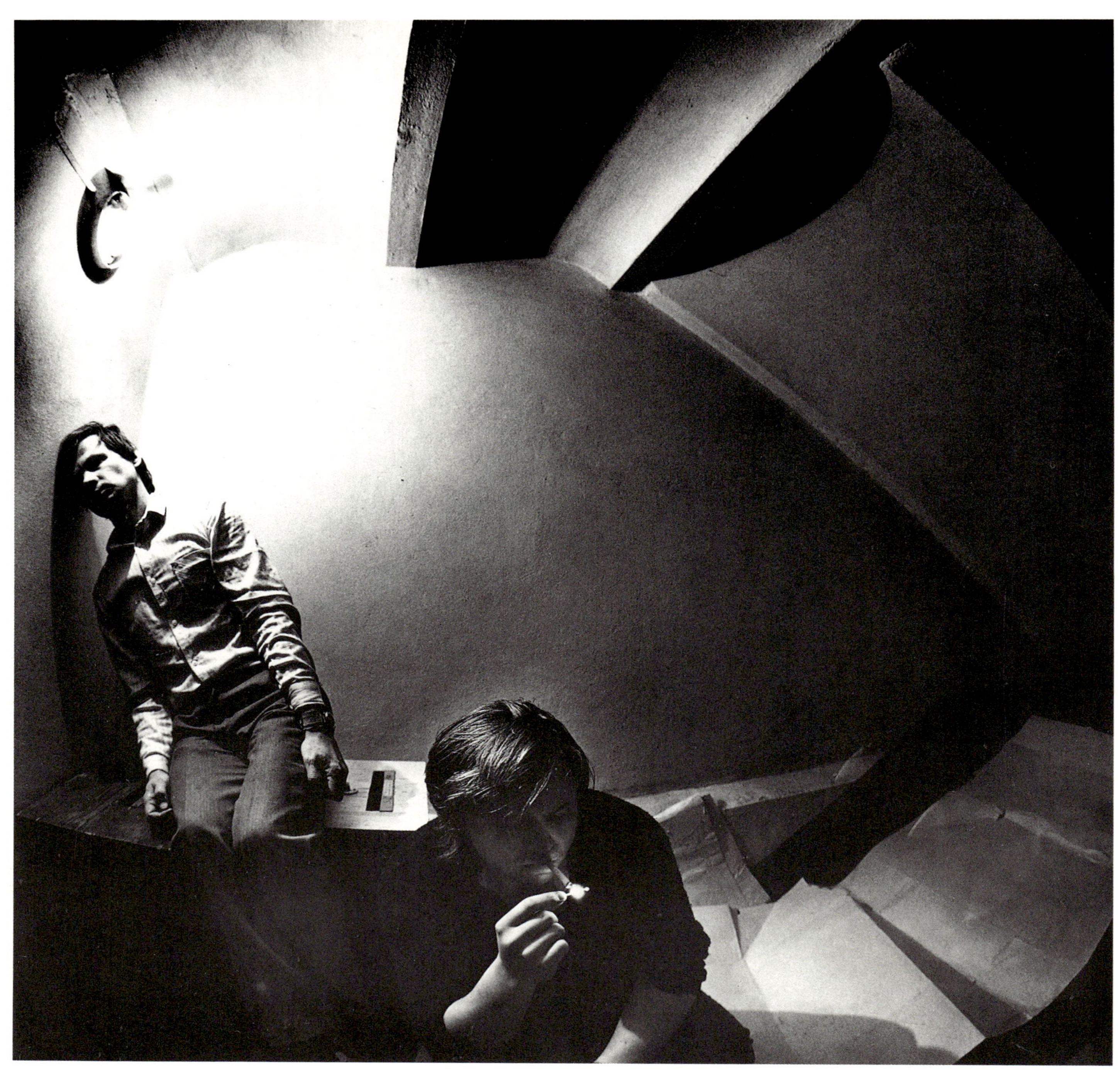

SERGEY OSMACHKIN, KUIBYSHEV
THE END OF THE YEAR TIREDNESS, 1988
11 × 11″

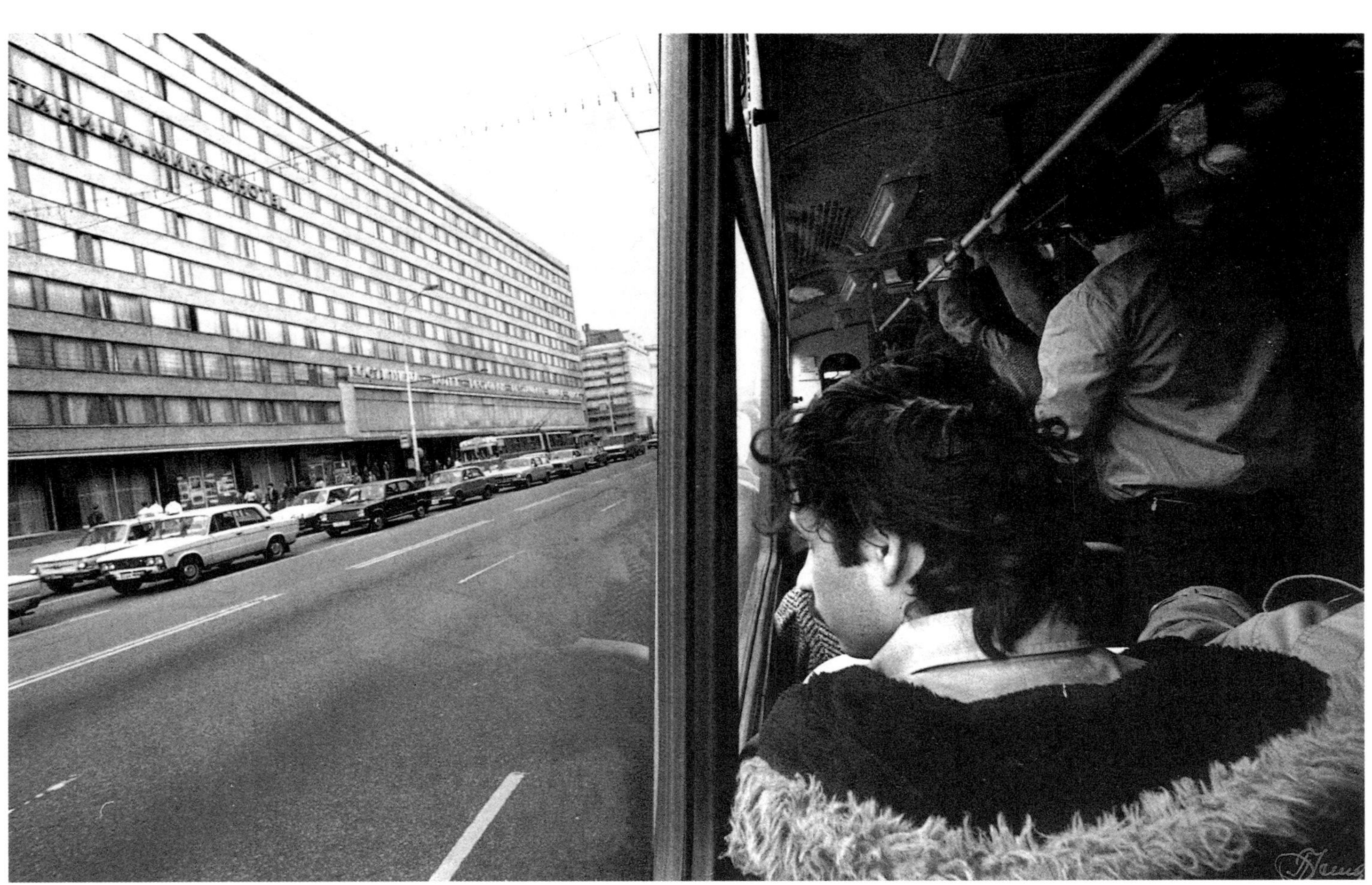

PAVEL KISELEV, MOSCOW
THE WORLD OF THE STREET/THE WORLD OF THE TROLLEY BUS, 1988
5½ × 8½″

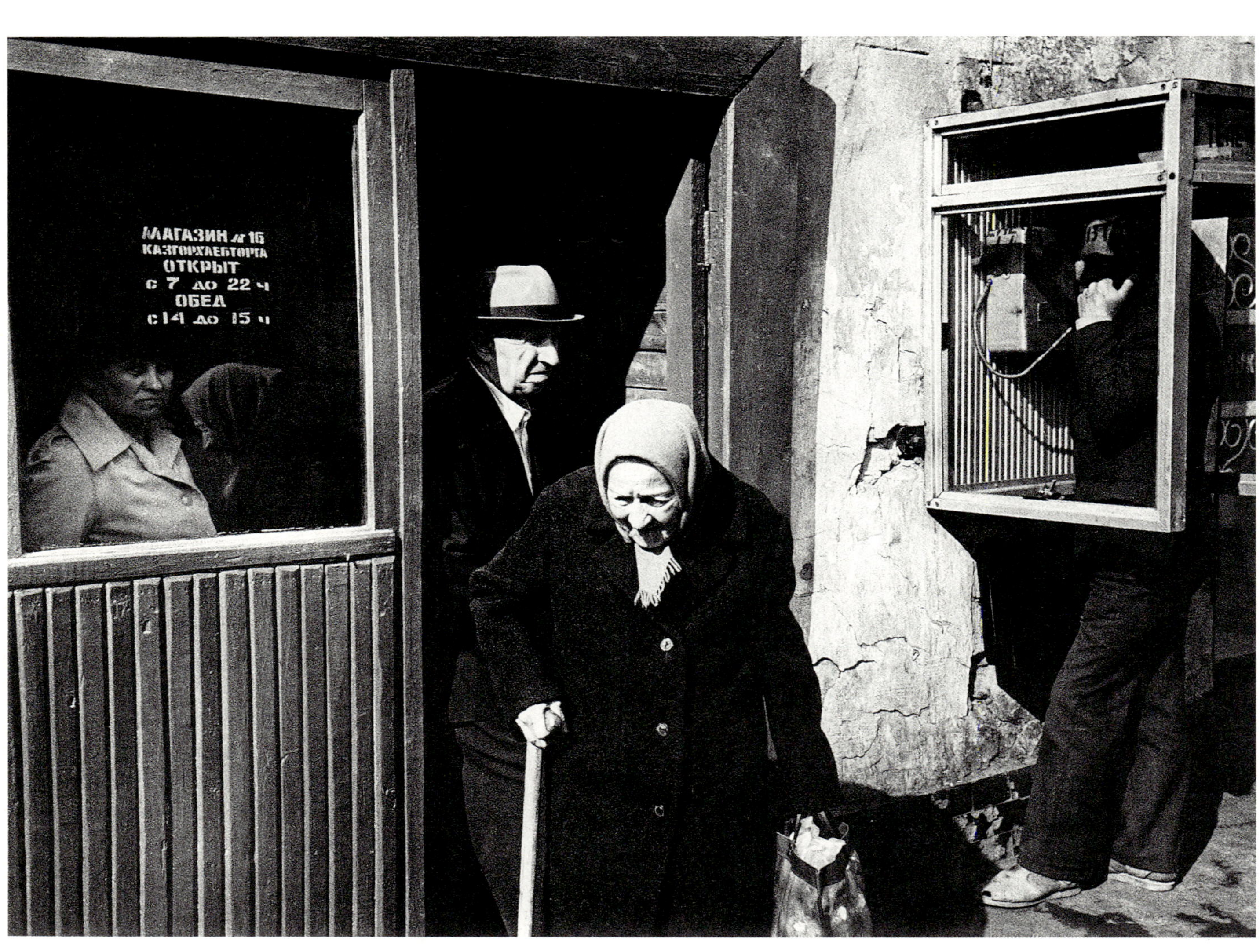
МАГАЗИН № 16
КАЗГОРХЛЕБТОРГА
ОТКРЫТ
с 7 до 22 ч
ОБЕД
с 14 до 15 ч

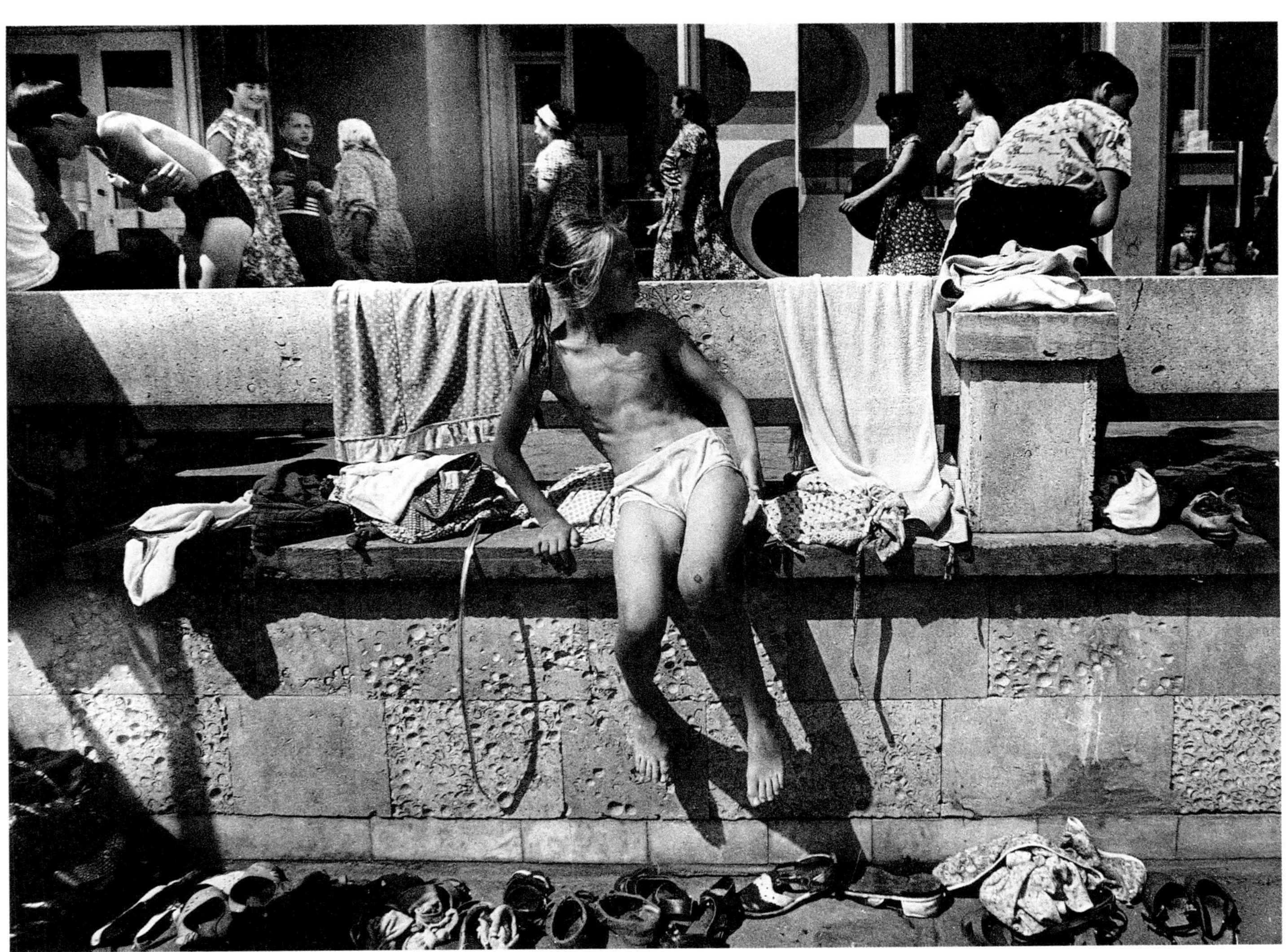

MIKHAIL LADEISHIKOV, CHEBOKSARY
UNTITLED, c.1989
12 × 15½" (each)

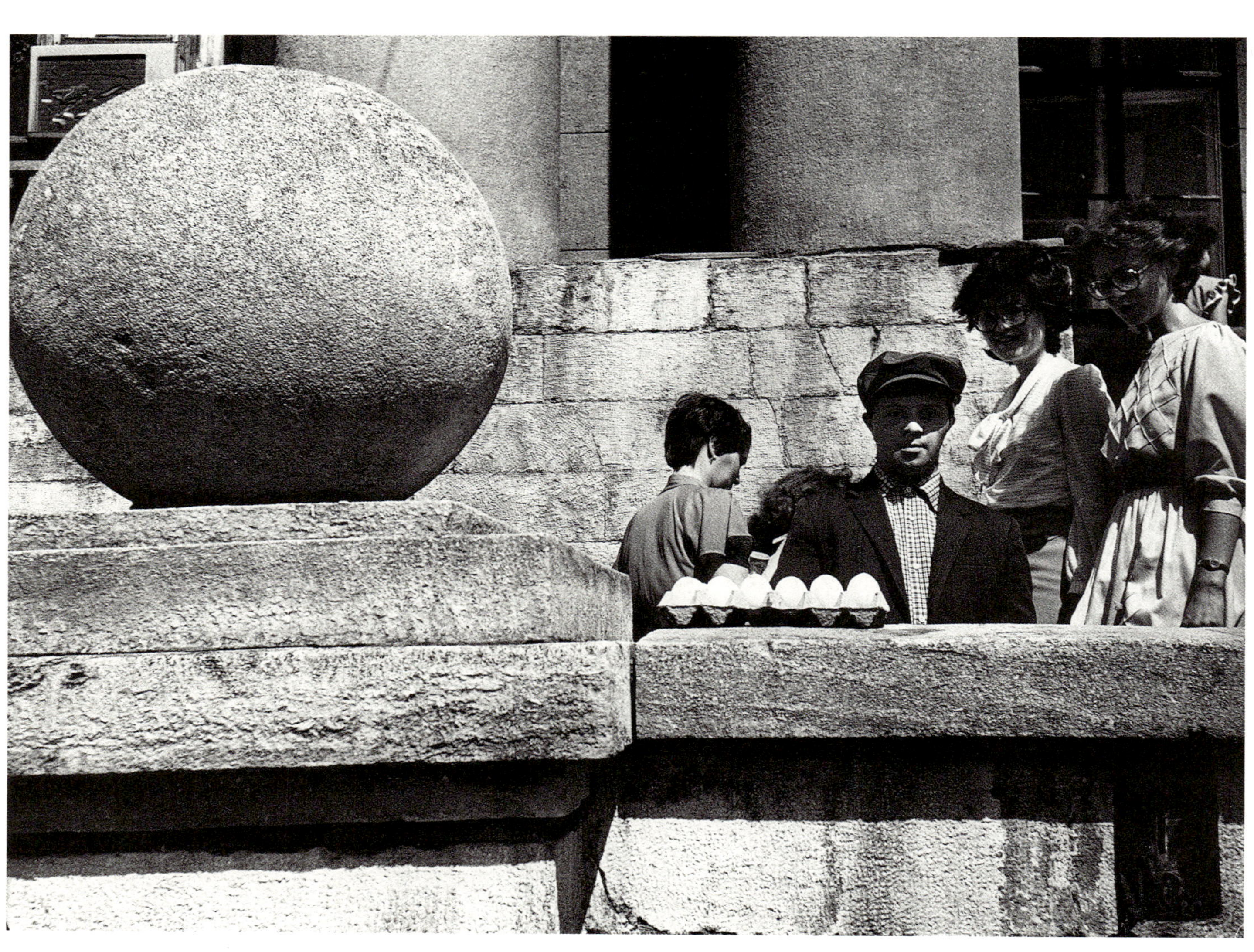

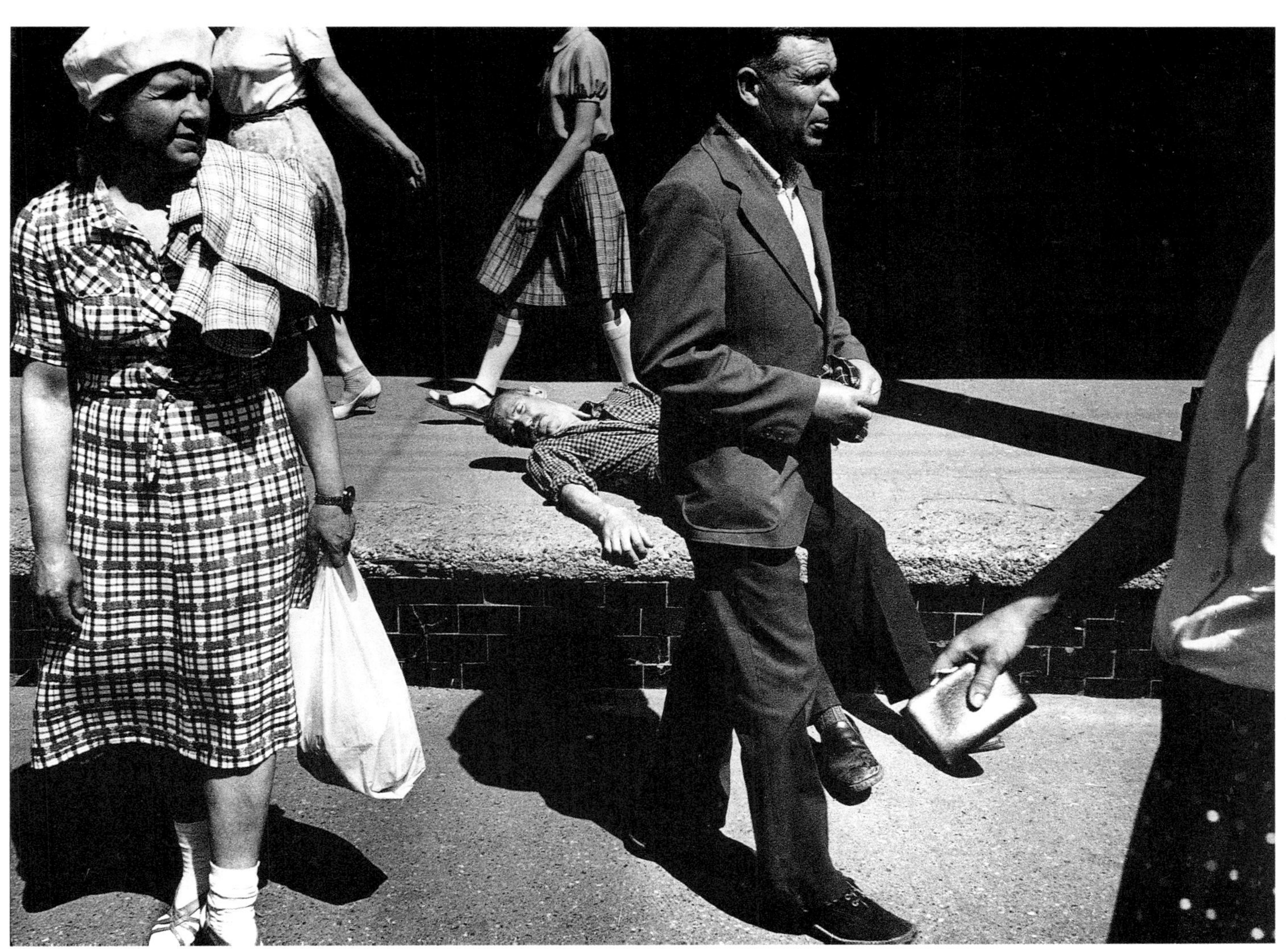

MIKHAIL LADEISHIKOV, CHEBOKSARY
UNTITLED, c.1989
12 × 15½″ (each)

ALEXANDER LAVRENTIEV • NIKOLAI LAVRENTIEV • IRINA PRESNETSOVA • VARVARA RODCHENKO • KATYA LAVRENTIEVA

RODCHENKO-STEPANOVA FAMILY WORKSHOP

The Rodchenko-Stepanova Family Workshop comprises three generations of descendants of the pioneering avant-garde husband-and-wife team of Alexander Rodchenko and Varvara Stepanova, who worked together from 1918 until Rodchenko's death in 1956.

The workshop is also a family that has chosen art as a way of life. The family members' practical experience in various media plus their extensive art historical knowledge is brought to bear on both their joint and individual artistic projects. The five family members live and work in the Moscow studio originally used by Rodchenko and Stepanova and have utilized their historically unique circumstance—their lineage from the foremost Soviet constructivists—as a resource for the study and creation of art that carries on the traditions of the family.

ALEXANDER LAVRENTIEV
DIAGONAL, 1984
11 × 11" (each)

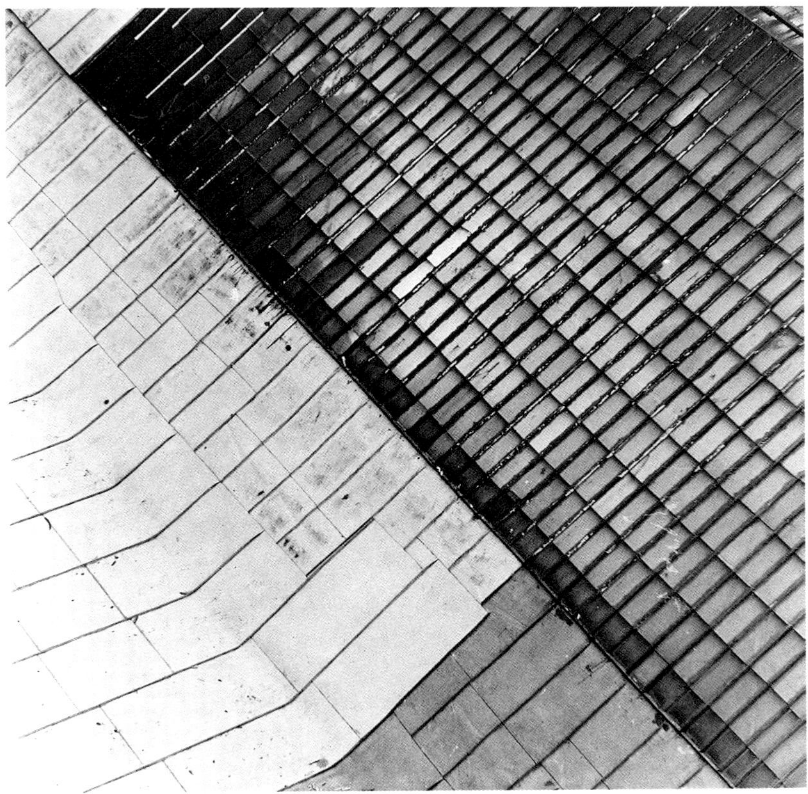

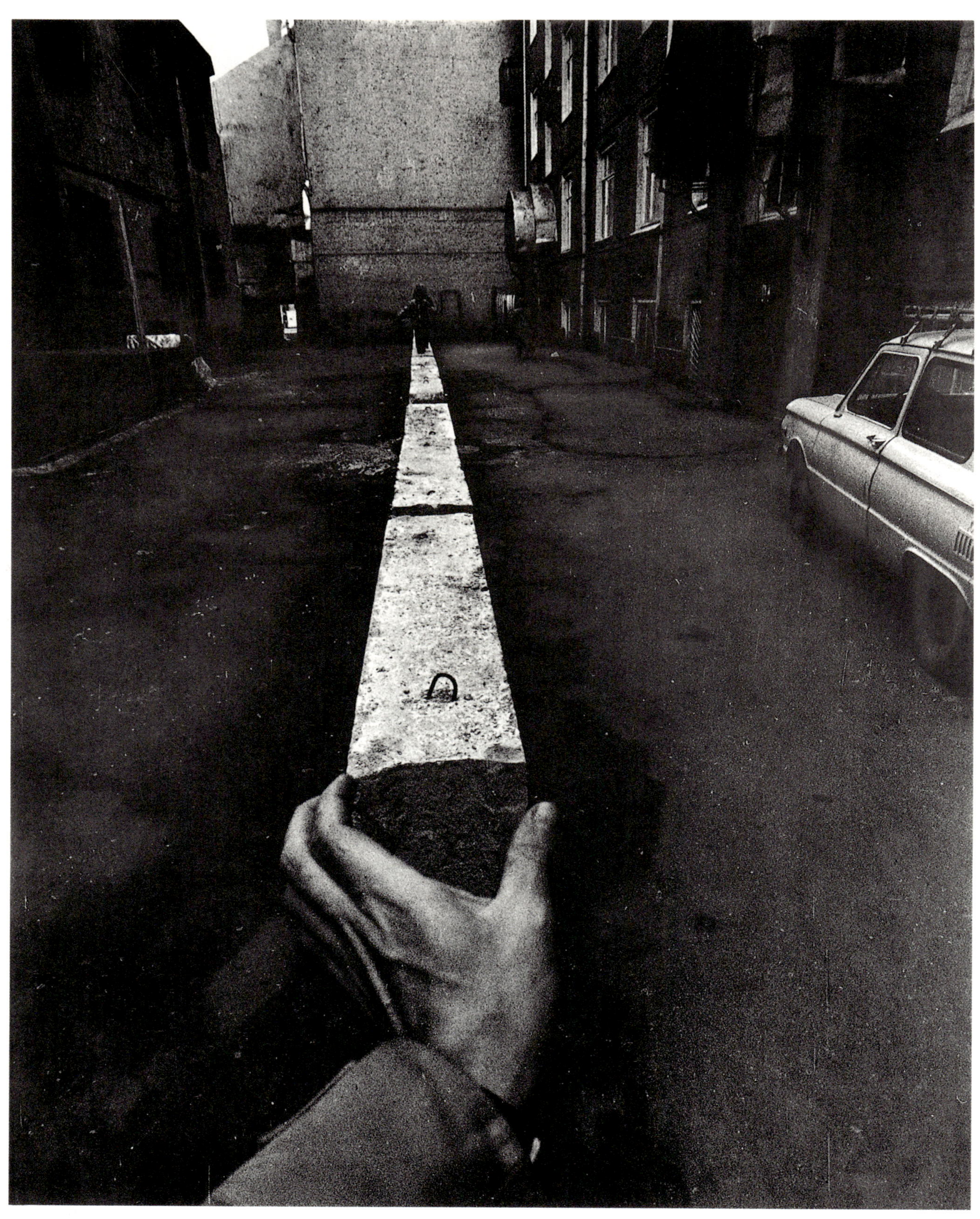

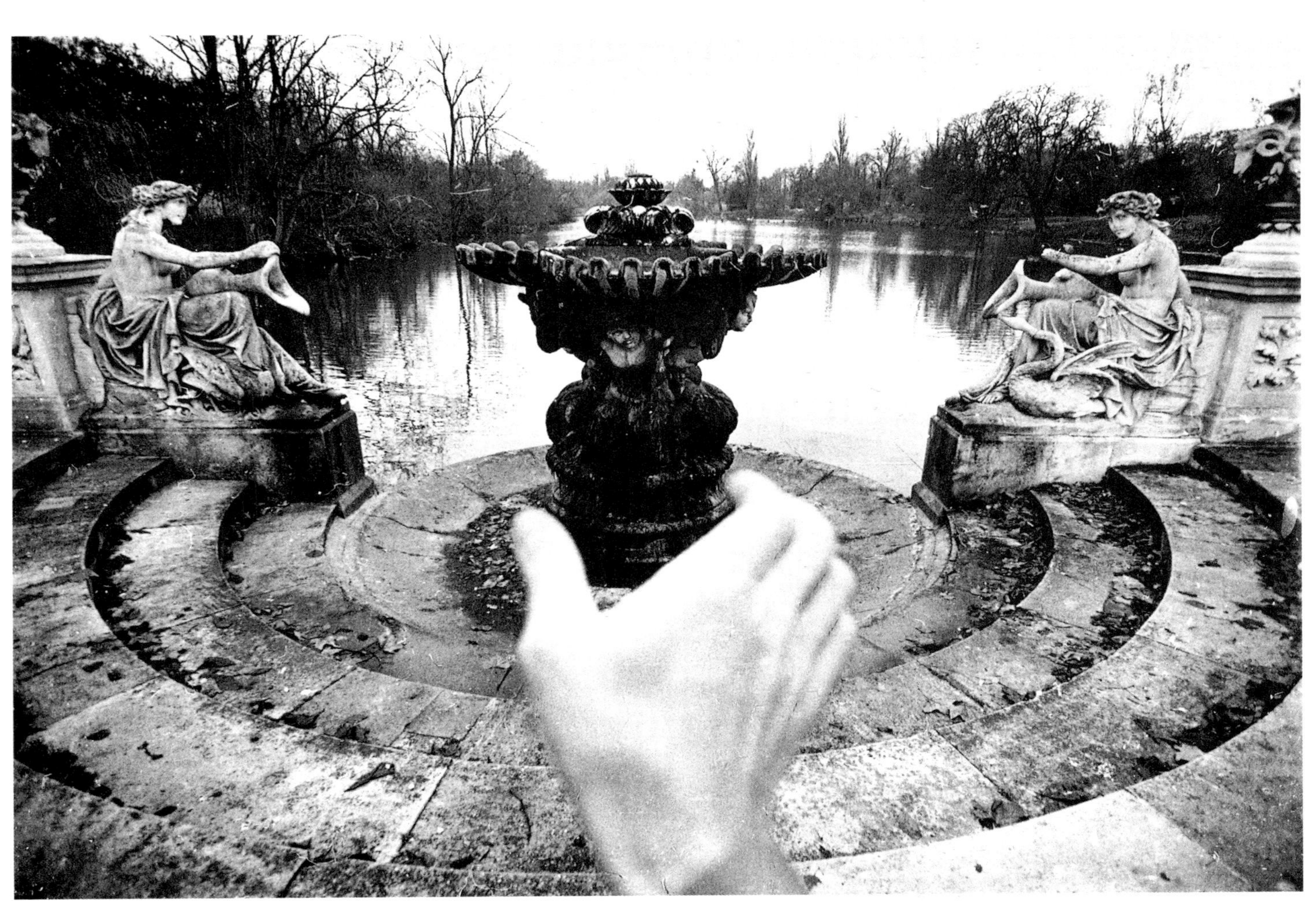

ALEXANDER LAVRENTIEV
from the series: A TOUCH OF ENGLAND, 1989
6½ × 9″

ALEXANDER LAVRENTIEV
from the series: WHO BUILT A FENCE IN MY YARD?, 1990
10½ × 8½″

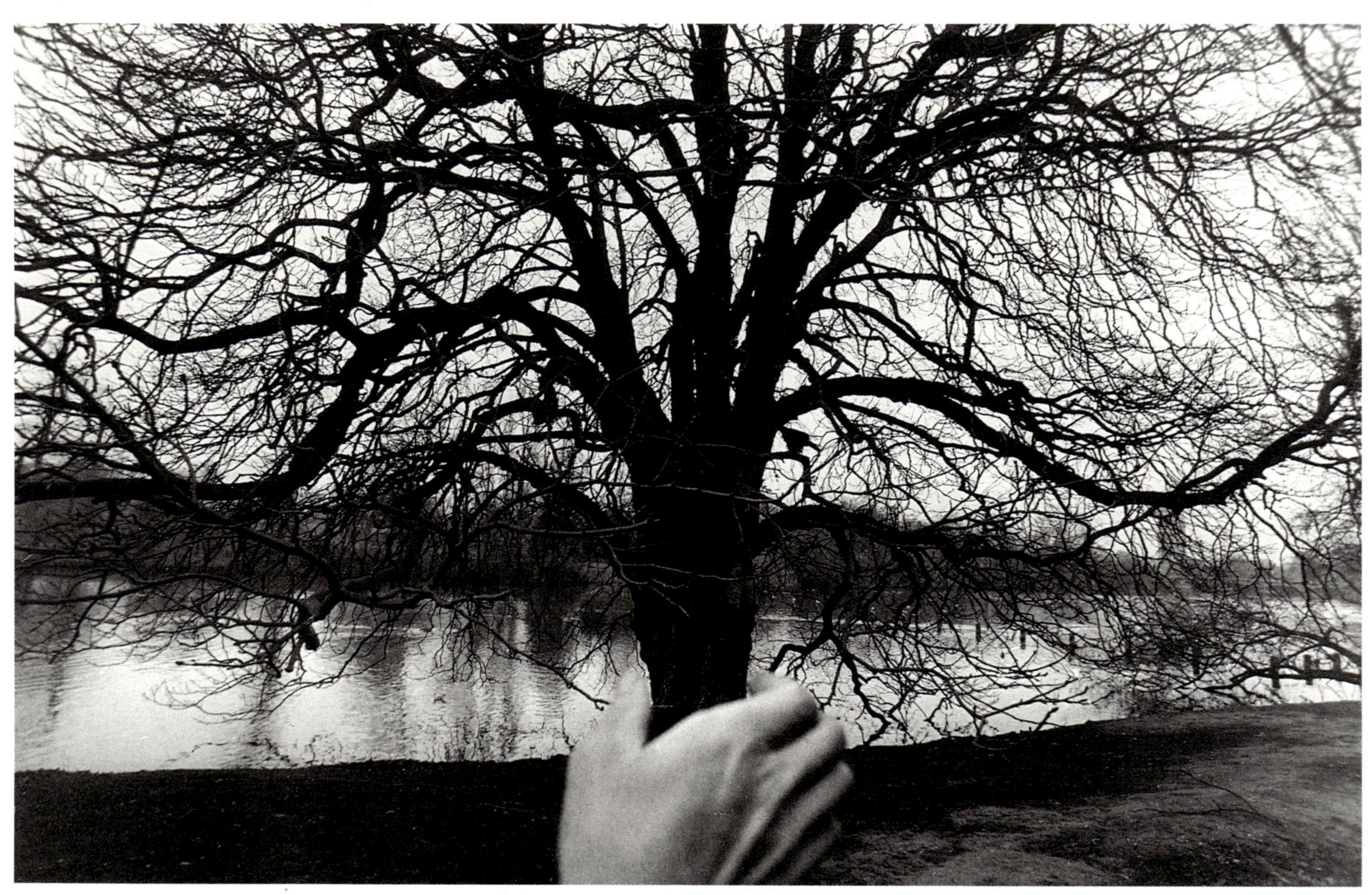

ALEXANDER LAVRENTIEV
from the series: A TOUCH OF ENGLAND, 1989
11 × 15½″

ALEXANDER LAVRENTIEV
INTERFERENCE, 1989
8 × 5½″

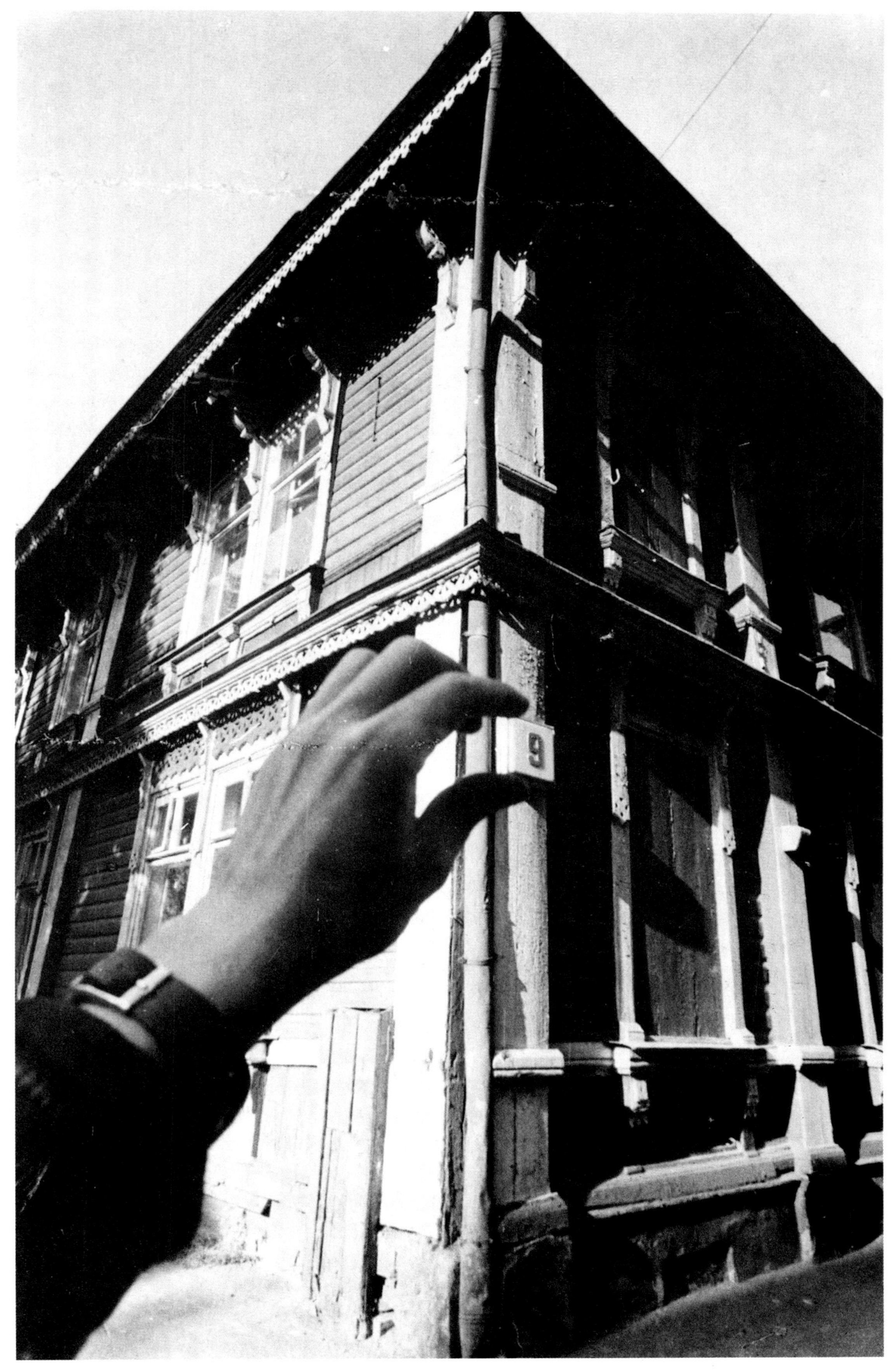
9

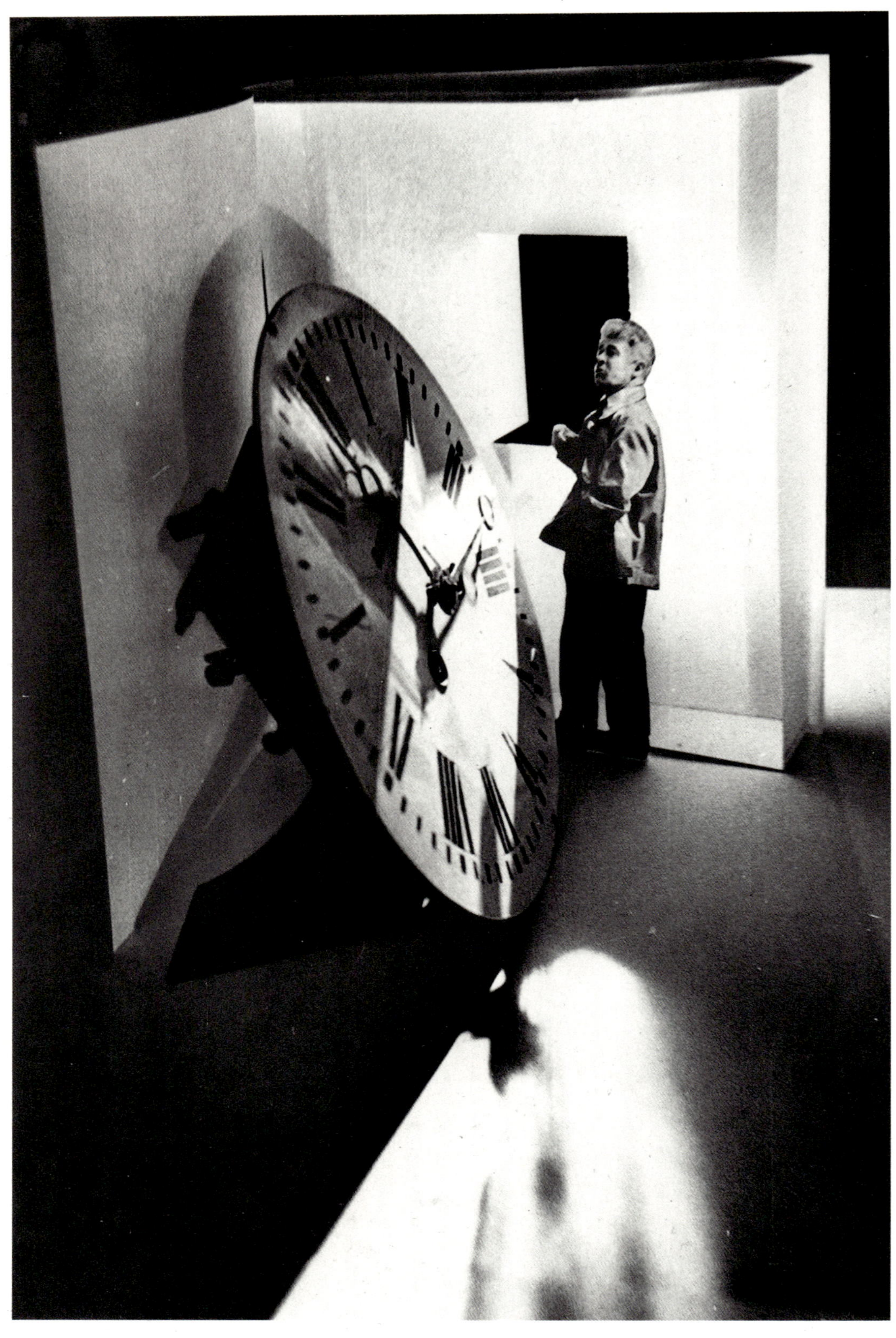

ALEXANDER LAVRENTIEV
PHOTO ILLUSTRATION FOR A BOOK ABOUT THE POET SEMEN KIRSANOV, 1985
8½ × 5½″

Opposite:
ALEXANDER LAVRENTIEV
EVENTS BEHIND THE SCREEN, 1989
15½ × 11″

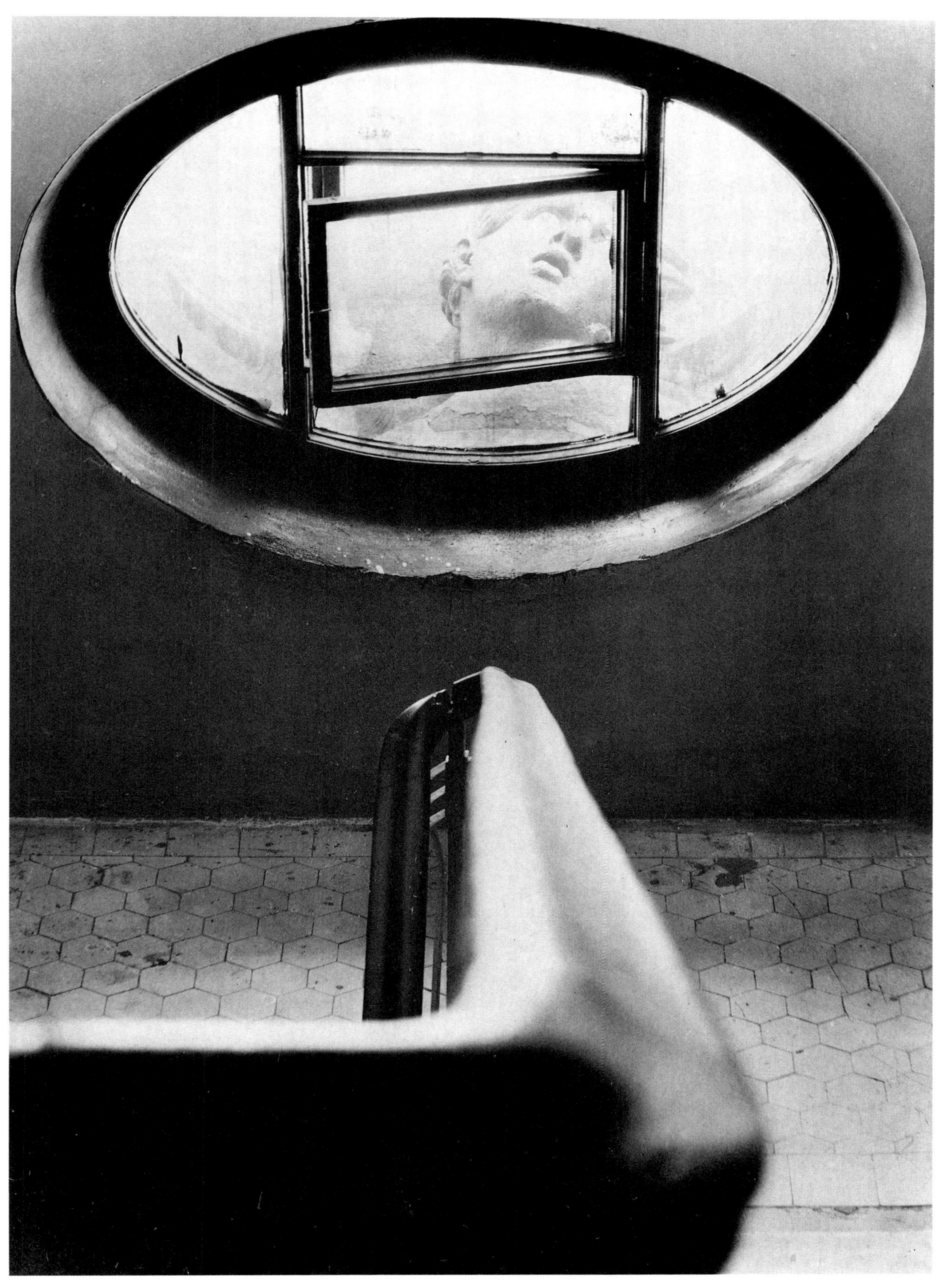

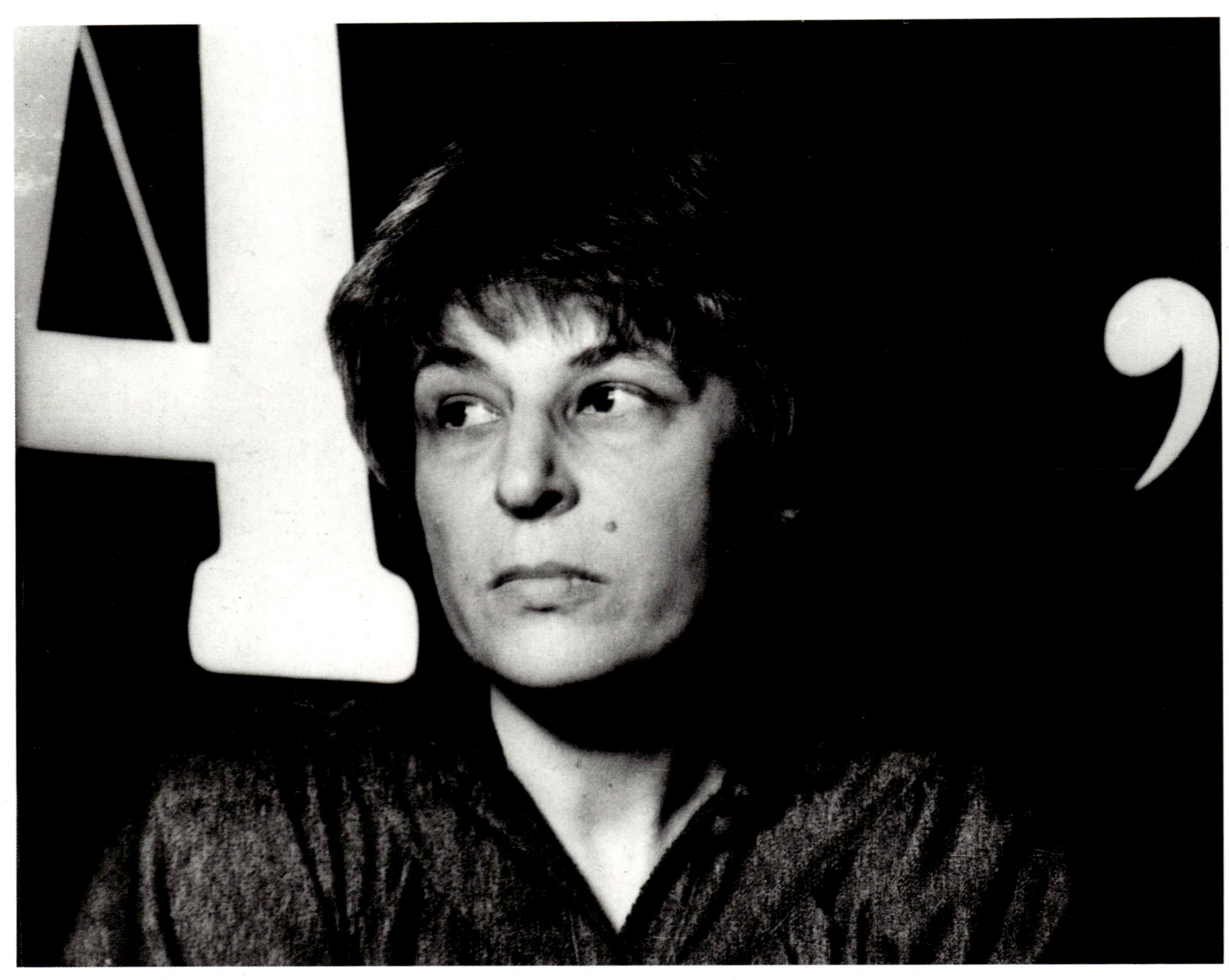

NIKOLAI LAVRENTIEV
POET, YUNNA MORIZ, 1989
6½ × 8″

NIKOLAI LAVRENTIEV
PHOTOGRAPHER PETER C. COSTAS,
MOSCOW, 1989
9 × 7″

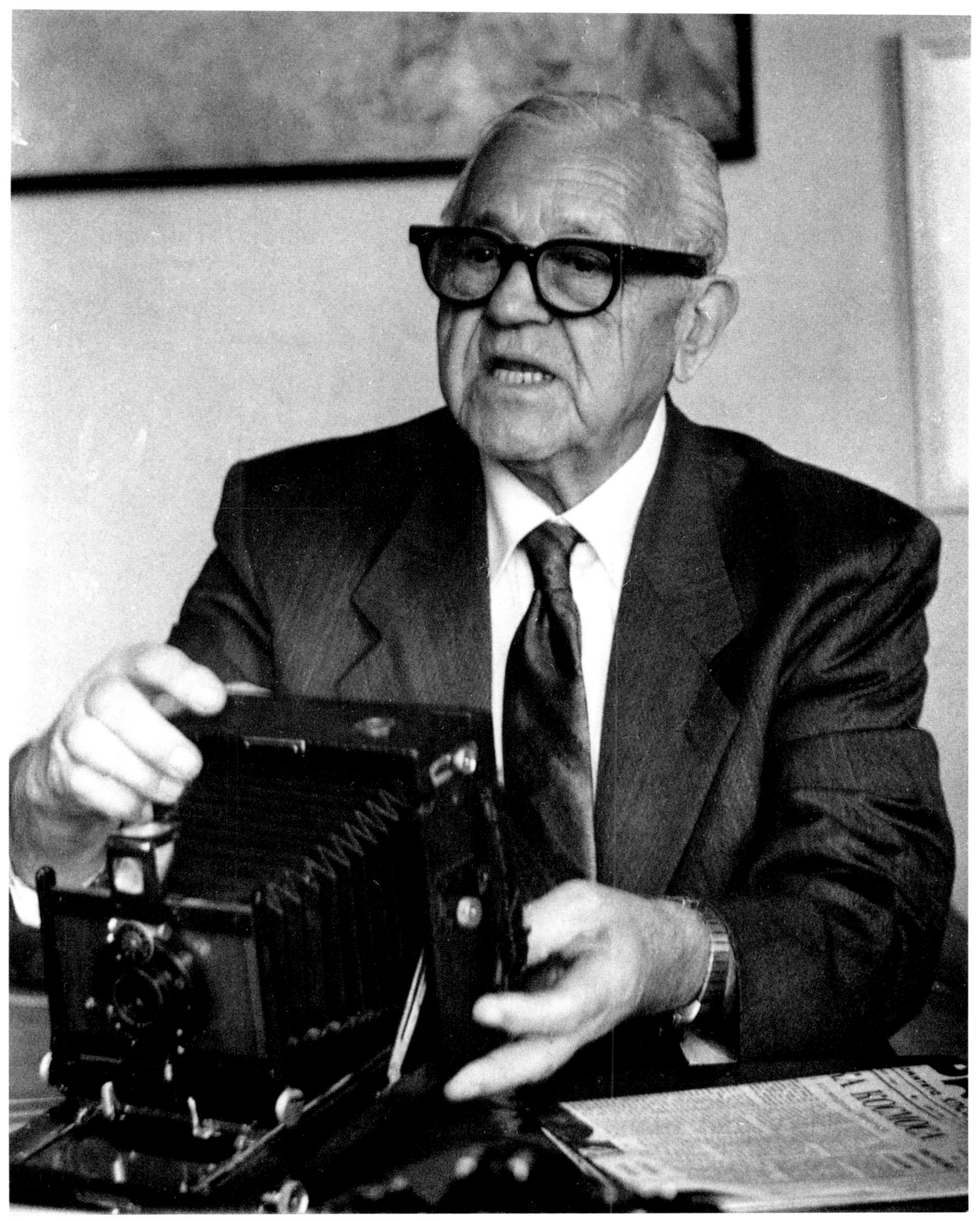

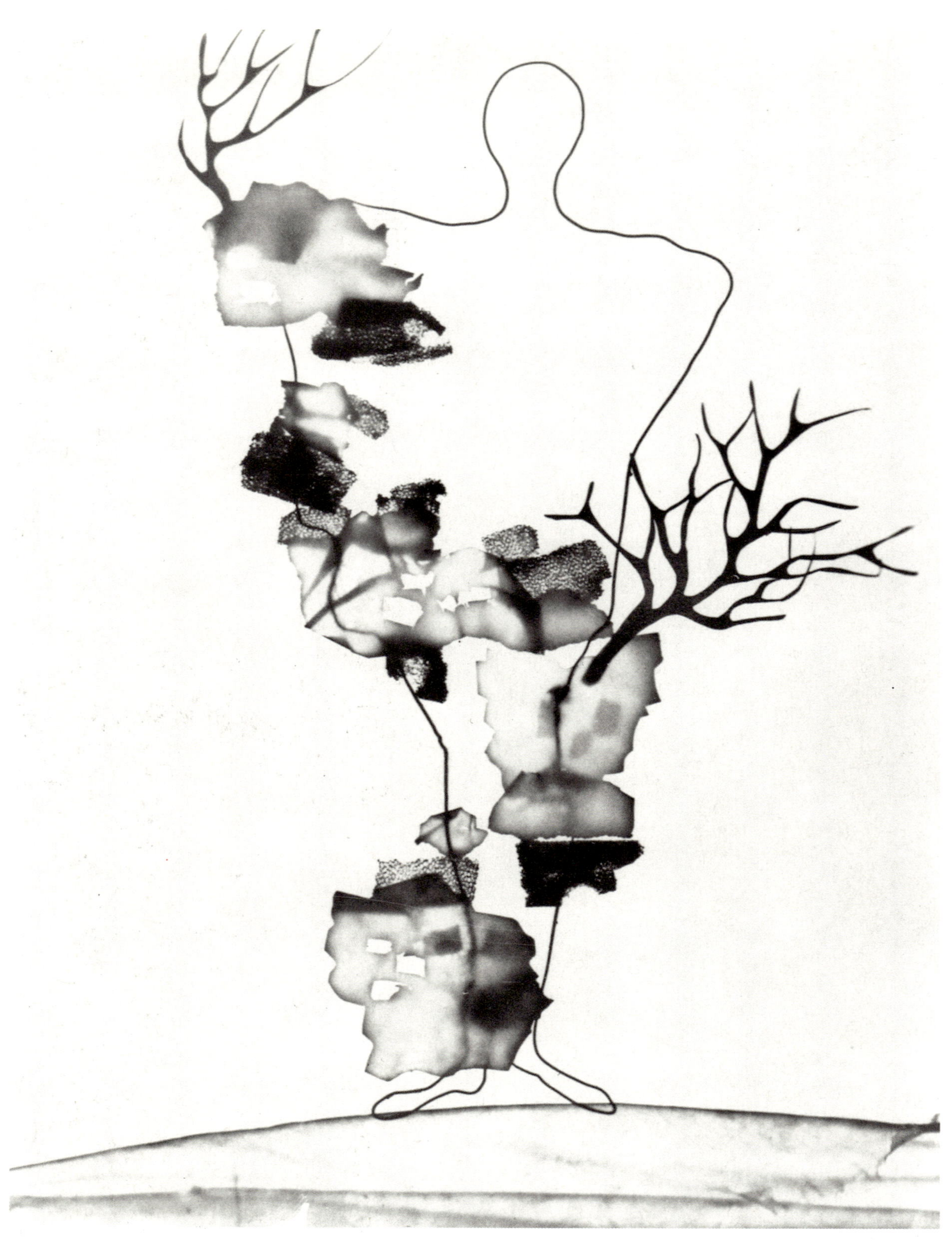

IRINA PRESNETSOVA
UNTITLED, 1989
9½ × 7″

Opposite:
IRINA PRESNETSOVA
UNTITLED, 1989
9½ × 5″

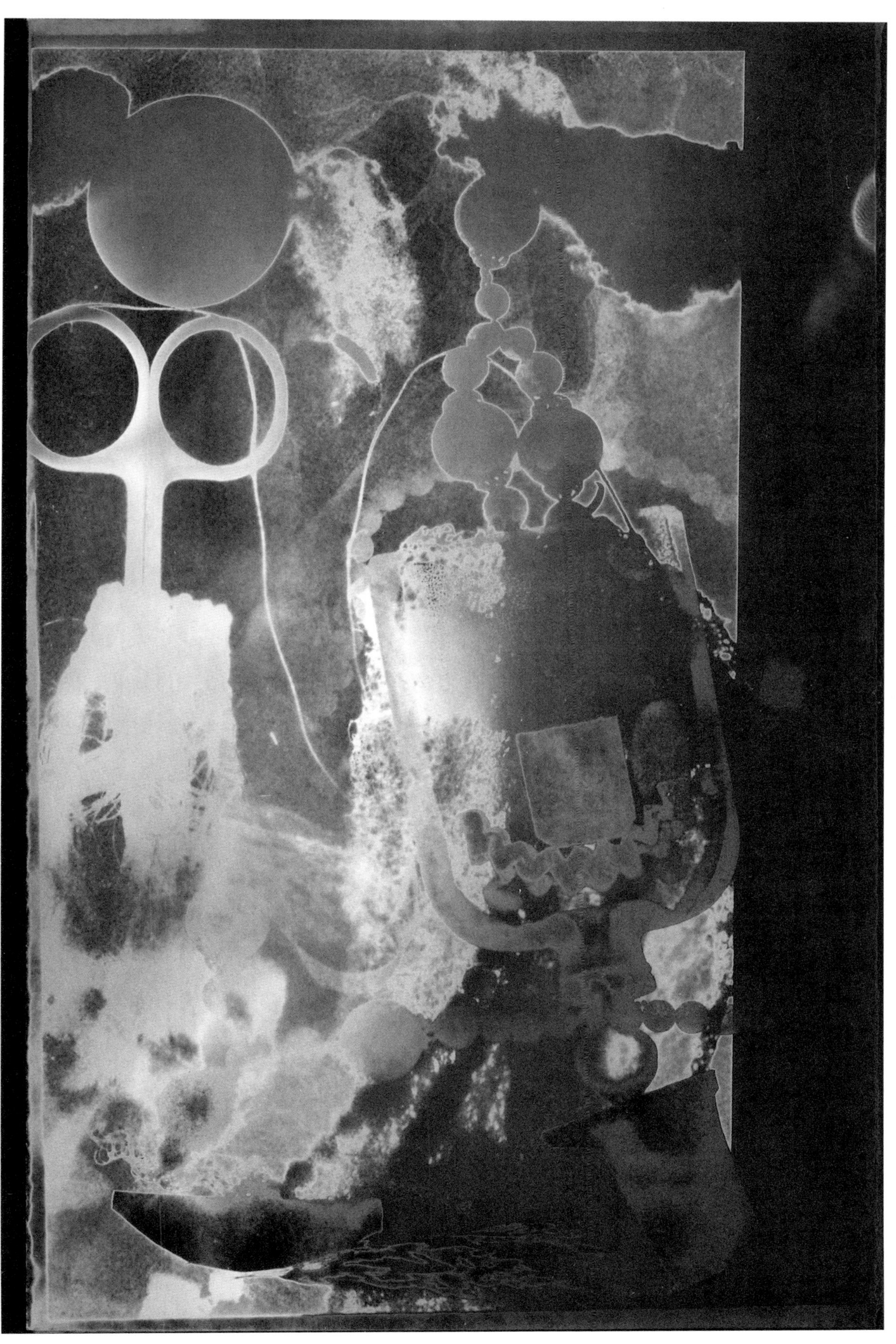

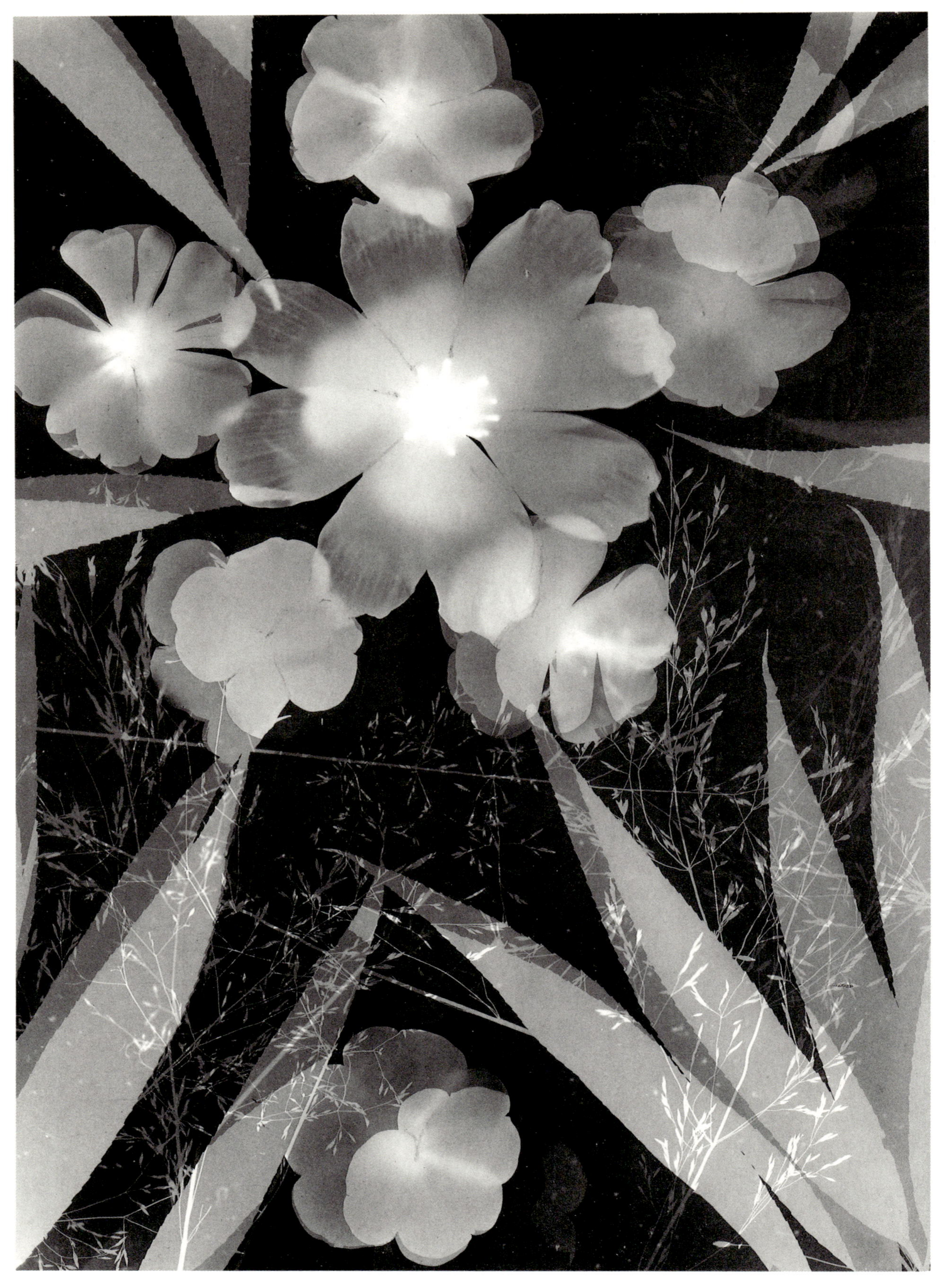

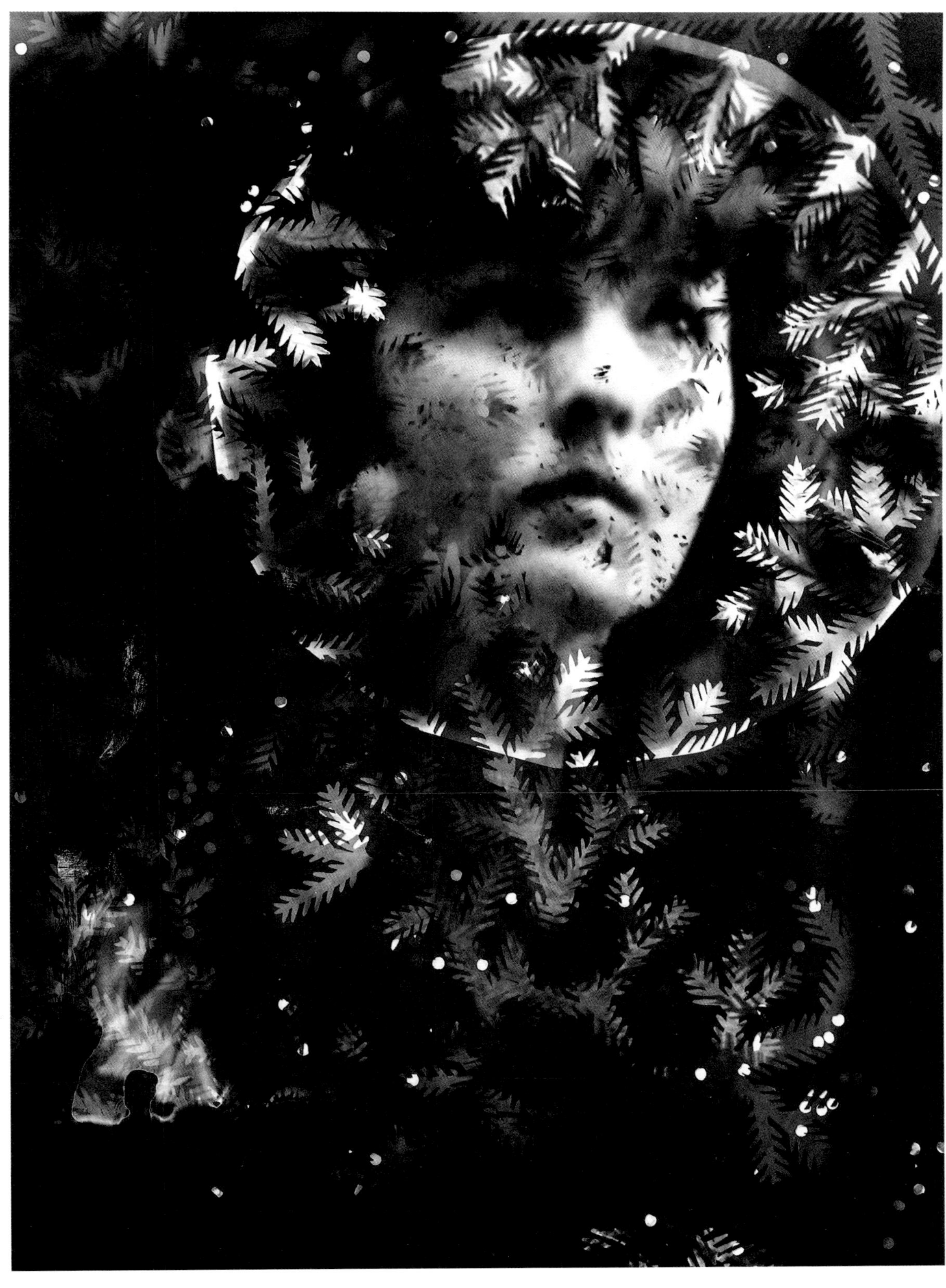

Opposite:
VARVARA RODCHENKO
FLOWER STILL LIFE, 1985
9 × 6½″

VARVARA RODCHENKO and NIKOLAI LAVRENTIEV
POET BELLA AKHMADULINA, 1988
9 × 6″

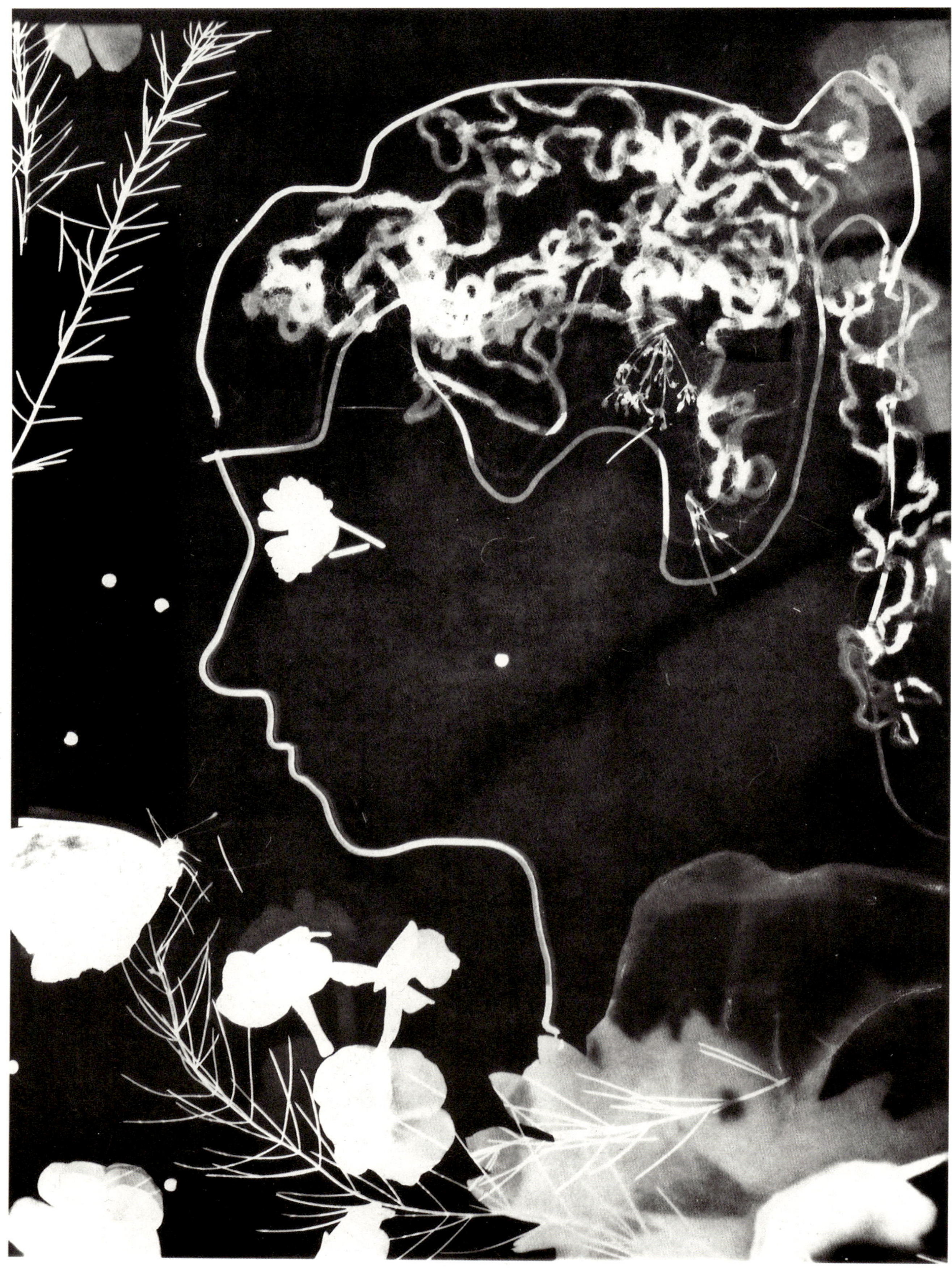

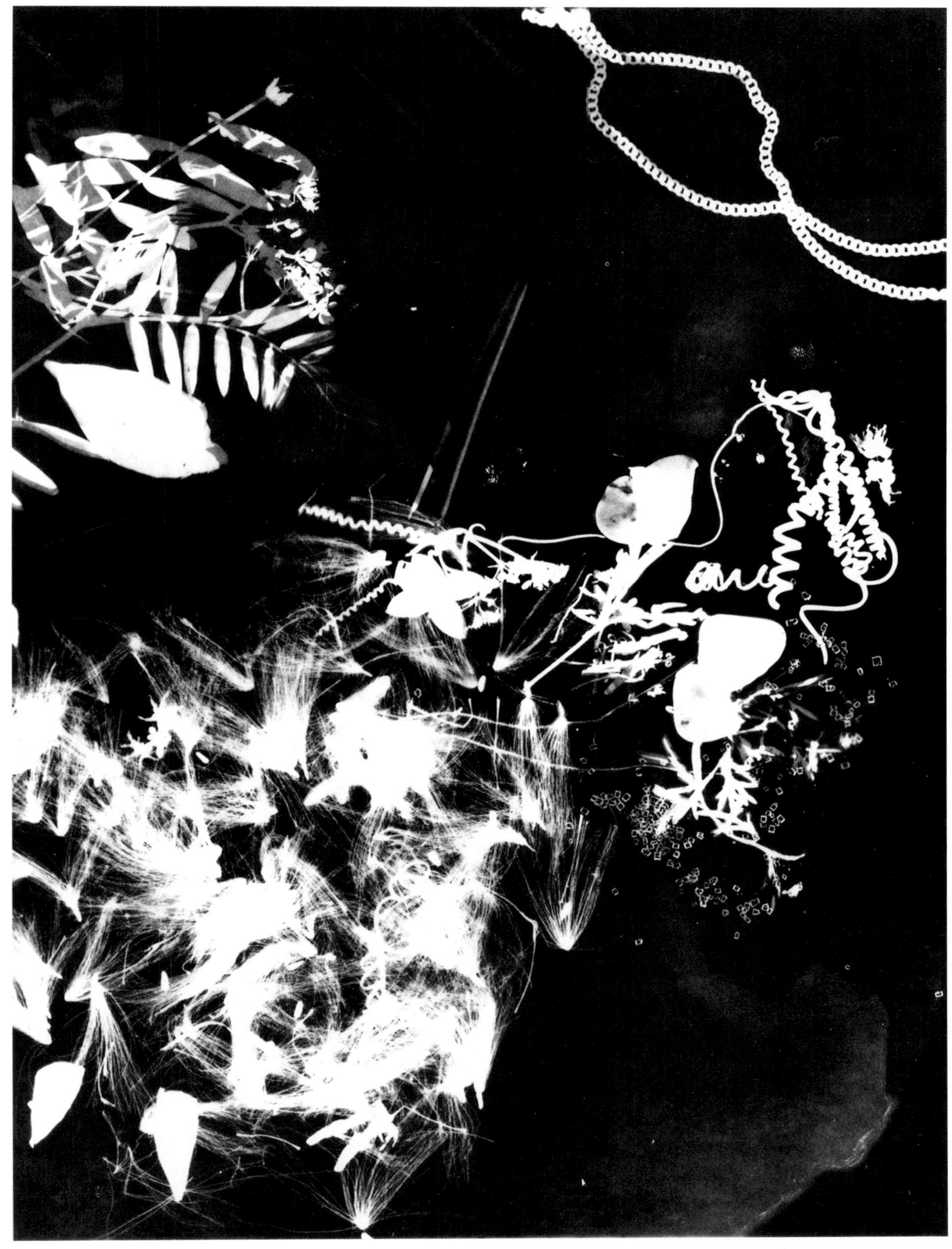

Opposite:
VARVARA RODCHENKO
PORTRAIT OF THE GRANDDAUGHTER, 1990
9 × 6½"

KATYA LAVRENTIEVA
PRINCESS PHOTOGRAM, 1990
9 × 6½"

IMAGE OF A PRAYER

IRINA RACHEYEVA

At first glance you are embarrassed. Is it a mural, a painting, a poster, or a still from a film? Before your eyes is a photograph on sensitized tissue, close to six feet high and twelve feet long, of the workers at one of the mechanical engineering plants near Moscow. This plant has the same equipment and the same work conditions it had before the 1917 Great October Socialist Revolution. Among themselves the workers call this plant Buchenwald. Under the portrait you see a line from a prayer, "God, don't abandon me."

My generation was not raised on prayers. Regretfully, we heard words very different from the words of prayer. Now we regard with distaste the copybook morality we learned and we are tired of official slogans and dogmas. But even in the ocean of formal, bureaucratic words that surround us, we carry in our memory certain other lines from childhood. Though none of us can remember the words exactly, they were the words that stirred in us our civic duty and courage, our humanity, our inalienable participation in native and world cultural tradition. Lacking our own words, expressions such as "for whom the bell tolls . . ." lifted us from the commonplace, as prayers saved the generation of our great-grandfathers.

My people . . . There is a difficult, centuries-old history, indissoluble ties of existence and the ordinary life. You see these faces and realize that the same people struggled with the Mongols and Tatars half a thousand years ago and with the fascist invasion half a century ago. Now they fight again, but for democracy, glasnost, and perestroika. Today the symbols of Russia are not the fields, flowers, and birch trees, but the people, their pain and their suffering, and their human nature. They bear in their hearts the hope that life must be better. They are the people in this work of art and it seems as if you know them very well. You live certain that they are here, near you, with a shoulder to lean on, to help you, to save you.

The words of prayer are written by the artist so that some letters and syllables are repeated. It is the speech of a man so overwhelmed by emotion that he stutters. His words come directly from his heart and that is why they cannot be

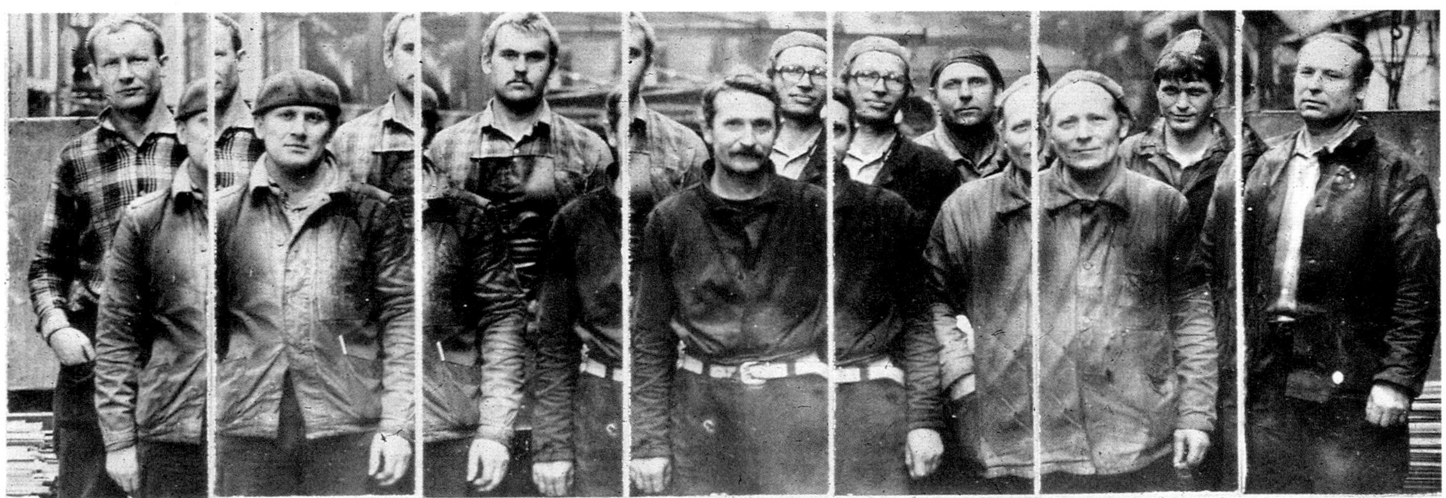

VLADIMIR KUPREJANOV
MIDDLE RUSSIAN LANDSCAPE, 1990
"God, don't turn your face away from me."
104¼ × 242¼"

untrue. His is the one voice that begins to sing before the chorus joins in unison. At once the souls and thoughts of people unite. We see these faces as the faces of saints who plead "God, do not abandon us." This is the portrait of our generation, and the portrait of our anxious, uneasy time.

The rhythm of the text is similar to the repetition and superposition of fragments of the figures in the portrait. The strict verticals serve as ribs of rigidity to hold the surface of the work. And is it by chance that you are reminded of a prison? The compositional fractionality gives a dynamic depth to the image. It seems that the people are approaching you, that more and more are coming . . .

They are the faces of our citizens, our contemporaries. It is unscrupulous and impossible to deceive them with political twaddle and economic confusion. You cannot cheat the people. It is stupid to deceive yourself so. From this canvas your own pained conscience looks back at you.

There is no hypocrisy and no banality in this work. The unity of text and image creates a new reality, gives birth to complex associations and connections that help us to more fully understand the artist's idea. Everything is alive: real people and timeless words. This work becomes a symbol of our life, the real image of the soul of the people.

"God, don't abandon us." These words are addressed not only to God but to each of us. The sincere words of the prayer are like a last refuge, as in childbirth a young mother-to-be, almost unconscious from the pain of delivering a new child to the world, whispers parts of a prayer only half-remembered from childhood. It seems that today the half-remembered, quiet words of prayer are mightier than the loud voices of strikes, demonstrations, and rallies. These words unite us and must be heard.

INDEX

Designed by Diana M. Jones
Composed in Caslon Old
Face and Akzidenz by
Trufont Typographers,
Hicksville, New York
Printed and bound by
Arnoldo Mondadori
S.P.A., Verona, Italy